T0350899

Second Edition

COMPUTER NETWORK TIME SYNCHRONIZATION

The Network Time Protocol on Earth and in Space

Second Edition

COMPUTER NETWORK TIME SYNCHRONIZATION

The Network Time Protocol on Earth and in Space

David L. Mills

CRC Press
Taylor & Francis Group
Boca Raton London New York

CRC Press is an imprint of the
Taylor & Francis Group, an **informa** business

The illustration on the cover is a logical map of the early Internet in 1979. It included the ARPAnet, consisting of over a hundred participating institutions interconnected by 50-kb/s leased lines, as well as domestic and international satellite. MILNET was an ARPAnet clone serving military users. WIDEBAND was a 3-Mb/s domestic satellite network. SATNET (lower right center) was a 64-kb/s international satellite network. This author's sandbox was the DCN oval near the top center of the map.

CRC Press
Taylor & Francis Group
6000 Broken Sound Parkway NW, Suite 300
Boca Raton, FL 33487-2742

© 2011 by Taylor and Francis Group, LLC
CRC Press is an imprint of Taylor & Francis Group, an Informa business

No claim to original U.S. Government works

Printed in the United States of America on acid-free paper
10 9 8 7 6 5 4 3 2 1

International Standard Book Number: 978-1-4398-1463-5 (Hardback)

Library of Congress Cataloging-in-Publication Data

Mills, David L.
    Computer network time synchronization : the Network Time Protocol on Earth and in space / David L. Mills. -- 2nd ed.
        p. cm.
    "A CRC title."
    Includes bibliographical references and index.
    ISBN 978-1-4398-1463-5
    1. Network Time Protocol (Computer network protocol) 2. Synchronous data transmission systems. 3. Computer networks--Management. 4. Synchronization. I. Title.

TK5105.575.M55 2011
004.6'2--dc22   2010009969

Visit the Taylor & Francis Web site at
http://www.taylorandfrancis.com

and the CRC Press Web site at
http://www.crcpress.com

This opus is dedicated to Beverly Mills, singer and musician, Eileen Mills,

BlackBerry virtuoso, and Keith Mills, globe-trotting photojournalist.

Contents

List of Illustrations

List of Tables

Preface

Mumpsimus (n): Middle English noun denoting an incorrigible dogmatic old pendant—jokingly called a *foolosopher* about 1550—which grew to include any incorrect opinion stubbornly clung to.

Jeffrey Kacirk
Forgotten English, 1997

This book is all about wrangling a herd of network computers so that all display the correct time. This may seem like a really narrow business, but the issues go far beyond winding the clock on your display taskbar. Carefully coordinated, reliable, and accurate time is vital for traffic control in the air and on the ground, buying and selling things, and TV network programming. Even worse, ill-gotten time might cause domain name system (DNS) caches to expire and the entire Internet to implode on the root servers, which was considered a serious threat on the eve of the millennium in 1999. Critical data files might expire before they are created, and an electronic message might arrive before it was sent. Reliable and accurate computer time is necessary for any real-time distributed computer application, which is what much of our public infrastructure has become.

This book speaks to the technological infrastructure of time dissemination, distribution, and synchronization, specifically the architecture, protocols, and algorithms of the Network Time Protocol (NTP). NTP has been active in one form or another for over almost three decades on the public Internet and numerous private networks on the nether side of firewalls. Just about everything today that can be connected to a network wire has support for NTP: print servers, WI-FI access points, routers and printers of every stripe, and even battery backup systems. NTP subnets are in space, on the seabed, onboard warships, and on every continent, including Antarctica. NTP comes with most flavors of Windows as well as all flavors of Unix. About 25 million clients implode on the NTP time servers at the National Institute of Standards and Technology (NIST) alone (J. Levine, NIST, personal communication).

This book is designed primarily as a reference book but is suitable for a specialized university course at the senior and graduate levels in both computer engineering and computer science departments. Some chapters may go down more easily for an electrical engineer, especially those dealing with mathematical concepts, others more easily for a computer scientist, especially those dealing with computing theory, but each will learn from the other. There are things for mathematicians, cryptographers, and spacefarers, even something for historians.

Welcome to the second edition of this book. The original 16 chapters of the first edition remain, but some have been rewritten, updated, and new material added. Four new chapters have been added, two of which discuss timekeeping in space missions. The presentation begins in Chapter 1 with a general overview of the architecture, protocols, and algorithms for computer network timekeeping. This includes how time flows from national time standards via radio, satellite, and telephone modem to hundreds of primary time servers, then via NTP subnets to millions of secondary servers and clients at increasing stratum levels. Chapter 2 describes the principal components of an NTP client and how it works with redundant servers and diverse network paths. Chapter 3 contains an in-depth description of the critical algorithms so important for the consistency, accuracy, and reliability that any good computer scientist will relish. The actual algorithm used to adjust the computer clock is so special that Chapter 4 is completely dedicated to its description and operation. As the word *network* is prominent in the title of this book, Chapter 5 presents an overview of the engineering principles guiding network configuration and resource discovery.

Along about now, you should ask how well the contraption works. Chapter 6 evaluates the performance of typical NTP subnets with respect to network delay variations and clock frequency errors. It shows the results of a survey of NTP servers and clients to determine typical time and frequency error distributions. It then analyzes typical NTP configurations to determine such things as processor and network overhead and engineered defenses against flood attacks.

An NTP subnet ultimately depends on national and international means to disseminate standard time to the general population, including Internet computers. Chapter 7 describes a number of systems and drivers for current radio, satellites, and telephone modem dissemination means. Chapter 8 describes specialized kernel software used in some computer systems to improve timekeeping accuracy and precision, ultimately to the order of nanoseconds.

In modern experience we have learned that computer security is a very serious business, and timekeeping networks are not exempt. What may be different for NTP subnets is that, by their very nature, the data exchanged are public values transmitted from public servers over public networks, so servers and clients of public networks might be seen as very inviting targets for tempo-terrorists. In addition, there are devilishly intricate issues when dated material such as cryptographic certificates must be verified by the protocol that uses them. Chapter 9 describes the NTP security model and authentication protocol, which shares headers with NTP, while Chapter 10 describes a number of cryptographic algorithms designed to prove industrial-strength group membership.

Computer network timekeeping, like many other physical systems, is not without errors, both deterministic and stochastic. Chapter 11 contains an intricate analysis of errors inherent in reading the system clock and disciplining its time and frequency relative to the clock in another computer. Chapter 12 is on modeling and analysis of the computer clock, together with a mathematical description of its characteristics.

Timekeeping on the global scale is a discipline all its own. Chapter 13 describes how we reckon the time according to the stars and atoms. It explains the relationships between the international timescales TAI, UTC, and JDN dear to physicists and navigators and the NTP timescale. If we use NTP for historic and future dating, there are issues of rollover and precision. Even the calendar gets in the act as the astronomers have their ways and the historians theirs. Since the topic of history comes up, Chapter 19 reveals the events of historic interest since computer network timekeeping started almost three decades ago. Finally, Chapter 20 is a bibliography of articles, reports, and other documents relevant to computer network timekeeping.

While a detailed description of the NTP reference implementation is beyond the scope of this book, it may be of some interest to explore its general architecture, organization, and operation. Chapter 14 includes a set of flowcharts, state variables, processes, and routines of the current public software implementation, together with an explanation of how it operates.

Chapters 15 through 18 are new to this edition. Chapter 15 includes an intricate cocktail of hardware and software algorithms to implement a truly awesome and precise system clock. It introduces the notions of softstamp, drivestamp, and hardstamp and includes an overview of the Institute of Electrical and Electronics Engineers (IEEE) 1588 Precision Time Protocol (PTP) and how it might interoperate with NTP. Chapter 16 describes the interleave modes new to NTP and how these new concepts can be exploited.

Chapters 17 and 18 have motivated the subtitle of this book, "The Network Time Protocol on Earth and in Space." Chapter 17 explains why timekeeping is so different from earthlings to martians, as now we must consider light-time and relativistic effects. This chapter also discusses space hardware issues and the Proximity-1 space data link protocol, which might boost NTP to a Mars orbiter fleet. Finally, Chapter 18 discusses time transfer issues for deep space missions at and beyond Mars.

The book in its entirety would certainly be of interest to an NTP administrator as a reference volume. It would be useful as a case study involving a widely deployed, distributed application with technology drawn from diverse interdisciplinary fields. The algorithms described in various chapters could be useful as a companion to a computer science book on algorithms. As a case study in cryptographic techniques, the material in Chapters 9 and 10 is particularly relevant as the security model for NTP is complicated by the need to authenticate the server and reckon the time simultaneously. Astronomers and physicists will find the clock discipline algorithm described in Chapter 4 similar to but different from the algorithms they use. Engineers will find Chapters 4, 11, and 12 relevant to a course on control feedback systems. Planetary scientists and space navigators might find the material in Chapters 17 and 18 useful in the design of new spacecraft hardware and instruments.

The development, deployment, and maintenance of NTP in the Internet have created a daunting task made possible by over four dozen volunteers from several professions and from several countries. NTP enthusiasts have much in common with radio amateurs (including me, W3HCF), even if the boss sees little need to wind the clock to the nanosecond. We have been fortunate that several manufacturers have donated radio and satellite receivers, computers, and cool gadgets over the years. Especially valued is the mutual support of Judah Levine at NIST and Richard Schmidt at the U.S. Naval Observatory (USNO), intrepid timekeepers in their own right. Many thanks to Interneteers Danny Mayer and Dave Hart of the NTP Public Services Project, who reviewed the entire book, and to Simon Wu and John Veregge of NASA (National Aeronautics and Space Administration) Jet Propulsion Laboratory, who reviewed the new chapters.

Finally, a word about the Parting Shots sections sprinkled at the end of most chapters. While the main text explores the timescape up to the cutting edge of the cliff, these sections rappel over the edge. Some are speculative, others offer proposals, and still others present an alternate view. All in all, they have been great fun.

David L. Mills

About the Author

Dr. David L. Mills is professor emeritus of electrical and computer engineering and computer and information sciences at the University of Delaware. He has been an active contributor for many years to the field of Internet technology, particularly computer network time synchronization. He is the original developer of the Network Time Protocol and has authored over 30 articles and technical reports on the subject, including the current operative standards documents. His doctoral degree in computer science was conferred by the University of Michigan in 1971. He is a member of the National Academy of Engineering and a Fellow in both the Association for Computing Machinery and the Institute of Electrical and Electronics Engineers.

1

Basic Concepts

It is possible to own too much. A man with one watch knows
what time it is; a man with two watches is never quite sure.

Lee Segall
1940s radio personality

We take for granted that computers on a network have some means to set their
clocks to the nominal time of day, even if those means amount to eyeball and
wristwatch. How accurate can this be done in practice? Most folks who have
to get to work on time set their wristwatch within a minute or two of radio or
TV time and expect it to drift less than a minute over the month. This amounts
to a rate error of about 23 parts per million (PPM), not bad for a temperature-
stabilized wrist. Real computer clocks can be set by wristwatch usually within
a minute or two, but some have rate errors 10 times that of a wristwatch.
Nevertheless, in many applications the accuracy maintainable by a herd of
wristwatch-wrangled network timekeepers might well be acceptable.

In a lackadaisical world where the only serious consequence of clock errors
may be that electronic mail occasionally arrives before it is sent, it may not
matter a lot if a clock is sometimes set backward or accumulates errors more
than a minute per month. It is a completely different matter in a distributed
airline reservation system in which a seat can be sold twice or not at all. In
fact, there may be legal consequences when an online stock trade is completed before it is bid or the local station begins its newscast a minute before
the network commercial. But, as Liskov [1] pointed out, there are a number of
things you probably have not thought about for which synchronized clocks
make many missions easier and some even possible.

1.1 Time Synchronization

Computer scientists like to model timekeeping in a distributed computer
network as a *happens-before* relation; that is, every event that occurs in one
computer must happen before news of that event gets to another computer.
In our universe where the arrow of time is always increasing and nothing
travels faster than light, if such a message contains the sending time, then

1

the receiving time on arrival must always be later. In Lamport's [2] scheme, all computer clocks are assumed to run at the same rate. Every message contains the time it was sent according to the sender's clock. If that time is later than the receiver clock, the receiver clock is advanced to that time. The happens-before relation would always be satisfied, even if the station stops were wrong according to the train schedule.

In Lamport's [2] scheme, time is never set backward, which would surely violate the happens-before relation. However, real network clocks can run at significantly different rates, and it takes a while for news of an earthquake in California to arrive in New York. So, an electronic timekeeping protocol needs some wiggle room to adjust the rate of each clock to maintain nominal time agreement with the national timescale. To do this, a distributed network clock synchronization protocol is required that can read a server clock, transmit the reading to one or more clients, and adjust each client clock as required. Protocols that do this include the topic of this book, the Network Time Protocol (NTP) [3], as well as the Digital Time Synchronization Service (DTSS) [4] protocol and others found in the literature.

Simply stated, NTP is a distributed service that synchronizes the computer clock to an ensemble of sources, either remote via the Internet or local via a radio, satellite, or telephone modem service. We speak of the *server clock*, which offers synchronization, and one or more *client clocks* that accept it. When the meaning is clear from context, we refer to the local clock in some client or server as the *system clock*. NTP aligns the system clocks in participating computers to Coordinated Universal Time (UTC)* used by most nations of the world. UTC is based on the solar day, which depends on the rotation of Earth about its axis, and the Gregorian calendar, which is based on revolution of Earth around the Sun. The UTC timescale is disciplined with respect to International Atomic Time (TAI) by inserting leap seconds at intervals of about two years. UTC time is disseminated by various means, including radio, satellite, telephone modem, or portable atomic clock. Chapter 13 includes an extensive discussion of these topics.

In spite of the name, NTP is more than a protocol; it is an integrated technology that provides for systematic dissemination of national standard time throughout the Internet and affiliated private and corporate networks. The technology is pervasive, ubiquitous, and free of proprietary interest. The ultimate goal of NTP is to synchronize the clocks in all participating computers to the order of less than a millisecond or two relative to UTC. In general, this can be achieved with modern computers and network technologies. This is easily good enough to detect things like stalled central processing unit (CPU)

---

* "In 1970 the Coordinated Universal Time system was devised by an international advisory group of technical experts within the International Telecommunication Union (ITU). The ITU felt it was best to designate a single abbreviation for use in all languages in order to minimize confusion. Since unanimous agreement could not be achieved on using either the English word order, CUT, or the French word order, TUC, the acronym UTC was chosen as a compromise" (NIST Web site).

fans and broken heating or cooling systems by calibrating the measured frequency offset to the ambient temperature. Performance may be somewhat less when long Internet paths with many router hops are involved and somewhat better if certain hardware and software functions are available as described in Chapter 8. As demonstrated in that chapter, the ultimate accuracy at the application program interface (API) of a modern computer with access to a precision timing source is on the order less than a microsecond.

Synchronization directly to UTC requires a specialized radio or satellite receiver or telephone modem service. Such sources, called *reference clocks* in this book, are available for many government dissemination services, including the Global Positioning System (GPS) and Long Range Navigation System (LORAN-C) radio navigation systems, WWV/H and WWVB radio time/frequency stations, U.S. Naval Observatory (USNO), and National Institute of Standards and Technology (NIST; formerly National Bureau of Standards [NBS]) telephone modem services in the United States, as well as similar systems and services in other countries. If every computer were equipped with one of these clocks and rooftop space was available for their antennas, NTP would not be needed, and this book could be recycled. But, a purpose-designed NTP server with a GPS antenna on one end and an Ethernet connection on the other cost $3,000 as this was written. Nonetheless, a clever electronic technician can hotwire a $100 Garmin GPS receiver to a serial port on a junkbox personal computer (PC) and do a decent job. The NTP software distribution even has drivers for it.

For reasons of cost and convenience, it is not possible to equip every computer with a reference clock. Furthermore, the reliability requirements for time synchronization may be so strict that a single clock cannot always be trusted. Therefore, even if a reference clock is available, most operators run NTP anyway with other redundant servers and diverse network paths. However, it is possible to equip some number of computers acting as primary time servers to wrangle a much larger herd of secondary servers and clients connected by a common network. In fact, USNO and NIST in the United States and their partners in other countries operate a fleet of Internet time servers providing time traceable to national standards. How this is done is the dominant topic of this book.

1.2 Time Synchronization Protocols

The synchronization protocol determines the time offset of a client clock relative to one or more server clocks. The various synchronization protocols in use today provide different means to do this, but they all follow the same general model. The client sends a request to the server, and the server responds with its current time. For the best accuracy, the client needs to measure the server-client propagation delay to determine the true time offset relative to the server. Since it is not possible to determine the one-way delays, unless the actual time offset is known, NTP measures the total round-trip delay and assumes that the propagation times are statistically equal in each direction. In general, this is a useful approximation; however, in the Internet of today, network paths and the associated delays can differ significantly, causing errors up to one-half the path delay difference. An extensive discussion and analysis of errors is in Chapter 11.

The community served by the synchronization protocol can be large. For instance, there is an extensive network, referred to in this book as the *public NTP subnet*, consisting of some hundreds of servers and millions of clients. NIST estimates 25 million clients of its dozen public servers (J. Levine, personal communication). In addition, there are numerous private NTP subnets that do not exchange time values with the public subnet for one reason or another. It is the usual practice to use multiple redundant servers and diverse network paths to protect against broken software, hardware, and network links, as well as misbehaving hackers, so there are many more synchronization paths than there are servers and clients.

The NTP protocol operates in multiple stratum levels where time values flow from servers at one stratum to clients at the next-higher stratum. Clients can also function as servers for the next-higher stratum in turn. Each NTP subnet graph is organized as a forest of trees with the primary (stratum 1) servers at the roots and dependent secondary servers at each increasing stratum from the roots. Primary servers are synchronized to UTC as disseminated via radio, satellite, or telephone modem service. Secondary (stratum 2) servers are synchronized to the primary servers and to other secondary servers at the same stratum. Individual corporations and institutions often operate private NTP servers behind firewalls and synchronized to public servers via holes bored in the firewalls. Private subnets may not require synchronization to national standards, in which case one or more servers are arbitrarily designated primary, and all other servers synchronize directly or indirectly to them.

Synchronization protocols work in one or more association modes, depending on the protocol association design. There are three kinds of associations: persistent, preemptable, and ephemeral. *Persistent* associations are mobilized as directed by the configuration file and are never demobilized. *Preemptable* associations are also mobilized by the configuration file but are demobilized if the server has not been heard for some time. Ephemeral associations are mobilized on receipt of a packet designed for that purpose, such as a broadcast mode packet, and are demobilized if the server has not been heard for some time.

Use of the term *broadcast* in this book should be interpreted according to the Internet Protocol Version 4 (IPv4) and Version 6 (IPv6) address family conventions. In IPv4, broadcast is intended for multiple delivery on the same subnet, while multicast is intended for multiple delivery on the Internet at large. In IPv6, multicast is intended for multiple delivery on the Internet at large as selected by the IPv6 address prefix. Notwithstanding this distinction and for simplicity in this book, the term *broadcast* applies equally to both address families and to both broadcast and multicast modes.

Client/server mode, also called master/slave mode, is supported in both DTSS and NTP. In this mode, a client synchronizes to a stateless server as in the conventional remote procedure call (RPC) model. NTP also supports symmetric modes, which allows either of two peer servers to synchronize to the other, to provide mutual backup. DTSS and NTP support broadcast mode, which allows many clients to synchronize to one or a few servers, reducing network traffic when large numbers of clients are involved.

Configuration management can be an engineering challenge in large subnets. Various schemes that index public databases and network directory services are used in DTSS and NTP to discover servers. Creative domain name system (DNS) schemes such as the NTP pool described in Chapter 5 can be used to automatically distribute load over a number of volunteer servers. Especially in networks with large client populations, clients can use broadcast mode to discover servers, but since listen-only clients cannot calibrate the propagation delay, accuracy can suffer. NTP clients can determine the delay at the time a server is first discovered by temporarily polling the server in client/server mode and then reverting to listen-only broadcast client mode. In addition, NTP clients can broadcast a special *manycast* message to solicit responses from nearby servers and continue in client/server mode with the respondents. NTP system engineering and configuration management are discussed in Chapter 5.

A reliable network time service requires provisions to prevent accidental or malicious attacks on the servers and clients in the network. NTP includes provisions for access control using a mask-and-match scheme and can shed messages that might arrive in a clogging attack. NTP clients can cryptographically authenticate individual servers using symmetric key or public key cryptography. Symmetric key cryptography authenticates servers using shared secret keys. In public key cryptography, industry standard X.509 certificates reliably bind the server identification credentials and associated public keys. The purpose-designed Autokey protocol, now navigating the standards process, authenticates servers using timestamped digital signatures. The protocol is specially crafted to reduce the risk of intrusion while maximizing the synchronization accuracy and to minimize the consumption of processor resources. Security issues are discussed in Chapters 9 and 10.

1.3 Computer Clocks

Most computers include a quartz or surface acoustic wave (SAW) resonator-stabilized oscillator and oscillator counter that interrupt the processor at intervals of a few milliseconds, called the *tick*. At each tick interrupt, this value is added to a system variable representing the clock time. The clock can be read by system and application programs and set on occasion to an external reference. Once set, the clock readings increment at a nominal rate, depending on the value of the tick. Typical Unix system kernels provide a programmable mechanism to increase or decrease the value of the tick by a small, fixed amount to amortize a given time adjustment smoothly over multiple ticks. Think of this as how Big Ben timekeepers in London adjust the clock time by periodically placing and removing coinage on its pendulum. Very likely the last farthings, halfpennies, and tuppence, no longer in circulation, are in the Big Ben toolbox.

Clock errors are due to systematic variations in network delay and latencies in computer hardware and software (jitter) as well as clock oscillator wander. The time of a computer clock relative to ideal time can be expressed as

$$T(t) = T(t_0) + R(t - t_0) + D(t - t_0)^2 + x(t),$$

where t is the current time, t_0 is the time at the last measurement update, T is the time offset, R is the frequency offset, D is the drift due to resonator aging, and x is a stochastic error term exposed in some detail in Chapter 11. The first three terms include systematic offsets that can be corrected and the last random variations that cannot. Some protocols, including DTSS, estimate only the first term in this expression, while others, including NTP, estimate the first two terms. Errors due to the third term, while important to model resonator aging in precision quartz oscillators, are usually dominated by errors in the first two terms.

The synchronization protocol estimates T (and R, where relevant) at regular *update intervals* and adjusts the clock to minimize $T(t)$ in future t. In common cases, R can have nominal values up to several hundred parts per million with random variations in the order of 1 PPM due to ambient temperature changes. If R is neglected, the resulting errors can accumulate to seconds per day. Analysis of quartz-resonator-stabilized oscillators shows that residual errors due to oscillator wander are a function of the averaging time, which in turn depends on the update time. With update times less than about 15 min, errors are usually dominated by network jitter, while at intervals greater than this, errors are usually dominated by oscillator wander.

As a practical matter, for nominal accuracies on the order of a millisecond, this requires clients to exchange messages with servers at intervals of not more than about 15 min. However, if the accuracy requirement can be relaxed to a few tens of milliseconds, the update time can be increased to a day and a half. In NTP, the errors that accumulate from the root to the leaves of the tree are estimated and incorporated into a comprehensive error budget defined in Chapter 11. This allows real-time applications to adjust audio or video play-out delay, for example.

1.4 Processing Time Values

Applications requiring reliable time synchronization, such as air traffic control and stock transactions, must have confidence that the system clock is correct within some bound relative to a given timescale such as UTC. There is a considerable body of literature that studies correctness principles with respect to various failure models such as fail-stop and Byzantine traitors. While these principles and the algorithms based on them inspire much confidence in a theoretical setting, most require multiple message rounds for each measurement and would be impractical in a large computer network such as the Internet.

Inspired by this work, a suite of correctness assertions has evolved over the years to bound the errors inherent in any configuration. For instance, it is shown in Chapter 11 that the worst-case error in reading a remote server clock cannot exceed one-half the round-trip delay measured by the client. The maximum error is inherited and augmented by each client along the synchronization path. This is a valuable insight since it permits strong statements about the correctness of the timekeeping system. There are many gems like this exposed in Chapter 2.

NTP is an exceedingly large and complex real-time system with intricately engineered algorithms and carefully structured protocol operations. There is an extensive suite of NTP grooming and mitigation algorithms that are the topic of the following chapters. They select only the best server or combination of servers and the best samples from each server. In a very real sense, the NTP algorithms operate as a gigantic digital signal processor and utilize many principles of that engineering field, including linear and nonlinear signal processing and adaptive-parameter feedback loops. Following is a capsule summary of these algorithms; details are in Chapter 3.

By its very nature, clock synchronization is a continuous sampling process by which time offset samples are collected on a regular basis from each of possibly several servers. Accuracy can be improved if the samples from each server are processed by an engineered filter algorithm. Algorithms described in the literature are based on trimmed-mean and median methods. The clock filter algorithm used in NTP and described in Chapter 3 is based on the observation that incidental errors increase with increasing round-trip delays. The algorithm accumulates time offset/delay samples in a window of several samples and selects the offset sample associated with the minimum delay.

Computer time is so precious and so many bad things can happen if the clock breaks or a hostile intruder climbs over the firewall that serious attention must be given to the issues of redundancy and diversity. Obviously, single points of failure in the network or server population must be avoided. More to the point, the select algorithm that sorts the *truechimers*, whose clocks gloriously tell the truth, from the *falsetickers*, whose clocks lie viciously, must be designed with verifiable correctness assertions. The computer science literature is stocked with algorithms that do this, but only a few are viable in a practical system. The one used in NTP finds the largest clique of truechimers in the server population.

Even under peacetime conditions, the truechimers surviving the select algorithm might have somewhat different time offsets due to asymmetric delays and network jitter. Various kinds of cluster and combine algorithms have been found useful to deliver the best time from the unruly bunch. The one used in NTP sorts the offsets by a quality metric, then repeatedly discards the outlier with the worst quality until further discards will not reduce the residual error or until a minimum number of servers remain. The final clock adjustment is computed as a weighted average of the survivors.

At the heart of the NTP synchronization paradigm is the algorithm used to adjust the system clock in accordance with the final offset determined by these algorithms. This is called the *discipline algorithm* or simply the *discipline*. Such algorithms can be classed according to whether they minimize the time offset, the frequency offset, or both. For instance, the discipline used in DTSS minimizes only the time offset, while the one used in NTP and described in Chapter 4 minimizes both time and frequency offsets. While the DTSS algorithm cannot remove residual errors due to systematic frequency offsets, the NTP algorithm is more complicated and less forgiving of design and implementation mistakes.

The NTP discipline algorithm functions as a feedback loop, with each round of measured offsets used to adjust the system clock time and frequency. The behavior of feedback loops is well understood and modeled by mathematical analysis, as described in Chapter 12. The significant design parameter is the time constant, or responsiveness to time and frequency variations, which depends on the client *poll interval*. For typical computer clocks, the best accuracy is achieved when the poll interval is relatively small, but this can result in unacceptable network overhead. In practice and with typical network configurations, the optimal value varies between 1 min and 20 min for Internet paths. In some cases involving toll telephone modem paths, much longer intervals of a day or more are suitable with only moderate loss of accuracy.

1.5 Correctness and Accuracy Expectations

One of the most important goals for the NTP design is that it conforms to strict correctness principles established by the computer science theory community. The thread running through just about all the literature on time business is that the intrinsic frequency error of the computer clock must be strictly bounded by some number. As a practical matter, this number has been set at 500 PPM, which works out to 0.5 ms/s, or 1.8 s/h, or 43 s/day. This is a large error and not found often; more often, the error is less than 100 PPM. It is not a showstopper if the actual error is greater than 500 PPM, but NTP will not be able to reduce the residual time offset to zero.

A real showstopper lies in the way NTP calculates time values using 64-bit arithmetic. This requires the computer clock to be set within 34 years of the current time.* There are two reasons for this. First, this avoids overflow in the computation of clock offset and round-trip delay as described in Chapter 2; second, this allows reliable determination of the NTP era number as described in Chapter 13. The 34-year limit is very real, as in early 2004 NTP tripped over the age of the Unix clock, which began life in 1970.

Correctness principles establish the frequency and time bounds representing the worst behavior of the computer clock; however, we are often more concerned with the expected behavior. For the ultimate accuracy, the discipline algorithm would have to control the hardware clock directly, and this has been done in experimental systems. Advances in computer timekeeping technology have raised the accuracy bar over the decades from 100 ms, when the Internet was teething, to a few microseconds in the adolescent Internet of today. However, the ultimate accuracy can be achieved only when the clock can be disciplined with exquisitely intimate means. In practice, this requires the discipline algorithm, normally implemented in the NTP software, to be implemented in the operating system kernel.

There have been two generations of kernel discipline algorithms: one over a decade ago designed to provide microsecond resolution and the latest to provide nanosecond resolution. The original discipline was implemented for Sun Solaris, Digital (now HP) Tru64, FreeBSD, Linux, and perhaps others. It has been included in Solaris and Tru64 releases for many years. The new discipline has been implemented for all of these systems as well but is not yet a standard feature in Solaris and Tru64. It is included in the current FreeBSD release and is an option in the current Linux release. A description of the kernel provisions along with a performance assessment is in Chapter 8.

How accurate is NTP time on a particular architecture, operating system, and network? The answer depends on many factors, some of which are discussed in Chapter 5. Absolute accuracy relative to UTC is difficult to determine unless a local precision reference clock is available. In point of fact, systematic errors are usually fixed and unchanging with time, so once calibrated they can be ignored. An exception is the error due to asymmetric delays, by which the transmission delay in one direction is significantly different from that in the reciprocal direction. Experience shows that these delays change from time to time as the result of network reconfigurations by Internet service providers, at least for paths spanning large parts of the Internet copper, glass, and space infrastructure. A common case is when one leg of the Internet path is via satellite and the other is via landline.

---

* In current NTP software, a simple trick using 64-bit integer first-order differences and floating-double second-order differences increases the 34-year aperture to 68 years without loss of precision.

It is easier and usually more useful to interpret the jitter and wander statistics produced by NTP as accuracy metrics. Certainly, this is the most important statistic in the provision of real-time audio and video services. The short answer for accuracy expectations is probably a few milliseconds in the vast Internet prairies covering the planet with occasional mountain peaks of a few tens of milliseconds due to network congestion. With slow, congested links to East Jabip,* accuracies may be in the 100-ms range. In quiet, full-duplex 100-Mb Ethernets where collisions are forbidden and hubs are lightning quick, the performance can be much better. Typical accuracies are better than 100 µs at a primary server degrading to a millisecond at a secondary server, but these expectations can be demolished if a rapid temperature change occurs or a server is rebooted.

The reference implementation includes software drivers for over 40 radio and satellite receivers and telephone modem services for every known means of national and international time dissemination service operating today. Where a sufficiently pristine external discipline signal such as a pulse-per-second (PPS) signal from a GPS receiver or calibrated atomic clock is used and the kernel discipline is available, the accuracy can be improved to a microsecond or better under most conditions. An engineering description of the design, interface, and performance of primary servers using these signals is given in Chapter 7.

1.6 Security

It may seem a little weird to bring up the topic of security, but doing secure time synchronization over a public network is as attractive as it is dangerous. Obviously, bad things can happen if a terrorist compromises the time so that trains are dispatched to collide, stocks are sold before they are bought, and the evening news comes on at midnight. There is a more sinister side as well if the time is warped sufficiently to purge domain name caches or invalidate prescriptions, disk quotas, or income tax returns.

There are many defenses already implemented in the NTP protocol design as described in Chapter 2, including protection against replay and spoofing attacks, as well as various kinds of protocol and packet format misdirection. The Byzantine select algorithm avoids disruptions that might be provoked by a terrorist cell as long as the number of terrorists are only a minority clique. Just for good measure, the reference implementation includes purpose-engineered access controls and clogging avoidance.

---

* East Jabip is a movable place found at the end of the current longest, most congested links in the Internet geography.

The Kerberos security scheme originally implemented at the Massachusetts Institute of Technology (MIT) might have been the first system to recognize that these defenses are not sufficient to keep out a determined hijacker attempting to masquerade as a legitimate source. The problem anticipated by the designers was security of the timestamped tickets used to validate access controls. If a student prank managed to torque the clock forward by a day or two, even for a short time, all tickets would instantly expire, and nobody could get anything done.

The solution to the Kerberos problem was implemented by NTP in the form of symmetric key cryptography, by which a secret key is shared between the time servers and time clients in the system. This scheme has worked well over the years, but it requires secure distribution and management of the keys themselves. Modern schemes use public key cryptography in which servers create a public/private key pair in which the public key is exposed for anybody who asks, but the private key is never divulged. As described in Chapter 9, the client obtains from its servers a set of cryptographic credentials verifying membership in a trusted group. Using these and a low-overhead protocol, the client can securely authenticate other servers in the group.

But, how do the clients know an evil middleman has not managed to pry between the client and a legitimate server and construct bogus credentials? A server proves identity to its clients using a public certificate containing digital signatures to bind selected identity credentials, such as its host name, to its public key. The binding process continues as a certificate trail beginning with the client via intermediate certificate authorities (CAs) and ending at a root CA, which is independently trusted by other reliable means.

NTP supports public key cryptography and certificate trails using the Autokey protocol described in Chapter 9. This protocol runs in parallel with the NTP protocol and uses the same packets. It is specifically designed to minimize intrusion and resist clogging attacks while providing strong defense against cryptographic malfeasance. The Autokey protocol provides for mutual overlapping groups using private group keys and crafted identity algorithms, some of which are properly described as zero-knowledge proofs. In a zero-knowledge proof, the server can prove identity without revealing the key itself. Identity schemes are described in Chapter 10.

In recent experience with the public NTP subnet, the most serious security violations have been accidental or malicious clogging attacks, by which large numbers of clients are configured for the same server or the same few servers. In one incident [5], a router intended for home office use was configured by the manufacturer to send packets at 1-s intervals to a single designated server. Ordinarily, this would not be a severe problem if only a small number of these routers was involved, but there were 750,000 of them sold, all ganging up on the same service providers and victim server. There is nothing in the Internet constitution that forbids this misbehavior, only a set of best practices and volunteer compliance. This kind of problem is not unique to NTP, of course, and the incident could be a warning of what might lie ahead.

1.7 NTP in the Internet

It is said that engineers start out knowing nothing about everything, then learn more and more about less and less until knowing everything about nothing. This may indeed characterize the field, more like the back porch, of computer network timekeeping. Boiled to essentials, really the only thing the protocol does is occasionally read the clock in another machine, tell whether the system clock is fast or slow, and nudge the clock oscillator one way or the other, just like the Big Ben timekeepers in London. Of course, the devil is in the details.

All NTP servers and clients in the Internet are expected to conform to the NTP Version 3 (NTPv3) protocol specification published by the Internet Engineering Task Force (IETF) as Request for Comments RFC-1305 [6]. Users are strongly encouraged to upgrade to the NTP Version 4 (NTPv4) protocol, which is the main topic of this book. NTPv4 consists of a suite of extensions to NTPv3, but a definitive protocol specification is not yet available, even after 4 years of review by the IETF. While a formal protocol specification for NTPv4 is beyond the scope of this book, it is expected to be based on the flowcharts and related discussion in Chapter 14 of this book. There is a subset of NTP called the Simple Network Time Protocol Version 4 (SNTPv4) defined in RFC-2030 [7] that is compatible at the protocol level with both NTPv3 and NTPv4 but does not include the mitigation algorithms of the full NTPv4 reference implementation. SNTP server mode is intended for dedicated products that include a GPS receiver or other external synchronization source. SNTP client mode is intended for PCs or low-end workstations that for one reason or another cannot justify running the full NTP implementation and do not have clients of their own.

In previous NTP specifications, a distinction was made between what was in the specification and what was in the reference implementation. The specification specifically defined the architecture, protocol state machine, transition function, and protocol data unit. The specification explicitly did not require the crafted grooming, mitigation, and discipline algorithms that are the heart of this book and left open the option to use different algorithms in different NTP implementations. However, the many NTP servers and clients in the Internet have become an interconnected forest of tightly coupled oscillators and feedback loops that now behave as one integrated system. To preserve stability in the forest, a full protocol specification now needs to encompass these algorithms.

If some NTP forest grove is not deep and there are no intermediate servers between the primary synchronization source (not necessarily stratum 1) and dependent clients, the particular algorithms might not matter much, even if suboptimal. But, experience has proven that the dynamics of larger NTP woodlands require a systematic approach to algorithm design, most importantly the algorithm that disciplines the system clock time and frequency.

Even small perturbations can excite a string of dependent servers and clients with badly matched discipline parameters something like the crack of a whip. For this reason, the discipline algorithm described in Chapter 4 is likely to become an integral component of future specifications.

1.8 Parting Shots

The latest NTPv4 software, called the *reference implementation* in this book, is the product of almost three decades of development and refinement by a team of over four dozen volunteer contributors and countless deputized bug catchers in the field. The volunteer corps represents several countries, professions, and technical skill sets—the copyright page in the NTP documentation acknowledges all of them. While this book is mostly about NTPv4, there still are a number of timekeepers running legacy versions, so this book speaks to older versions as well. When necessary, differences between versions are identified in context. Much more about the development process and milestones is revealed in Chapter 19.

NTP in one version or another has been running for almost three decades in the Internet. In fact, a claim can be made that it is the longest-running continuously operating application protocol in the Internet. NTP is widely deployed in hosts and routers in the Internet of today, although only a fraction have been surveyed [8]. The protocol and algorithms have continuously evolved from humble beginnings and have adapted over the years as the Internet itself grew up. Thus, it is important that new developments do not make older versions obsolete. The current protocol implementation is backward compatible with previous versions but includes several new features described in other chapters.

NTP has spawned a commercial enterprise of its own. Several firms make NTP servers integrated with a GPS receiver or telephone modem. NTP is used by research projects, service providers, broadcasters, air traffic control, brokerage houses, and the intranets of many large corporations and universities. NTP time is disseminated using public servers operated by the national standards laboratories of the United States and many other countries of the world. In fact, not only does the Sun never set on NTP, but also it now never even gets close to the horizon. NTP subnets have been discovered on ships and airplanes all over the world, on the seafloor and space vehicles, and most recently in Antarctica. A deployment on the Moon and Mars is anticipated in the near future.

The current software and documentation release is available free of charge (but see the copyright notice) via the Web at http://www.ntp.org. The distribution has been ported to almost every computer architecture known from PCs to Crays (but only as a server on IBM mainframes) and embedded in products. The build-and-install process is largely automatic and requires no architecture or operating system configuration. Much more is said about this in the documentation included in the software distribution on the Web. Online resources at this Web site include many articles and reports cited in this book, together with topical briefings, project descriptions, mail, and newsgroups. A Google for "network time protocol" at the time of this writing returned 21.8 million hits.

References

1. Liskov, B. Practical uses of synchronized clocks in distributed systems. *Proceedings 10th Annual ACM Symposium on Principles of Distributed Computing* (Montreal, April 1991), 1–9.
2. Lamport, L. Time, clocks and the ordering of events in a distributed system. *Commun. ACM 21, 7* (July 1978), 558–565.
3. Mills, D.L. Internet time synchronization: the Network Time Protocol. *IEEE Trans. Commun. COM-39, 10* (October 1991), 1482–1493. Also in Yang, Z., and T.A. Marsland (Eds.), *Global States and Time in Distributed Systems*. IEEE Computer Society Press, Los Alamitos, CA, 1994, 91–102.
4. *Digital Time Service Functional Specification Version T.1.0.5*. Digital Equipment Corporation, 1989.
5. Mills, D.L., J. Levine, R. Schmidt, and D. Plonka. Coping with overload on the Network Time Protocol public servers. *Proceedings Precision Time and Time Interval (PTTI) Applications and Planning Meeting* (Washington, DC, December 2004), 5–16.
6. Mills, D.L. *Network Time Protocol (Version 3) Specification, Implementation and Analysis*. Network Working Group Report RFC-1305, University of Delaware, Newark, March 1992, 113 pp.
7. Mills, D.L. *Simple Network Time Protocol (SNTP) Version 4 for IPv4, IPv6 and OSI*. Network Working Group Report RFC-2030, University of Delaware, Newark, October 1996, 18 pp.
8. Mills, D.L., A. Thyagarajan, and B.C. Huffman. Internet timekeeping around the globe. *Proceedings Precision Time and Time Interval (PTTI) Applications and Planning Meeting* (Long Beach, CA, December 1997), 365–371.

Further Reading

IEEE Standard 1344. IEEE Standard for Synchrophasors for Power Systems. 1995 (Revised 2000).

2

How NTP Works

"The time has come," the Walrus said,
"To talk of many things:
Of shoes—and ships—and sealing wax—
Of cabbages—and kings—
And why the sea is boiling hot—
And whether pigs have wings."

Lewis Carroll
Through the Looking Glass

The Network Time Protocol (NTP) is three things: the NTP software program, called a *daemon* in Unix and a *service* in Windows; a protocol that exchanges time values between servers and clients; and a suite of algorithms that process the time values to advance or retard the system clock. In this book, especially in this chapter, we speak of NTP "doing something." This is rather loose terminology since the acronym NTP is a descriptive noun and uncomfortable with an action verb. More properly, it is the NTP daemon that does something and that depends on the implementation. Nevertheless, in this book we sometimes animate the acronym.

One of the things that NTP has been "doing" is evolving in five versions over almost three decades.* With few exceptions, the last four versions are interoperable, and all can exchange time values and synchronize the system clock. However, the timekeeping quality has much improved over the versions, and many features have been added. If needed, the version is specified as NTPv3 for version 3 and NTPv4 for version 4; if not, the generic NTP is used. The current NTPv4 reference implementation, ntpd, is designed to run in a multitasking environment as an independent, self-contained program. This program sends and receives time values with each of possibly several NTP servers running elsewhere in the Internet.

This chapter is organized as follows: First discussed is set of general requirements for NTP to do its job and be a good network citizen. Next is a discussion of how NTP reckons the time with respect to sources elsewhere in the Internet. The discussion continues with how the various program units fit together and operate to determine the time offset of the system clock relative to possibly several remote servers. Next a discussion of how the system clock time and frequency are adjusted to minimize the offset over time is

---

* The first version had no version number and was later assigned version 0.

15

presented. NTP can operate in several modes, such as client/server, symmetric, and broadcast, depending on the configuration. These modes and the associations that define them are discussed next. NTPv4 introduces new methods to discover servers and automatically select among them for the most precise timekeeping. The chapter concludes with an overview of the security model, access controls, and system monitoring.

2.1 General Infrastructure Requirements

NTP must operate in the Internet of today with occasional server failures, traffic emergencies, route flaps, hacker attacks, and facility outages. Following is a set of assertions that have served as the developer's road map.

1. The protocol and algorithms must perform well over a wide range of conditions and optimize the various algorithm parameters automatically for each server, network path, and computer clock. Good performance requires multiple comparisons over relatively long periods of time. For instance, while only a few measurements are usually adequate to determine local time in the Internet to within a millisecond or two, a number of measurements over several hours are required to reliably stabilize frequency to less than 1 part per million (PPM).

2. The NTP subnet architecture must be hierarchical by stratum, where synchronization flows from *primary servers* at the lowest stratum successively to *secondary servers* at progressively higher strata. The primary servers must be reliably synchronized to national standards by radio, satellite, telephone modem, or calibrated atomic clock. All primary and secondary servers must deliver continuous time based on UTC, even when leap seconds are inserted in the UTC timescale. The servers must provide accurate and precise time, even with significant network jitter and oscillator wander.

3. The subnet must be reliable and survivable, even under unstable network conditions and where connectivity may be lost for periods up to days. This requires redundant time servers and diverse transmission paths, as well as a dynamically reconfigurable subnet architecture. Failing or misoperating servers must be recognized and reconfiguration performed automatically without operator direction or assistance.

4. The synchronization protocol must operate continuously and provide update information at rates sufficient to compensate for the expected wander of the room temperature quartz oscillators used in ordinary computer clocks. It must operate efficiently with large numbers of time

servers and clients in continuous-polled and procedure-call modes and in broadcast and unicast configurations. The protocol must operate in existing Internets, including a spectrum of architectures ranging from personal workstations to supercomputers, but make minimal demands on the operating system and infrastructure services.

5. Security provisions must include cryptographic protection against accidental or willful intrusion, including message modification, replay, and clogging attacks. Means must be available to securely identify and authenticate servers and protect against masquerade, intended or accidental. Some implementations may include access controls that selectively allow or refuse requests from designated networks and limit the rate of requests serviced.

6. Means must be provided to record significant events in the system log and to record performance data for offline analysis. Some implementations may include the ability to monitor and control the servers and clients from a remote location using cryptographically secure procedures. Some implementations may include the ability to remotely enable and disable specific protocol features and to add, modify, and delete timing sources.

7. Server software, especially client software, must be easily built, installed, and configured using standard system tools. It must operate in most if not all computer architectures and operating systems in common use today. The software must be available free of charge and without limitations on use, distribution, or incorporation in products for sale.

2.2 How NTP Represents the Time

In a very real sense, this book is all about time values. Every computer operating system has means to read the system clock and return a time value representing the current time of day in one format or another. Time values are ephemeral; in principle, every reading returns a value greater than the previous reading. In other words, time never stands still or runs backward. Since time values are represented in words or structures with a limited number of bits, they can represent only a limited range of time, called an *era*, and a limited resolution within the era.

Most of the discussion in this book is centered about NTP, so its time format is a natural choice, as shown in Figure 2.1. There are two formats: a 64-bit unsigned *timestamp* format, which represents time in packet headers exchanged between clients and servers, and a 128-bit signed *datestamp* format, which can represent dates from the dawn of the universe to when the Sun grows dim. In both formats, the high-order bits represent time in

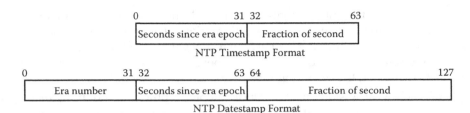

FIGURE 2.1
NTP time formats.

seconds since the NTP base epoch in era 0, 0 h 1 January 1900, while the low-order bits represent the fraction of the second.

In datestamp format, era 0 represents the years from the beginning in 1900 to some time in 2036 when era 1 begins, while era –1 represents the years from 1900 to some time in 1854 when era –2 ended. In timestamp format, the years span from the beginning of an era to the end of that era 136 years later, while in datestamp format the years span the age of the universe. In timestamp format, the second can be represented to 232 ps, which seems tiny, but computers are getting so fast that this might soon be the precision-limiting factor. In datestamp format, the second can be represented to about 500 atto-seconds, or about a tenth of the time light takes to pass through an atom.

There is a special value for both formats when both the seconds and fraction fields are zero, which designates a condition in which the system clock is unsynchronized. Datestamp values are considered twos complement, signed values as used in ordinary 128-bit arithmetic, so negative values represent times before era 0. Timestamp values are considered unsigned; the only computations allowed are differences between 64-bit values producing a 63-bit signed result. Furthermore, the calculations producing clock offset and round-trip delay are differences between 63-bit signed values producing a 62-bit signed result. The 30-bit signed seconds field can represent only from 34 years in the past to 34 years in the future. This is an intrinsic characteristic of any time synchronization protocol using 64-bit integer arithmetic. However, while it is necessary to use 64-bit integer arithmetic for the first-order differences to preserve precision, the second-order differences can be done after conversion to 64-bit floating-double representation without diminishing precision. Further discussion of these issues is in Chapter 13.

There are only two operations possible with time values: subtraction of one time value from another (time interval) and signed addition of a constant to a time value (time adjustment). Having survived the millennium rollover in 2000, the anxious reader will ask what happens when era 0 rolls over in 2036? The answer is that as long as the computer clock is set within 68 years of the correct time, NTP will synchronize correctly, even if an adjustment spans an era boundary.

To set the clock correctly means setting the era number, which presumably comes from the real-time clock or the file system. It does not have to be accurate, just within 68 years of the time to which NTP will eventually steer. To see why this is so, consider the subtraction operation in twos-complement arithmetic. First, the second number (subtrahend) is ones complemented, then incremented by one, then added to the first number. Assume the two numbers are in adjacent eras but within 68 years of each other. Then, the sum of the two numbers considered as a signed number cannot overflow the 32-bit seconds field.

Note with emphasis that nothing in this book says anything about the system clock format, whether seconds and microseconds, seconds and nanoseconds, or seconds and fraction. To be consistent with present-day means that to disseminate conventional civil time, the NTP timescale is coincident with UTC, including leap seconds. It says nothing about the local time zone or standard/daylight time, which is established by the operating system. It says nothing about how NTP timestamps are converted to external representation or displayed in a message or on the task bar. These things are completely determined by the operating system and application programs that interpret the system clock values.

2.3 How NTP Reckons the Time

To understand how NTP works, it may be helpful to describe in general how it reckons the time. The NTP daemon implements several semiautonomous cooperating sequential processes. There is a peer process and poll process and related state variables, called an *association*, for each remote NTP server and local reference clock, such as a radio or satellite receiver or telephone modem. The poll process sends messages to the server at intervals varying from less than a minute to over a day. The actual intervals are determined on the basis of expected time quality and allowable network overhead, as described further in this chapter. The peer process receives the reply and calculates the time offset and other values.

The peer and poll processes animate the protocol described in Chapter 3. First, client A sends the current time T_1 to server B. On arrival, B saves T_1 along with the current time T_2. Server B does not have to respond immediately since it might have other things to do or simply wants to pace the client and avoid runaway loops. Some time later, B sends the current time T_3 along with the saved T_1 and T_2 to A. On arrival, A reads its clock T_4 and proceeds to compute both time offset θ and round-trip delay δ of B relative to A:

$$\theta = \frac{1}{2}[(T_2 - T_1) + (T_3 - T_4)] \text{ and } \delta = (T_4 - T_1) - (T_3 - T_2). \qquad (2.1)$$

The offset and delay values are groomed by the clock filter algorithm described in Chapter 3 and saved along with related variables separately for each association. Note that while this method is described as a client/server exchange, it is symmetric and operates as well in a peer–peer exchange in which either peer can function as a server for the other as a client. Also note that the protocol provides a way to detect duplicate and bogus packets.

The time values from Equation 2.1 are processed by the clock filter algorithm, which selects the best from among the previous eight values. The system process runs as new values are produced by the clock filter algorithm. These values are processed by a suite of three concatenated algorithms, including the select, cluster, and combine algorithms, which are discussed in Chapter 3. The job of the select algorithm is to find and discard falsetickers and pass the truechimers on to the cluster algorithm. The job of the cluster algorithm is to select from among the truechimers the most reliable and accurate time values on the basis of statistical principles. Assuming a sufficient number of truechimers are available, statistical outliers are discarded until only three candidates survive. The combine algorithm averages the survivor offsets weighted by a statistic called the *root distance*.

The result of the algorithms to this point is a single time value representing the best guess of the system clock offset with respect to the server population as a whole. This value is redetermined as each message arrives and results in a new offset update. The updates are processed by the loop filter, which is part of the feedback loop that implements the discipline algorithm discussed in Chapter 4. The clock adjust process closes the feedback loop by amortizing the offsets between updates using incremental adjustments at 1-s intervals. The adjustments are implemented by the system clock, which operates as a variable-frequency oscillator (VFO). The VFO implements the system clock from which the timestamps are determined and closes the feedback loop.

The NTP subnet is a forest of multiple trees in which each client has a network path to each of a number of configured servers, and each of these servers has a network path to each of their configured servers, and so on. Each of these paths is associated with a metric computed from the number of server hops (strata) to the primary servers at the roots of the forest. The NTP algorithms operate as a distributed Bellman-Ford routing protocol to construct a shortest-path spanning tree among these paths. This results in minimum-distance paths from each primary server at the root via intervening secondary servers to every configured client at the leaves of the tree. The roots for secondary servers and clients in different regions of the subnet may have different primary servers, but the overall distance to each primary server will always be the minimum over all available paths. As a practical matter, this approach provides the most accurate, most reliable timekeeping in the subnet as a whole.

2.4 How NTP Disciplines the Time

Every NTP host has a hardware system clock, usually implemented as a counter driven by a quartz crystal or surface acoustic wave (SAW) oscillator. The counter interrupts the processor at intervals of 10 ms or so and advances the software system clock by this interval. The software clock can be read by application programs using a suitable application program interface (API) to determine the current clock time. In some architectures, software time values can be interpolated between interrupts using a processor chip counter called the processor cycle counter (PCC) in Digital systems and the timestamp counter (TSC) in Intel systems. In most computers today, several application programs can be running at once, and each can read the clock without interference from other programs. Precautions are necessary to avoid violating causality; that is, the clock reading operation is always atomic and monotone-definite increasing.

In Unix operating systems of today, the system clock is represented in seconds and microseconds or nanoseconds with a base epoch of 0 h 1 January 1970. The Unix system clock can be set to run at a nominal rate and at two other rates slightly fast and slightly slow by 500 PPM or 0.5 ms/s. A time adjustment is performed by calculating the length of an interval to run the clock fast or slow to complete the specified adjustment. Unix systems include the capability to set the clock to an arbitrary time, but NTP does this only in exceptional circumstances.

No computer clock is perfect; the intrinsic frequency can vary from computer to computer and even from time to time. In particular, the frequency error can be as large as several hundred parts per million, depending on the manufacturing tolerance. For instance, if the frequency error is 100 PPM and no corrective means are available, the time error will accumulate at the rate of about 8 s per day. In addition, the frequency can fluctuate depending on the ambient temperature, associated circuit components, and power supply variations. The most important contribution to frequency fluctuations is the ambient temperature. A typical temperature coefficient is 1 PPM per degree celsius.

The discipline algorithm described in Chapter 4 implements corrections for both the intrinsic frequency and frequency fluctuations once each second. Thus, in the example after 1 s the time error will be 100 μs, which is generally considered good timekeeping on a local-area network (LAN). For better accuracy, the clock adjustments must be done in the kernel using techniques discussed in Chapter 8. By way of comparison, a modern workstation with kernel timekeeping support can attain nominal accuracy in the low microseconds.

Each computer clock can have a different intrinsic frequency and different frequency fluctuations with temperature. This can be a valuable diagnostic aid; the intrinsic frequency can serve as something like a unique fingerprint which identifies a particular computer. More usefully, the fluctuation with temperature can be recorded and used as a machine room or motherboard thermometer. In fact, failures in room air conditioning and central processing unit (CPU) fans have been alarmed in this way. In passing, an NTP frequency surge has often been the first indication that a power supply fan, CPU fan, or air conditioner is failing.*

2.5 How NTP Manages Associations

Recall that an NTP client has an association for each remote server and local reference clock. There are three types of associations: persistent, preemptable, and ephemeral. *Persistent* associations are explicitly configured and mobilized at startup. *Preemptable* associations are mobilized at startup or as the result of a server discovery scheme described later. *Ephemeral* associations are mobilized by protocol operations described in this chapter. Persistent associations are never demobilized, although they may become dormant when the associated server becomes unreachable. Preemptable associations are demobilized when discarded by the cluster algorithm. Ephemeral associations are demobilized after some interval when the server is no longer heard. Since an intruder can impersonate a server and inject false time values, ephemeral associations should always be cryptographically authenticated.

In the following, a careful distinction is made among *server*, *client*, and *peer* operations. A *server* provides synchronization to a client but never accepts it. A *client* accepts synchronization from a server but never provides it. On the other hand, *peers* operate in pairs; either peer can provide or accept synchronization from the other, depending on their other sources. What may be confusing is that a particular NTP host can operate with any combination of modes—server, client, and peer—depending on configuration. This provides flexibility in subnet design and fault confinement. A primary server is synchronized by external means, such as a GPS receiver, and accepts synchronization from no other source, while a secondary server accepts synchronization from another server and provides synchronization to other servers and clients.

The NTP specification includes a subset called the Simple Network Time Protocol (SNTP), which has the same on-wire packet format and protocol but not necessarily the full suite of NTP mitigation and grooming algorithms. For instance, a primary server can run SNTP because it does not accept synchronization, while a client can run SNTP because it does not provide synchronization. However, since a secondary server both accepts

---

* All other things being equal, frequency changes can record the fraction of floating-point instructions in the instruction mix.

and provides synchronization, it is part of a cascaded chain of feedback loops that must have a controlled impulse response with specified rise time and overshoot. Therefore, a secondary server must conform to the full NTP specification.

There are three principal modes of operation: client/server, symmetric, and broadcast. These modes are selected based on the scope of service, intended flow of time values, and means of configuration. In all modes, the reference implementation supports both the traditional Internet Protocol Version 4 (IPv4) and its sixth version (IPv6) defined in Request for Comments (RFC) 3513 [1]. Ordinarily, the use of either IP version is transparent to the NTP time and security protocols with minor exceptions noted in the user documentation.

Client/server mode is probably the most common configuration in the Internet today. It operates in the classic remote procedure call (RPC) paradigm with stateless servers. In this mode, a client sends a request to the server and expects a reply at some future time. In some contexts, this would be described as a *pull* operation, in that the client pulls the time values from the server. In the reference implementation, a client specifies one or more persistent client associations in the configuration file by DNS (domain name system) name or IP address; the servers require no prior configuration.

Symmetric active/passive mode is intended for configurations in which a clique of low-stratum peers operates as mutual backups for each other. Each peer normally operates with one or more sources, such as a reference clock, or a subset of primary and secondary servers known to be reliable and authentic. Should one of the peers lose all reference clocks or simply cease operation, the other peers will automatically reconfigure so that time values can flow from the surviving peers to all the others in the subnet. In some contexts, this would be described as a *push–pull* operation, in that each peer either pulls or pushes the time values depending on the particular configuration and stratum.

Symmetric peers operate with their sources in some NTP mode and with each other in symmetric modes. In the reference implementation, a peer specifies one or more persistent symmetric active peer associations in the configuration file by DNS name or IP address. Other peers can also be configured in symmetric active mode; however, if a peer is not specifically configured, a symmetric passive association is mobilized on arrival of a message from a symmetric active peer.

Broadcast mode is intended for configurations involving one or a few servers and possibly a large client population. In the reference implementation, the configuration file specifies one or more persistent broadcast associations with subnet address or multicast group address, as appropriate. A broadcast client is declared in the configuration file with optional subnet address or group address. The Internet Assigned Numbers Authority (IANA) has assigned IPv4 multicast group address

224.0.1.1 to NTP, but this address should be used only when the span can be reliably constrained to protect neighbor networks. The IANA has assigned permanent IPv6 broadcast address 101 to NTP. This is ordinarily used with the site-local prefix ff05. Further explanation can be found in RFC-3513 [1].

The broadcast server generates messages continuously at intervals usually on the order of a minute. In some contexts, this would be described as a *push* operation, in that the server pushes the time values to configured clients. A broadcast client normally responds to the first message received after waiting an interval randomized to avoid implosion at the server. Then, the client polls the server in client/server mode using the burst feature (discussed further in this section) to reliably set the system clock and authenticate the source. This normally results in a volley of eight exchanges over a 16-s interval during which both the synchronization and the cryptographic authentication protocols run concurrently. When the volley is complete, the client sets the clock and computes the offset between the broadcast time and the client time. This offset is used to compensate for the propagation time between the broadcast server and client and is extremely important in the common cases when the unicast and broadcast messages travel far different paths through the IP routing fabric. Once the offset is computed, the server continues as before, and the client sends no further messages.

There are two new modes recently added to the NTPv4 reference implementation that can significantly reduce the effects of queuing and scheduling delays in the operating system. *Interleaved symmetric mode* and *interleaved broadcast mode* are described in Chapter 16, while the principles on which they are based are described in Chapter 15. Briefly, the on-wire protocol is modified to put the output packet interrupt timestamp in the next following packet. This is also the basis of the proposed Proximity-1 space data link synchronization protocol described in Chapter 17.

In the reference implementation, a burst feature can be enabled for each persistent client/server association separately. When enabled, a single poll initiates a burst of eight client messages at intervals of 2 s. The result is not only a rapid and reliable setting of the system clock but also a considerable reduction in network jitter. The burst feature can be enabled when the server is unreachable, reachable, or both. The unreachable case is intended when it is important to set the clock quickly when an association is first mobilized. The reachable case is intended when the network attachment requires an initial calling or training procedure for each poll and results in good accuracy with intermittent connections typical of Point-to-Point Protocol (PPP) and Integrated Services Digital Network (ISDN) services. The burst feature is useful also in cases of excessive network jitter or when the poll interval is exceptionally large, like over a day.

2.6 How NTP Discovers Servers

For a newbie confronting NTP for the first time, the most irksome task to overcome is the selection of one or more servers appropriate to the geography at hand. Over the years, this has become something of a black art and the origin of urban legends. There are four schemes to discover candidate servers: ordinary broadcast mechanisms, public lists maintained at the NTP Web site (http://www.ntp.org), the pool scheme based on DNS, and the manycast scheme based on an expanding ring search. These schemes are described in detail in Section 5.8.

There are two public server lists, one for stratum 1 primary servers and the other for stratum 2 secondary servers. The servers on these lists are operated for the Internet at large and come with certain rules of engagement, as indicated in each entry. They are scattered all over the world, with some in exotic places, some behind very long wires, and, soon, some on the Moon. Prominent among them are many operated by government agencies like the NIST and U.S. Naval Observatory (USNO) disseminating UTC from national standards. Potential users are cautioned to avoid the primary servers unless they support sizable NTP subnets of their own. A newbie is advised to scan the secondary server list for two or three nearby candidates and follow the access rules and notification directions.

An automatic discovery scheme called *pool* has been implemented and is now in regular use. A client includes a number of servers in the configuration file, all specifying the same server http://www.pool.ntp.org or associated country-specific subdomains like us.pool.ntp.org. The DNS server responds with a list of five NTP servers for that country randomly selected from a large pool of participating volunteer servers. The client mobilizes associations for each configured server. Subsequently, statistical outliers are systematically pruned and demobilized until the best three remain.

Manycast is an automatic discovery and configuration paradigm new to NTPv4. It is intended as a means for a client to troll the nearby network neighborhood using broadcast mode and an expanding-ring search. The object is to (1) find cooperating servers, (2) validate them using cryptographic means, and (3) evaluate their time values with respect to other servers that might be lurking in the vicinity. The intended result is that each unicast client mobilizes client associations with the best three of the available servers yet automatically reconfigures to sustain this number of servers should one or another fail.

Note that the manycast paradigm does not coincide with the anycast paradigm described in RFC-1546 [2], which is designed to find a single server from a clique of servers providing the same service. The manycast paradigm uses an expanding-ring search to find a plurality of redundant NTP servers and then prune the population until only the highest-quality survivors are left. There are many details about the protocol operations and configuration that can be found in the user documentation and on the Web.

2.7 How NTP Deals with Stale Time Values

During the lifetime of an association, which can be the lifetime of the computer and operating system on which it runs, there may come an hour, a day, or a week when one or another server becomes unreachable or shows only stale time values. What is a client to do when it has no time to chime? This happens often enough that a carefully engineered policy has been evolved. The following principles apply:

- A client starts out unsynchronized (leap indicator 3). When the client has synchronized for the first time, it can provide valid time (leap indicator 0) to its applications. It can continue to provide valid time forever, although it might not be very accurate.

- A statistic called the *peer dispersion* is initialized as each valid clock update is received from a server. The peer dispersion is a component of the root distance, which also depends on the root delay and residual jitter components. Both the root dispersion and root delay are included in the NTP packet header.

- Once initialized, the peer dispersion and thus the root distance increase at a fixed rate commensurate with the frequency tolerance of the disciplined oscillator, by default 15 PPM.

- NTP clients have a configurable parameter called the *distance threshold*, by default 1.5 s. If the root distance exceeds this threshold, it is no longer a selectable candidate for synchronization.

So, what happens when a server loses all synchronization sources? Assuming the server is reachable, a client sees increasing root distance until tripping over the threshold. After initialized by the latest update, the distance will increase by 15 PPM and trip in a little over 1 day. Since the round-trip delay to the Moon is much longer than on Earth, about 2 s, the threshold for clients on the Moon should be about 3.5 s.

Now, assume that the server has been working normally but then stops responding to polls. If the server does not respond after four polls, the peer dispersion is increased by a substantial amount at each subsequent poll. Eventually, the root distance exceeds the distance threshold and the server becomes unselectable for synchronization. If it does not reply within eight poll intervals, the poll interval is doubled at each subsequent poll until reaching the maximum poll interval, by default 1,024 s. This is done in the interest of reducing unneeded network traffic. Once the server is heard again, the poll interval resumes its normal value.

2.8 How NTP Manages Network Resources

Think of the global NTP subnet as a vast collection of coupled oscillators, some nudging others faster or slower to huddle around UTC. Whatever algorithm is used to wrangle the oscillator herd, it must be stable, not given to ugly stampedes and endure milling about as oscillators join and leave the herd or lurch in response to a thermal insult. NTP acts to exchange time offsets between oscillators, which by nature involves averaging multiple samples. However, the most important things NTP needs to know are the averaging time constant and the sample interval, which in NTP is called the poll interval.

For every averaging time constant, there is an associated poll interval resulting in a critically damped response characteristic. This characteristic generally produces the fastest response consistent with the best accuracy. If the poll interval is much larger than the critically damped value, the oscillators may exhibit various degrees of instability, including overshoot and even something like congestive collapse. This is called *undersampling*, and the algorithms described in this book try hard to avoid it. If the poll interval is smaller than the critically damped value, stability is preserved, even if unnecessary network loads result.

The discipline algorithm operates with a variable time constant as described in Chapter 4. The best time constant is usually the Allan intercept, which is about 2,000 s, but can swing over a wide range depending on network jitter and oscillator wander. When the NTP daemon starts up, the time constant is relatively small to rapidly converge the clock frequency. Under typical conditions when the system jitter has settled within a millisecond or two and the oscillator wander to within a part per million or two, the algorithm increases the time constant and matching poll interval to reduce the load on the network and servers.

Each peer association polls the server autonomously at intervals to be determined but not beyond the span allowed by the minimum and maximum poll intervals configured for the association. For NTPv4, these default to 64 s and 1,024 s, respectively, but can be configured between 8 s and 36 h. Ephemeral associations are assigned minimum and maximum values depending on mode. Under ordinary circumstances, the association polls the server at the largest interval consistent with the current time constant but not outside the allowed span.

There are two rules required to maintain stability: The first is that the time constant is clamped from above by the maximum poll interval of the system peer and to a default minimum if no system peer is available. This ensures that the feedback loop is not undersampled. The second is that in symmetric modes the time constant in both peers cannot become unbalanced, which would lead to undersampling of one peer and oversampling of the other. The NTP packet format includes a field called the *peer poll interval*. Either peer sets this field equal to the poll interval in each packet it sends. The peer receiving this packet sets the association poll interval to the minimum of its own host poll interval and the packet value. While this algorithm might result in some oversampling, it will never result in undersampling.

2.9 How NTP Avoids Errors

Years of accumulated experience running NTP in the Internet suggest the most common cause of timekeeping errors is a malfunction somewhere on the NTP subnet path from the client to the primary server or its synchronization source. This could be due to broken hardware, software bugs, or configuration errors. Or, it could be an evil mischief maker attempting to expire Kerberos tickets. The approach taken by NTP is a classic case of paranoia and is treatable only by a dose of Byzantine agreement principles. These principles require in general multiple redundant sources together with diverse network paths to the primary servers. In most cases, this requires an engineering analysis of the available servers and Internet paths specific to each server. Engineering principles for NTP subnet configuration are covered in Chapter 5.

The Byzantine agreement principles discussed in Chapter 3 require at least three independent servers, so that if one server turns traitor, the client can discover which one by majority clique. However, the raw time values can have relatively large time variations, so it is necessary to accumulate a number of them and determine the most trusted value on a statistical basis. Until a minimum number of samples has accumulated, a server cannot be trusted, and until a minimum number of servers has been trusted, the composite time cannot be trusted. Thus, when the daemon first starts up, there will be a delay until these premises have been verified.

To protect the network and busy servers from implosive congestion, NTP normally starts out with a poll interval of 64 s. The present rules call for at least four samples from each server and for this to occur for a majority of the configured servers before setting the clock. Thus, there can be a delay on the order of 4 min before the clock can be considered truly valid. Various distributed network applications have at least some degree of pain with this delay, but if justifiable by network loads, it is possible to use the burst feature described in this chapter. Using this feature, the delay is usually not more than 10 s.

It can happen that the local time before NTP starts up is relatively far (like a month) from the composite server time. To conform to the general spirit of extreme reliability and robustness, NTP has a *panic threshold* of 1,000 s earlier or later than the local time in which the server time will be believed. If the composite time offset is greater than the panic threshold, the daemon shuts down and sends a message to the log advising the operator to set the clock manually. As in other thresholds, the value can be changed by configuration commands. In addition, the daemon can ignore the panic threshold and set the clock for the first time but observe it for possible subsequent occasions. This is useful for routers that do not have battery backup clocks.

Another feature, or bug depending on how you look at it, is the behavior when the server time is less than the panic threshold but greater than a *step threshold* of 128 ms. If the composite time offset is less than this, the clock is disciplined in the manner described; that is, by gradual time and frequency adjustments. However, if the offset is greater than this, the clock is stepped instead. This might be considered extremely ill mannered, especially if the step is backward in time. To minimize the occasions when this might happen, due, for example, to an extreme network delay transient, the offset is ignored unless it continues beyond the step threshold for a *stepout threshold* of 900 s. If a succeeding offset less than the step threshold is found before reaching the stepout threshold, the daemon returns to normal operation and amortizes offsets. Further details are in Chapters 4 and 13.

There are important reasons for this behavior. The most obvious is that it can take a long time to amortize the clock to the correct time if the offset is large. Correctness assertions require a limit to the rate that the clock can be slewed, in the most common case no more than 500 PPM. At this rate, it takes 2,000 s to slew 1 s and over 1 day to slew 1 min. During most of this interval, the system clock error relative to presumably correct network time will be greater than most distributed applications can tolerate. Stepping the clock rather than slewing it if the error is greater than 128 ms is considered the lesser of two evils. With this in mind, the operator can configure the step threshold to larger values as necessary or even avoid the step entirely and accept the consequences.

When the daemon starts for the first time, it must first calibrate the intrinsic frequency correction of the hardware clock. In the general case, it may take a surprisingly long time to determine an accurate correction, in some cases several hours to a day. To shorten this process when the daemon is restarted, the current correction is written to a local file about once per hour. When this file is detected at restart, the frequency is reset immediately to that value. If the daemon is started without this file, it executes a special calibration procedure designed to calculate the frequency correction directly over a period of 15 min. The procedure begins the first time the clock is set in normal operation and does not adjust the clock during the procedure. After the procedure, the frequency correction is initialized, and the daemon resumes normal operation.

2.10 How NTP Performance Is Determined

No discussion of NTP operation is complete without mention of where timekeeping errors originate and what NTP does about them. There are several sources of errors due to network delay and clock frequency variations, asymmetric delays, and others discussed in detail in Chapter 11. However, for the purposes of discussion here, it is necessary only to describe how the errors are interpreted and how the error budget is compiled and passed along the chain from the primary servers through intervening servers to the clients.

In the normal course of operation, the NTP data-grooming and discipline algorithms keep track of both deterministic and nondeterministic errors. *Deterministic errors* are those that can be measured and corrected, such as the quasi-constant components of the time error and oscillator frequency error. *Nondeterministic errors* are estimated from measured root-mean-square (RMS) offset differences between samples from the server (*peer jitter*) and between samples from different servers (*select jitter*). In addition, the discipline algorithm has two statistics: *clock jitter*, computed from clock update time differences, and *oscillator wander*, computed from clock update frequency differences.

The *peer dispersion* statistic ε represents the error due to the clock oscillator maximum frequency error φ or *tolerance* and clock reading maximum error ρ or *precision*. (A glossary of the Greek symbols used in this book is shown in Figure 11.3.) When a server update is received, the round-trip delay δ is calculated, and ε is initialized with the sum of the remote server and local client precisions, usually something in the low microseconds, then increases at a fixed rate of 15 μs for each second after that until reset by a subsequent update. The peer jitter statistic φ is an average of the offset differences between the last several updates. There are two derived statistics included in the server update message: *root delay* Δ and *root dispersion* E. These represent, respectively, the accumulated delay and dispersion of the server relative to the root of the NTP synchronization subnet. These statistics are updated as packets arrive for each association separately.

To assess the quality of service, a metric interpreted as the *root distance* Λ is defined in Equation 11.11 and reproduced here for convenience:

$$\Lambda = \frac{\delta + \Delta}{2} + \varepsilon + E + \varphi.$$

There are two statistics available to application programs using the kernel API, *maximum error* and *expected error*. In Chapter 3, it is shown that the maximum error must be bounded by half the round-trip delay plus the dispersion from the primary server to the client, which we know as the root distance. This is the deterministic upper bound that the actual time offset can never exceed. The expected error represents the nondeterministic uncertainty of the offset as estimated from the various jitter contributions, which we know as the peer jitter. This is an important distinction since different applications may need one or the other or both of these statistics.

2.11 How NTP Controls Access

Most NTP servers provide service to an intended client population usually defined by a geographic or organization affiliation. In the case of public NTP servers, this is specified in the lists of public servers maintained at http:// www.ntp.org. If all NTP clients obeyed the rules specified in these lists, server access controls would not be needed. Unfortunately, such is not the case in modern life, and up to half the clients found on some servers have violated the rules of engagement. On one hand, it must be admitted that actually serving the scofflaws may be in fact just as expensive as detecting the scoff and dropping their packets. On the other hand, in the finest Internet tradition, the most effective way to notify a sender that packets are unwanted is simply to drop them without prejudice.

It is not the intent in the formal NTP specification to require access controls or prescribe the way they must operate. However, as an optional feature the reference implementation provides access controls using an access control list specified in the configuration file. Each entry on the list includes an address and mask and one or more bits for various functions, such as provide time, allow monitoring, allow configuration change, and so forth. A default entry is provided that matches any address not matching another on the list. If the IP address of an incoming packet matches an entry on the list, the associated bits define the service it can receive.

There is another access control function to protect against accidental or malicious clogging attacks. It is called *call-gap* after a similar function designed to protect telephone networks in cases of national alarm, like an earthquake. As an example, some nefarious implementation attempted to send 256 packets to a USNO time server as fast as possible and without waiting for responses. USNO servers are provisioned by fairly awesome networks, but the nefariot was able to jam network and server queues for each blast, which was repeated at intervals of 1 s.

The call-gap function maintains a list of recent NTP packets with distinct source addresses. As each message arrives, the list is searched for a matching address. If found, that entry goes to the head of the list; if not, an entry is created at the head of the list. In either case, the time of arrival is recorded in the entry. Using these means, the NTP daemon discards packets that exceed a peak rate over one per 2 s and an average rate over one per 5 s. On violation, the daemon also sends a special *kiss-o'-death* packet to the nefariot. By design, this kills the client association and sends a nasty message to the system log.

Of course, the call-gap and kiss-o'-death packet are much more expensive than either servicing the packet or simply dropping it, but sometimes desperate means are required to provoke the system administrator's attention. Apparently, a few of them are not watching things since it is not uncommon for a besieged server to drop 20 percent of all arriving packets due to call-gap. Sadly, it is not uncommon to see the same client be repeatedly gapped and for this to continue for a long time. This is not an exaggeration. Some nefariot is still beating on an address once used by one of our time servers that was abandoned several *years* ago.

2.12 How NTP Watches for Terrorists

That serious havoc can result if the computer clocks supporting stock trading, airline reservation, and transportation systems are terrorized is self-evident. A determined hacker or terrorist could crash an airplane, invalidate a corporate buyout, or dismantle the telephone system, not to mention steal credit cards and render online commerce unusable. When the AT&T telephone network suffered a meltdown on 15 January 1990, the most likely cause first imagined by the system operators was a terrorist attack.* Thus, NTP is sensitive to the issue of server authentication and the provision of cryptographically authenticated time values.

The NTPv4 and NTPv3 versions support secure authentication using symmetric key cryptography as described in Chapter 9. When available and enabled, symmetric key cryptography allows a client to verify that a server shares the same secret key. If practiced by all servers on the path to a primary server, these means ensure an unbroken chain of trust between the dependent clients and the primary servers. We call this chain, actually the transitive closure of the authentic relation, the *provenance* of the client and define new vocabulary as to proventicate a client or provide proventic credentials (see Chapter 9 for a discussion of these terms).

In symmetric key cryptography, every message contains a message authentication code (MAC), which is appended to the NTP header in the message.

---

* It was not terrorists; it was a software bug that resulted in continuous reboot for all 114 4ESS switches in the network and lasted 10 h.

The MAC is calculated using a cryptographic hash algorithm that produces a mathematical fingerprint serving to uniquely identify each message. This calculation involves a secret key known only to the server and clients of that server. The server uses the key to construct the MAC; the client uses it to construct its own MAC. If the MAC values match, the client concludes the message indeed came from the intended server and could not have been manufactured by an intruder.

While symmetric key cryptography has been available for over 18 years, it has several shortcomings. The most obvious is the need to distribute keys in advance by secure means. Previously, this was done by generating a table of random keys and transmitting it to clients using PGP messaging or the equivalent. This scheme is complicated by the need to refresh the table contents when the keys get old. While these operations can be partially automated, it is necessary to hide the keys and procedures from prying hackers and Web robots.

In NTPv4, an alternate scheme based on public key cryptography has become available. Called Autokey, the scheme is based on two keys, one public and the other private. The private key is used to construct a digital signature and is never revealed. The public key is distributed by insecure means and used by the clients to verify the signature. The mathematical basis of public key cryptography is basically mature, and protocols based on them are widely available. However, for reasons discussed in Chapter 9, the existing protocols cannot be directly incorporated in Autokey. The basic fact to recognize is that cryptographic media such as public certificates are ephemeral; that is, they have a defined lifetime relative to an ordinary calendar. The fact that valid certificates require correct time and correct time requires valid certificates creates a potential circularity. The protocol that exchanges the public keys and related values, as well as automatically validates each NTP message, is the topic of Chapter 9.

2.13 How NTP Clocks Are Watched

The NTP software distributions include several utility programs that provide remote monitoring, control, and configuration functions. Ordinarily, these programs are used to detect and repair broken servers, find and fix bugs in the software, and monitor timekeeping performance. Two monitoring protocols and programs have been developed: ntpq to monitor the operation and overall performance of selected servers and clients and ntpdc to search for specific causes of failures, improper operation, and misconfiguration. The ntpq program uses the control and monitoring protocol defined in the NTPv3 specification, while the ntpdc program uses a proprietary protocol.

An observer may ask why the Internet standard Simple Network Monitoring Protocol (SNMP) is not used for NTP. The simple answer is that the NTP monitoring protocols preceded SNMP by several years, and the NTP volunteer maintenance corps has resisted making more work than seems necessary. The long answer has two parts. First, the NTP subnet and monitoring protocols have been a valuable Internet monitoring tool since the NTP daemons run continuously, chat with each other, and can record statistics in some detail in local files or send them over the net to remote monitoring programs. On several occasions, these programs and the monitoring data they produce have facilitated the identification and repair of network problems unrelated to NTP. Second, the NTP monitoring tools are designed for the continuous observation of dynamic behavior and intricate statistical variations, not just snapshots of event counters and traps as in SNMP. The real answer is the loss of fidelity with SNMP, which is most useful for machine interpretation, while ntpq is most useful for human interpretation. A project is under way to design a suitable MIB and use it in a remote agent that communicates with NTP using the ntpq protocol.

NTP has other debugging tools as well, including ntptrace to walk the NTP forest from the client to the primary server and display the successive secondary servers. Along the trip, it displays statistics such as time offset, root distance, and reference identifier. Other programs can be used to generate cryptographic keys for both the symmetric key and public key authentication functions.

2.14 Parting Shots

While incorrect time values due to improperly operating NTP software or protocol design are highly unlikely, hazards remain due to incorrect software external to NTP. These hazards include the Unix kernel and library routines that convert Unix time to and from conventional civil time in seconds, minutes, hours, days, years, and especially centuries. Although NTP uses these routines to format monitoring data displays, they are not used to discipline the system clock. They may in fact cause problems with certain application programs, but this is not an issue that concerns NTP correctness.

It is possible that some external source to which NTP synchronizes may produce a discontinuity that could then induce an NTP discontinuity. The NTP primary servers, which are the ultimate time references for the entire NTP population, obtain time from various sources, including radio and satellite receivers and telephone modems. Not all sources provide year information, and of those that do, not all of them provide the year in four-digit form. In point of fact, the reference implementation does not use the year information, even if available. Instead, it uses a combination of the time-of-year (TOY) chip and the file system, as described in Chapter 13.

It is essential that any synchronization protocol such as NTP include provisions for multiple-server redundancy and multiple-route diversity. Past experience has demonstrated the wisdom of this approach, which protects clients against hardware and software faults as well as incorrectly operating reference clocks and sometimes even buggy software. For the most reliable service, the NTP configuration should include multiple reference clocks for primary servers, such as a backup radio or satellite receiver or telephone modem. Primary servers should run NTP with other primary servers to provide additional redundancy and mutual backup should the reference clocks themselves fail or operate incorrectly. These issues are further elaborated in Chapter 5.

References

1. Hinden, R., and S. Deering. *Internet Protocol Version 6 (IPv6). Addressing Architecture.* Network Working Group RFC-3513, Nokia, April 2003, 26 pp.
2. Partridge, C., T. Mendez, and T. Milliken. *Host Anycasting Service.* Network Working Group RFC-1536, Bolt Beranek Newman, November 1992, 9 pp.
3. Cain, B., S. Deering, I. Kouvalas, B. Fenner, and A. Thyagarajan. *Internet Group Management Protocol, Version 3.* Network Working Group RFC-3376, Cereva Networks, October 2002, 53 pp.

Further Reading

Meyer, D., and P. Lothberg. *GLOP Addressing in 233/8.* Network Working Group RFC-2770, Cisco Systems, February 2000, 5 pp.

Meyer, D. *Administratively Scoped IP Multicast.* Network Working Group RFC-2365, University of Oregon, Eugene, July 1998, 8 pp.

Ramanathan, P., K.G. Shin, and R.W. Butler. Fault-tolerant clock synchronization in distributed systems. *IEEE Computer 23, 10* (October 1990), 33–42.

3

In the Belly of the Beast

And, as in uffish thought he stood,
The Jabberwock, with eyes of flame,
Came whiffing through the tulgey wood,
and burbled as it came!

Lewis Carroll
Through the Looking Glass

In this chapter we are truly in the belly of the beast. At the very navel of the belly are the algorithms used to groom time values from a flock of redundant servers via diverse network paths and produce the most accurate and reliable time. In fact, the most defining characteristic of the NTP as distinct from other synchronization means such as the Digital Time Synchronization Service (DTSS) and Unix timed daemon is the suite of data grooming algorithms developed specifically for rowdy Internet network paths and meandering computer clock oscillators. Since Internet path characteristics vary widely and computer clocks wander in haphazard ways, the algorithms must be robust and adaptable and defend against the sludge of misconfiguration, misrepresentation, and stupid mistakes as well.

NTP is certainly the best known technology for synchronizing clocks in the Internet, but there is a wide field of related technology developed in the computer science and electrical engineering communities. This chapter begins by summarizing the related technology, including the ancestors of many NTP algorithms. It then describes the various NTP algorithms, including the filter, select, cluster, and combine algorithms that represent the heavy machinery. The discipline algorithm is so important that it has a chapter all its own (Chapter 4). Finally, it describes miscellaneous algorithms, including the huff-'n-puff, orphan mode, rate control, and wickedly intricate mitigation algorithms.

3.1 Related Technology

NTP is not the only network timekeeping technology. Other mechanisms have been specified in the Internet protocol suite to record and transmit the time at which an event takes place, including the Daytime protocol [1], Time protocol [2], ICMP (Internet Control Message Protocol) Timestamp message [3], and IP (Internet Protocol) Timestamp option [4]. Other synchronization algorithms are discussed in Cole and Foxcroft [5], the Digital Equipment Corporation [6], Gusella and Zatti [7], Halpern et al. [8], Lundelius and Lynch [9], Marzullo and Owicki [10], Rickert [11], Schneider [12], and Tripathi and Chang [13], while protocols based on them are described in the Digital Time Service Functional Specification Version T.1.0.5 [6], Tripathi and Chang [13], and Gusella and Zatti [14]. Clock synchronization algorithms, not necessarily for time, are discussed in Liao, Martonosi, and Clark [15] and Lu and Zhang [16].

The Daytime and Time protocols are the simplest ways to read the clock of a remote Internet host. In either protocol a client sends an empty message to the server, which then returns the time since 0 h 1 January 1900 as binary seconds (Time) or as a formatted date string (Daytime). The protocol can run above the Transmission Control Protocol (TCP) or the User Datagram Protocol (UDP); however, TCP requires a much larger resource commitment than UDP and provides very little reliability enhancement.

The Digital Time Synchronization Service (DTSS)* [6] has many of the same service objectives as NTP. The DTSS design features configuration management and correctness principles when operated in a managed network environment, while the NTP design features accuracy and stability when operated in the unmanaged Internet environment. In DTSS, a synchronization subnet consists of time providers, couriers, servers, and clerks. A DTSS time provider is synchronized to UTC via a radio or satellite receiver or telephone modem. A courier imports time from one or more distant servers for local redistribution, and a local server provides time for possibly many local clerks. In NTP, the time provider is called a reference clock, while generic NTP servers operate in the roles of DTSS couriers, servers, and clerks depending on the subnet configuration. Unlike NTP, DTSS does not need or use mode or stratum information and does not include provisions to filter, select, cluster, and combine time values or compensate for inherent frequency errors.

The Unix 4.3bsd time daemon timed [7] uses a single master time daemon to measure offsets of a number of slave hosts and send periodic corrections to them. In this model the master is determined using an election algorithm [14] designed to avoid situations in which either no master is elected or more than one master is elected. The election process requires a broadcast capability, which is not a ubiquitous feature of the Internet. While this model has been extended to support hierarchical configurations in which a slave on one network serves as a master on the other [13], the model requires handcrafted configuration tables to establish the hierarchy and avoid loops. In addition to the burdensome, but presumably infrequent, overhead of the election

---

* Digital changed the name from Digital Time Service (DTS) to Digital Time Synchronization Service (DTSS) after Reference 6 was published.

process, the offset measurement/correction process requires twice as many messages as NTP per update.

A scheme with features similar to NTP is described in Kopetz and Ochsenreiter [17]. It is intended for multiserver local-area networks (LANs) in which each of possibly many time servers determines its local time offset relative to each of the other servers in the set. It uses periodic timestamped messages, then determines the local clock correction using the fault-tolerant average (FTA) algorithm of Lundelius and Lynch [9]. The FTA algorithm, which is useful where up to k servers may be faulty, sorts the offsets, discards the k highest and k lowest, and averages the rest. This scheme is most suitable for LAN environments that support broadcast but would result in unacceptable overhead in the general Internet environment. In addition, for reasons given further in this chapter, the statistical properties of the FTA algorithm are not likely to be optimal in an Internet environment with highly dispersive delays.

A good deal of research has gone into the issue of maintaining accurate time in a community in which some clocks cannot be trusted. As mentioned in a previous chapter, a *truechimer* is a clock that maintains timekeeping accuracy to a previously published (and trusted) standard, while a *falseticker* is a clock that does not. Falsetickers can display erroneous or inconsistent times at different times and to different watchers. Determining whether a particular clock is a truechimer or falseticker is an interesting abstract problem.

The fundamental abstraction from which correctness principles are based is the *happens before* relation introduced by Lamport [18]. Lamport and Melliar-Smith [19] show that clocks are required to determine a reliable time value if no more than m of them are falsetickers, but only clocks are required if digital signatures are available. Byzantine agreement methods are introduced in Pease, Shostak, and Lamport [20] and Srikanth and Toueg [21]. Other methods are based on convergence functions.

A convergence function operates on the offsets between multiple clocks to improve accuracy by reducing or eliminating errors caused by falsetickers. There are two classes of convergence functions: those involving inter-active-convergence algorithms and those involving interactive-consistency algorithms. Interactive-convergence algorithms use statistical cluster techniques such as the FTA and CNV algorithms of Lundelius and Lynch [9], the majority-subset algorithm of Mills [22], the non-Byzantine algorithm of Rickert [11], the egocentric algorithm of Schneider [12], the intersection algorithm of Marzullo and Owicki [10], and the select algorithm described in this chapter.

Interactive-consistency algorithms are designed to detect faulty clock processes that might indicate grossly inconsistent offsets in successive readings or to different readers. These algorithms use an agreement protocol involving successive rounds of readings, possibly relayed and possibly augmented by digital signatures. Examples include the fireworks algorithm of Halpern et al. [8] and the optimum algorithm of Srikanth and Toueg [21]. However, these algorithms require large numbers of messages, especially when large numbers of clocks are involved, and are designed to detect faults that have rarely been found in the Internet experience. For these reasons they are not considered further in this chapter.

The particular choice of offset and delay computations used in NTP is a variant of the returnable-time algorithm used in some digital telephone networks [23]. The filter and select algorithms are designed so that the clock synchronization subnet self-organizes as a hierarchical master–slave configuration, as in Mitra [24]. The select algorithm is based on the intersection algorithm of Marzullo and Owicki [10], together with a refinement algorithm similar to the self-stabilizing algorithm of Lu and Zhang [25]. What makes the NTP model unique among these schemes is the adaptive configuration, polling, filtering, selection, and discipline mechanisms that tailor the dynamics of the system to fit the ubiquitous Internet environment.

3.2 Terms and Notation

Recall that t represents the epoch according to the tick counter, called *process time*, while $T(t)$ represents the *real time* displayed by a clock at that epoch. Then,

$$T(t) = T(t_0) + R(t - t_0) + D(t + t_0)^2 + x(t), \qquad (3.1)$$

where t_0 is some epoch in process time when $T(t_0)$ is the UTC time, $R(t_0)$ is the frequency, $D(t_0)$ is the drift (first derivative of frequency), and $x(t)$ is some stochastic noise process yet to be determined. It is conventional to represent both absolute and relative (offset) values for T and R using the same letters, where the particular use is clear from context. In the conventional stationary model used in the literature, T and R are estimated by some statistical process, and the second-order term D is ignored. The random nature of the clock is characterized by x, usually in terms of time or frequency distributions or the Allan deviation statistic introduced in Chapter 12.

The time offset of clock i relative to clock j is the time difference between them $T_{ij}(t) \equiv T_i(t) - T_j(t)$ at a particular epoch t, while the frequency offset is the frequency difference between them $R_{ij}(t) \equiv R_i(t) - R_j(t)$. It follows that $T_{ij} = -T_{ij}$, $R_{ij} = -R_{ij}$, and $T_{ii} = R_{ii} = 0$ for all t. In this chapter, reference to offset means time offset unless indicated otherwise.

A computer clock is characterized by stability, accuracy, resolution, precision, and tolerance, which are technical terms in this book. *Stability* is how closely the clock can maintain a constant frequency, while *accuracy* is how closely its time compares with UTC. *Resolution* is the smallest increment of the hardware clock, which is equivalent to the number of significant seconds-fraction bits in a clock reading. *Precision* is the maximum error in reading the system clock at the user level; that is, the latency inherent in its reading.* *Tolerance* is the maximum oscillator frequency error inherent in the manufacturing process and operating environment.

A source, whether the system clock or another remote clock in the network, is characterized by jitter, wander, and reliability. *Jitter* is the root-mean-square (RMS) differences between a series of time offsets, while *wander* is the RMS differences between a series of frequency offsets. Finally, the *reliability* of a timekeeping system is the fraction of the time it can be kept connected to the network and operating correctly relative to stated accuracy and stability tolerances. While sufficiently rigorous for the purposes of this chapter, these terms are given precise definitions in Chapter 12.

In Equation 3.1, a careful distinction is made between the time of a happening in real time, called a *timestamp*, and the ordering of this happening in process time, called an *epoch*. It is sufficient that epochs be ordered only by a sequence number, but we adopt the convention that the sequence number increments in ticks of the (undisciplined) system clock oscillator. In this chapter, we adopt the convention that a timestamp is represented by uppercase T, while the ordering of an epoch in process time is indicated by lowercase t. It is convenient to scale the value of tick so that the rate that time progresses in real time is close to the rate that time progresses in process time:

$$T(t) - T(t_0) \approx t - t_0.$$

The remainder of this chapter follows the journey of an NTP packet on arrival at a client. First, the packet is inspected, cleaned, and scrubbed of dirt that may have been picked up in transit or even as soil from an intruder. Next, the clock filter algorithm selects the best of the recent packets and extracts several statistics for later use. As there may be several such journeys running at the same time, the select algorithm classifies the truechimers and falsetickers according to formal agreement principles. The survivors are further processed by the cluster algorithm to cast off imprecise outliers, and the resulting candidates are averaged. The final result is passed on to the discipline algorithm discussed elsewhere in this book.

3.3 Process Flow

The NTP daemon itself is an intricate, complex, real-time system program. It usually operates simultaneously with multiple servers and may have

---

* Technically speaking, it is possible that the latency in reading the clock is less than the resolution, as when no means is available to interpolate between ticks. In such cases, the precision is defined as equal to the resolution.

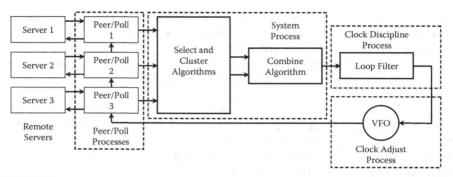

FIGURE 3.1
Process organization.

multiple clients of its own. The overall organization of the processes is illustrated in Figure 3.1. For every server, there are two processes a peer process that receives and processes each packet and a companion poll process that sends packets to the server at programmed intervals. State variables and data measurements are maintained separately for each pair of processes in a block of memory containing the peer state variables. The peer and poll processes together with their variables collectively belong to an *association*.

We speak of *mobilizing* an association when it begins life and *demobilizing* it when its life is over. An association is mobilized either by prior configuration or by a network event, such as the arrival of an unsolicited packet or as the result of a server discovery scheme. Associations that live forever are called *persistent*, while others mobilized and demobilized as life continues are called *preemptable* or *ephemeral*. A careful distinction is made between the last two in how they are demobilized. A preemptable association is demobilized when discarded by the cluster algorithm, described further in this chapter, after time-out. An ephemeral association is demobilized when the server has been unreachable after time-out. Note that the designations of preemptable and ephemeral are not mutually exclusive and can be applied to configured associations as well.

As each packet arrives, the server time is compared to the system clock and an offset specific to that server is determined. The system process grooms these offsets using the select, cluster, and combine algorithms and delivers a correction to the discipline process, which functions as a low-pass filter to smooth the data and close the feedback loop. The clock adjust process runs at 1-s intervals to amortize the corrections in small adjustments that approximate a continuous, monotonic clock.

The following sections describe how an NTP packet navigates these algorithms. There are some minor simplifications relative to the reference implementation flowcharts in Chapter 14, but for the present purpose these details can be ignored.

3.4 Peer Process

Received packets are first checked for correct format and version and discarded if invalid. While currently not required by the specification, as a configuration option the IP source address must match an entry in the access control list, where each entry contains an IP address, mask, and capability bits. Also not required by the specification, as a configuration option the IP address and arrival time for the most recent packets received is saved in a most recently used (MRU) list to catch and discard denial-of-service (DOS) attacks. It could be argued that the machine cycles spent to reject unwanted packets might be more than needed to actually service the request; however, in the finest Internet tradition, the best way to discourage unwanted traffic is simply to discard it.

Packets are next subject to cryptographic checks involving either symmetric key or public key cryptography as described in Chapter 9. If NTP extension fields are present, they are processed by the Autokey protocol to instantiate the public certificates, identity parameters, and related cryptographic values. Packets failing the authentication checks are discarded. In some cases documented in Chapter 14, a special message called a crypto-NAK (negative acknowledgment) is returned to the sender.

At this point, the packet is acceptable but might contain invalid data or even have been manufactured or mangled by a hacker. A summary of the tests performed at this point is shown in Table 3.1, in which the enumeration is from the reference implementation.* If any of these tests are true, the packet is discarded. Otherwise, the packet is accepted.

Next, the IP source address and port number are matched with each association in turn. Note that the IP destination address and port have already been matched by the UDP protocol. If the address and port match an association, the mode number is the mode of that association; otherwise, the mode number is zero. Next, one of the following actions is taken based on the mode number and the mode of the packet:

1. Client packet matching no association. Return a server packet without mobilizing an association.
2. Broadcast packet matching no association. Mobilize a broadcast client association in temporary client mode. Discard the packet; the mobilized association will continue the protocol.
3. Symmetric active packet matching no association. Mobilize a symmetric passive association. Process the packet.

---

* Test 7 is intended for networks on Earth or Mars or in orbit about either planet. The value 1.5 s must be increased to at least 3.5 s for Earth–Moon paths. NTP is probably not directly suited to paths from Earth–Mars or deep-space missions, but we have other methods for that as discussed in Chapter 18.

TABLE 3.1

Packet Error Checks

Test	Name	Description
1	Duplicate	The packet is an old duplicate. This may be due to a hacker attack but could also happen in symmetric modes if the poll intervals are uneven.
2	Bogus	The packet is not a reply to the most recent packet sent. This may be due to hacker attack but could also happen in symmetric modes if the poll intervals are uneven.
3	Invalid	One or more timestamp fields are invalid. This normally happens in symmetric modes when one peer sends the first packet to the other and before the other has received its first reply.
4	Access	The access controls have blacklisted the source address.
5	Authentication	The cryptographic message digest does not match the message authentication code.
6	Unsynchronized	The server has not synchronized to a valid source.
7	Distance	The root distance is greater than 1.5 s.
8	Autokey	Public key cryptography has failed to authenticate the packet.
9	Crypto	There are mismatched or missing cryptographic keys or certificates.

4. Error cases. Discard the packet.

5. Other cases. Process the packet and execute the on-wire protocol in Section 3.6.

3.5 Poll Process

The poll process generates output packets at regular poll intervals and determines the state of the association as reachable, unreachable, or time-out. In the normal course of operation, it sometimes happens that a server becomes erratic or unreachable over the Internet. NTP deals with this using good Internet engineering principles developed from the ARPANET (Advanced Research Projects Agency Network) experience. Each client association has a reach register of eight bits. When a message is sent to the server, the register is shifted left by one bit, with zero replacing the vacant bit. When a valid message is received from the server, the rightmost bit is set to one. If one or more bits are set, the server is considered reachable; otherwise, it is not.

From a system management point of view, the reach register has proved to be a good indicator of server and network problems. The operator quickly learns from the pattern of bits whether the server is first coming online or going offline or the network paths have become lossy. If the rightmost four bits of the reach register become zero, the server is probably going down, so a dummy update is sent to the clock filter algorithm (see below) with peer dispersion equal to the maximum of 16 s. This causes the root distance to increase, eventually exceeding the distance threshold and causing the server to become unselectable.

It is sometimes useful to send a burst of packets instead of a single packet at each poll opportunity. At initial startup when associations are first mobilized, the system clock can be set within 10 s rather than waiting 4 min without the burst. Also, in cases with moderate-to-severe network congestion, especially with relatively large poll intervals, the clock filter algorithm performance can be considerably improved. Finally, when a dial-up connection is required, such as with DSL (digital subscriber line) and ISDN (Integrated Services Digital Network) services, there may be a delay of several seconds after the first packet is sent to the modem for it to complete the call. There are two options to enable burst mode: the `iburst` option, which is effective when the server is unreachable, and the `burst` option, which is effective when it is reachable. Either or both options can be enabled by configuration commands. In either option, if the packet is to be sent, a burst of six packets is sent instead.

The burst algorithm is carefully constrained to minimize excess traffic on the network. After the first packet in the burst is sent, the algorithm waits for a reply from the server before sending the remaining packets in the burst at 2-s intervals. If no reply is received within a 64-s time-out, the second packet is sent, and after another 64-s time-out the third packet, and so forth until all packets in the burst have been sent. In addition, the burst algorithm is constrained by the rate control mechanisms described in Section 3.14.

There are two timers among the poll process variables: the poll timer and the unreach timer. At each poll event, the poll timer is set to the number of seconds until the next poll event. After the event, the poll timer decrements once each second until reaching zero and initiating the next poll event. The unreach timer increments once each second until reaching a defined time-out threshold. On reaching this threshold for a persistent association, the association is placed in a time-out state and the poll interval set at the maximum of 1,024 s. On reaching this threshold for an ephemeral or preemptable association, the association is demobilized. For all except preemptable associations, the unreach timer is set to zero on arrival of a valid packet. For a preemptable association, the unreach timer is set to zero only in the case that there are not less than a defined minimum number of survivors of the cluster algorithm in Section 3.9 and the association is among those survivors. The intent is to leave some wiggle room should servers of similar quality bob in and out of the survivor population.

3.6 On-Wire Protocol

Packet processing continues to update the peer variables included in the association and run the on-wire protocol that computes the clock offset and round-trip delay. Figure 3.2 shows the basic on-wire protocol and how timestamps are numbered and exchanged between hosts A and B. The state variables appear in lowercase, while the timestamps appear in uppercase. The arrows show the direction of packet transmission. The head of the arrow shows the transmit timestamp; the tail shows the receive timestamp. Note that the numbering applies where A is the server and B is a client, B is the server and A is a client, or A and B are peers in the symmetric modes protocol. Let $T_1, T_2, \ldots, T_8$ be the timestamps as shown and, without loss of generality, assume the partial orders $T_1 < T_4 \leq T_5 < T_8$ and $T_2 \leq T_3 < T_6 \leq T_7$; that is, clocks never run backward.* The nominal poll interval for A is $T_5 - T_1$, while the nominal poll interval for B is $T_7 - T_3$.

The on-wire protocol has two simple rules:

- When transmitting a packet, first copy *xmt* to t_{org} and *rec* to t_{rec}, then read the system clock and save to t_{xmt} and *org*.

- When receiving a packet, if t_{xmt} matches *xmt*, the packet is a duplicate and is discarded. If t_{org} does not match *org*, the packet is bogus and is discarded. In this case and otherwise, copy t_{org} to *org* and t_{xmt} to *xmt*, then read the system clock and save to *rec*.

For example, in its most general form with symmetric modes, the protocol begins when host A reads its clock T_1, saves the value in *org*, and sends packet T_1 containing T_1 to B. On arrival, B reads its clock T_2 and saves the timestamp and T_1 in *rec* and *org*, respectively. Some time later, B reads its clock T_3, saves the timestamp in *org*, and sends packet T_3 containing T_1, T_2, and T_3 to A. On arrival, A reads its clock T_4 and saves the timestamp and T_3 in *rec* and *org*, respectively. Host A now has the four timestamps T_1, T_2, T_3, and T_4 necessary to calculate clock offset and round-trip delay. However, at the same time A is collecting timestamps using packets T_1 and T_3, B is doing the same with packets T_3 and T_5. The protocol continues as shown in the figure.

In client/server mode, the server saves no state variables. It updates the header fields of the client packet, copies t_{rec} and t_{xmt} of the request to t_{org} and t_{rec} of the reply, then reads the clock, saves the timestamp in t_{xmt}, and sends the server packet. There is no need to validate the header fields other than to check that the packet version number is equal to or less than the current version and send the reply with the same version number as the request.

---

* These relations do not necessarily hold if there is significant uncorrected frequency difference between the clocks of A and B.

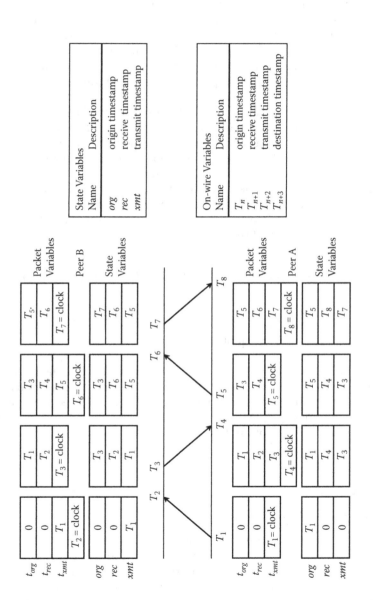

FIGURE 3.2
NTP on-wire protocol.

In all modes, if t_{xmt} is equal to *xmt*, the packet is a replay of the last one received (duplicate). This could happen if the network duplicates a packet because of a redundant retransmission or if an intruder intercepts and replays it. In client/server and symmetric modes, if t_{org} is not equal to *org*, the packet is not a response from the last packet sent (bogus). In both cases, the prudent action is to drop the packet but in the latter case to save the time-stamps. It does no harm if the A and B poll intervals are mismatched and either no packets or more than one packet are received during a poll interval. In symmetric modes, the on-wire protocol is not vulnerable to replays of packets such as T_1 and T_3 since T_1 duplicates are discarded by B and T_3 dupli-cates are discarded by A. In broadcast mode, there is no T_1, and T_3 duplicates are discarded by A. In client/server mode, B immediately responds to the T_1 packet with the T_3 packet, so there is negligible chance a spurious duplicate could arrive at A before the legitimate T_3 packet.

For the moment, assume the clocks of A and B are stable and run at the same rate. If the packet numbering scheme adopted in Figure 3.2 is used, for *i* equal to any multiple of 4 beginning at 4, the clock offset θ_{AB} and round-trip delay δ_{AB} of A relative to B at time T_i are

$$\theta_{AB} = \frac{1}{2}\left[(T_{i-2} - T_{i-3}) + (T_{i-1} - T_i)\right] \text{ and } \delta_{AB} = (T_i - T_{i-3}) - (T_{i-1} - T_{i-2}). \quad (3.2)$$

The offset θ_{BA} and delay δ_{BA} of B relative to A at time T_{i+2} are obtained by replacing *i* with *i* + 2 in Equation 3.2. Each NTP packet includes the lat-est three timestamps T_{i-3}, T_{i-2}, and T_{i-1}, while the fourth T_i is determined on arrival. Thus, both peers A and B can independently calculate delay and offset using a single bidirectional message stream. This is a symmetric, con-tinuously sampled time transfer scheme similar to those used in some digi-tal telephone networks [23]. Among its advantages are that it does not matter if messages cross in flight or are lost or duplicated.

3.7 Clock Filter Algorithm

The NTP clock filter algorithm is designed to select the best sample data while rejecting noise spikes due to packet collisions and network congestion. Recall that the clock offset θ and round-trip delay δ samples are computed from the four most recent timestamps. Without making any assumptions about the delay distributions but assuming the frequency difference or *skew* between the server and peer clocks can be neglected, let (θ, δ) represent the offset and delay when the path is otherwise idle and thus the true val-ues. The problem is to produce an accurate estimator $(\hat{\theta}, \hat{\delta})$ from a sample sequence (θ_i, δ_i) collected for the path over an appropriate interval under ambient traffic conditions.

The design of the clock filter algorithm was suggested by the observation that packet-switching networks are most often operated well below the knee of the throughput-delay curve. This means that packet queues are mostly small with relatively infrequent packet bursts. In addition, the routing algorithm most often operates to minimize the number of packet-switch hops and thus the number of queues. Not only is the probability that an NTP packet finds a busy queue in one direction relatively low, but the probability of packets from a single exchange finding busy queues in both directions is even lower. Therefore, the best offset samples should occur with the lowest delays.

The characteristics of a typical Internet path are illustrated in Figure 3.3, called a *wedge scattergram*. Scattergrams like these plot samples $(y_i, x_i) = (\theta_i, \delta_i)$ over intervals of hours to months. Network delays in this and other plots in this chapter were constructed using the NTP simulator, which includes all the algorithms of the reference implementation, driven by zero-mean exponential distributions with specified standard deviation σ. As demonstrated in Chapter 12, this is a good model that fits closely the observed data and is free from distractions. The particular path models seven networks and 12 routers and was among the most complex in the Internet of 1986. The choice $\sigma = 10$ ms was made by inspection from old tattered performance plots unsuitable for reproduction here.

As explained in Chapter 11, the limb lines of the wedge have slope ±0.5. The shape of the wedge reveals intimate details about the network path characteristics, as explained in Chapter 6. Under low-traffic conditions, the points are concentrated about the apex of the wedge and begin to extend rightward

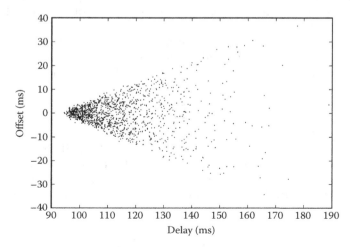

FIGURE 3.3
Wedge scattergram.

along the limb lines as network traffic increases. As the traffic continues to increase, the points begin to fill in the wedge as it expands even further rightward. From these data, it is obvious that good estimators $(\hat{\theta}, \hat{\delta})$ are points near the apex, which is exactly what the clock filter algorithm is designed to produce.

This observation suggests the design of what is called here a *minimum filter* consisting of a shift register holding samples $(\theta_i, \delta_i, \varepsilon_i, t_i)$ $(0 \le i \le n)$. On arrival of a packet, a new entry $(\theta_0, \delta_0, \varepsilon_0, t_0)$ shifts into the register, and the oldest one is discarded. Here, $\theta_0 = \theta_{AB}$ and $\delta_0 = \delta_{AB}$ are from Equation 3.2, and $t_0 = t$ is the epoch at T_4. The ε_0 is initialized with the precision, then grown at a constant rate $\phi = 15$ PPM, as described in Chapter 11. It is used to represent missing data as well as a component of the quality metric discussed later. If a packet has not arrived for four successive poll intervals, a dummy sample $(0, 0, \infty, t)$ is shifted into the register, where $\infty = 16$ s represents missing data. While missing data samples are never used in subsequent calculations, they shove very old samples out of the register to prevent them from being used.

Next, the register contents are copied to a temporary list and sorted by the metric λ designed to avoid missing data and devalue samples older than the Allan intercept, which is about 2,000 s, discussed in Chapter 12:

$$\text{if } \delta_j + \varepsilon_j \ge \infty \text{ then } \lambda_j = \infty;$$
$$\text{else if } t_j - t > \sigma_y(x) \text{ then } \lambda_j = \delta_j + \varepsilon_j;$$
$$\text{else } \lambda_j = \delta_j.$$

The intended algorithm is an exchange sort; however, an exchange is not made unless to do so would reduce the metric by at least the value of the precision. In other words, it does not make sense to change the order in the list, which might result in the loss of otherwise good samples, unless the metric change is significant.

The first entry $(\theta_0, \delta_0, \varepsilon_0, t_0)$ on the temporary list represents the lowest delay sample that is used to update the peer offset $\theta = \theta_0$ and peer delay $\delta = \delta_0$. The peer dispersion ε is calculated from the temporary list:

$$\varepsilon = \sum_{k=0}^{n-1} \frac{\varepsilon_k}{2^{k+1}}.$$

Finally, the temporary list is trimmed by discarding all entries $\lambda_j = \infty$ and all but the first devalued entry, if one is present, leaving m $(0 \le m \le n)$ surviving entries on the list. The peer jitter φ is used by the cluster algorithm as a quality metric and in the computation of the expected error

$$\varphi = \left(\frac{1}{m-1} \sum_{k=1}^{m-1} (\theta_k - \theta_0)^2 \right)^{\frac{1}{2}} \quad (m > 1). \tag{3.3}$$

A *popcorn spike* is a transient outlier, usually only a single sample, that is typical of congested Internet paths. The *popcorn spike suppressor* is designed to detect and remove them. Let θ' be the peer offset determined by the previous message and φ the current peer jitter. If $|\theta - \theta'| > K_s \varphi$, where K_s is a tuning parameter that defaults to 3, the sample is a popcorn spike and is discarded. Note that the peer jitter will increase to protect a legitimate step change.

As demonstrated by simulation and practical experience, it is prudent to avoid using samples older than the latest one used. Let t_p be the epoch that the peer variables were last updated and t_0 be the epoch of the first sample on the temporary list. If $t_0 \le t_p$, the new sample is a duplicate or earlier than the last one used. If this is true, the algorithm exits without updating the system clock; otherwise, $t_p = t_0$, and the offset can be used. Note that this can result in the discard of all but one sample in the clock filter, but there will always be one sample. The components of the tuple (θ, δ, ε, φ, t_p) are called the *peer variables* elsewhere in this book. Note that if a burst option is enabled, the system clock is not updated until the last packet in the burst.

Several experiments were made to evaluate this design using measurements between NTP primary servers so that delays and offsets could be determined independently of the measurement procedure itself [22]. The experiments were performed over several paths involving ARPANET, NSFNET (National Science Foundation Network), and various LANs and using minimum filters and various other algorithms based on median and trimmed-mean statistics. The results showed consistently lower errors for the clock filter algorithm when compared with the other algorithms. Perhaps the most dramatic result with the clock filter algorithm was the greatly reduced maximum error with moderate-to-severe network congestion.

For example, Figure 3.4 shows the offsets simulated for a typical Internet path over a 24-h period with a 64-s poll interval. In this case, the network delays were modeled as a zero-mean exponential distribution with $\sigma = 10$ ms. Figure 3.5 shows a cumulative distribution function (CDF) for the raw offsets (right curve) and filtered offsets (left curve). The result is a decrease in maximum error from 37 to 7.6 ms and a decrease in standard deviation from 7.1 to 1.95 ms.

3.8 Select Algorithm

To provide reliable synchronization, NTP uses multiple redundant servers and multiple disjoint network paths whenever possible. When a number of associations are mobilized, it is not clear beforehand which are truechimers and which are falsetickers. Crucial to the success of this approach is a robust algorithm that finds and discards the falsetickers from the selectable server

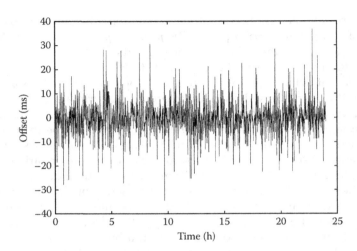

FIGURE 3.4
Raw offset.

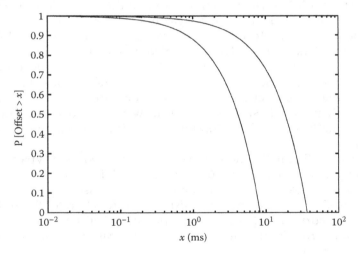

FIGURE 3.5
Raw (right) and filtered (left) offset CDF.

population. This is especially important with broadcast client mode since the servers may have no a priori pedigree. The clock select algorithm determines from among all associations a suitable subset of truechimers capable of providing the most accurate and trustworthy time using Byzantine principles similar to those of Vasanthavada and Marinos [26].

A brief summary of the nomenclature used here will be helpful. An association that has valid peer variables is called a *candidate*. A candidate is *selectable* if it passes the peer error checks in Table 3.2. A selectable is a *truechimer* if it is among the products of the select algorithm. A truechimer is a *survivor* if

TABLE 3.2

Peer Error Checks

Test	Name	Description
10	Stratum	The stratum is greater than 15.
11	Distance	The root distance is greater than 1.5 s.
12	Loop	The client is synchronized to this server, forming a timing loop.
13	Synchronized	The server is not synchronized to a valid source.

it is among the products of the cluster algorithm of the next section. A survivor is the *system peer* if it is the (only) product of the mitigation algorithms of Section 3.11. Only selectable candidates are considered for further processing by the select algorithm.

In Chapter 11, it is proved that the true offset θ of a correctly operating clock relative to UTC must be contained in a computable range, called the *confidence interval*, equal to an interval of size twice the root distance centered at the current offset. Marzullo and Owicki [10] devised an algorithm designed to find the *intersection interval* containing the correct time given the confidence intervals of m clocks, of which no more than f are considered incorrect. The algorithm finds the smallest intersection interval containing points in at least $m - f$ of the given confidence intervals. If f is less than $m/2$, a majority clique has been found, and its members are the truechimers; the rest are falsetickers.

Figure 3.6 illustrates the operation of this algorithm with a scenario involving four clocks A, B, C, and D, given the confidence interval for each and with the measured offset indicated at the center of each correctness interval. In fact, any point in an interval may represent the actual offset associated with that clock. If all clocks are correct, there must exist a nonempty intersection interval including points in all four confidence intervals, but clearly this is not the case for D in the figure. However, if one of the clocks is incorrect (e.g., D), it might be possible to find a nonempty intersection interval including all but one of the confidence intervals. If not, it might be possible to find a nonempty intersection interval including all but two of the intervals and so on.

The algorithm used in DTSS is based on these principles. It finds the smallest intersection interval containing at least one point in each of $m - f$ confidence intervals, where m is the total number of clocks and f is the number of falsetickers, as long as $f < m/2$. For the scenario illustrated in Figure 3.6, it computes the intersection interval for clocks, three of which turn out to be truechimer, and one is the falseticker. The interval marked DTSS is the smallest intersection interval containing points in three confidence intervals, with one interval outside the intersection interval considered incorrect.

There are some cases for which this algorithm can produce anomalistic results. For instance, consider the case where the left endpoints of A and B

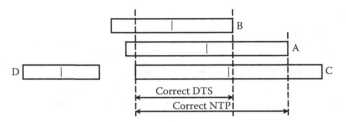

FIGURE 3.6
Correctness intervals.

are moved to coincide with the left endpoint of D. In this case, the intersection interval extends to the left endpoint of D in spite of the fact that there is a subinterval that does not contain at least one point in all confidence intervals. Nevertheless, the assertion that the correct time lies somewhere in the intersection interval remains valid.

One problem is that while the smallest interval containing the correct time may have been found, it is not clear which point in that interval is the best estimate of the correct time. Simply taking the estimate as the midpoint of the intersection interval throws away a good deal of useful statistical data and results in large peer jitter, as confirmed by experiment. Especially when the network jitter is large, some or all of the calculated offsets (such as for C in Figure 3.6) may lie outside the intersection interval. For these reasons, in the NTP algorithm the DTSS algorithm is modified to include at least $m - f$ of the confidence intervals where the midpoints must all lie in the intersection interval. The revised algorithm finds the smallest intersection $m - f$ of intervals containing at least $m - f$ midpoints. As shown in Figure 3.6, the modified algorithm produces the intersection interval marked NTP and including the calculated time for C.

The algorithm shown in Figure 3.7 starts with a set of variables for each of the i ($1 \leq i \leq m$) selectable servers including the clock offset θ_i, root delay Δ_i, and root dispersion E_i. To be selectable, a server has to survive the tests shown in Table 3.2, where the enumeration follows the reference implementation. If any of these tests is true, the server is rejected; otherwise, the server is selectable. The root variables represent the statistics for the entire path to the primary servers, as described in Chapter 11. The root distance for the ith server is defined

$$\Lambda_i = \frac{\delta_i + \Delta_i}{2} + \varepsilon_i + E_i + \varphi_i, \tag{3.4}$$

where Δ_i and E_i are, respectively, the root delay and root dispersion of the ith server, as provided in the received packet. However, the root distance is bounded from below by the `mindist` option of the `tos` configuration command. The default value of 1 ms ensures that small variations between multiple servers sharing the same wire do not result in an empty correctness

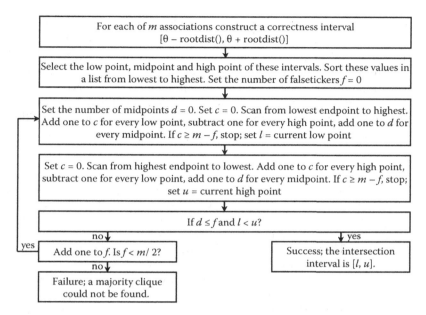

For each of *m* associations construct a correctness interval
[θ – rootdist(), θ + rootdist()]

Select the low point, midpoint and high point of these intervals. Sort these values in a list from lowest to highest. Set the number of falsetickers *f* = 0

Set the number of midpoints *d* = 0. Set *c* = 0. Scan from lowest endpoint to highest. Add one to *c* for every low point, subtract one for every high point, add one to *d* for every midpoint. If *c* ≥ *m* – *f*, stop; set *l* = current low point

Set *c* = 0. Scan from highest endpoint to lowest. Add one to *c* for every high point, subtract one for every low point, add one to *d* for every midpoint. If *c* ≥ *m* – *f*, stop; set *u* = current high point

If *d* ≤ *f* and *l* < *u*?

no

yes

Add one to *f*. Is *f* < *m*/ 2?

no

yes

Success; the intersection interval is [*l*, *u*].

Failure; a majority clique could not be found.

FIGURE 3.7
Select algorithm.

interval. As demonstrated in Chapter 11, the confidence interval for the *i*th server extends from $\theta_i - \Lambda_i$ at the lower endpoint to $\theta_i + \Lambda_i$ at the upper endpoint. The algorithm constructs for each server a set of three tuples of the form $(\theta - \Lambda, -1)$ for the lower endpoint, $(\theta, 0)$ for the midpoint, and $(\theta + \Lambda, +1)$ for the upper endpoint. These entries are placed on a list and sorted by *offset*. The job of the select algorithm is to determine the lower and upper endpoints of an intersection interval containing at least $m - f$ truechimers. Let $n = 3m$ be the number of entries in the sorted list and *f* be the number of presumed falsetickers, initially zero. Also, let *l* designate the lower limit of the intersection interval and *u* the upper limit. The algorithm uses *c* as a counter of endpoints and *d* as the number of midpoints found outside the intersection interval.

1. Set both *c* and *d* equal to zero.
2. Starting from the lowest *offset* of the sorted list and working toward the highest, for each entry (*offset*, *type*) subtract *type* from *c*. If $c \geq m - f$, the lower endpoint has been found. In this case, *l* = *offset* and go to step 3. Otherwise, if *type* is zero, increment *d*, then continue with the next entry.
3. At this point, a tentative lower limit *l* has been found; however, the number of midpoints has yet to be determined. Set *c* again to zero, leaving *d* as is.
4. In a similar manner as in step 2, starting from the highest *offset* of the sorted list and working toward the lowest, for each entry (*offset*, *type*)

add *type* to *c*. If $c \geq m - f$, set $u = offset$ and go to step 5. Otherwise, if *type* is zero, increment *d*, then continue with the next entry.

5. If $l < u$ and $d \leq f$, the midpoints of truechimers have been found, and all are within the intersection interval $[l, u]$. In this case, declare success and end the procedure. If $l \geq u$ or $d > f$, then the interval does not exist, or one or more midpoints is not contained in the interval. So, add one to *f* and try again. If there is a majority clique of truechimers, that is, $f < m/2$, continue in step 1; otherwise, declare failure and end the procedure.

Sometimes, the select algorithm can produce surprising results, especially with fast machines and precision sources for which the confidence intervals are very small. In such cases, the confidence intervals may not overlap due to some small neglected systematic error, and a majority clique is not possible. This problem most often occurs with a precision GPS clock with pulse-per-second (PPS) assist, as described in Chapter 7. The obvious remedy for this problem is to find and remove the systematic error; however, this may be in the low microseconds, and a more charitable remedy might be to increase the root distance assigned the clock driver. For this reason, the root distance is increased by measured peer jitter components described in Chapter 11.

The original (Marzullo and Owicki) algorithm produces an intersection interval that is guaranteed to contain the correct time as long as fewer than half the clocks are falsetickers. The modified algorithm produces an interval containing the original interval, so the correctness assertion continues to hold. Since the measured offsets associated with each interval are contained in the interval, a weighted average of these offsets, such as computed by the combine algorithm, is contained in the intersection interval as well. This represents the fundamental correctness assertion applicable to the NTP algorithm.

3.9 Cluster Algorithm

NTP configurations usually include several servers to provide sufficient redundancy for the select algorithm to determine which are truechimers and which are not. When a sizable number of servers are present, the individual clock offsets for each are not usually the same, even if each server is closely synchronized to UTC by one means or another. Small systematic differences on the order of microseconds to milliseconds are often due to operating system and network latencies. Larger differences are due to asymmetric delays and, in the extreme, due to asymmetric satellite or landline delays.

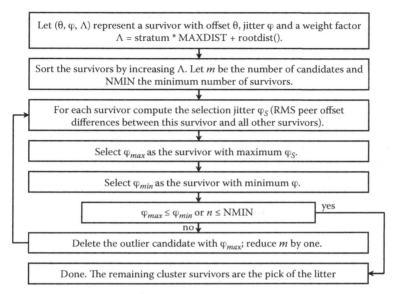

FIGURE 3.8
Cluster algorithm.

The cluster algorithm shown in Figure 3.8 sifts the truechimers of the select algorithm to identify the survivors providing the best accuracy. In principle, the shift could result in a single survivor and its offset estimate used to discipline the system clock; however, a better estimate usually results if the offsets of a small number of survivors are averaged together. The *select jitter* is defined as the RMS average of the differences between survivor offsets relative to a designated survivor:

$$\varphi_{s,j} = \left(\frac{1}{m-1} \sum_{k=1}^{m-1} \left(\theta_k - \theta_j \right)^2 \right)^{\frac{1}{2}} \; (m > 1),$$

where k ranges over all survivors, and j is the designated survivor. This is a good measure of the "noise" resulting from selecting survivor j as the system peer. Let ϕ_i be the peer jitter from Equation 3.3 for survivor i. So, a balance must be struck between reducing the select jitter by repeatedly casting off outliers and improving the offset estimate by including more survivors in the average.

The algorithm operates in succeeding rounds in a manner similar to one described by Paxson [27]. Let m be the number of truechimers revealed by the select algorithm and $n_{\min}$ be the minimum number of survivors and $n_{\min} < m$. For each survivor i, let s_i be the stratum, Λ_i the root distance (from Equation 3.4), and θ_i the offset. Begin by constructing a list $(\lambda_i, \theta_i, \varphi_i)$, $(0 \le i < m)$, where

$$\lambda_i = \frac{\Lambda_i + \phi t_p}{\Lambda_{max}} + s_i$$

is a sort metric in which Λ_{max} is the select threshold, and t_p is the interval from the current time to the time of the next poll event. Since the root dispersion rises until the next poll event, this minimizes unhelpful switches from one source to another or *clockhop*, as the root dispersion rises until the next poll event. Sort the list by increasing λ_i, then do the following:

1. Compute φ_{max} as the maximum $\varphi_{s.i}$ $(0 \le i < m)$ and φ_{min} as the minimum φ_j $(0 \le j < m)$;
2. If $m \le n_{min}$ or $\varphi_{max} \le \varphi_{min}$, exit;
3. From the m survivors at this step, discard the one with φ_{max} and reduce m by one. Continue in step 1.

Figure 3.9 illustrates how the algorithm works. The algorithm starts with four survivors on the left, where the diameter of the white circles represents the peer jitter and the diameter of the gray circle represents the select jitter. Since the largest select jitter is greater than the smallest peer jitter, the survivor with the largest metric x_i, here assumed R1, is removed, leading to the three survivors shown on the right. The largest select jitter is now less than the smallest peer jitter, so the algorithm terminates. The algorithm also terminates when the number of survivors reaches a configurable parameter called `minclock`, which by default is 3, leaving the remaining survivors for the combine algorithm.

The sort strategy is designed to produce a rank order of survivors from the most favored to the least favored. The first survivor remaining on the list is

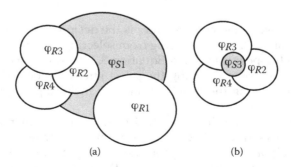

(a)   (b)

FIGURE 3.9
Cluster algorithm example.

the most favored; it becomes the system peer, and its related clock filter variables are inherited by the system variables. However, the actual clock offset is averaged from the survivors as described in the next section.

It is not always best to select the system peer as the first survivor on the survivor list. The current system peer might be occasionally disadvantaged by a spike and temporarily displaced as the first survivor on the list. To deselect it under these circumstances invites unwanted clockhop. To minimize clockhop in such cases yet respond to legitimate changes, an *anticlockhop* algorithm is used when the previous system peer is among the survivors but is not first on the list.

The algorithm uses a persistent system variable *hop*, initially zero. Let θ_0 be the first survivor on the list, θ_s the current system peer, and $x = |\theta_0 - \theta_s|$ the difference between their offsets. Then, if x is greater than the mindist option of the tos command described in Section 5.9, set *hop* to zero, select θ_0, and continue. If not and *hop* is zero, set *hop* to mindist; otherwise, multiply *hop* by 0.5. If x does not exceed *hop*, select θ_s and continue. If it does, set hop to zero, select θ_0, and continue.

With the default value for mindist of 1 ms, the algorithm works well with fast Ethernets and closely matched sources. With a pair of GPS clock devices on the same Ethernet and a client configured for both of them, the clockhop incidence is reduced by an order of magnitude while improving the accuracy. With larger values of mindist, the algorithm can be useful in cases of moderate-to-severe network congestion.

3.10 Combine Algorithm

The select and cluster algorithms described previously operate to select a single system peer based on stratum and root distance. The result is that the NTP subnet forms a forest of trees with the primary servers at the root and other servers at increasing stratum levels toward the leaves. However, since each server on the tree ordinarily runs the NTP protocol with several other servers at equal or lower stratum, these servers can provide diversity paths for backup and cross-checking. While these other paths are not ordinarily used directly for synchronization, it is possible that increased accuracy can be obtained by averaging their offsets according to appropriately chosen weights.

The result of the cluster algorithm is a set of survivors (there must be at least one) that represent truechimers or correct clocks. If there is only one survivor or if the prefer peer (see Section 3.11) is among the survivors, that peer becomes the system peer, and the combine algorithm is not used. Otherwise, the final clock correction is determined by the combine algorithm.

Let the tuples $(\theta_i, \varphi_i, \Lambda_i)$ represent the peer offset, peer jitter, and root distance, respectively, for the ith survivor. The combined peer offset and peer jitter are, respectively,

$$\Theta = a \sum_i \frac{\theta_i}{\Lambda_i} \text{ and } \varphi_r = \left(a \sum_i \frac{\varphi_1^2}{\Lambda_i} \right)^{\frac{1}{2}},$$

where a is the normalizer

$$a = \frac{1}{\displaystyle\sum_i \frac{1}{\Lambda_i}}.$$

The result Θ is the system offset processed by the discipline algorithm described in Chapter 4. Note that by design, the root distance cannot be less than the precision, which is always greater than zero, so awkward divide exceptions cannot happen.

Let φ_s represent the select jitter associated with the system peer and φ_r as above. Then, the system jitter is defined:

$$\vartheta = \left(\varphi_r^2 + \varphi_s^2 \right)^{\frac{1}{2}}.$$

The system jitter ϑ represents the best estimate of error in computing the clock offset Θ. It is interpreted as the expected error statistic available to the application program.

At this point, the major grooming algorithms—clock filter, select, cluster, and combine—have been described, but we are just getting started. As is often the case, the devil is in the details. In the following, reference is made to a number of commands and options that can be set using the configuration commands described in Section 5.9. As in conventional Web documentation, the commands and options are represented in `teletype` monospace font.

3.11 Mitigation Rules and the Prefer Peer

To provide robust backup sources, clients are often operated in a diversity configuration with a number of remote servers sometimes in addition to one or more local reference clocks. However, because of small but significant systematic offsets between the cluster algorithm survivors, it is in general not possible to achieve the lowest errors in these configurations. The select algorithm tends to *clockhop* between survivors of substantially the same root distance but showing small systematic offsets between them. The reference implementation provides a mechanism to select one or more associations as a *prefer peer*. In addition, there are a number of configurations involving special reference clock drivers for precision pulse sources and configured backup services. Whether a combined source, a single source, or no source at all is used becomes extremely complicated, so a set of carefully contrived mitigation rules is necessary. This section explores these issues in some detail.

3.11.1 The Prefer Peer

The mitigation rules are designed to provide an intelligent selection between various sources of substantially the same statistical quality without compromising the normal operation of the select, cluster, and combine algorithms. As the result of normal operations, there may be a system peer or none at all following these algorithms; if a system peer exists, there may be one or more survivors included in the weighted average computation. One or more associations can be designated *prefer peer*, which enjoys special privileges as described here. A prefer peer can be any source but is most commonly a reference clock.

In the prefer scheme, the cluster algorithm is modified so that the prefer peer is never discarded; on the contrary, its potential removal becomes a termination condition. If the original algorithm were about to toss out a prefer peer, the algorithm would terminate immediately. A prefer peer can still be discarded by the sanity checks and select algorithm, but if it survives them, it will always survive the cluster algorithm. If it does not survive or for some reason it fails to provide updates, it will eventually become unselectable, and the clock selection will remitigate to select the next-best source.

The combine algorithm is not used when a prefer peer is selected; instead, the prefer peer offset is used exclusively to discipline the system clock. In the usual case involving a reference clock and a flock of remote primary servers, and with the reference clock designated the prefer peer, the result is that the high-quality reference time disciplines the system clock as long as the reference clock itself remains a truechimer.

3.11.2 Peer Classification

The behavior of the various algorithms and mitigation rules involved depends on how the various synchronization sources are classified. This depends on whether the source is local or remote and, if local, the type of source. This is determined by examining each selectable association in turn. A *selectable association* is one that survives the peer error checks in Table 3.2. The following classes are defined:

- Associations configured for a remote server or peer are classified simply as *servers*. All other associations are classified as *device drivers* of one kind or another. In general, one or more sources of either or both classes will be configured in each installation.

- If all sources have been lost and the orphan stratum has been specified by the orphan option of the tos command, one or more pseudoservers called the *orphan parents* are created with offset and jitter both zero and operating at the orphan stratum. If a selectable association has synchronized to an orphan server, it is an *orphan child*. If there is more than one orphan parent on the same wire, one of them is selected by a tie-break procedure based on a hash of the orphan parent IP address, so all orphan children select this same orphan parent.

- When an undisciplined local clock driver is found, it is designated a *local driver*. This driver is used either as a backup source (stratum greater than zero) should all sources fail or as the primary source (stratum zero). Normally, the local driver is used only if no other sources are available. If it is designated a prefer peer, the first one found will become the only source, and all other sources will be ignored; if not, it will be used only if there are no other available sources. The local driver is operated as a prefer peer when the kernel time is controlled by some means external to NTP, such as the NIST *lockclock* algorithm or another time synchronization protocol such as DTSS.

- When an Automated Computer Time Service (ACTS) driver is found, it is designated the *modem driver*. This driver is used either as a backup source should all other sources fail or as the (only) primary source. Ordinarily, the interval between modem calls is many times longer than the interval between polls of other sources, so it is not a good idea to operate with a modem driver and other sources at the same time. Therefore, the modem driver operates in one of two ways. If it is designated a prefer peer, the first one found will become the only source, and all other sources will be ignored; if not, it will be used only if there are no other available sources.

- When a PPS driver is among the truechimers and valid PPS signals are being received, the first one found is designated the *PPS driver*. This PPS driver provides precision clock discipline only within ±0.5 s, so it is always associated with another source or sources to provide the seconds-numbering function. If this source is a reference clock driver, it may include provisions to monitor the signal and disable it if operating incorrectly.

- When an association designated prefer peer is among the truechimers, the first one found is designated the *prefer peer*.

3.11.3 Mitigation Rules

The mitigation algorithm proceeds in three steps in order:

1. If there are no survivors, the modem driver becomes the only survivor if there is one. If not, the local driver becomes the only survivor

if there is one. If not, the orphan child becomes the only survivor if there is one. If the number of survivors at this point is less than the minsane option or the tos command (see the following sections), the algorithm is terminated without producing a system peer, and the system variables remain unchanged. Note that minsane is by default 1 but can be set at any value, including 0.

2. If the prefer peer is among the survivors, it becomes the system peer. Otherwise, the combine algorithm computes the system variables from the survivor population, and the survivor with minimum root distance becomes the system peer.

3. If there is a PPS driver and the system clock offset at this point is less than 0.4 s, and if there is a prefer peer among the survivors or if the PPS peer is designated as a prefer peer, the PPS driver becomes the system peer, and its offset and jitter are inherited by the system variables. This overrides any variables already computed in step 1. Note that a PPS driver is present only if PPS signals are actually being received and enabled by the associated reference clock driver.

If none of the above is the case, the system variables remain as they are without producing a system peer.

3.11.4 The minsane Option

The minsane option of the tos command specifies the minimum number of survivors required to synchronize the system clock. A common scenario is a GPS reference clock driver with a serial timecode and PPS signal. The PPS signal is disabled until the system clock has been set by some means, not necessarily the GPS driver. If the serial timecode is within 0.4 s of the PPS signal, the GPS driver is designated the PPS driver, and the PPS signal disciplines the system clock. If no GPS satellites are in view or if the PPS signal is disconnected, the GPS driver stops updating the system clock and disables the PPS signal, so eventually it becomes unreachable and is replaced by other sources. If no other sources are available and minsane is other than zero, the host coasts according to its last update.

Whether the GPS driver disables the PPS signal when unreachable is at the discretion of the driver. Ordinarily, the PPS signal would be disabled in this case; however, when the GPS receiver has a precision holdover oscillator, the driver may elect to continue PPS operation driven by the holdover oscillator. In this case, the PPS signal continues to discipline the system clock, and minsane should be set to zero. According to the mitigation rules, the clock will continue to be disciplined by the PPS signal indefinitely.

3.12 Huff-'n-Puff Filter

One of the things hard to fix in an NTP subnet is errors due to asymmetric delays. It is in fact not possible to correct these errors, even if an interlocking network of servers is available. However, there is one scenario for which errors due to asymmetric delays can be very much reduced. Consider when the access link to an information services provider is relatively slow and all other links between the provider and the information source are relatively fast. Furthermore, consider when the access link is heavily congested in one direction but not the other. This is typically the result of a large download or upload file for which fat data packets flow one way, and only skinny acknowledgment (ACK) packets flow the other.

Returning to the arguments made in connection with the clock filter algorithm, note that the scattergram in such cases will be highly asymmetric, with the vast majority of the points concentrated on one of the two limbs of the scattergram. If the coordinates of the apex could be determined one way or another, the points further out the limb could be corrected and used to discipline the clock. Such would be the case if the lowest-delay samples could be determined. This is not easy as the periods during which the link is congested can last for hours.

The huff-'n-puff filter is designed to determine the lowest-delay samples in periods ranging up to several hours. It does this by using a shift register and circular pointer by which delay samples appear to shift in one end and old samples shift off the other. Occasionally, the register is searched to find the lowest-delay sample m. If (θ_i, Λ_i) represents an offset and delay sample,

$$\text{if } \theta_i > 0 \ \text{ then } \theta = \theta_i - \frac{\delta_i - m}{2} \, ;$$
$$\text{else } \theta = \theta_i + \frac{\delta_i - m}{2}.$$

Note that this works only if the system clock offset is relatively small; in other words, it works better as the differential delays get larger. Typically, the register holds 4 h of samples and is searched for the minimum every 15 min.

Figure 3.10 shows the scattergram for a badly asymmetric Internet path simulating a DSL modem at the subscriber end. As before, the network delays are simulated by zero-mean exponential distributions, but with $\sigma = 10$ ms in one direction and $\sigma = 1$ ms in the other. Figure 3.11 shows the cumulative distribution function for the unfiltered samples (right) and filtered samples (left). The result with the huff-'n-puff filter is a reduction in mean error from 45 to 6.4 ms and a reduction in standard deviation from 48 to 9.7 ms.

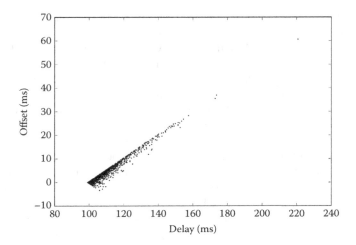

FIGURE 3.10
Huff-'n-puff wedge scattergram.

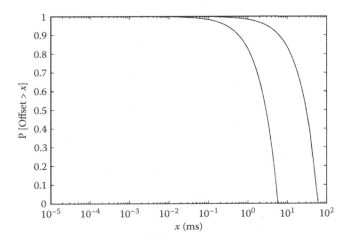

FIGURE 3.11
Huff-'n-puff raw (right) and filtered (left) offset CDF.

3.13 Orphan Mode

Sometimes, an NTP subnet becomes isolated from all UTC sources, such as a local reference clock or remote Internet time servers. In such cases, it may be necessary that the subnet servers and clients remain synchronized to a common timescale, not necessarily the UTC timescale. Previously, this function was provided by the local clock driver described in Section 7.4. It simulates a UTC source when no other source is present according to the mitigation rules of Section 3.11. A server with this driver can synchronize other hosts in the subnet directly or indirectly. However, there are many disadvantages using the local clock driver, primarily that the subnet is vulnerable to single-point failures, and multiple-server redundancy is not possible. Orphan mode is intended to replace the local clock driver. It provides a single simulated UTC source with multiple servers and provides seamless switching as servers fail and recover.

A common configuration for private networks includes one or more core NTP servers operating at the lowest stratum. Good practice is to configure each of these servers as a backup for the others using symmetric or broadcast modes. As long as at least one core server can reach a UTC source, the entire subnet can synchronize to it. If no UTC sources are available to a core server, it operates as an *orphan parent* to provide a simulated UTC source for other hosts in the subnet. However, only one orphan parent can simulate the UTC source, and all *orphan children* directly dependent on them must select the same one.

A host is enabled for orphan mode by specifying the *orphan stratum* using the orphan option of the tos command. The orphan stratum is less than 16 and greater than any anticipated stratum that might occur with configured subnet time servers. However, sufficient headroom should remain so that every subnet host dependent on the orphan children has stratum less than 16. Where no associations for other servers or reference clocks are configured, the orphan stratum can be set to 1. These are the same considerations that guide the local clock driver stratum selection.

For orphan mode to work well, each core server should operate at the same stratum. All core servers and directly dependent clients should specify the same orphan stratum. Each client should maintain associations for all core servers. An orphan parent with no sources shows stratum equal to the orphan stratum. While ordinary NTP clients use a selection metric based on stratum and root distance, orphan children use a metric computed as a hash of the IP address of the orphan parent. Each orphan child chooses the orphan parent with the smallest metric.

For example, consider the symmetric peer network configuration in Figure 3.12 in which two or more campus primary or secondary servers A and B are configured with reference clocks or public Internet servers and with each other using symmetric modes. Clients are configured in two groups: one with orphan child C and the other with orphan child D. With this configuration, a server that loses all sources continues to discipline the system clock using the other servers as backup. If all sources are lost by all core servers, they operate as orphan parents, and all orphan clients agree on only one of them as their source.

As another example, consider the broadcast configuration in Figure 3.13. For broadcast networks, each core server is configured in both broadcast server and broadcast client modes. Orphan children operate as broadcast clients of all core servers. As in symmetric peer networks, the core servers back up each other, and only if all sources fail do the core servers operate as orphan parents.

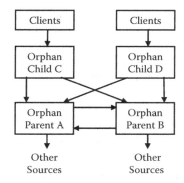

FIGURE 3.12
Symmetric mode orphan subnet.

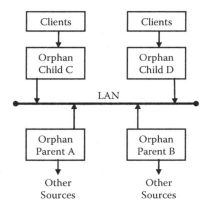

FIGURE 3.13
Broadcast mode orphan LAN.

3.14 Rate Control and the Kiss-o'-Death Packet

Some national time metrology laboratories, including NIST and USNO, use the reference implementation in their busy public time servers. They operate multiple servers behind load-balancing devices to support aggregate rates up to several thousand packets per second. The servers need to defend themselves against all manner of broken implementations that can clog the server and network infrastructure. On the other hand, friendly clients need to avoid configurations that can result in unfriendly rates.

This section describes provisions in the reference implementation for clients to limit sending rates to avoid overloading servers and for servers to defend against clients sending at excessive rates. The provisions are optional and work well only if the client and server implement them. There are several features designed to defend the servers, clients, and network against accidental or malicious flood attack. On the other hand, these features are also used to ensure that the client is a good citizen, even if configured in unfriendly ways. The ground rules are as follows:

- Send at the lowest rate consistent with the nominal accuracy expectations.
- Maintain strict minimum average headway and guard times, even if multiple burst options or the Autokey protocol are in use.
- When the first packet of a burst is sent to a server, do not send further packets until the first packet has been received from the server.
- On receiving a kiss-o'-death (KoD) packet (discussed in Section 3.14.2), immediately reduce the sending rate.

Rate management involves two algorithms to manage resources: (1) average headway and guard time and (2) the KoD packet. These are described in the following sections.

3.14.1 Average Headway and Guard Time

There are two features of the poll algorithm designed to manage the interval between one packet and the next. These features use a set of two counters: a client output counter for each client association and a server input counter for each distinct client IP address. Each counter increments by a value called the *headway* when a packet is processed and decrements by one each second. The default minimum average headway is 8 s, but this can be increased using the `average` option of the `discard` command.

If the `iburst` or `burst` options are present, the poll algorithm sends a burst of packets instead of a single packet at each poll opportunity. The NTPv4 specification requires that bursts contain no more than eight packets; so, starting from an output counter value of zero, the maximum counter value or output ceiling can be no more than eight times the minimum poll interval set by the `minpoll` option of the `server` command. However, if the burst starts with a counter value other than zero, there is a potential to exceed the ceiling. The poll algorithm avoids this by computing an additional headway time so that the next packet sent will not exceed the ceiling. Additional headway time can result from Autokey protocol operations. Designs such as this are often called *leaky buckets*.

The server input packet routine uses a sorted list of entries, one entry for each distinct client IP address found. Each entry includes an IP address, input counter, and interval since the last packet arrival. The entries are ordered by interval from the smallest to the largest. As each packet arrives, the IP source address is compared to the IP address of each entry in turn. If a match is found, the entry is removed and inserted first on the list. If the IP source address does not match any entry, a new entry is created and inserted first on the list, possibly discarding the last entry on the list if it is full.

In the least recently used (LRU) virtual memory paging algorithm, the entry replaced is the last, whereas here the entry replaced is the first, so this is a most recently used (MRU) algorithm. The input counter is decreased by the interval since it was last referenced but not below zero. If the value of the counter plus the headway is greater than the input ceiling set by the `aver-age` option of the `discard` command, the packet is discarded. Otherwise, the counter is increased by the headway, and the packet is processed. The result is that, if the client maintains an average headway not less than the input ceiling and transmits no more than eight packets in a burst, the input counter will not exceed the ceiling.

A review of past client abuse incidents showed that the most frequent scenario is a broken client that attempts to send a number of packets at rates of one per second or more. On one occasion, due to a defective client design, over 750,000 clients fell into this mode [28]. There have been occasions when this abuse persisted for days at a time. These scenarios are the most damaging as they can threaten not only the victim server but also the network infrastructure.

In the intended design, the minimum headway between the last packet received and the next packet is called the *guard time*. If the headway is less than the guard time, the packet is discarded. The guard time defaults to 2 s, but this can be changed using the `minimum` option of the `discard` command.

3.14.2 The Kiss-o'-Death Packet

Ordinarily, packets denied service are simply discarded with no further action except incrementing statistics counters. Sometimes, a more proactive response is needed to force the client to slow down. A special packet format has been crafted for this purpose called the kiss-o'-death (KoD) packet. KoD packets have leap indicator 3, stratum 0, and the reference identifier set to a four-character ASCII (American Standard Code for Information Interchange) code.

A client receiving a KoD packet is expected to slow down; however, no explicit mechanism is specified in the protocol to do this. In the reference implementation, the poll interval in the server packet is set as the maximum of the poll interval in the client packet and the average headway. For KoD packets (only), if the packet poll interval is greater than `minpoll`, `minpoll` is set to the packet poll interval and the output counter increased by that value. This forces the client to reduce the rate to a value acceptable by the server.

At present, there is only one KoD packet with code RATE. To make sure that the client notices the KoD, the receive and transmit timestamps in the packet are set to the transmit timestamp and all other fields left as in the client packet. Thus, even if the client ignores the KoD, it cannot do any useful time computations. KoDs themselves are rate limited in the same way as arriving packets to deflect a flood attack.

3.15 Parting Shots

A few words are offered at this point to explain why these algorithms are so squirrelly. The short answer is that they have to work well over a very wide range of ambient network jitter, oscillator wander, and system clock resolution. They have to deliver good results when the network jitter is in the hundreds of milliseconds and when it is fractions of a microsecond and when the system clock resolution is 20 ms all the way down to 1 ns. The algorithms are designed to optimize operations by adapting to the prevailing network and hardware conditions. They also have to operate with very small residuals in the order of the time to read the system clock. That is why fanatic attention to detail is required. An even higher degree of fanatic detail is discussed in Chapter 11 on the error budget.

The long answer is that the algorithms are the result of a continuing refinement from the days when the computer clock was based on the power grid to modern days when some systems salute atomic clocks. In the last almost 30 years, much has been learned about how a huge network like the Internet behaves, and the Internet behavior itself has changed in dramatic ways. Compare the ARPANET scattergram of Figure 3.3 with the DSL huff-'n-puff scattergram of Figure 3.10. The ARPANET was slow by the standards of today; most links were slower than the dial-up telephone modem of today. The ARPANET had over 200 packet switches in its heyday, and most of that traffic was between time-sharing machines and ASCII terminals. So, the scattergram shows symmetry and moderately long queue sizes. This means a good deal of the end-end delays were for packets waiting in intermediate queues.

Currently, the typical network path is lightning quick compared to the delay on the customer tail circuit, with the result that the delays are often dominated by propagation delay rather than queuing delay. Thus, the delay distribution is typically due to occasional spikes that the NTP algorithms are specifically designed to handle.

References

1. Postel, J. *Daytime Protocol*. Network Working Group Report RFC-867, USC Information Sciences Institute, May 1983.
2. Postel, J. *Time Protocol*. Network Working Group Report RFC-868, USC Information Sciences Institute, May 1983. Postel, J. *User Datagram Protocol*. Network Working Group Report RFC-768, USC Information Sciences Institute, August 1980.
3. *Internet Control Message Protocol*. Network Working Group Report RFC-792, USC Information Sciences Institute, September 1981.

4. Su, Z. *A Specification of the Internet Protocol (IP) Timestamp Option*. Network Working Group Report-781, SRI International, May 1981.

5. Cole, R., and C. Foxcroft. An experiment in clock synchronisation. *Computer J. 31, 6* (1988), 496–502.

6. *Digital Time Service Functional Specification Version T.1.0.5*. Digital Equipment Corporation, 1989.

7. Gusella, R., and S. Zatti. *The Berkeley UNIX 4.3BSD Time Synchronization Protocol: Protocol Specification*. Technical Report UCB/CSD 85/250, University of California, Berkeley, June 1985.

8. Halpern, J.Y., B. Simons, R. Strong, and D. Dolev. Fault-tolerant clock synchronization. *Proceedings ACM Third Annual Symposium on Principles of Distributed Computing* (August 1984), 89–102.

9. Lundelius, J., and N.A. Lynch. A new fault-tolerant algorithm for clock synchronization. *Proceedings Third Annual ACM Symposium on Principles of Distributed Computing* (August 1984), 75–88.

10. Marzullo, K., and S. Owicki. Maintaining the time in a distributed system. *ACM Operating Syst. Rev. 19, 3* (July 1985), 44–54.

11. Rickert, N.W. Non Byzantine clock synchronization—a programming experiment. *ACM Operating Syst. Rev. 22, 1* (January 1988), 73–78.

12. Schneider, F.B. *A Paradigm for Reliable Clock Synchronization*. Department of Computer Science Technical Report TR 86-735, Cornell University, Ithaca, NY, February 1986.

13. Tripathi, S.K., and S.H. Chang. *ETempo, a Clock Synchronization Algorithm for Hierarchical LANs—Implementation and Measurements*. Systems Research Center Technical Report TR-86-48, University of Maryland, 25 pp.

14. Gusella, R., and S. Zatti. TEMPO—A network time controller for a distributed Berkeley UNIX system. *IEEE Distributed Processing Technical Committee Newsletter 6*, NoSI-2 (June 1984), 7–15. Also in *Proceedings Summer 1984 USENIX* (Salt Lake City, June 1984).

15. Liao, C., M. Martonosi, and D. Clark. Experience with an adaptive globally-synchronizing clock algorithm. In *Proceedings 11th Annual ACM Symposium on Parallel Algorithms and Architecture* (June 1999), 106–114.

16. Lu, M., and D. Zhang. Analysis of self-stabilizing clock synchronization by means of stochastic Petri nets. *IEEE Trans. Computers 39, 5* (May 1990), 597–604.

17. Kopetz, H., and W. Ochsenreiter. Clock synchronization in distributed real-time systems. *IEEE Trans. Computers C-36, 8* (August 1987), 933–939.

18. Lamport, L. Time, clocks and the ordering of events in a distributed system. *Commun. ACM 21, 7* (July 1978), 558–565.

19. Lamport, L., and P.M. Melliar-Smith. Synchronizing clocks in the presence of faults. *JACM 32, 1* (January 1985), 52–78.

20. Pease, M., R. Shostak, and L. Lamport. Reaching agreement in the presence of faults. *JACM 27, 2* (April 1980), 228–234.

21. Srikanth, T.K., and S. Toueg. Optimal clock synchronization. *JACM 34, 3* (July 1987), 626–645.

22. Mills, D.L. *Experiments in Network Clock Synchronization*. DARPA Network Working Group Report RFC-957, M/A-COM Linkabit, September 1985.

23. Lindsay, W.C., and A.V. Kantak. Network synchronization of random signals. *IEEE Trans. Commun. COM-28, 8* (August 1980), 1260–1266.

24. Mitra, D. Network synchronization: analysis of a hybrid of master-slave and mutual synchronization. *IEEE Trans. Commun. COM-28, 8* (August 1980), 1245–1259.
25. Lu, M., and D. Zhang. Analysis of self-stabilizing clock synchronization by means of stochastic Petri nets. *IEEE Trans. Computers 39, 5* (May 1990), 597–604.
26. Vasanthavada, N., and P.N. Marinos. Synchronization of fault-tolerant clocks in the presence of malicious failures. *IEEE Trans. Computers C-37, 4* (April 1988), 440–448.
27. Paxson, V. On calibrating measurements of packet transit times. *Proceedings Joint Internet Conference on Measurements and Modelling of Computer Systems* (June 1998), 11–21.
28. Mills, D.L., J. Levine, R. Schmidt, and D. Plonka. Coping with overload on the Network Time Protocol public servers. *Proceedings Precision Time and Time Interval (PTTI) Applications and Planning Meeting* (Washington, DC, December 2004), 5–16.

Further Reading

Braun, W.B. Short term frequency effects in networks of coupled oscillators. *IEEE Trans. Commun. COM-28, 8* (August 1980), 1269–1275.

Dolev, D., J. Halpern, and H. Strong. On the possibility and impossibility of achieving clock synchronization. *Proceedings 16th Annual ACM Symposium on Theory of Computing* (Washington, DC, April 1984), 504–511.

Jones, R.H., and P.V. Tryon. Continuous time series models for unequally spaced data applied to modelling atomic clocks. *SIAM J. Sci. Stat. Comput. 4, 1* (January 1987), 71–81.

Lamport, L., and P.M. Melliar-Smith. Synchronizing clocks in the presence of faults. *JACM 32, 1* (January 1985), 52–78.

Levine, J. An algorithm to synchronize the time of a computer to universal time. *IEEE Trans. Networking 3, 1* (February 1995), 42–50.

Mills, D.L. The fuzzball. *Proceedings ACM SIGCOMM 88 Symposium* (August 1988), 115–122.

Mills, D.L. *Internet Delay Experiments.* DARPA Network Working Group Report RFC-889, M/A-COM Linkabit, December 1983.

Percival, D.B. The U.S. Naval Observatory Clock Time Scales. *IEEE Trans. Instrum. Measure. IM-27, 4* (December 1978), 376–385.

Tryon, P.V., and R.H. Jones. Estimation of parameters in models for cesium beam atomic clocks. *J. Res. Natl. Bur. Stand. 88, 1* (January–February 1983).

4

Clock Discipline Algorithm

Macavity's a Mystery Cat: he's called the Hidden Paw—
For he's the master criminal who can defy the Law.
He's the bafflement of Scotland Yard, the Flying Squad's despair:
For when they reach the scene of crime—*Macavity's not there!*

T. S. Elliot
Old Possum's Book of Practical Cats

If the last chapter was the belly of the beast, this chapter is the navel of the belly. In the navel is the discipline algorithm that synchronizes the system clock to the best and final time correction produced by the mitigation algorithm. The discipline algorithm, shortened to *discipline*, is the main topic of this chapter. It has evolved from humble beginnings to a sophisticated design that automatically adapts to changes in operating environment without manual configuration or real-time management functions. The discipline has been implemented both in the NTP daemon and, for the highest accuracy, in the operating system kernel. However, the discipline could be used in principle with any protocol that provides periodic time corrections.

Recall the key concepts of resolution, precision, and accuracy. *Resolution* is the degree to which one hardware clock reading can be distinguished from another, normally equal to the reciprocal of the clock oscillator frequency. For a modern 3-GHz processor with a readable cycle counter, the resolution is 0.33 ns or about the time light travels 3 inches. When processors get much faster, the ultimate resolution limit will be the NTP timestamp itself, which is 0.232 ns. However, in modern operating system kernels, the time is maintained in seconds and nanoseconds, so the resolution is limited to 1 ns.

Precision is the degree to which an application can distinguish one clock reading from another, defined as the latency to read the system clock, and is a property of the hardware and operating system. As hardware has become faster, the precision has been reduced from 58 μs on a Sun Microsystems SPARC IPC 15 years ago to less than 1 μs today on a Sun Blade 1500.

Accuracy is ordinarily defined as the degree to which a clock reading differs from real time as disseminated by national standards, but this is not the central issue in this chapter. The discipline is presented with periodic time corrections. It adjusts the clock time, compensates for the intrinsic frequency error, and adjusts the various parameters dynamically in response to measured system jitter and oscillator wander. The goal of the discipline is to minimize the residual time offset with respect to the updates produced by the grooming and mitigation algorithms.

4.1 Feedback Control Systems

We need to talk about feedback control systems before plunging into the mathematics. The NTP discipline is a feedback control system, and as such it must conform to the basic principles of physics. To shed light on this point, consider how you use the accelerator pedal to maintain speed on a crowded freeway. The headway between you and the car in front of you can be expressed in time, distance, or the number of wheel rotations. In electronic terms, the angular position of a wheel is the phase, and the rate that the angle changes is the velocity or frequency. In this chapter, we use the terms time difference and phase difference interchangeably or just offset when the meaning is clear from context.

In the sense that your eye measures the headway, it measures the number of wheel rotations or phase difference between your wheel and the wheel of the car in front of you. If the car is receding ahead of you, you press down on the accelerator, which increases the angular velocity and thus the frequency; if you are gaining on the car, you ease back on the accelerator to decrease the frequency. The accelerator pedal, engine, transmission, and wheels are analogous in electronic terms to a variable-frequency oscillator (VFO). Your headway perception is analogous in electronic terms to a phase detector. Your brain functions as the filter that closes the feedback loop; if it takes too long to decide what to do, a transient may result, and you may go over the speed limit, at least momentarily. Obviously, the impulse response of the brain is an important freeway design consideration.

The NTP discipline functions as a combination of two philosophically quite different feedback control systems. A client sends messages to each server with a *poll interval* $T_s = 2^\tau$, as determined by the time constant T_c. In the NTPv4, τ is called the *poll exponent* and can range from 3 (8 s) through 17 (131,072 s, about 36 h). The algorithms in this chapter have been scaled so that $T_c = 2^{\tau+5}$. The reason for expressing the interval as a power of two will become clear in this discussion.

A server responds with messages at update intervals of μ seconds. Usually, but not necessarily, $\mu \approx 2^\tau$, and the update intervals for all servers are about equal. In a phase-lock loop (PLL) design, periodic phase updates at intervals μ are used directly to minimize the time error and indirectly the frequency error. In a frequency-lock loop (FLL) design, periodic frequency updates at intervals μ are used directly to minimize the frequency error and indirectly the time error. As shown in this chapter, a PLL usually works better when system jitter dominates, while an FLL works better when oscillator wander dominates.

The NTPv4 discipline design described in this chapter is slightly modified from the design described in Mills [1]. The new design shows a substantial improvement in the performance over the earlier algorithm. In addition, the discipline automatically selects the optimum combination of FLL and PLL corrections over a wide range of system jitter and oscillator wander characteristics while in regular operation and does not require initial calibration. Perhaps the most striking result is that the discipline is effective with poll intervals well over 1 day, which is an attractive feature when telephone toll charges are involved.

Figure 3.1 shows how the discipline process interacts with the other important algorithms in NTPv4. The output of the combine algorithm represents the best estimate of the system clock offset relative to the server ensemble. The discipline adjusts the frequency of the VFO to minimize this offset. Finally, the timestamps of each server are compared to the timestamps derived from the VFO to calculate the server offsets and close the feedback loop.

The discipline is implemented as the feedback control system shown in Figure 4.1. The variable θ_r represents the combined server reference phase, and θ_c is the control phase of the VFO. Each update received from a server produces a signal V_d representing the instantaneous phase difference $\theta_r - \theta_c$. The clock filter for each server functions as a tapped delay line, with the output taken at the tap selected by the clock filter algorithm. The select, cluster, and combine algorithms combine the data from multiple filters to produce the signal V_s. The loop filter, with impulse response $F(t)$, produces the signal V_c, which controls the VFO frequency ω_c and thus its phase $\theta_c = \int \omega_c dt$, which closes the loop. The V_c signal is generated by an adjustment process that runs at intervals of 1 s in the NTP daemon discipline or one tick in the kernel discipline. The characteristic behavior of this model, which is determined by $F(t)$ and the various gain factors, is studied in Chapter 12, many textbooks, and summarized in Mills [1].

The original NTPv3 discipline was based on a conventional PLL. The NTPv4 discipline includes an FLL capability as well. The selection of which

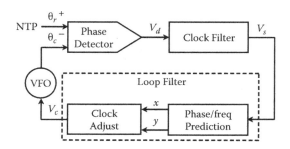

FIGURE 4.1
Discipline algorithm.

mode to use, FLL or PLL, and in what combination is made on the basis of the poll exponent τ. In the NTPv4 design, PLL mode is used at smaller values of τ, while FLL mode is used at larger values. The FLL improves the clock accuracy and stability, especially for poll intervals larger than the Allan intercept discussed in Chapter 12.

4.2 Phase and Frequency Discipline

An overview will suffice to describe how the prediction algorithms and adjustment process work. The details, which are given in Mills [2], are beyond the scope of this book. The transient behavior of the hybrid PLL/FLL feedback loop is determined by the impulse response of the loop filter $F(t)$. The loop filter shown in Figure 4.2 is implemented using two subalgorithms, one based on a conventional PLL and the other on an FLL design suggested in Levine [3]. Both predict a phase adjustment x as a function of V_s, but this becomes ineffective for poll intervals above the Allan intercept, which for most commodity computer oscillators is about 2,000 s. The PLL predicts a frequency adjustment y_{PLL} as an integral $\int V_s \mu dt$, but this is used only when the poll interval is below the Allan intercept. Above that, the FLL predicts an adjustment y_{FLL} as a function of V_s/μ. The x and y are then used by the clock adjust process to control the VFO frequency V_c and to close the feedback loop.

In PLL mode y is a time integral over all past values of V_s, so the PLL frequency adjustment required by the theory discussed in Chapter 12 is

$$y_{PLL} = \frac{V_s \mu}{(4K_p T_s)^2},$$

(4.1)

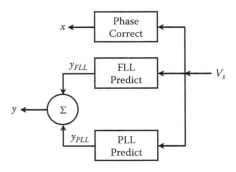

FIGURE 4.2
FLL/PLL prediction functions.

where $K_p = 16$ is a constant chosen to control the feedback loop damping factor. In FLL mode, y_{FLL} is an average of past frequency changes as computed from V_s and μ. The goal of the algorithm is to reduce V_s to zero; so, to the extent this has been successful in the past, previous values can be assumed zero, and the average becomes

$$y_{FLL} = \frac{V_s - x}{K_f \mu},\tag{4.2}$$

where x is the residual phase error computed by the clock adjust process. The constant $K_f = 4$ is an averaging factor determined from experience with typical clock frequency wander. Note the $V_s - x$ term, which at first glance would seem to be unnecessary tedium. At the previous update, the y_{FLL} prediction was made on the assumption that the x would be zero at the next update. If not, then V_s should be reduced by that value so that y_{FLL} reflects only adjustments due to frequency changes. This isolates the frequency prediction from the phase prediction, which is important during the initial frequency measurement at startup for the first time.

Finally, in both PLL and FLL modes, set the phase $x = V_s$ and frequency $y = y + y_{PLL} + y_{FLL}$, but note that the y_{FLL} term is included only for T_s above the Allan intercept where the effects of y_{PLL} become very small. Once each second, the adjustment process computes a phase increment $z = \frac{x}{K_p T_s}$ and new phase adjustment $x = x - z$. The phase increment z is passed to the kernel time adjustment function, usually the adjtime() system call. This continues until the next update, which recomputes x and y.

For good PLL stability, T_c must be at least twice the total loop delay, which, because of the clock filter algorithm, can be as much as eight times the update interval. When the discipline is first started, a relatively small poll interval of 64 s is required to achieve the maximum capture range of 500 PPM. Following the stability rule, $T_c \geq 2 \times 8 \times 64 = 1,024$ s. In fact, at this poll interval $T_c = 2,048$ s, giving a margin factor of two. At this value, the PLL response to a time step has a rise time of 53 min, an overshoot of 5 percent, and a 63 percent response to a frequency step of 4.2 h.

Ordinarily, the update interval increases substantially once the frequency has stabilized, and these values increase in proportion. In this design, as T_c is increased, the shape of the transient response characteristic remains the same, but the rise time scales inversely with T_c. However, even as the influence of the FLL kicks in, the transient response characteristic is preserved.

The performance of the discipline algorithm has been evaluated using simulation and confirmed by experiment. There are three reasons for this, rather than testing the algorithm exclusively in the context of the reference implementation. First, evaluation of these algorithms can take long wall clock times since the intrinsic time constants are often quite long—several hours to days. Simulation time runs much faster than wall clock time, in fact by several orders of magnitude. Second, the simulation environment is not burdened by the infrastructure in which the real software must operate, such as input/output (I/O) and monitoring code. Third, the simulator code itself consists mainly of the actual reference implementation in which the system clock and I/O functions have been replaced by synthetic generators. The simulator then becomes a convincing proof-of-performance demonstration of the program in actual operation.

4.3 Time and Frequency Response

Figures 4.3, 4.4, and 4.5 illustrate the discipline response to a time step of 100 ms. The behavior for small values of τ for which the PLL response dominates is shown in Figure 4.3 for the time response and Figure 4.4 for the frequency response. In both cases, the left trace is for $\tau = 4$ (16 s), the middle trace for $\tau = 6$ (64 s), and the right trace for $\tau = 8$ (256 s). Note that while the time response converges relatively quickly, the frequency response takes much longer.

The behavior for large values of τ where the FLL response dominates is shown in Figure 4.5 for the time response with the left trace for $\tau = 13$ (2.2 h) and $\tau = 16$ (9 h) relatively smooth and overlap to the left on the figure. This is because, while the interval is quadrupled, the time constant is reduced by the same factor, so the transient response is similar, and the step threshold has not been exceeded. On the other hand, the

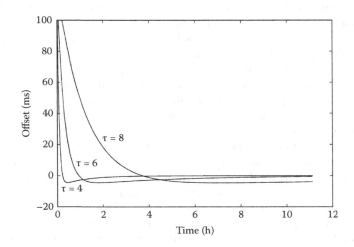

FIGURE 4.3
PLL time response to a 100-ms time step ($\tau = 4, 6, 8$).

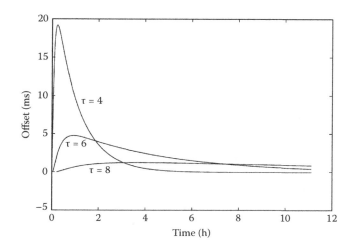

FIGURE 4.4
PLL frequency response to a 100-ms time step ($\tau = 4, 6, 8$).

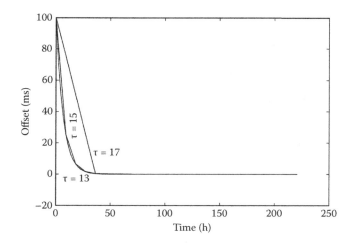

FIGURE 4.5
FLL time response to a 100-ms time step ($\tau = 13, 15, 17$).

trace for $\tau = 17$ (36 h) is different because the step threshold has been exceeded and the frequency calculated directly. In all three cases, the FLL frequency prediction is near perfect and the error too small to show on the same scale as Figure 4.4.

Figures 4.6 and 4.7 illustrate the discipline response to a frequency step of 5 PPM. The behavior for small values of τ for which the PLL response dominates is shown in Figure 4.6 for the time response and Figure 4.7 for the frequency response. In Figure 4.6, the most rapid response is for $\tau = 4$ (16 s),

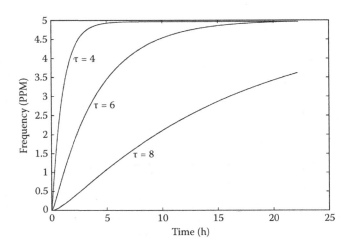

FIGURE 4.6
PLL frequency response to a 5-PPM frequency step (τ = 4, 6, 8).

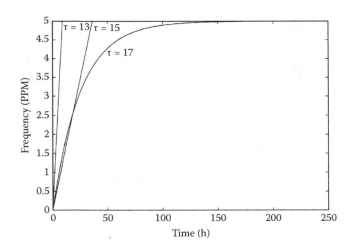

FIGURE 4.7
FLL frequency response to a 5-PPM frequency step (τ = 13, 15, 17).

the next slower for τ = 6 (64 s), and the slowest for τ = 8 (256 s). Obviously, the PLL can take well over a day to adapt to a frequency step, especially at the larger poll intervals.

The behavior for large values of τ for which the FLL response dominates is shown in Figure 4.7 for the frequency response. In the rightmost curve with τ = 13 (2.2 h), the step threshold has not been exceeded and the response is smooth, while in the leftmost curve with $\tau = 15$ (9 h) and middle curve with $\tau = 17$ (36 h), the threshold has been exceeded and the time and frequency calculated directly, resulting in very small error. The effect is most dramatic with the frequency response, where the frequency is corrected in less time than at the lowest τ.

4.4 Poll Interval Control

NTP time servers and clients operate today using network paths that span the globe. In many cases, primary servers operate with several hundred clients or more. It is necessary to explore every means with which the poll interval can be increased without significantly degrading clock accuracy or stability. The discipline algorithm allows a significant increase in the interval without compromising accuracy, while at the same time adapting dynamically to widely varying network jitter and oscillator wander regimes. Since the network overhead decreases as the interval increases, a method is needed to select the best compromise interval between required accuracy and acceptable overhead. This is most important in configurations for which a toll charge is incurred for each poll, as in Integrated Services Digital Network (ISDN) and telephone modem services.

In the NTP design, the minimum and maximum poll exponents default to values appropriate for almost all network and computer configurations. For NTPv3 network clients, τ can range from 6 (64 s) to 10 (1,024 s) and for telephone modem clients from 10 to 14 (16,384 s). However, in NTPv4 it can range from 3 (8 s) to 17 (131,072 s or about 36 h). The discipline automatically manages τ within these ranges in response to the prevailing system jitter and oscillator wander. An important point is that it is not necessary to clamp τ to the minimum when switching among different synchronization sources as in NTPv3. In cases of moderate-to-severe network jitter and with multiple sources, this sometimes causes frequent *clockhop*, which in turn degrades accuracy.

The NTPv4 algorithm attempts to set the averaging time somewhere near the Allan intercept. A key to this strategy is the measured system jitter and oscillator wander statistics. The system jitter model described in Chapter 12 describes white phase noise typical of network and operating system latencies. The oscillator wander model describes random-walk frequency noise typical of computer clock oscillators. The clock jitter is estimated from phase differences $\varphi_c = \sqrt{\langle \Delta x^2 \rangle}$, where x is from Figure 4.2, and the brackets indicate exponential average. The oscillator wander is estimated from frequency differences $\varphi_f = \sqrt{\langle \Delta y^2 \rangle}$. As τ increases, we expect φ_c to decrease and φ_f to increase, depending on the relative contributions of phase noise and frequency noise. As a general rule, the errors due to network jitter decrease by a factor of two for every twofold increase of the poll interval, while errors due to oscillator wander increase by a factor of two for every fourfold increase.

In practice, φ_f is difficult to measure directly, especially at the larger poll intervals. An effective strategy is to compare the values of x to the clock jitter φ_c. In the NTPv4 algorithm, at each update a jiggle counter is incremented by the current value of τ if x is within the bound $|x| < K_s \varphi_c$, where the jiggle threshold $K_s = 3$ is determined by experiment, and decremented by 2τ otherwise. To avoid needless hunting, a degree of hysteresis is built into the algorithm. If the counter reaches the upper jiggle threshold 30, τ is increased by one; if it reaches the lower jiggle threshold -30, τ is reduced by one. In either case, the counter is reset to zero. Under normal conditions, τ slowly increases in stages from a default lower limit of 6 (64 s) to a default upper limit of 10 (1,024 s). However, if the wander increases because the oscillator frequency is deviating too fast, τ is quickly reduced. Once the oscillator wander subsides, τ is slowly increased again. Under typical operating conditions, τ hovers close to the maximum, but on occasions of a heat spike when the oscillator wanders more than about 1 PPM, it quickly drops to lower values until the wander subsides.

4.5 Popcorn and Step Control

Computer networks are noisy places. Incidental network jitter varies over a wide range, and spikes are not infrequent. The clock filter algorithm greatly reduces network jitter and removes most spikes for each server separately, but spikes can also occur when switching from one server to another. Specific provisions have been incorporated in the discipline to further attenuate these disturbances in the form of spike suppressors, noise gates, and the aptly named huff-'n-puff filter. While not strictly a grooming provision, the step threshold and panic threshold are designed to protect against broken hardware or completely insane servers.

As a practical matter, a not uncommon hazard in global Internet timekeeping is an occasional large offset spike, called a *popcorn spike*, due to some transient phenomenon in the network. Popcorn spike suppressors are used in the clock filter and discipline algorithms to avoid these spikes. They operate by tracking the exponentially averaged jitter and discarding a spike that exceeds a threshold equal to some multiple of the average. The spike itself is then used to update the average, so the threshold is self-adaptive. Popcorn spike suppressors are effective for only a single spike or two and not under extreme conditions of network jitter as on some international Internet circuits.

A more refined grooming provision, called a noise gate, is incorporated in the state machine described in the next section. It operates under conditions of very large network jitter typical of heavily congested network paths. Offset spikes on these paths can range up to a second or more and tend to occur in bursts. However, the bursts are not a large fraction of the total offset population. Unlike the popcorn spike suppressor, which has a self-adaptive threshold, the noise gate has a fixed step threshold, typically 128 ms. Spikes greater than the step threshold are ignored unless they persist for a relatively long time, like 15 min. In operation, a watchdog counter counts the seconds since the first offset sample exceeded the step threshold. If a sample arrives with offset less than this, the counter stops and is reset to zero. If the counter reaches 900 s, called the *stepout threshold*, the next sample is believed, and the clock stepped to its value.

In practice, clock steps in the Internet are very rare and almost always indicate a hardware, software, or operational failure. Historically, the most common case has been when the operating system has been warned in advance of a pending leap second and correctly stepped the clock at the epoch, but some attached reference clock has not yet recognized that the leap second has occurred. It may take up to 15 min for the reference clock to resynchronize to the radio signal, during which its time is incorrect but disregarded by the noise gate. Happily, once the radio has resynchronized, the offsets are again less than the step threshold, and operation continues normally.

While considered extremely rare, forward and backward clock steps are possible. While forward steps are not in principle damaging, backward steps would violate Lamport's happens-before relation. There has been considerable discussion about the implications of this behavior since backward steps are much feared in the distributed database community. The arguments have to be considered carefully. First, in NTPv4 both the step and stepout thresholds can be changed by configuration commands, and it is easily possible to make the step threshold a year and the stepout threshold zero. However, this is a simplistic approach and fraught with ugly implications.

In time-sensitive applications, it is important that the time offsets between network clocks never exceed the step threshold, whatever its value, without being declared unhealthy. In general, formal correctness principles impose a maximum frequency tolerance that the clock oscillator can never exceed. This means both the oscillator frequency tolerance and the additional frequency deviation provided by the discipline have a strict upper bound called the *slew limit*. The Unix adjtime() system call used to slew the system time adds a fixed, signed slew increment to the clock value at every tick interrupt, which has the effect of introducing a fixed frequency offset for a computed interval depending on the adjustment.

The NTPv4 implementation assumes the slew limit is 500 PPM or about 1.8 s per hour, which is typical of Unix kernels. If the actual limit is greater than this, formal correction assertions can be violated. If the actual oscillator frequency error is greater than the slew limit, NTP cannot reduce the systematic offset to zero. It is possible to avoid a step by setting the step threshold to values larger than 128 ms; however, in case of a large time offset like 10 min, it may take a very long time to slew the clock to within an acceptable margin of error. Meanwhile, the system clock must be considered unhealthy, and application programs cannot assume the time is correct. In such cases, it may be better simply to step the clock, even if it steps backward.

In almost all modern workstations (but not in many routers), a time-of-year (TOY) clock chip maintains the time when the machine power is off, although the time is often maintained only to the second. The operating system restores the system clock from the TOY chip when power is restored, after which NTP disciplines the time and frequency as expected. Occasionally, the operating system resets the TOY chip time to the system time as disciplined by NTP. If for some reason the time offset computed by NTP is found to be very large, like over 1,000 s, called the *panic threshold*, something may be seriously wrong with the hardware, software, or server. If this happens, the ordinary action is to exit the daemon with a message to the system log that manual operator intervention is required. Some systems (usually dedicated routers) do not have a TOY chip, so in these cases the panic threshold is disregarded, and the first update received resets the clock to any value. However, subsequent updates respect the panic threshold.

4.6 Clock State Machine

The discipline algorithm must operate over an extremely wide range of network jitter and oscillator wander conditions without manual intervention or prior configuration. As determined by past experience and experiment [1], the data-grooming algorithms work well to sift good data from bad, especially under conditions of light-to-moderate network and server loads. Especially at startup and under conditions of extreme network or server congestion or large systematic frequency errors, the hybrid PLL/FLL discipline algorithm may perform poorly and even become unstable. The clock state machine functions something like a safety valve that short circuits some discipline functions under these conditions, especially when the poll interval must operate at relatively large values.

The clock state machine is necessary to cope with two common conditions. Without prior knowledge of the intrinsic frequency error of the clock oscillator, it can take a surprisingly long time for the frequency to converge to a nominal value. Once the frequency has converged, the nominal value is saved in a file. If the daemon is restarted after reboot, for example, it initializes the frequency from the file system, thus avoiding the convergence time. However, when toll charges accrue for every NTP message, as with a telephone modem service, it is important that the initial frequency convergence be as rapid as possible, especially if the interval between telephone calls must be an hour or more.

The second function of the state machine is to deal with occasional surges due to temporary fits of congestion or transients due to network delay spikes. These phenomena are similar to the popcorn spike suppressor in the clock filter algorithm described in Section 3.7 but are designed for disruptions that last much longer, up to 15 min.

The clock state machine transition function is shown in Table 4.1. It determines the action and next state when an update with specified offset occurs in the state shown in the first column. The second column shows what happens if the offset is less than the step threshold; the third shows what happens when the offset is greater than the step threshold. The fourth and last column contains comments meant to clarify the actions. Each table entry defines the actions and the next state indicated by the → symbol. Some states are conditional based on the time resident in that state. For instance, in FREQ state the machine remains in that state for 900 s, called the *stepout threshold*, after which the action and state transition are taken.

The actions include adjust frequency, step frequency, adjust time, and step time. Here, adjust time and adjust frequency mean to use the hybrid PLL/FLL algorithm described in this chapter, while step time means to abruptly set the time to the correct value. The step frequency action is to calculate the frequency offset directly rather than allowing the feedback loop to do that. This has to be done carefully to avoid contamination of the frequency estimate by the phase adjustment since the last update.

The machine can be initialized in two states: FSET if the frequency file is present or NSET if it has not yet been created. If the file is not present, this may be the first time the discipline has ever been activated, so it may have to quickly determine the oscillator intrinsic frequency offset. It is important to realize that a number of NTP messages may be exchanged before the mitigation algorithms determine a reliable time offset and call the discipline algorithm. When the first valid offset arrives in NSET state, (1) the time is stepped to that offset, if necessary; (2) the watchdog counter is started; and

TABLE 4.1

Clock State Machine Transition Function

State	$|\Theta| < 128$ ms	$|\Theta| \geq 128$ ms	Comments
NSET	Adjust time, →FREQ	Step time, → FREQ	No frequency file
FSET	Adjust time, → SYNC	Step time, → SYNC	Frequency file present
SPIK	Adjust frequency, adjust time, → SYNC	Step frequency; step time, → SYNC	Outlier detected
FREQ	If (<900 s) → FREQ else step frequency, adjust time, → SYNC	If (<900 s) → FREQ else step frequency, step time, → SYNC	Initial frequency
SYNC	Adjust frequency; adjust time, → SYNC	If (<900 s) → SYNC else → SPIK	Normal operation

(3) the machine exits to FREQ state. Subsequently, updates will be ignored until the stepout threshold has been reached, at which time the frequency is stepped, the time is stepped if necessary, and the machine exits to SYNC state. When the first valid offset arrives in FSET, the frequency has already been initialized, so the machine does the same things as in NSET but exits to SYNC state.

In SYNC state, the machine watches for outliers exceeding the step threshold. If one is found, it is ignored, and the watchdog timer continues to increment. If another offset less than the step threshold is found, the counter is stopped and set to zero, and the machine exits to SYNC state. If the watchdog timer reaches the stepout threshold, the machine exits to SPIK state. At the first update received after that, the time is stepped as required, and the machine exits to SYNC state. The SPIK state allows a single outlier to be ignored when the poll interval is greater than the stepout threshold.

A refinement not shown in Table 4.1 is used when, for some reason, usually as the result of a hardware fault, the frequency error surges to a large value, typically over 400 PPM. In such cases, the accrued time error becomes so large that only a single update is possible between step corrections. Under these conditions, the discipline converges only slowly, typically a fraction of a PPM for every step correction. The solution for this problem is a test: If the interval between step corrections is less than twice the stepout threshold, the discipline is forced to the FREQ state. On reaching the step threshold, the discipline resumes normal operation with a much reduced frequency error.

4.7 Parting Shots

The discipline algorithm is probably the most often tinkered algorithm in the NTP algorithm suite. It started out as a type I feedback loop that only had to deal with daily excursions in the power grid frequency; accuracy within several hundred milliseconds was the best it could do. As quartz oscillators replaced the power grid, expectations increased to tens of milliseconds, and the type II design described in this chapter was developed. As the squirrelly behavior of the computer clock became better understood and expectations increased to below the millisecond, the Allan deviation analysis helped to explain the behavior at very small and very large poll intervals. This led to the hybrid PLL/FLL design in this chapter. Talk about improving technology when you need it and then read Chapter 15.

It can be argued that we are about as far as we can go in increasing expectations. Sure, we can split the microsecond, zap pesky hardware and software latencies, and fill up all the NTP timestamp fraction with valid bits. But, the ultimate barrier is the dirty rotten clock oscillator. If and until computer manufacturers see the need to use a good clock rock, perhaps a temperature-compensated crystal oscillator (TCXO) or, like many communications-grade radio receivers now, a TCXO option, we may have conquered the mountain and are stuck at the peak.

References

1. Mills, D.L. Improved algorithms for synchronizing computer network clocks. *IEEE/ACM Trans. Networks* (June 1995), 245–254.
2. Mills, D.L. *Clock Discipline Algorithms for the Network Time Protocol Version 4.* Electrical Engineering Department Report 97-3-3, University of Delaware, Newark, March 1997, 35 pp.
3. Levine, J. An algorithm to synchronize the time of a computer to universal time. *IEEE Trans. Networking 3, 1* (February 1995), 42–50.

Further Reading

Mills, D.L., A. Thyagarajan, and B.C. Huffman. Internet timekeeping around the globe. *Proceedings Precision Time and Time Interval (PTTI) Applications and Planning Meeting* (Long Beach, CA, December 1997).

5

NTP System Engineering and Configuration

I'm nobody! Who are you?
Are you nobody too?
Then there's a pair of us—don't tell!
They'd banish us, you know.

How dreary to be somebody!
How public like a frog
To tell your name the livelong day
To an admiring bog!

Emily Dickenson
Poems, 1891

Probably most NTP timekeepers are not concerned about designing and deploying large NTP subnets since their needs may simply be to find a convenient server or three somewhere and plug a few lines into the NTP configuration file. If that is the case, read only Sections 5.6 and those that follow it on configuration issues and put the rest off until you might need it. However, system and network administrators should understand the basic principles of NTP system engineering since it can be easy to do something evil, like generate the same configuration file for 1,000 machines all pointing to a dinky time server on the other side of the planet. This has happened more than once. Another popular evil is when some stalwart server changes its Internet Protocol (IP) address for some reason, and hundreds of clients continue hammering on the old address for *years* afterward. This also has happened more than once.

The system engineering issues discussed in Section 5.1 and those sections that follow it focus on large corporate and campus systems and home office and small business systems. Reliable time synchronization is rather like an uninterruptable power source (UPS); when the clocks wind down or come up on the wrong century, serious trouble can happen, so we need an NTP UPS. The remedy, of course, is always redundancy and diversity. This is the most important concept to learn from the engineering issues discussed in this chapter. The chapter begins by a presentation of the basic principles of NTP systems engineering followed by an overview of large corporate and campus systems with up to thousands of servers and clients. Example configurations used by selected corporations are given. This is followed by a discussion of issues confronted by home and small business networks and the effects of network technology on accurate timekeeping.

The configuration issues discussed in Section 5.6 and those that follow it are based on the reference implementation discussed in Chapter 14. The example configuration items have been drawn from this implementation but are intended as generic. Any implementation providing equivalent functionality would need to address these same configuration items in one way or another. Much of the discussion on configuration issues is about how to select the servers and what to put on the configuration command lines. Finally, it is not the intention of this chapter to provide specific instructions; the only definitive place to find them is the reference implementation documentation itself.

5.1 Core Engineering Principles

This section explains the redundancy and diversity principles that are at the core of the NTP robustness model. As explained here, the principles apply to the core subnet, usually operated at stratum 1 with GPS receivers as the ultimate sources, although the principles apply at any given stratum. The principles presented are extensible; that is, given a requirement to survive a certain number of failures of a certain type, the number of servers and manner of their interconnection are immediately evident.

It has become the practice at the national laboratories (NIST and U.S. Naval Observatory [USNO]) to avoid backup paths between primary servers, so that in case of failure a server either shows an unsynchronized condition or stops operating entirely. However, it is the recommended practice in large, multiple-stratum subnets to interconnect the core subnet using multiple diversity links operating in symmetric mode. This not only provides backups should one or more servers fail but also provides protection should one or more of them, for whatever reason, turn falseticker. A client must have at least one source but normally has more than one to be consistent with the robustness principles. The optimum number of sources is subject to many and conflicting engineering issues.

There are two kinds of server failure events, fail-stop and fail-Byzantine. In a fail-stop event, the server loses power or the software crashes. In a fail-Byzantine event, the server clock is disrupted and declared a falseticker; however, to be declared a falseticker, there must be more truechimers than falsetickers; that is, there must be a majority clique. In any case, if a server fails, all links connected to it fail and vice versa. Since a communication link between two servers must be full duplex, it fails if transmission in either direction fails.

We assume that a source or sources such as a GPS receiver is attached to each server in the NTP core subnet. The symmetric mode protocol operates over the communication links to provide the offset and delay of every core server relative to every other core server; thus, every core server has an almost identical view of the entire core subnet. A source, such as a GPS receiver, is represented by an association just as for the other core servers. Clients of the core subnet are expected to configure some or all core servers and operate at a stratum one greater than the core subnet. If a core server has lost all outside sources or those sources have turned Byzantine, it synchronizes to other core servers and continues at a stratum one greater than the core subnet. If all sources for all core servers are lost and orphan mode is configured, as described in Section 3.13, one of the core servers will become the orphan parent, and the clients will become orphan children.

The core subnet topology can be formally defined as a graph where the nodes represent the core servers and the arcs represent the communication links between them. A *path* is an unbroken sequence of adjacent arcs from one node to another. Note that while a falseticker cannot provide synchronization, it can provide packet transport between links as that does not require a clock. A graph is connected if there is a path from every node to every other node. Given a connected graph with defined topology, we ask whether it remains connected in the face of an arbitrary number of server failures, either fail-stop or fail-Byzantine, or link failures. It is convenient to define two new terms, *n*-redundant and *n*-Byzantine. A graph is *n*-redundant if it remains connected when an arbitrary set of *n* arcs is removed. A graph is *n*-Byzantine if a majority clique remains when an arbitrary set of *n* nodes turns falseticker.

Consider Figure 5.1, which shows three graphs representing topologies that might be considered for a highly reliable core subnet. In these graphs, the communication links are shown point to point, although they might be implemented using local-area network (LAN) broadcast media. As a trivial case, a tree topology as in Figure 5.1a is 0-redundant since a fail stop of node 2 or the removal of any arc results in a nonconnected graph. However, the graph is 1-Byzantine since if any node turns Byzantine, a majority clique survives. Now consider Figure 5.1b, which is a ring of three nodes. The graph is

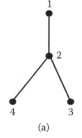

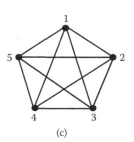

(a)   (b)   (c)

FIGURE 5.1
NTP subnet graphs.

1-redundant since removing any single arc leaves the graph connected. The graph is 1-Byzantine since if any node turns falseticker, a majority clique survives. However, on removal of a node or two arcs, the resulting graph is not connected and has no possible majority clique. The most general case is Figure 5.1c, which is a ring of five nodes, each with an arc to every other node. Removing any three arcs leaves the graph connected, so the graph is 3-redundant, but not 4-redundant, since removing four arcs from any node isolates that node. Remove any two nodes and the resulting three-node graph degenerates to the graph of Figure 5.1b, so the caveats in that case apply. Turn any two nodes falseticker, and the remaining three nodes can form a majority subset, so the graph is 2-Byzantine but not 3-Byzantine. In general, for any $n \geq 3$, the graph is $(n - 2)$ redundant and $(n - 2)$ Byzantine.

5.2 Engineering Large Corporate and Campus NTP Systems

Engineering an NTP subnet configuration for a large corporation or institution requires consideration of many factors, some conflicting, that reflect the goals of the project. Sometimes, the goal is the best accuracy by any means possible; other times, the goal is the most resilient timekeeping in the face of unlikely failures and insidious attacks. Still other times, the goal is the least intrusion on the public network and server infrastructure; other times, the goal is simplicity and convenience in the configuration process itself. There is a huge spectrum of specific requirements for NTP subnets, including whether to provide primary servers or use servers elsewhere in the Internet, which modes to use, which access controls are needed, and which security functions are required.

Consider, for example, a large university with both centralized and distributed computing services plus dozens of routers and department servers of various types and thousands of workstations and personal computers (PCs). The subnet hierarchy is organized by stratum and administrative unit. The information technology (IT) office provides the network infrastructure connecting the various administrative units and connections to the outside world, so this would be the logical place for the core servers. There are several manufacturers of self-contained devices, including Spectracom, Symmetricom, EndRun, and Meinberg, that provide NTP services via Ethernet. Alternatively, a junkbox PC equipped with an inexpensive GPS navigation receiver makes an effective core server. A number of these, perhaps three, can form the NTP core subnet.

Stratum-2 secondary servers are assigned to the various administrative units, such as the College of Arts and Sciences and the various engineering departments, as they tend to field large numbers of workstations and PCs. Note that the logical hierarchy of the NTP subnet does not have to coincide with the physical hierarchy; a primary time server administered by the IT office could well be located in another building with easy access to a rooftop GPS antenna.

The stratum for each server should be carefully considered as it affects the preferred order in the cluster algorithm. In general, multiple servers should be selected at the same stratum as the cluster algorithm can make decisions based on quality of service without prior bias. As a general rule, busy campus backbone routers not equipped with reference clocks ordinarily operate with external primary servers and possibly with each other as backup, therefore operating at stratum 2. Department servers and domain controllers ordinarily operate at stratum 3. Workstations and PCs ordinarily operate at stratum 4 using unicast or broadcast modes. Of necessity, Windows PCs support only client/server mode, so the decision is which server to type in the Internet Time dialog box. Students are a special case; they should be told not to use outside servers but to use one or more of the campus secondary servers assigned for this purpose. A case involved a horrendous onslaught on a dinky time server near the ends of Earth because some dormitory geek said that was the best place. The victim lamented that 2,000 packets were raining on his server, all coming from the same campus network. Operators should steer the horde inside the firewall.

Unix workstations and even some or all stratum-2 secondary servers on the same subnet should use broadcast mode since this considerably simplifies the infrastructure management and allows the configuration file to be cloned and automatically distributed. If the clients and servers are on different subnets, multicast mode is just as convenient. At the University of Delaware, campus networks have several dozen subnets, one of which has two primary servers operating in multicast mode for all subnets. Using multicast mode has vastly simplified infrastructure management.

5.3 Examples of Large Corporate NTP Systems

A typical subnet configuration for a large university campus is shown in Figure 5.2, in this case at the University of Delaware. There are two primary campus servers, each connected to a different GPS receiver. Each server operates in symmetric active mode with the other, so if either GPS receiver fails or its antenna is knocked down, the other server can back it up. These servers are used by other department stratum-2 secondary servers on dedicated LANs interconnected by switches and routers. The department LAN servers in some cases have hundreds of PC and workstation clients, many using unicast, broadcast, or multicast modes.

A key point to make about this configuration is the use of outside sources should one or both core servers lose the GPS receiver. These outside sources take the form of other trusted campuses running configurations like this. In point of fact, there are several university campuses using each other as backup in this manner. While not shown in the figure, there are two additional GPS devices on campus, each consisting of a GPS receiver integrated with an NTP server packaged with an Ethernet port. These lurk in the background to serve an itinerant population. Also not shown in the figure, the GPS radios are connected to multiple clients that do not operate as servers. The patch bay connecting these radios and clients is shown in Figure 5.3.

Figure 5.4 shows the configuration used by a major health care insurance company. The company operates three data centers in different parts of the

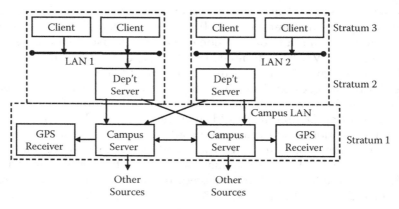

FIGURE 5.2
Typical campus NTP subnet configuration.

FIGURE 5.3
Patch bay for GPS receivers.

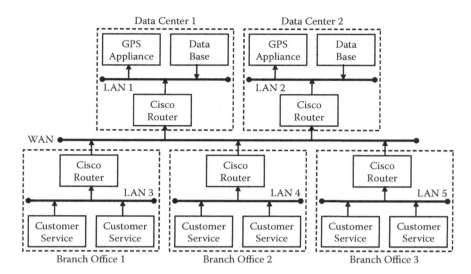

FIGURE 5.4
NTP subnet for health care insurer.

country. Each data center has a mainframe, possibly other computers, and a GPS device connected to a LAN. The data centers are connected to other core routers via a DS3 frame relay network. The branch offices include a core router and a number of workstations and point-of-service (POS) devices. The core router network is used to distribute stratum 2 time to all branch offices in the network.

In this design, redundancy is provided by the core router network. With respect to time distribution, it can survive the loss of two of the three data centers. The timing source for the core routers at the data centers are the GPS devices, while the remaining machines in the network configure their source as the local core router. The core routers run NTP with each of the GPS devices plus one or more other core routers. In case all GPS devices become unreachable, a core router will continue at stratum 3 with other core routers.

Figure 5.5 shows the configuration used by a large telephone company. The company operates a large database service designed for high survivability in case of a natural or unnatural disaster. There are three data centers located in different states. Each data center has two identical servers, one online and the other a hot spare. Each processor has a duplicate database operated as a redundant array of independent disks (RAID). Each processor is connected to both a GPS receiver and a WWVB receiver, thus providing redundancy of the radio medium as well. As in the previous example, the data centers and up to 30,000 routers, servers, and clients all over the country are interconnected by routers, wide-area networks (WANs), and LANs.

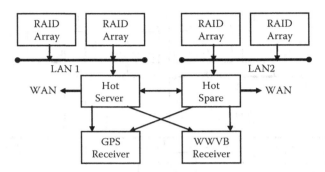

FIGURE 5.5
NTP subnet for large telephone company.

5.4 Engineering Home Office and Small Business NTP Systems

The home office of today has sprouted his and her computers, bridges, routers, print servers, fax machines, and even UPS servers. The Internet connection of choice is some Integrated Services Digital Network (ISDN), digital subscriber line (DSL), or cable/fiber variant and possibly intermittent connectivity to a remote time server. Those of us with home silicon farms have learned the value of fiber between the basement and upstairs offices since a vertical wire is as much a network link as the secondary of a transformer triggered by a nearby lighting strike. In general, ISDN and cable services have less availability outside the metropolitan areas than DSL; however, current tariffs make full-period ISDN connectivity generally unaffordable outside a Centrex span. There is a healthy and growing competition between high-speed fiber (Verizon) and cable (Comcast) services in urban and suburban areas.

A common deployment of NTP using ISDN or DSL transport is to work offline most of the time and then nail up a call occasionally to clear the queues and wind the clock. An inherent problem with this approach is that in most routers the call is triggered by a packet arrival. If that arrival is an NTP packet, there can be a considerable delay for the downtown telephone switch to complete the call. Normally, a burst of eight packets is sent at nominal 2-s intervals, but in the reference implementation the second packet in a burst is not sent until the reply to the first packet is received. The remaining packets in the burst are sent at 2-s intervals. This gives the switch more time to complete the call while ensuring a substantial degree of redundancy to reliably set the clock. Alternatively, a modem driver can be used to call the NIST or USNO telephone time service at infrequent intervals. The calls can be inexpensive or free on some calling plans.

Traffic flows on home network and small business networks are often highly asymmetric. Downloading a large file may take tens of minutes, during which the delay due to other traffic on the download path may be much higher than on the upload path. If NTP is running at the time, huge time errors can result. At times like this, the huff-'n-puff filter described in Section 3.12 can make a dramatic improvement.

5.5 Network Considerations

NTP timestamps are exchanged between time servers and clients over one networking technology or another. Each technology imposes a different set of engineering constraints on delay and jitter. Probably the most common technology is the ubiquitous 10/100/1,000-Mb/s Ethernet. Once upon a time, a typical 10-Mb/s Ethernet consisted of bulky half-inch RG/8 coaxial cable occasionally broken by transceivers with either type N connectors or vampire taps. The cable and half-duplex transceivers were in the ceiling plenum, and the transceiver cables dangled down to the $3,000 network interface card. Sometimes, the Ethernet cable was several hundred meters long and connected a fairly large number of computers. The problem with these old Ethernets, as far as good timekeeping is concerned, was that the network load could become moderate to high, collisions could occur, and various retry and back-off schemes could cause significant jitter and seriously degrade timekeeping quality.

Today, these cable plants are no longer seen since modern Ethernets use standard house wiring by which the Ethernet and telephone lines go from offices to wiring closets and connect to bridges, switches, or routers with varying degrees of intelligence. In many cases, the connections are full duplex, and the switch data paths are buffered, so that collisions are rare to nonexistent. However, collisions have been replaced by buffer queues in which packets can be delayed for previously received traffic going out the same wire. The situation gets more interesting when VLANs (virtual LANs) and tag switching and port switching schemes are in use, but that gets just too complicated for this book. However, the bottom line is that the cost per port of a 100-Mb/s network has fallen dramatically with a 1,000-Mb/s network to deploy in future. It does not seem likely that the technology will be a significant hazard to good timekeeping, at least not until the 3-GHz machines of today become even faster in the future.

One alternative to the 100-Mb/s Ethernet broadcast bus technology is the 100-Mb/s fiber distributed data interface (FDDI) token ring technology. While collisions cannot occur in this technology, queues can build up and cause significant delays, especially since packets travel around the ring from one interface to another, possibly via a number of other interfaces. What is even worse from a timekeeping point of view is that the delay from a client to a server part way around the ring can have a far different delay from the server to the client. This is an inherent feature of all rings, not just FDDI, and there is little that can be done about it.

Ethernet and FDDI technology are the typical technologies used for workstations and routers today. Network paths spanning longer distances in campus and service provider networks typically use heavily aggregated Synchronous Optical Network (SONET) and Asynchronous Transfer Mode (ATM) links of 155 Mb/s or higher, but as evident in Chapter 6, the utilization is typically low, at least for the present. The result is that packets today spend most of the time in flight along the wire or glass and less time in router queues. Aggregation is good in the sense that the network jitter process becomes more noise-like and can be modeled as discussed in Chapter 12. The NTP data-grooming algorithms are effective at minimizing jitter impairments in these networks.

The real killer with service provider networks is that transmission paths often have quite different delays in either direction of transmission. This is the case when packets fly one way via undersea cable and the other way via satellite. Geosynchronous satellite links have an inherent round-trip propagation delay near 270 ms, while cable delay is usually much less. Unless traffic goes both ways by cable or both ways by satellite, the timekeeping error can exceed 100 ms. While such situations may be discouraging, the current trend is that routing policy depends more on political and economic purposes than on engineering principles.

An example is the growing problems in connecting various backbone networks such as vBNS, Abilene, Internet 2, and others in a rational way. Some of these backbones have restrictions on the traffic they carry; some permit only educational traffic, and others limit traffic only between participating institutions. The result can be a most circuitous path between participating institutions. The ultimate case observed by this timekeeper was a path between a router at University College London and a time server in Newark, Delaware. One way went via a commercial provider under the Atlantic in a reasonably rational way. The other way went back under the Atlantic, then for unknown reasons meandered to California and from there back across the United States to Delaware. The path differences with this contraption were truly awesome.

5.6 General Configuration Considerations

When selecting a potential server from among a candidate population, it is useful to determine which are better than others. To assess the quality of service, a metric computed from the server stratum and root distance is used. The candidates are ranked first by increasing stratum, then, for those at the same stratum, by increasing root distance. Note that the root distance changes with every update and increases with time after an update is received. A server is assumed unusable for synchronization under the conditions specified in Table 3.2, which includes a test of whether the root distance exceeds the select threshold with default 1.5 s. This can be changed using the maxdist option of the tos command. These and other commands and options are described in Section 5.9. The default value is appropriate for paths spanning Earth and spacecraft in geosynchronous orbits, but not the Moon, where a more appropriated value is 3.5 s. If a Mars colonist configures a server on Earth, keep in mind that the round-trip light time ranges from 20 to 40 m; however, more practical means are described in Section 18.5.

An association is mobilized using the server and peer configuration commands, which specify the domain name system (DNS) name or IP address of the server or peer. These commands have a number of options, which are summarized in Section 5.9. These include the minpoll and maxpoll options that determine the minimum and maximum poll intervals, respectively. Unless there is a clear and present reason to change them, they should be left alone. Except for the modem clock driver described in Section 7.3, their use with other reference clock drivers might cause erratic operation. The key and autokey options can be used for the symmetric key and public key authentication schemes described in Chapter 9. The burst and iburst options should be used only in client/server mode, while the remaining options can be used as needed. See the server options page in the program documentation for details.

In the clock select algorithm of Section 3.8, the *correctness interval* for a server is defined as the current clock offset plus and minus the root distance plus a "shim" value that defaults to 1 ms. The *truechimers* are defined as the intersection of the correctness intervals. As demonstrated in Section 3.8, if the root distances are small, minor offset differences between sources can cause the correctness intervals not to intersect, possibly preventing a majority clique. This rarely happens with remote servers and long network paths as the root distance tends to be relatively large. However, in cases with Ethernet LANs and fast computers, even minor wiggles can result in nonintersecting correctness intervals. If circumstances justify, the shim can be increased using the mindist option of the tos command.

The cluster algorithm described in Section 3.9 discards outlier candidates until no less than three survivors remain. This number of survivors is a compromise between excess select jitter with a higher number and less combine algorithm effectiveness with a lower number. In special cases, the number can be changed using the minclock option of the tos command. The system clock is considered synchronized only if the number of survivors is at least one. This can be changed using the minsane option of the tos command. Additional considerations about this option are discussed in Section 3.11.

5.7 Manual Server Discovery

This and the following sections discuss how to find appropriate remote servers for a local client. In many cases, the search begins, and quite likely ends, with well-known servers in the same organization on either side of the firewall or a friendly router operated by the service provider. If more than these are needed, the search can continue with two lists maintained at http://www.ntp.org, one for public primary (stratum 1) servers and the other for public secondary (stratum 2) servers. Each entry in both lists includes the server DNS name, IP address (optional), operating organization and contact representative, country/state, service area, and access restrictions. Even if an IP address is given, it is always best to use the DNS name as this allows the operator to change to a new address and avoid unwanted traffic at the old address. All servers listed are operated as a voluntary resource for the Internet community, so it is vital to obey the access restrictions. It is important to note that these resources are made available without charge, and the operators make no guarantees on service quality or continuity.

In general, the public primary servers are intended to serve stratum 2 secondary servers that themselves serve a moderate-to-large population of stratum 3 secondary servers and clients. As the load on the public primary servers is heavy and always increasing, other private servers and clients should avoid using the public primary servers whenever possible. As a general rule, a private secondary server should use a public primary server only under the following conditions:

- The server provides synchronization for a sizable population of other servers and clients on the order of tens or more.
- The server operates with other secondary servers in a common synchronization subnet designed to provide reliable service, even if some servers or the links connecting them fail.
- The administrators that operate these servers should coordinate other servers within the region to reduce the resources required outside that region. Note that at least some interregional resources are required to resist failures and configuration errors.
- No more than two servers or clients on the same network should use the same public primary server on another network.
- In the case of the NIST and USNO public primary servers, secondary servers and clients should spread access evenly over the NIST and USNO satellite servers elsewhere in the country and avoid the servers in Washington, D.C., and Boulder, Colorado.

It is not practical to examine and evaluate even a significant fraction of the servers on the lists, so the initial selection must be done by hand. There is a good deal of searchable information in the public lists. For instance, when it is necessary to provide synchronization traceable to national laboratories, the lists can be filtered by organization, such as http://nist.gov for NIST servers or http://www.usno.navy.mil for USNO servers. It may also be useful to filter the lists by country or state.

Without actually mobilizing an association with a candidate server, the available information may be only the server location and service area. If this is the case, near is dear, so rank the candidates in order of geographical distance. For a client in New York, a server in Chicago is usually, but not always, better than a server in London, but today there is a blinding fast link between Sweden and California, so for a client in Stockholm a server in San Jose may be better than a server in Istanbul.

Another approach is to use the Unix traceroute (Windows tracert) program to determine the path route and number of router hops. The program produces a line for each hop, together with the DNS name or IP address of the router and the total round-trip delay. There is a certain amount of craft when evaluating the routes. Usually, the route with the shortest source-destination round-trip delay is preferred; however, sometimes two routes with substantially the same round-trip delay are found. In this case, the wise choice is the route with the fewest number of hops.

5.8 Automatic Server Discovery

In some cases the server discovery process can be automated partially or completely using automatic server discovery tools. There are three such tools in the reference implementation: broadcast/multicast, manycast, and pool. These schemes troll the Internet by one means or another to mobilize a number of candidate associations, the survivors of which are allowed to synchronize the system clock at least temporarily. Then, the cluster algorithm discards the outliers until only three survivors remain. After a suitable time-out, the outliers are demobilized and operation continues only with the survivors.

Outliers are demobilized only if the association is marked preemptable. In some schemes, this is automatic, while in others it depends on the `preempt` option of the `serve` or `peer` configuration command. In all schemes, it is possible and often convenient to filter the candidates to include only those in a defined stratum range. The `floor` option of the `tos` command rejects candidates below the option value, while the `ceiling` option of the `tos` command rejects candidates at or above the option value. To help remember the behavior, think that you can sit on the floor, but you cannot sit on the ceiling. Ordinarily, candidates of the same stratum as the client are rejected, but the `cohort` option of the `tos` command specifically allows this.

The maximum number of candidates that can be mobilized is ordinarily 10, but this can be changed using the maxclock option of the tos command. A typical configuration would set maxclock 5 and minclock 3, so that originally five candidates would be solicited within the specified stratum range, then the population reduced to the best three of them.

5.8.1 Broadcast/Multicast Discovery

Many organizations large and small operate with a broadcast communication infrastructure such as Ethernet and Wi-Fi. It is convenient for these organizations to operate from one to a few core broadcast servers providing synchronization to possibly many broadcast clients. When a broadcast packet is first received by a client, it automatically mobilizes an ordinary client association and begins a calibration exchange to measure the round-trip delay. Once this is complete, the client corrects the broadcast spanning tree offset relative to the unicast spanning tree offset measured by the first broadcast packet received, then continues in listen-only mode. If more than one broadcast server is present, the clients will mobilize an association with each of them.

It is good practice to limit the scope of Internet Protocol Version 4 (IPv4) broadcast packets to a single subnet on a LAN, although it could include several LAN segments interconnected by bridges. The scope of multicast packets is determined by the spanning tree algorithm and the group membership protocol. Multicast mode requires that the host and routers support the Internet Group Multicast Protocol (IGMP) and either Distance Vector Multicast Routing Protocol (DVMRP) or Protocol Independent Multicast Protocol (PIMP). Both protocols form spanning trees with the multicast group sources as roots and the group destinations as leaves. It is conventional for all NTP multicast servers within the span of the connected group to use the same multicast group number specified by the server and clients, but it is possible to use different group addresses for different servers. In this way, the client can select individual servers by group address.

It may be counterintuitive, but a single machine can operate as both a broadcast server and a broadcast client. This is the basis of the orphan mode described in Section 3.13. Orphan mode is used to select a single server when all broadcast servers have lost all remote or local time sources.

A broadcast server association is mobilized by the broadcast command specifying the broadcast or multicast group address. Broadcast clients are enabled by the broadcastclient command. A multicast client is enabled by the multicastclient command specifying the multicast group address. See the server options page in the program documentation for details. When a broadcast client association is mobilized, the iburst and preempt options are configured and the minpoll and maxpoll options set to the peer poll interval in the broadcast server packet. In this case, the poll options apply only when the client is operating in the calibrate mode.

5.8.2 NTP Manycast Discovery

The manycast discovery scheme provides a way for a client to actively survey a local area in multicast mode and listen for responding servers in unicast mode. The manycast client sends an ordinary client request message to a multicast group address. One or more manycast servers in scope listen on this group address and respond with an ordinary unicast server message, and the operation continues in client/server mode. The scope limit is determined from the IP time-to-live (TTL) field, which is measured in router hops. On receipt, the client mobilizes a preemptable association and continues service in the ordinary way.

To minimize disruption in large subnets, the manycast client starts with a TTL of one and collects all the servers it finds. If less than `maxclock` are found after time-out, the TTL is increased by one, and the client tries again. Replies that duplicate the servers already found are ignored, and new ones are added. This expanding ring search continues until at least `maxclock` servers are found. If this does not happen when a maximum TTL is reached, the time-out is increased to a nominal interval to avoid harassing the environment. If for some reason a server drops out of the survivor population, the manycast client begins to troll the environment as before.

The manycast server and manycast client are configured with the `manycastserver` and `manycastclient` commands. See the server options page in the program documentation for details. When a new unicast client association is created for a manycast server, the association options are copied from the manycastclient configuration command.

5.8.3 NTP Pool Discovery

One of the things that simplifies system and network administration is to hide the IP address and require clients to resolve some generic name like ntp. udel.edu at startup. In many cases, the name is actually a DNS CNAME for (one of) the real names of the server and one or more of its IP addresses. This way the servers can be moved around the network, and the IP addresses can be changed just by amending the DNS records. Historically, it was important that the IP address be included in the public lists since not all clients had DNS resolvers, and some had no connectivity to the DNS. Today, these considerations are probably overtaken by events, and the IP address is considered an endangered species.

However, and especially in the case of USNO and NIST servers, it is always helpful to spread the load from a sizable number of clients over the available servers in some round-robin or random fashion. Late-model DNS servers can be configured to do this. Using this feature, all the workstations and PCs in a department can have the same NTP configuration file pointing to http://ntp.udel.edu, for example, and the actual server determined only at the time the client association is mobilized and a DNS query is generated. Multiple-server redundancy can be provided using CNAMEs such as ntp1.udel.edu, ntp2.udel, and so forth.

A particularly effective means for server discovery exploits this technique. There is a cooperative project, currently a work in progress, involving about 2,000 volunteer NTP servers and DNS servers in many countries. A client configures between one and several servers with names like 0.pool.ntp.org, 1.pool.ntp.org, or 2.pool.ntp.org. On receiving a query for one of these names, the resolver returns a number of randomized DNS resource records that comprise a list of servers, currently about five, scattered all over the world. The servers associated with each name are nonoverlapping; that is, every server occurs only once.

The pool discovery scheme is based on crafted DNS tables maintained by a number of volunteer domain keepers. The servers are provided as a public service by volunteer operators. The server operators have agreed to allow unrestricted access but expect clients to be well mannered. At present, most of these servers operate at stratum 2, but some operate at stratum 1 and some higher than 2. It is not clear whether the latter are under a temporary handicap. One reason why this is yet a work in progress is that there is now no way to replace preempted entries once the NTP program has started normal operations.

There is a distinguished zone pool.ntp.org reserved for NTP server discovery and subzones associated with geographic regions and countries of the world. Table 5.1 shows the various global areas of the world, the DNS zone, and the number of pool servers in that area. Alternatively, a country name such as bs (Bahamas) can be used instead of the global area, in this case, bs.pool.ntp.org. Each DNS query returns a block of five servers randomized over the zone. The order of the servers is randomized for each query, so even if the client DNS resolver uses only the first entry but is configured with multiple queries using the same name, the IP addresses will be for different servers. Additional blocks of servers are available by prefixing the name with "n.", where n can be 0, 1, 2, or 3, depending on the size of the zone. If a query happens to respond with a server already mobilized, the response is discarded.*

The pool servers are configured with the pool configuration command. Multiple commands can be used for the same or different areas or countries. See the server options page in the program documentation for details. When

---

* The pool discovery scheme also works in Windows using the native Microsoft SNTP (Simple Network Time Protocol) client. To use, enter the DNS zone name in the Control Panel → Date and Time → Internet Time dialog box.

TABLE 5.1

Pool Servers by Global Area

Global Area	DNS Zone	Servers
Africa	africa.pool.ntp.org	8
Asia	asia.pool.ntp.org	114
Europe	europe.pool.ntp.org	1,114
North America	north-america.pool.ntp.org	564
Oceana	oceana.pool.ntp.org	75
South America	south-america.pool.ntp.org	24
Global	pool.ntp.org	1,703
All pool servers		1,807

a new client association is created for a pool server, the association options are copied from the `pool` configuration command.

5.9 Configuration Commands and Options

This section contains a partial list of configuration commands in the reference implementation. They may be useful when crafting the configuration file for a typical installation. The description of each command and option is not intended as a definitive reference guide; the software documentation is the place to find that. The descriptions are intended as general information about what the command or option is for and how it might be used. In the descriptions, the default option values are enclosed in parentheses. By convention, specific command and option names are represented in monospace font, sometimes called teletype, but not many other than this old buzzard have seen, heard, and used one.

There are three classes of commands described: association configuration, type of service, and tinker. The association commands are used to mobilize an association when the NTP program is started. The type of server and tinker commands provide ways to tune the protocol in various ways to adapt to unusual conditions. They probably should be left alone unless the knob twiddler knows exactly what the result will be.

5.9.1 Association Configuration Options (`server`, `peer`, and the Like)

The `server`, `pool`, and `manycastclient` commands mobilize an association in client/server mode; the `peer` command mobilizes an association in symmetric active mode; the `broadcast` command mobilizes an association in broadcast or manycast server mode. These commands have a required argument represented as the IPv4 or IP Version 6 (IPv6) address or the DNS name of the remote server or peer. The following options can be used with these commands. The default values are enclosed in parentheses:

minpoll (6), maxpoll (10)

> These options specify the minimum and maximum poll exponent range, respectively, in log2 seconds. The default range is from 6 (64 s) set by the minpoll parameter to 10 (1,024 s) set by the maxpoll parameter. However, minpoll can be as small as 3 (8 s), and maxpoll can be as large as 17 (36 h). Ordinarily, there is no need to change the default range since the poll interval algorithm automatically selects the optimum interval depending on the prevailing network jitter and oscillator wander. In some cases, it may be reasonable to change the range limits. For instance, with the pulse-per-second (PPS) driver it is usually better to change the minpoll and maxpoll to 4 (16 s) since that allows more precise compensation for oscillator wander. With the modem driver, minpoll should be set appropriately for the minimum call interval, ordinarily 12 (4,096 s). The maxpoll can be set at the same value up to 17 (36 h), depending on the acceptable error.

burst, iburst

> These switches replace a single poll with a burst of eight polls at 2-s intervals. The burst and iburst features are specific to each server separately and can be activated in two ways, depending on whether the server is reachable. If iburst is set, the burst is sent only if the server is unreachable. This results in quickly setting the system clock when first coming up. If burst is set, the burst is sent only if the server is reachable. This usually results in better performance at poll intervals of 1,024 s and higher. It is advisable to use both options with poll intervals in the order of hours. This causes the clock filter algorithm to effectively groom the samples at each poll opportunity.

key, autokey

> These options activate the authentication schemes described in Chapter 9.

noselect, preempt, true, prefer, xleave

> These switches affect the mobilization state of the association. The noselect switch declares the association to be unselectable,

so it will never be used for synchronization. This is useful to watch a remote server for evaluation or test. The preempt switch activates the preemption algorithm that demobilizes the association if not useful for synchronization. The true switch declares the association to be a truechimer no matter how good or evil that might be. The need for this switch for other than testing is problematic. The prefer switch is used by the mitigation algorithm described in Section 3.11. The xleave switch activates interleaved mode as described in Chapter 16.

5.9.2 Type of Service Options (tos)

The tos command is used to set various options that affect tuning parameters of the grooming and mitigation algorithms. The following options can be used with this command:

floor (0), ceiling (16), cohort (0)

These parameters select the stratum range of eligible servers. Packets from servers with stratum less than floor or greater than or equal to ceiling are discarded. In addition, if cohort is not set, packets with the same stratum as the client are discarded; otherwise, they are accepted.

For example, consider the case with a number of redundant primary servers and a designated set of secondary servers for which the intent is to disregard a configured primary server if for some reason its stratum becomes greater than one. In this case, ceiling can be set in the designated secondary servers to two so that they will accept packets only from primary servers with properly operating reference clocks.

These parameters are useful with automatic server discovery schemes to impose structure on an otherwise flat-stratum subnet. Consider a large subnet with this configuration operating in manycast mode. The primary and secondary servers operate as manycast servers; the secondary and tertiary servers operate as manycast clients. To ensure that tertiary servers mobilize associations only with the secondary servers, they are configured with floor 2.

mindist (1 ms)

This is the shim included in the root distance calculation to avoid spurious falsetickers with fast networks and computers. Lower values increase the selectivity of the mitigation algorithms, which may be useful with very fast networks and computers. Larger values reduce the degree of clockhop with relatively high network jitter and asymmetric delay.

maxdist (1.5 s)

This is also called the *select threshold*. This is the root distance above which a server is considered unfit and below which it is eligible for synchronization. When an association first starts up or returns after a long absence, the root distance is dominated by peer dispersion, by default 16 s. At each update, the peer dispersion is halved; after four updates, the root distance is normally about 1 s. The threshold can be raised, which reduces the time for eligibility, or lowered, which reduces the false alarm rate. Values above 1.5 s will be necessary for outposts on the Moon.

minclock (3)

As described in Chapter 3, the select and cluster algorithms operate to cull the worst survivors from the population of configured servers in successive rounds as long as the remaining number of servers is greater than minclock. This can be changed to fit special circumstances such as a threat of terrorist attack.

maxclock (10)

This is the maximum number of preemptable associations that can be mobilized in addition to the configured servers. This is most useful with the automatic server discovery schemes.

minsane (1)

This is the minimum number of eligible servers needed to synchronize the clock. Purists might want to increase this number in the interest of the highest confidence. It might even be set to zero under the conditions described in Section 3.11.

orphan (16)

This specifies the orphan stratum described in Section 3.13. Orphan parents with no available synchronization sources operate at this stratum. Orphan clients sharing the same network recognize orphan parents and select the one with the lowest address hash.

5.9.3 Tinker Options (`tinker`)

The `tinker` command is used to set various options that affect tuning parameters of the discipline algorithm. The following options can be used with this command:

`allan` (11)

> This specifies the Allan intercept in log2 seconds. There are some minor optimizations that depend on the Allan intercept described in Chapter 12. Changing the value of `allan` would only be indicated if the Allan intercept for the particular computer clock oscillator was determined by measurement.

`dispersion` (15 PPM)

> This is the rate the maximum error increases to account for the disciplined oscillator frequency tolerance. It is a compromise between the real world and the theoretical world, where `dispersion` would have to be at least the intrinsic tolerance of the undisciplined clock oscillator frequency, assumed to be 500 PPM. It is unlikely that the disciplined frequency error even comes close to 15 PPM, and in that case, it would strongly suggest broken hardware. This parameter is included for the computer theorist, who will quickly realize the need to use something less than 500 PPM.

`freq` (0 PPM)

> This parameter defines the initial frequency offset. It can be used in special circumstances when it is not possible to set the initial frequency from a file, such as in embedded systems.

`huffpuff` (900 s)

> This is the window over which the huff-'n-puff filter searches for minimum delay. This parameter should be set to the maximum period during which substantial asymmetric delays are anticipated.

`step` (128 ms), `stepout` (900 s), `panic` (1,000 s)

> These commands specify the step, stepout, and panic thresholds, respectively, described in Section 4.6. If the clock offset persists beyond the step threshold for at least the stepout threshold, the clock is set directly rather than slewed. While a step adjustment is rare and almost certainly indicates broken hardware or reference clocks, some operators might want to increase the step

threshold or eliminate steps entirely by setting the step threshold to zero. In most computer systems, a TOY chip sets the clock when first powered up. If for some reason the clock offset is greater than the panic threshold, then the program exits with an operator request to set the clock within this threshold and restart. If there is no TOY chip, most famously in Cisco routers, the panic threshold can be set to zero, effectively disabling it. Using a command line switch, the NTP daemon will set the clock at the first update, no matter what the value, but enforce the panic threshold after that.

5.10 Parting Shots

One might ask if there is a magic protocol that could somehow solve the asymmetric delay problem with possibly several to many auxiliary servers that babble among themselves to determine the one-way delays. Sadly, as confirmed by a recent doctoral dissertation, even with a raft of servers that read all other clocks, there is no system of equations that yields the desired answer. The only solution is an independent reference clock other than NTP itself.

Further Reading

Mills, D.L., A. Thyagarajan, and B.C. Huffman. Internet timekeeping around the globe. *Proceedings Precision Time and Time Interval (PTTI) Applications and Planning Meeting* (Long Beach, CA, December 1997), 365–371.

Mills, D.L. Measured performance of the Network Time Protocol in the Internet system. *ACM Comput. Commun. Rev. 20, 1* (January 1990), 65–75.

6

NTP Performance in the Internet

Down time's quaint stream
Without an oar,
We are enforced to sail,
Our Port a secret
Our Perchance a gale.
What Skipper would
Incur the risk,
What Buccaneer would ride,
Without a surety from the wind
Or schedule of the tide?

Emily Dickenson
Poems, 1891

NTP was and is designed to wander the mountain ranges and vast prairies of the global Internet, where congestion storms over the planet and Web squalls rain on the routers. The question is, how well does timekeeping really work in the current Internet? What is the current state of the NTP global subnet? What kind of reasonable guarantees can be made about accuracy? These are not trivial questions, and they do not have comforting answers. By its very nature, the Internet is a statistically noisy place, and timekeeping can be just as noisy.

This chapter begins with a brief summary of the measurement tools available in the reference implementation. It continues with a set of measurements designed to show the system clock latency characteristics for a modern workstation and then the error characteristics with a directly connected reference clock. Next is a performance comparison between primary servers at faraway places. This is designed to calibrate the errors due to network jitter and congestion events. A performance assessment for modern workstations connected to a fast local-area network (LAN) then follows. This is followed by the results of a survey designed to assess the quality of clock hardware and NTP subnet configuration. Last is an analysis of the hardware and software resources required to provide NTP services to a large client population.

6.1 Performance Measurement Tools

The reference implementation includes a monitoring and measurement subsystem used to capture and record performance statistics for later retrieval, analysis, and display in the form of the graphs in this chapter. It includes packet timestamps, time and frequency offsets, and various counters and status indicators for system monitoring and performance evaluation. At present, there are seven different families of data, each identified by a unique file name consisting of a prefix followed by a datestamp. The data currently collected are as follows:

- Rawstats. One line of data is appended to this file for every valid received packet update. The data include the server, peer, or clock driver Internet Protocol (IP) address followed by the four packet timestamps T_1, T_2, T_3, and T_4 as received. The wedge scattergrams displayed in this chapter are generated from these data.

- Peerstats. One line of data is appended to this file for every valid clock filter update. The data include the server, peer, or clock driver IP address and status code followed by the peer clock offset, round-trip delay, dispersion, and jitter. The server plots displayed in this chapter are generated from these data.

- Loopstats. One line of data is appended to this file for every valid discipline algorithm update. The data include the combined clock offset, system jitter, oscillator frequency, oscillator frequency wander, and poll exponent. The frequency plots displayed in this chapter are generated from these data.

- Sysstats. One line of data is appended to this file every hour. The data include packet counters at various processing checkpoints.

- Clockstats. One line of data is appended to this file for every valid reference clock update. The data include reference clock timecode strings and error events.

- Protostats. One line of data is appended to this file for every significant protocol event. The data include mobilization, synchronization, and error events.

- Cryptostats. One line of data is appended to this file for every significant cryptographic event. The data include exchange values, error conditions, and key refresh events.

Each line of data includes a datestamp consisting of the modified Julian date (MJD) and the seconds past midnight followed by the data itself. At specified intervals, usually at midnight, a new file is created with the same prefix and a new datestamp. This operation is atomic, so that no data are lost. In some instances, a shell script reads the data file, looks for trouble, and appends summary data to the system log. In one instance, if trouble is found the shell script turns up a cell phone and beeps the administrator.

6.2 System Clock Latency Characteristics

The latency to read the system clock has decreased steadily from 58 µs 20 years ago on a Sun SPARC IPC to less than 1 µs today on modern machines. However, claims like this do not tell the whole story. The fact is that there are other things going on in the hardware and operating system, and sometimes the machine is doing something else when the clock is to be read. The questions are, how often does this occur? What can be done about it?

In an experiment to quantify the answer, a program was written that reads the system clock as fast as possible using the most precise system call available, in this case with nanosecond resolution. The program first zeros an array to avoid page faults and swaps, then records the interval between executions for about 30,000 times. The array is then processed by Matlab programs to produce the figures discussed here.

The time series for the measurements is shown in Figure 6.1, where the horizontal line shows a slight variation around 1 µs between successive calls punctuated by spikes up to 35 µs on a regular basis and where every fifth spike is a little larger than the rest. Note that the interval between spikes is

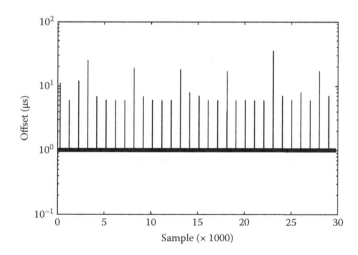

FIGURE 6.1
System clock reading latency.

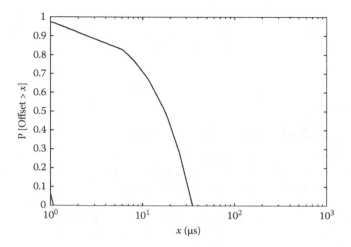

FIGURE 6.2
System clock reading latency CDF.

about 1 ms, so at 1 μs an execution the spikes are probably the tick interrupt for a 1,024-Hz clock oscillator. One would expect additional, larger spikes to occur as the result of device interrupts but would expect the likelihood of two or more spikes in a row to be very small.

This suggests a simple scheme to minimize the effect of the spikes by taking the minimum of two successive readings, here called the bottom fisher. The result might be off by a microsecond, but the spikes would be rare. The cumulative distribution function (CDF) is shown in Figure 6.2 for both the raw series (right curve) and bottom fisher series (smidgen near the bottom left). The bottom fisher has reduced the latency for all practical purposes to 1 μs. The reference implementation exploits this method to determine the intrinsic kernel precision.

6.3 Characteristics of a Primary Server and Reference Clock

A primary server is by definition synchronized to an external source of precise time, most commonly a GPS receiver but others as well. There are several primary servers operating on the University of Delaware campus, department and research subnets, including public servers Rackety and laboratory server Malarky. This section describes a number of experiments designed to calibrate how well the system clock can follow the external source with respect to prevailing hardware and software latencies and oscillator wander.

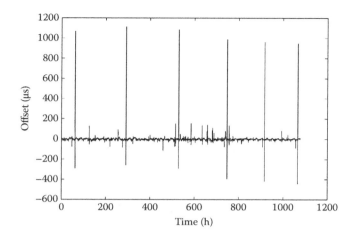

FIGURE 6.3
Rackety time offset.

Rackety lives in an old Pentium hulk rescued from the scrap heap and running recent FreeBSD 5.3. It is configured for a Spectracom GPS receiver via a 9,600-b/s serial port and a pulse-per-second (PPS) signal via a parallel port. It uses the nanosecond kernel discipline described in Chapter 8 but not the PPS kernel discipline. The machine is dedicated to NTP service and has several hundred clients.

Rackety is normally synchronized to the PPS signal with seconds numbering provided by the GPS receiver. The system clock offset over about a month is shown in Figure 6.3, which is a plot of offsets harvested from the loopstats files. What stands out in this figure is that most of the time the residual offset is very low, on the order of 3 μs; however, every 250 h there is a distinct spike with magnitude about 1 ms. There is no immediate explanation for this; however, the impact these spikes have on application time is negligible due to the popcorn spike suppressor and low-pass filter characteristic of the discipline algorithm. It is known from other measurements that the PPS interrupt latency and bus jitter are in the range of 1–2 μs, which shows that the median filter in the PPS signal driver is highly effective.

To maximize the response to oscillator wander, the poll interval is clamped at 16 s. Figure 6.4 shows the frequency over the same interval. There is a distinct diurnal variation of about 0.1 PPM, probably due to small temperature changes in the air-conditioned machine room. The characteristic is dominated by surges up to 0.5 PPM lasting several days or more, which is convincing evidence that the intrinsic oscillator frequency distribution has a distinctly heavy tail. This aspect is explored further in this chapter.

Malarky lives in a new Sun Blade 1500 running Solaris 10. It is connected to a telephone modem with all the latest X protocols via a 9,600-b/s serial port. The microsecond kernel discipline is available, but it is specifically disabled

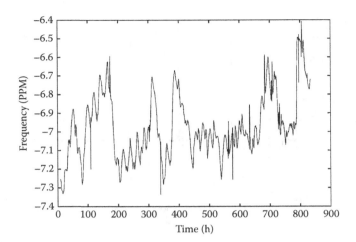

FIGURE 6.4
Rackety frequency offset.

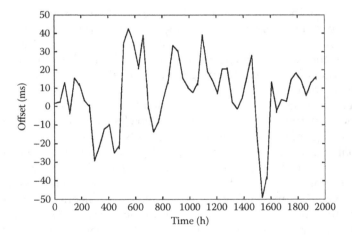

FIGURE 6.5
Rackety time offset.

due to the very large poll intervals used. Ordinarily, Malarky runs only typical office and software development applications.

Malarky calls the Automated Computer Time Service (ACTS) in Boulder, Colorado, to synchronize the system clock once each poll interval, which starts at 4,096 s and gradually increases to 36 h. Figure 6.5 shows the offsets from the loopstats data harvested over a 3-month interval. While this is not definitive, one might draw the conclusion that, even at such a large poll interval the clock can be kept generally within 50 ms of ACTS time. The crucial observation is that the frequency must be reliably predicted within

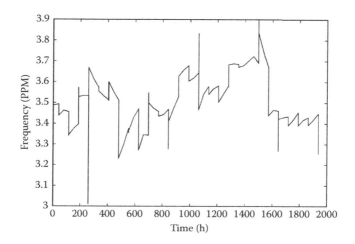

FIGURE 6.6
Malarky frequency offset.

0.39 PPM to attain that accuracy and that small excursions due to temperature changes be accurately compensated. Figure 6.6 shows the frequency over the same interval for which the frequency changes over a range of about 0.7 PPM, yet the frequency predictions for each 36-h interval are accurate within 0.2 PPM.

6.4 Characteristics between Primary Servers on the Internet

The next set of experiments was designed to evaluate timekeeping performance over typical Internet paths spanning the globe. In this section, three network paths were selected as representative of the Internet at large. Experience with paths like these suggests that statistics like mean and standard deviation are insufficient to accurately characterize network delay. This is because the delay distribution can be decidedly nonexponential and have a heavy tail characteristic that appears as long-range dependency (LRD). There are two statistical displays that do show these characteristics: the wedge scattergram described in Chapter 3 and a new one, called the variance-time plot.

The variance-time plot is constructed in a way similar to the Allan deviation plot described in Chapter 12. Consider a series of N time offset measurements, $X = x_1, x_2, \ldots, x_N$ and let x_k be the kth measurement and τ the interval between measurements. Define

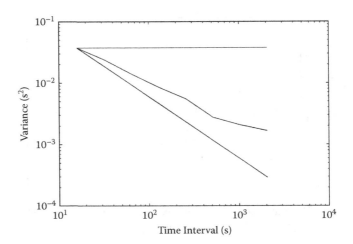

FIGURE 6.7
Boulder variance-time plot.

$$\sigma_v(n,\tau) \equiv \sigma(X_n), \tag{6.1}$$

where $X_n = x_n, x_{2n}, x_{3n}, \ldots$ is a subinterval of X and $n = 1, 2, 4, 8, \ldots$. The character of the plot in log-log coordinates determines the degree of LRD. Consider Figure 6.7, which shows the variance-time plot for three functions: an exponential distribution, a random-walk distribution, and a distribution formed from round-trip network delays between a time server at the University of Delaware and the NIST time server at Boulder. This slope of the characteristics determines the degree of LRD. Random functions with mutually independent, identically distributed (iid) distributions, such as the exponential distribution, show characteristic slopes near the limb line with slope –1. Random functions that display random-walk behavior or Brownian motion show characteristic slopes near the limb line with slope 0. Other functions, including the Boulder function, show some slopes in between. The NIST path is generally uncongested and the delay relatively small, so the expected path delays should be exponentially distributed. Note that the Boulder path, while tending toward exponential, departs significantly from it.

Returning to the study of network paths, consider Figure 6.8, which is a scattergram for the Boulder path considered. The server at each end of the path is connected to a precision source, a cesium oscillator at Boulder and a calibrated GPS receiver at Delaware. At first glance, it would appear that the apex is somewhat blunt, suggesting that the clocks at either end of the path wiggle some 0.4 ms, but the span is well centered about the expected zero relative offset. In other words, the residual error at the clock filter output will probably show peer jitter in the similar amount. Such is confirmed in Figure 6.9, which shows the offset over 1 day for the Boulder

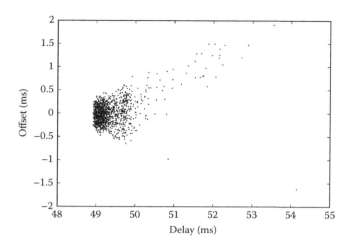

FIGURE 6.8
Boulder wedge scattergram.

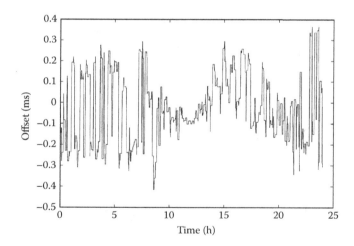

FIGURE 6.9
Boulder time offset.

path. Considering the network path involved and number of router hops (at least 15), the performance within 0.4 ms is remarkably good.

The next example looked at a path across the country from Delaware to an NIST server in Seattle, Washington. The scattergram shown in Figure 6.10 suggests that the outbound and inbound paths have a delay difference of 1.5 ms with peer jitter about 2 ms. Figure 6.11 confirms this but adds a little

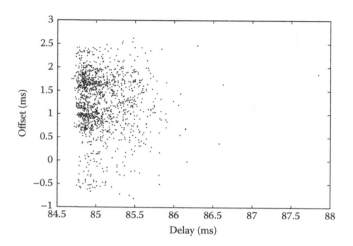

FIGURE 6.10
Seattle wedge scattergram.

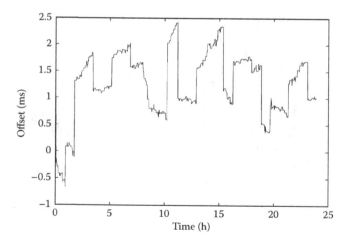

FIGURE 6.11
Seattle time offset.

mystery due to the apparent discontinuities. Further analysis shows that the server is itself synchronized by ACTS telephone from Boulder. The characteristic shows clearly that calls were made and the frequency recomputed about once per hour. One would think the discontinuous nature of the characteristic could degrade frequency stability, and this is confirmed in the

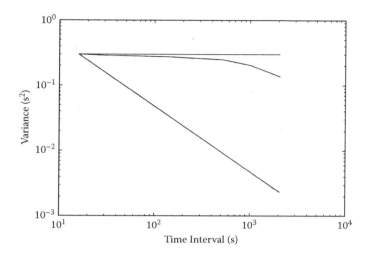

FIGURE 6.12
Seattle variance-time plot.

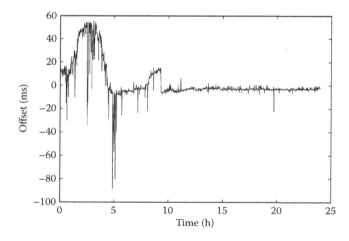

FIGURE 6.13
Malaysia time offset.

variance-time plot shown in Figure 6.12. Note that the path characteristics are much closer to random walk than exponential.

The final example represents one of the worst paths that could be found between Delaware and somewhere else, in this case on the other side of the world in Malaysia. Consider first the offsets over 1 day shown in Figure 6.13, where obviously something went bump during the local afternoon, a 50-ms bulge near hour 5. (All times on these figures are in UTC [Coordinated

Universal Time].) Now, consider the scattergram in Figure 6.14, which shows classic asymmetric delay characteristics. Most of the points are clustered about the apex, and most of the rest populate the upper limb. The result shown in Figure 6.15 with the huff-'n-puff filter shows that the bump has been flattened to about 10 ms. Casual experiment using the huff-'n-puff filter with symmetric delays shows that the performance is not materially degraded. This suggests that leaving it always turned on for paths like this might be a good idea. This should be a topic for further study.

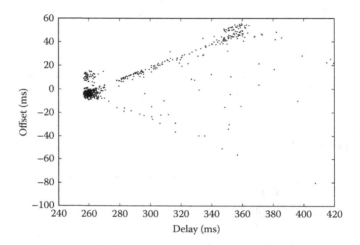

FIGURE 6.14
Malaysia wedge scattergram.

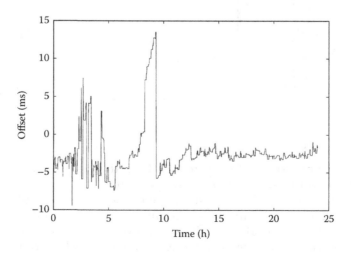

FIGURE 6.15
Malaysia huff-'n-puff time offset.

6.5 Characteristics of a Client and a Primary Server on a Fast Ethernet

Beauregard is a 2.4-GHz Pentium 4 machine running FreeBSD 5.3 and on the same 100-Mb/s wire as an EndRun Tempus Cntp code division multiple access (CDMA) server. This server synchronizes to the CDMA signal of the local wireless provider, which in turn synchronizes to GPS. The experiment is designed to do two things: evaluate the performance of a typical workstation on a fast LAN and evaluate the performance of CDMA as a means for computer network synchronization. In many respects, CDMA dissemination is preferable to GPS as it works anywhere a cell phone works and does not require line-of-sight view of the GPS constellation.

Beauregard is used as an archive server and ordinarily does nothing but volley NTP packets. For the experiment, the kernel discipline described in Chapter 4 was enabled. Data were harvested from the rawstats and peerstats files over a typical day and analyzed for time and frequency offset and LRD. Figure 6.16 shows the offset, and Figure 6.17 shows the frequency during the experiment. It is obvious from these figures that the dominant source of error is a wavy distortion with peak–peak amplitude about 200 ns and period about 5 h. It is not clear whether this was induced by CDMA protocol processing or the EndRun server itself, which is based on an embedded Linux system.

Figure 6.18 shows the CDF for both the rawstats data (right curve) and peerstats data (left curve). The maximum raw offset is 10 ms, while the maximum peer offset is 200 ns, a reduction factor of 50, again demonstrating the

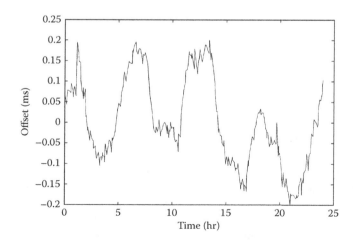

FIGURE 6.16
Beauregard time offset.

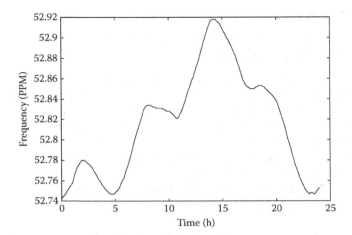

FIGURE 6.17
Beauregard frequency offset.

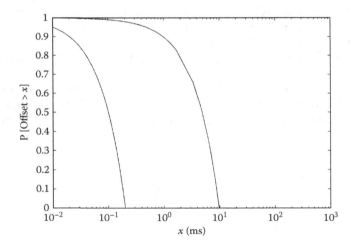

FIGURE 6.18
Beauregard time offset CDF.

improvement due to the clock filter algorithm. Figure 6.19 shows the round-trip delay characteristic over the experiment period. This includes all sources of latencies in the server and client Ethernet interfaces, device interrupts, and software queues. The effect of these contributions is largely suppressed by the clock filter and low-pass characteristic of the discipline algorithm. Figure 6.20 shows the variance-time plot and confirms that there is very little LRD, as expected.

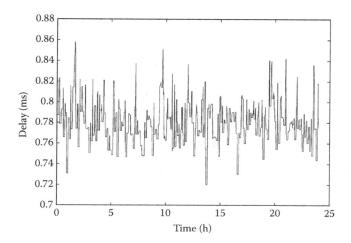

FIGURE 6.19
Ethernet time delay.

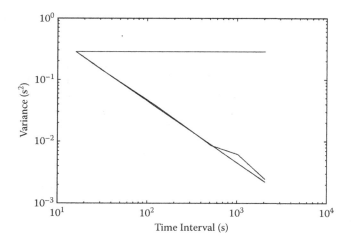

FIGURE 6.20
Ethernet time delay variance-time plot.

6.6 Results from an Internet Survey

There have been several comprehensive surveys of the Internet NTP population in the past, but such surveys are probably not possible today without setting off indexing alarms all over the place. The most recent in 1997 [1] found 38,722 NTP Version 2 (NTPv2) and Version 3 (NTPv3) hosts with

182,538 mobilized associations for an average of 4.7 associations per machine. About half of these associations were for servers on the same subnet. There is every reason to believe today that these figures are in the tens of millions (J. Levine, NIST, personal communication). While the survey may be historic, it does reveal insight in subnet configuration issues and especially expected system clock characteristics that remain valid today.

As determined from the 1997 survey [1], the distribution of associations by stratum is shown in Figure 6.21. While today the number of clients per server is much larger, there is every reason to suspect that the relative numbers are similar. Not surprisingly, the most associations were at the lower strata. The top 10 primary servers had over 400 clients and the busiest one over 700; however, the particular monitoring function used to collect these numbers does not count client numbers greater than 700, so there could be many more clients. Probably the most striking observation evident from the figure is the relatively low mean compared to the top 10. Especially in the case of the primary servers, the load is very unevenly distributed. Since the survey was conducted, NIST and the U.S. Naval Observatory (USNO) have installed over two dozen time servers, but the load on a few of them peaks at times over 2,000 packets per second (p/s). As an aside, the reason for at least some of this abuse is the occasion of some misguided NTP client implementation that squirts 256 packets as fast as it can for every measurement.

Figure 6.22 shows the CDF for time offsets measured by all associations in the 1997 survey [1]. At first glance, the rather heavy tail in this distribution is not pretty; the maximum is 686 ms, mean is 234 ms, and median is 23.3 ms. However, the Internet is a rowdy place, and these data show only the individual associations, not the actual host time offsets. The discipline algorithm considers only those associations showing less than 128-ms offset

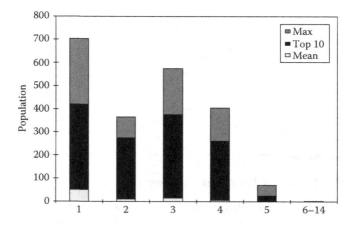

FIGURE 6.21
Clients per server per stratum.

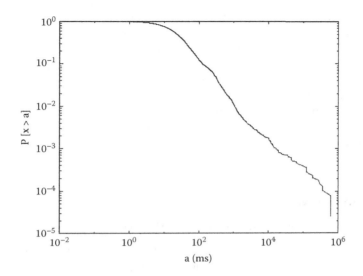

FIGURE 6.22
Measured time offset CDF.

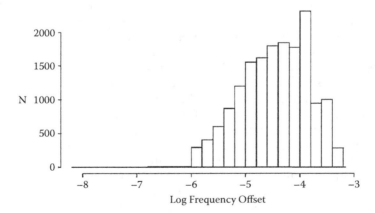

FIGURE 6.23
Measured frequency offset histogram.

as valid. If only those associations are included, the mean is 28.7 ms and median 20.1 ms. This is probably the best indicator of NTP nominal performance in the Internet of 1997. The experiments described in the previous section suggest that the Internet of today is much faster and timekeeping much more accurate.

Figure 6.23 is a histogram of frequency offsets ($\log_{10}$ PPM) measured in the 1997 survey [1], which probably remain valid today. This represents the systematic frequency error of the system clock, not the errors due to oscillator wander. The mean is 78.1 PPM and median is 38.6 PPM. However, 2.3 percent of the total population show zero frequency error, and 3.0 percent show errors greater than 500 PPM, which suggests that they were not properly synchronized. The histogram has an uncomfortably heavy tail, as indicated by the large mean compared to the median and in the histogram itself. While NTP measures and compensates for frequency errors, large errors result in correspondingly large sawtooth errors, as discussed in Chapter 4.

6.7 Server and Network Resource Requirements

Some idea of the resources required for a busy time server and network can be gained with a careful examination of a day in the life of Rackety, in its former life a Sun SPARC IPC running SunOS 4.1.3. Both the machine and the operating system would charitably be considered in their twilight years compared to modern silicon, but Rackety makes a good extreme to calibrate against. In addition to well over 600 clients, it has two GPS receivers, two WWVB receivers, and a PPS signal added to the interrupt load. It also watches three other primary servers for redundancy and backup.

To assess the impact on central processing unit (CPU) cycles and network load, the machine was left in place to collect statistics for running time R in seconds, packets received P, CPU time T in seconds, and number of clients n. The first two statistics are available using the ntpdc utility program in the NTPv4 software distribution, while the third is available using the Unix ps command and the fourth estimated from the most recently used (MRU) list maintained by the load management algorithm. Using these statistics, the mean packet arrival rate is $\lambda = P/R$ and mean service rate is $\mu = T/P$. Thus, the CPU time per packet is $t = T/P$, resulting in CPU utilization $\rho = \lambda/\mu = T/R$. Counting 48 octets for the NTP header, 8 octets for the User Datagram Protocol (UDP) header, 20 octets for the IP header, and 16 octets for the Ethernet header, an NTP packet has a total length of 92 octets or 1,360 bits, so the aggregate load on the network is $B = 1,360 \lambda$. The maximum arrival (redline) rate is $\lambda_{max} \leq (\lambda/2\rho)$, assuming that 50 percent of the available CPU cycles can be dedicated to NTP.

During the interval $R = 5.83 \times 10^4$ s, Rackety received $P = 3.18 \times 10^5$ packets for an aggregate rate $\lambda = 5.45$ p/s. The service time $T = 1,379$ s, so the processing time per packet $t = 4.34$ ms. This represents $\rho = 4.37$ percent of the available CPU cycles and 7.44 kb/s on the campus network. Projected to redline, this machine can handle 115 p/s using 156 kb/s on the network. The conclusion is that NTP cycles probably slip beneath the noise waves, even on an ancient 25-MHz machine.

If the MRU list held all clients for the recording interval and did not over-flow, the total population would be about 700 clients, so the mean poll interval for each client would be 454 s. However, it is most certain that the list did overflow, but not by how much. Therefore the true value is probably much lower than this value. These measurements were made using NTPv3, and its polling policy was more aggressive.

Compare these statistics with the NIST Boulder time server, which is a fast Alpha machine running Tru64. During an experiment in 1997 lasting $R = 8.03 \times 10^6$ s (about 93 days), it received $P = 3.22 \times 10^9$ NTP packets for an aggregate rate of $\lambda = 401$ p/s. The processing time per packet was 13.2 μs (measured on another Alpha of the same type), so the service time $T = 4.25 \times 10^4$ s and service rate $\mu = 75.8$ kp/s. This represents $\rho = 0.53$ percent of the available CPU cycles and 545 kb/s on the NIST network. Projected to redline, this machine can handle 37.8 kp/s using 51.4 Mb/s on the network. While the machine in principle will only begin to glow at this rate, the consequences would surely be noticed, and this does not count the crushing load due to Transmission Control Protocol (TCP) services, which are far more intrusive than UDP services.

Today, Boulder has three machines behind a load leveler serving an estimated total of 25 million customers who pour in thousands of packets per second. The following summary, compiled from Mills et al. [2], tells what modern life is like. The data are harvested by running a program on each machine at substantially the same time. After a number of filtering and sorting operations, the following conclusions result: In a 9-s window, 3,595 packets (400 p/s) were captured, about 13 percent of the total number of 27,853 arrivals. Of the total, 1,094 represent bursts from 574 different clients where the spacing between packets is less than 5 s. Altogether, the burst makers account for about 313 p/s. In effect, 14 percent of the clients account for 78 percent of the total load.

Of the 574 burst makers, 15 are sending at rates greater than 1 p/s (28 p/s total), 253 sending at rates between 1 and 2 p/s (166 p/s total), and the remaining 36 sending at rates between 2 and 5 p/s (120 p/s total). The most bizarre observation is the length of the bursts. Of the 574 burst makers, 379 lasted less than 1 min (214 p/s total), 189 lasted less than 1 h (93 p/s total), and 6 lasted over 1 day (6 p/s). The worst two sent at 2 p/s for over 2 days, which is the limit of observation and probably means they were sending continuously.

By contrast, redline on an even faster Sun Blade 1000 is about 70 kp/s. Do not get too comfortable with machines of the Blade class. A manufacturer who really should know better dumped some 750,000 routers on the market, each unchangeably configured to use a University of Wisconsin time server [2]. That seemed to almost work until a misconfigured firewall internal to the router prevented NTP server packets from reaching the NTP client. When the router received no reply to its packets, it began hammering the server at 1-s intervals. The result was a huge implosion at the server and access links that completely overwhelmed the campus network. The situation has not been completely resolved at this writing; certainly, the engineers and programmers need to practice good social behavior. But, there is every reason to suspect that this will not be the last incident of this type.

The situation with the audio drivers is somewhat different. These drivers do a good deal of digital signal processing and are voracious consumers of CPU cycles. For instance, the audio drivers burn 48 percent of SPARC IPC cycles and 5.2 percent of UltraSPARC 1 cycles. In the sunny days of the SPARC IPC, there was some concern about the interrupt overhead for reference clocks, but at the common serial port rate of 9,600 b/s today, the overhead is below the noise level.

6.8 Parting Shots

As the Internet was growing up, NTP served well as a network thermometer and rumble detector. But, something interesting has happened. In the bad old ARPANET (Advanced Research Projects Agency Network) days, it was easy to find congested but stable paths with good-looking scattergrams like the one shown in Figure 6.5. The scattergrams elsewhere in this chapter look nothing like that; in fact, it is hard to find a filled-in wedge cruising academic networks today. It seems that everybody, even in East Jabip, comes with a high-speed Internet access. The performance even on access to the overloaded NIST public servers is almost as good as via a local network. To find a "bad" path illustrating anticipated performance on a slow, overloaded path, I had to dip into the archives for a 7-year-old path between Newark, Delaware, and Washington, D.C., via a 1.5-Mb/s tail circuit.

References

1. Mills, D.L., A. Thyagarajan, and B.C. Huffman. Internet timekeeping around the globe. *Proceedings Precision Time and Time Interval (PTTI) Applications and Planning Meeting* (Long Beach, CA, December 1997), 365–371.
2. Mills, D.L., J. Levine, R. Schmidt, and D. Plonka. Coping with overload on the Network Time Protocol public servers. *Proceedings Precision Time and Time Interval (PTTI) Applications and Planning Meeting* (Washington, DC, December 2004), 5–16.

7

Primary Servers and Reference Clocks

They say that "time assuages"—
Time never did assauge;
An actual suffering strengthens,
As sinews do, with age.
Time is a test of trouble,
But not a remedy.
If such it prove, it prove too
There was no malady.

Emily Dickenson
Poems, 1891

It happens at the end of the fiscal year that there is some loose cash that must be spent or lost to the next budget cycle. So, Network Services splurges $3,000 for either a stand-alone NTP in a box with a GPS antenna connector on one side and an Ethernet connector on the other or a GPS receiver with a timecode suitable for a computer serial port. While these work well, they require an antenna on the roof with downlead threaded through the elevator shaft and ceiling plenums to the machine room. The GPS signal is line of sight, and the satellites can wander across the sky from any direction and elevation. This means that the GPS antenna must have a substantially clear shot from the zenith to maybe 10–20 degrees above the horizon, which means an antenna in a machine room window might not work. Also, note that the length of the downlead is usually limited to 50 or 100 feet, depending on model, beyond which an amplifier is required.

If the building is rented, most landlords have found the roof the most lucrative real estate in the building, and in any case getting a wire to the roof is maybe more pain than it is worth. Other things to consider are that the NTP in a box might not support some desired protocol modes like Internet Protocol Version 4 (IPv4) multicast, do not have the extensive suite of monitoring tools, and may not support authentication and access controls. Nevertheless, the temptation to buy one of these boxes and avoid the hassle interfacing the receiver to a real NTP server may be attractive. Where rooftop real estate is not possible but there is good reception for code division multiple access (CDMA) cell phones, NTP devices are available for which servers synchronize to the CDMA system. CDMA systems are synchronized via GPS and provide accuracy in the low microseconds.

Increasingly as time goes by, the preferred choice is a GPS receiver, but others using the WWVB radio service or equivalent services in Europe and Japan are good choices as well and might not require that antennas squint near the horizon, and the length of the downlead may be much more flexible. These services use long-wave frequencies at 40, 60, or 77.5 kHz, which are susceptible to conductive and radiative noise and lightning storms in the vicinity. Even after a transmitter upgrade at WWVB, the signals are not completely reliable in some parts of North America. The situation is better in Europe, both because distances are smaller and because of the generally higher latitudes, where the noise levels are lower. However, it has become a serious problem in some installations where battery backup systems are in use. These systems produce copious amounts of radio-frequency interference (RFI) at long-wave frequencies that can render these services useless.

GPS satellite and long-wave radio services are not the only options. Others are telephone modem services operated by the U.S. Naval Observatory (USNO) and NIST in the United States, NRC in Canada, and others in Europe. While it might not be typical, a 3-min telephone call from the University of Delaware to the Automated Computer Time Service (ACTS) in Boulder, Colorado, at one time cost nine cents but now is free in the calling plan. With NTP Version 4 (NTPv4), the intervals between calls can be over a day. Possible downsides to the modem approach are that the ACTS modem pool is becoming increasingly congested, and the time quality has considerably degraded in recent years. The degraded quality is a victim of modern digital signal processing. Once upon a time, modems were crude analog devices with no compression, equalization, or multilevel quantization. This said, old modems had essentially constant delays and made rather good time transporters. Modern modems are really microcomputers with all the above attitudes and rather severe jitter on the order of several milliseconds. This level of jitter and occasional busy signal might be acceptable in many applications.

This is money well spent, but where and how to connect a reference clock and to which machines? The best answer is to all the servers using dedicated serial ports. Most professional reference clocks have an Inter-Range Instrumentation Group (IRIG) output and a pulse-per-second (PPS) output in addition to a serial ASCII (American Standard Code for Information Interchange) timecode. The reference implementation includes software drivers for all of them. This chapter discusses the software drivers and driver interface of the reference implementation.

7.1 Driver Structure and Interface

NTP reference clock support maintains the fiction that the clock is actually an ordinary server in the NTP subnet. Ordinarily, reference clocks are assigned stratum 0, so that the server itself appears to clients at stratum 1. As shown in Figure 7.1, the clock driver manages the clock hardware and input/output interface, processes serial ASCII timecode, and performs certain filtering and grooming functions. The entire suite of NTP algorithms is available to filter the received data, select the best clocks or servers, and combine their offsets to synchronize the system clock. Using these algorithms, defective clocks can be detected and removed from the population. Note that the mitigation rules of Section 3.11 apply when both reference clocks and ordinary servers are included in the configuration.

The components of a typical reference clock driver and driver interface are shown in Figure 7.2. There are four interface functions: sample, receive, transmit, and second. The sample function parses the timecode data, either in the form of a serial ASCII timecode or a set of hardware registers that display the time continuously. In either case, the timecode data are reduced to canonical form and converted to an NTP timestamp in seconds and

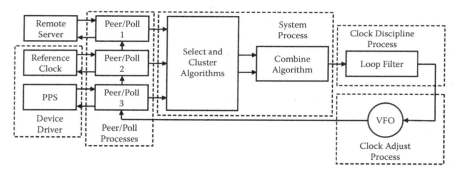

FIGURE 7.1
Reference clock drivers.

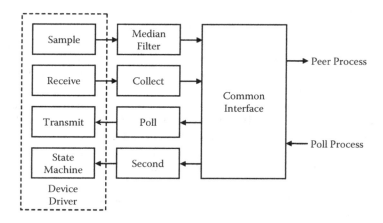

FIGURE 7.2
Driver interface.

fraction, called the *driver timestamp*. A system clock timestamp is captured at a designated on-time character in the timecode. The difference between the driver timestamp and system timestamp represents the clock offset. The driver then calls the sample function to save the offset in a circular buffer for use later.

The receive function is called by the driver to process the samples in the circular buffer. The n samples are sorted by offset and the median found. Then, a designated number k of samples above and below the median are averaged and the rest discarded. This algorithm, called a *median filter*, is effective for reducing the jitter due to the various latencies and has less bias than the traditional trimmed-mean filter. For convenience, the resulting offset is passed to the clock filter algorithm, which processes the samples in order since they all have zero delay. The principal advantage using the clock filter is that it properly handles missing samples and produces consistent statistics.

At each poll interval, the driver interface calls an optional transmit routine supplied by the driver. This can be used to activate the receive function or initiate a modem call or any other periodic function. Once each second, the driver interface calls an optional second routine supplied by the driver. Some drivers use this to send a poll message to the clock, while others use it to run a state machine that controls the clock functions.

The drivers require that the clock run in UTC; that is, it is not adjusted for local time zone. The drivers assume three timescales: UTC time maintained by a distant laboratory such as USNO or NIST, reference time maintained by the reference clock, and system time maintained by NTP. The reference clock synchronizes to UTC time via radio, satellite, or telephone modem. If this fails for some reason according to timecode indicators or if the clock does not respond, the driver does not call the receive interface function, so the peer dispersion will increase, and eventually the driver will appear unreachable just like an ordinary NTP server.

Most timecode formats include a synchronized indicator that shows that the clock has been synchronized; some include a leap second warning indicator. The drivers use these indicators to set the leap indicator of the association. If available, a quality indicator is used to set the initial peer dispersion, just as when a packet arrives from an NTP server. The reference time is determined as the system time when the most recent timecode was received. The round-trip delay, root dispersion, and root delay are ordinarily set to zero. Normally, the assigned driver stratum is 0, which becomes one as seen by the clients of this server. Some formats include indicators showing the DST state and UT1 − UTC adjustment called DUT1, but these are not used by the drivers.

Table 7.1 shows the reference clock drivers currently implemented in NTPv4. Most drivers operate with ASCII timecodes received via a serial port. Exceptions include the modem driver, local clock driver, PPS driver, and audio drivers. These drivers are described in the following sections.

TABLE 7.1

Reference Clock Drivers

Type	Description	Type	Description
1	Undisciplined local clock	23	Not used
2	Trak 8820 GPS receiver	24	Not used
3	PSTI/Traconex 1020 WWV/H receiver	25	Not used
4	Generic Spectracom receiver	26	Hewlett Packard 58503A GPS receiver
5	Generic TrueTime receiver	27	Arcron MSF receiver
6	Generic IRIG audio decoder	28	Shared memory driver
7	CHU audio demodulator/decoder	29	Trimble Palisade GPS receiver
8	Generic reference driver	30	Motorola UT Oncore GPS receiver
9	Magnavox MX4200 GPS receiver	31	Rockwell Jupiter GPS receiver
10	Austron 2200A/2201A GPS receivers	32	Chrono-Log K-series WWVB receiver
11	Arbiter 1088A/B GPS receiver	33	Dumb clock driver
12	KSI/Odetics TPRO/S IRIG interface	34	Ultralink WWVB receiver
13	Leitch CSD 5300 master clock controller	35	Conrad parallel port radio clock
14	EES M201 MSF receiver	36	WWV/H audio demodulator/decoder
15	Not used	37	Forum Graphic GPS dating station
16	Bancomm GPS/IRIG receiver	38	Hopf GPS/DCF77 6021 serial line
17	Datum precision time system	39	Hopf GPS/DCF77 6039 PCI-bus
18	Generic modem time service	40	JJY receivers
19	Heath WWV/H receiver	41	TrueTime 560 IRIG-B decoder
20	Generic NMEA GPS receiver	42	Zyfer GPStarplus receiver
21	TrueTime GPS-VME interface	43	RIPE NCC interface for Trimble Palisade
22	PPS clock discipline	44	NeoClock4X-DCF77/TDF serial line

7.2 Serial Timecode Drivers

Most radio and satellite receiver drivers shown in Table 7.1 work the same way. A typical clock produces an ASCII timecode similar to the format `sq yy ddd hh:mm:ss.fff ld sd`, where

s	Synchronized indicator shows ? if never unsynchronized, space after first synchronized
q	Quality indicator decodes the maximum error since the clock was last synchronized
yy	Year of century

ddd	Day of year
hh	Hour of day
mm	Minute of hour
ss	Second of minute
fff	Fraction of second
l	Leap warning shows L if pending leap second, space if not
d	DST shows S standard, D daylight, I daylight warning, O standard warning
sd	DUT1 correction shows s the sign and d a single digit 0–9 in deciseconds

By design, reference clock drivers set the association leap indicator to 3 if the synchronization indicator shows ? and 0 if space. If the leap warning shows L, the association leap indicator is set to 1. By design, the driver sets the reference timestamp and initial peer dispersion each time a timecode is received, and the peer dispersion provided to the clock filter algorithm increments from then. The initial peer dispersion is mapped from the quality indicator, if available.

In some designs, the clock must be polled to receive the timecode; others deliver the timecode automatically at 1-s intervals. The latter are preferred as each timecode produces a measurement for the median filter. In such cases, the poll routine at intervals of about 1 min processes the median filter samples, discards outliers, and averages the rest. This helps to minimize jitter due to the serial port hardware and operating system.

The on-time epoch is usually provided by a designated timecode character, often the CR or LF ending the ASCII timecode string. In some operating systems, in particular System V Streams, the latency and latency variations of the operating system routines can be tens of milliseconds, especially with older, slower machines. There have been several attempts in the past to mitigate these latencies, usually by modifying the serial port interrupt routine to capture a timestamp and insert it in the serial data stream when a designated input character is found. Modern machines are usually fast enough that such measures are not necessary.

The ubiquitous Unix serial interface termios provides a dazzling number of options for line editing, flow control, and device management. Historically, these were intended to service the bewildering variety of terminal and display devices marketed over the years. With respect to clock drivers, one of the most important is the selection of what is called raw and cooked mode. In raw mode, every character received is passed individually to the driver, while in cooked mode a line is formatted as an ASCII character string followed by a CR or LF. Cooked mode avoids the overhead of character-at-a-time interrupts but can result in poor accuracy unless the on-time character is a CR or LF. Once upon a time with slower computers, cooked mode was highly prized; however, with fast modern computers it may not make much difference.

The choice of raw mode brings with it another design issue. Since no particular character code is available to signal an interrupt, this function must be provided by another means. In an attempt to reduce the per-character interrupt load, the hardware and operating system avoid passing single characters to the driver during a burst, such as might be produced by the reference clock timecode. The Unix interface can be set to return a burst of characters if the kernel buffer fills up or a designated time-out is exceeded when no characters have been received. If raw mode is in use, the time-out directly detracts from the accuracy achievable. So, for the best accuracy, the interface should be set to return each character separately.

Another factor affecting accuracy is the widespread use of buffered UART chips used for serial ports. These chips include a first in, first out (FIFO) buffer of 16 characters or more. This can cause serious problems since the on-time character can be delayed several character times, causing errors up to several milliseconds. The only remedy for this problem is to disable the FIFO by an appropriate hardware BIOS (Basic Input/Output System) command. Notwithstanding the hardware FIFO, the ubiquitous Unix serial port driver often has a software FIFO buffer of its own. Its purpose is to reduce the number of software queue dispatches at the higher data rates. In some systems, the software FIFO can be disabled; in others, it cannot. Even when available, the appropriate kernel system call can be astonishingly hard to locate.

7.3 Generic Modem Driver

The generic modem driver (type 18 in Table 7.1) can operate with the ACTS telephone time service operated by NIST as well as similar services operated by USNO and several European countries. It operates much like the serial timecode drivers but with additional provisions to handle modem and telephone operations. The driver uses the ubiquitous Hayes modem control commands and a state machine with time-outs implemented using the second driver interface function. The state machine is used for modem control, dialing functions, and various error recovery functions. Ordinarily, the `minpoll` option of the `server` command described in Section 5.9 is set to 12 (4,096 s), so calls are placed initially at a rate of about one per hour. After a few hours, the call interval will increase, eventually to `maxpoll`, which can be set from `minpoll` to 17 (36 h) and continues at that interval. Up to five telephone numbers can be configured using the `phone` command; the driver will call each in turn if there is no answer or if the call fails for some reason. The driver recognizes each individual modem service automatically and needs no prior configuration.

The ACTS telephone modem service incorporates a clever means to calibrate the delay from Boulder to the user location. When using this service, the modem driver echoes each character received so the ACTS can measure the round-trip delay and adjust the transmitted times to compensate for the one-way delay. While this improves the accuracy in principle to less than a millisecond, at the relatively long intervals between calls, the errors are usually dominated by system clock oscillator wander.

The driver can be operated in two modes selected by the `prefer` option of the `server` command. If not present, the driver operates in backup mode and is not selected unless all other synchronization sources are lost. If present, it operates at all times along with other drivers and servers. This is not recommended as the modem driver poll interval is usually very large compared to the other drivers, and serious transients might occur if it becomes the only backup source. See the mitigation rules in Section 3.11 for further information.

7.4 Local Clock Driver

Some NTP subnets thrive where no connections to the public Internet are possible and no reference clocks are available. However, the several machines in the network may need to coordinate time, even if the time is not synchronized to UTC. The local clock driver (type 1 in Table 7.1) can be useful in subnets like these. It allows a designated machine to act as a primary time server providing synchronization to other clients in the same subnet. The operator sets the clock in this machine using the best means available, like eyeball and wristwatch. Then, the other machines in the network are configured either directly or indirectly with this machine.

The local clock driver provides updates to the core algorithms at intervals of about 1 min, although the indicated offset is always zero. The driver can be operated in two modes selected using the `prefer` option of the `server` command. If not present, the driver operates in backup mode and is not selected unless all other synchronization sources are lost. If present, it operates at all times along with other drivers and servers.

The stratum of this driver defaults to 5 but can be changed to another value, including 0, using the `stratum` option of the `server` command. This would be appropriate if a means other than NTP is used to discipline the system clock, such as the NIST lockclock program, which uses the ACTS telephone time service (but not the modem driver), or Digital Time Synchronization Service (DTSS), which runs on DCE machines. In this case, the stratum should be set at zero, indicating a bona fide stratum 1 source. In the case of DTSS, the system clock can have a rather large sawtooth error, depending on the interval between corrections and the intrinsic frequency error of the PPS interface and clock oscillator.

The local clock driver is useful as a backup even if other sources of synchronization are available. A typical application involves a firewall machine configured with one or more NTP servers in the public Internet and also configured with the local clock driver running at stratum 5. As long as no synchronization path to a public NTP server has a stratum greater than 5, the firewall will always use the public servers; however, if all public servers become unreachable, the local clock driver will be selected, and the clients track the vagrancies of the firewall clock. There may be a small transient when the public servers again become reachable, but this should not cause a time step unless the vagrancy lasts several days. See the mitigation rules in Section 3.11 for further information.

Used in this way, only one server can be configured with the local clock driver. The orphan mode feature described in Section 3.13 can be used when more than one server is available and is the preferred mechanism even if only one server is configured. It provides a managed failover and backup mechanism that exploits all available redundancy and diversity.

7.5 PPS Interface and Driver

A pulse-per-second (PPS) signal is produced by some radios and laboratory equipment for extremely accurate and precise synchronization. With proper interfacing, the system clock can be synchronized to it, usually within a few microseconds with modern computers. However, the PPS signal is inherently ambiguous in that it provides a precise seconds epoch but provides no way to number the seconds. This requires another source of synchronization, either the timecode from an associated reference clock or one or more remote NTP servers to number the seconds. In all cases, a specific, configured server must be designated as associated with the PPS signal as determined by the mitigation rules in Section 3.11. The PPS signal can be associated in this way with any source but is most commonly used with the reference clock generating the PPS signal.

The PPS signal can be connected to the computer in either of two ways: via the data carrier detect (DCD) pin of a serial port or via the acknowledge (ACK) pin of a parallel port, depending on the hardware and operating system. However, the PPS signal levels are usually incompatible with serial port signal levels, so a level converter might be required. One example is the gadget box described in the reference implementation documentation. It consists of a handful of electronic components assembled in a small aluminum box. A complete set of schematics, PCB artwork, and drill templates is available at http://www.ntp.org.

Ordinarily, the reference clock driver associated with the PPS signal calls the PPSAPI interface [1] to measure the difference between the PPS signal and the system clock and saves it in the median filter. The second function in the driver interface is a convenient way to do this. The poll routine calls the receive routine of the driver interface to process the median filter differences and delivers the resulting offset to the peer process. Alternatively, the driver calls the PPSAPI interface to enable the kernel to process the PPS signal directly, as described in Section 8.4. In any case, the PPS signal is considered valid only if the offset produced by the clock filter, select, cluster, and combine algorithms is within 400 ms of the PPS signal offset.

When the PPS signal is not associated with a device driver, a special device driver called the PPS driver (type 22 in Table 7.1) can be used. This driver performs all the PPS functions using the PPSAPI interface but has no provision for a serial timecode. The PPS driver includes extensive signal sanity checks and grooming algorithms. A range gate and frequency discriminator reject noise and signals with incorrect frequency. The median filter minimizes jitter due to hardware interrupt and operating system latencies. The selection of which sources provide the seconds numbering is determined by the mitigation rules in Section 3.11.

By default, the stratum assigned to the PPS driver is set automatically to the stratum of the prefer peer selected by the mitigation rules. If the prefer peer becomes unreachable or as the result of PPS signal loss, the PPS driver peer dispersion is managed as for ordinary servers. Alternatively, the stratum can be set by a configuration command. The PPS driver stratum can masquerade as a primary server by forcing the stratum to 0 if the prefer peer is a remote NTP server. This is decidedly dangerous as it invites timing loops.

7.6 Audio Drivers

There are some applications in which the computer time can be disciplined to an audio signal sent over a telephone circuit or received from a shortwave radio. In such cases, the signal can be connected via an ordinary sound card or baseboard audio codec and processed by one of the audio drivers in the reference implementation. The suite of NTP reference clock drivers currently includes three drivers suitable for these applications. They include the IRIG (type 6 in Table 7.1) for the Inter Range Instrumentation Group (IRIG) signals produced by many reference clocks and timing devices, the CHU driver (type 7) for the Canadian time/frequency radio station CHU in Ottawa, Canada, and the WWV driver (type 36) for the NIST time/frequency radio stations WWV in Ft. Collins, Colorado, and WWVH in Kauai, Hawaii.

The radio drivers are designed to work with ordinary inexpensive short-wave radios and may be one of the least-expensive ways to build a primary time server. The drivers include provisions to automatically tune the radio in response to changing radio propagation conditions throughout the day and season. The radio interface is compatible with the ICOM CI-V standard, which is a bidirectional serial bus operating at TTL (time-to-live) levels. The bus can be connected to a standard serial port using a level converter such as the CT-17. Further details are on the Reference Clock Audio Drivers page at http://www.ntp.org.

All three drivers process 8,000-Hz μ-law companded samples using sophisticated digital signal processing algorithms designed to efficiently extract timing signals from noise and interference. The drivers implement optimum linear demodulation and decoding techniques, including matched filter, maximum likelihood, and soft decision methods. The NTP documentation page for each driver contains an in-depth discussion of the algorithms and performance expectations. In some cases, the algorithms are further analyzed, modeled, and evaluated in technical reports available on the NTP project page at http://www.ntp.org.

The audio drivers include a number of common features designed to groom input signals, suppress spikes, and normalize signal levels. The drivers include provisions to select the input port and to monitor the input signal. An automatic gain control (AGC) feature provides protection against overdriven or underdriven input signals. It is designed to maintain adequate demodulator signal amplitude while avoiding occasional noise spikes. To ensure reliable operation, the signal level must be in the range where the AGC is effective.

In the IRIG and WWV/H drivers, the reference frequency is disciplined by the audio source and is assumed to have the same reliability and accuracy as an external radio or satellite receiver, so even if the audio signals are lost for some time, there will be minimal disruption when they reappear. This is done by stuffing or slipping codec samples as required to maintain exact frequency to the order of 0.1 PPM. For the driver to reliably lock on the audio signal, the sample clock frequency tolerance must be less than 250 PPM (0.025 percent) for the IRIG driver and 125 PPM for the WWV/H driver. The largest error observed so far is about 60 PPM, but it is possible some sound cards or codecs may exceed that tolerance.

The CHU and WWV/H drivers require an external shortwave radio with the radio speaker or headphone jack connected to either the microphone or line-in port of the sound card. The WWV/H and CHU transmitters operate on several frequencies simultaneously, so that in most parts of North America at least one frequency supports propagation to the receiver location at any given hour. While both drivers support the ICOM CI-V radio interface and can tune the radio automatically, computer-tunable radios are expensive and probably not cost effective compared to a GPS receiver. So, the radio frequency must usually be fixed and chosen by compromise. There is some degree of art in selecting the transmitter frequency, installing the antenna, and minimizing ambient noise and interference. While the drivers are highly sophisticated and efficient in extracting timing signals from noise and interference, it always helps to have as clear a signal as possible.

7.6.1 IRIG Driver

The IRIG driver supports the analog-modulated signal generated by several reference clocks, including those made by Arbiter, Austron, Bancomm, Meinberg, Odetics, Spectracom, Symmetricom, and TrueTime, among others, although it is often an add-on option. The signal is connected via an optional attenuator box and cable to either the microphone or line-in port of the sound card. The driver receives, demodulates, and automatically selects either the IRIG-B format at 1,000 Hz or the IRIG-E format [2] at 100 Hz using infinite impulse response (IIR) filters designed to reduce the effects of noise and interference.

The program uses a comb filter, envelope detector, and automatic threshold corrector to demodulate the amplitude-modulated signal. Cycle crossings relative to the corrected slice level determine the width of each pulse and its value: zero, one, or position identifier. The data encode 20 BCD digits, which determine the second, minute, hour, and day of the year and sometimes the year and synchronization condition. The comb filter exponentially averages the corresponding samples of successive baud intervals to reliably identify the reference carrier cycle.

For proper operation, the IRIG signal source should be configured for analog signal levels, not digital TTL levels. In most radios, the IRIG signal is driven ±10 V behind 50 ohms. In such cases, the cable should be terminated at the line-in port with a 50-ohm resistor to avoid overdriving the codec. Where feasible, the IRIG signal source should be operated with signature control so that, if the signal is lost or mutilated, the source produces an unmodulated signal rather than possibly random digits. The driver automatically rejects the data and declares itself unsynchronized in this case. Some devices, in particular Spectracom radio/satellite clocks, provide additional year and status indication; other devices may not.

In general and without calibration, the driver is accurate within 0.5 ms relative to the IRIG time. After calibrating relative to the PPS signal from a GPS receiver, the mean offset with a 2.4-GHz P4 running FreeBSD 6.1 is less than 20 μs with standard deviation 10 μs. Most of this is due to residuals after filtering and averaging the raw codec samples, which have an inherent jitter of 125 μs. The processor load due to the driver is about 0.6 percent on the P4.

7.6.2 WWV/H Driver

The WWV/H driver synchronizes the computer time using shortwave radio transmissions from NIST time/frequency stations WWV in Ft. Collins, Colorado, and WWVH in Kauai, Hawaii. Transmissions are made continuously on 2.5, 5, 10, and 15 MHz by both stations and on 20 MHz by WWV. An ordinary shortwave receiver can be tuned manually to one of these frequencies, or in the case of ICOM receivers, the receiver can be tuned automatically by the driver as propagation conditions change throughout the day and season.

Without calibration but with corrections for propagation delay, the driver is accurate to within 1 ms relative to the broadcast time when tracking a station. However, variations up to 0.3 ms can be expected due to diurnal variations in ionospheric layer height and ray geometry. In Newark, Delaware, 2,479 km from the transmitter, the predicted two-hop propagation delay varies from 9.0 ms in sunlight to 9.3 ms in moonlight. When not tracking the station, the accuracy depends on the codec oscillator stability, which is ordinarily better than 0.5 PPM.

The demodulation and decoding algorithms used by this driver are based on a machine language program developed for the TAPR DSP93 DSP unit, which uses the TI 320C25 DSP chip. The analysis, design, and performance of the program for this unit is described in Mills [3]. The original program was rebuilt in the C language and adapted to the NTP driver interface. The algorithms have been modified to improve performance, especially under weak signal conditions, and to provide an automatic frequency and station selection feature.

The WWV signal format is described in NIST Special Publication 432 (revised 1990) and also is available on the WWV/H Web site. It consists of three elements: a 5-ms, 1,000-Hz pulse, which occurs at the beginning of each second; an 800-ms, 1,000-Hz pulse, which occurs at the beginning of each minute; and a pulse-width modulated 100-Hz subcarrier for the data bits, one bit per second. The WWVH format is identical, except that the 5-ms, 1000-Hz pulses are sent at 1,200 Hz. Each minute encodes nine BCD digits for the time of century plus seven bits for the daylight savings time (DST) indicator, leap warning, and DUT1 correction.

The 1,000-/1,200-Hz pulses and 100-Hz subcarrier are first separated and voice modulation components removed using IIR filters. The minute pulse is extracted using an 800-ms synchronous matched filter and pulse grooming logic that discriminates between WWV and WWVH signals and noise. The second pulse is extracted using a 5-ms FIR matched filter for each station and a single 8,000-stage integrator. The phase of the 100-Hz subcarrier relative to the second pulse is fixed at the transmitter; however, the audio stage in many radios affects the phase response at 100 Hz in unpredictable ways. The driver adjusts for each radio using two 170-ms synchronous matched filters. The I (in-phase) filter is used to demodulate the subcarrier envelope, while the Q (quadrature-phase) filter is used in a type 1 phase-lock loop (PLL) to discipline the demodulator phase.

A bipolar data signal is developed from the 100-Hz subcarrier envelope using a pulse-width discriminator. The signal is exponentially averaged in a set of 60 correlators, one for each second, to determine the semistatic miscellaneous bits, such as DST indicator, leap second warning, and DUT1 correction. In this design, a data average value larger than a positive threshold is interpreted as +1 (hit) and a value smaller than a negative threshold as a −1 (miss). Values between the two thresholds, which can occur due to signal fades, are interpreted as erasures and result in no change of indication.

The BCD digit in each digit position of the timecode is represented as four data bits. The bits are correlated with the bits corresponding to each of the valid decimal digits in this position. If any of the four bits is invalid, the correlated value for all digits in this position is assumed zero. In either case, the values for all digits are exponentially averaged in a likelihood vector associated with this position. The digit associated with the maximum over all averaged values then becomes the maximum likelihood candidate for this position, and the ratio of the maximum over the next lower value represents the digit signal-to-noise ratio (SNR).

The decoding matrix contains nine row vectors, one for each digit position. Each row vector includes the maximum likelihood digit, likelihood vector, and other related data. The maximum correlator value for each digit of the nine digit positions becomes the maximum likelihood time of the century. A built-in transition function implements a conventional clock with decimal digits that count the minutes, hours, days, and years, as corrected for leap seconds and leap years. The counting operation also rotates the likelihood vector corresponding to each digit as it advances. Thus, once the clock is set, each clock digit should correspond to the maximum likelihood digit as transmitted.

A logical master clock is derived from the audio codec clock. Its frequency is disciplined by a frequency-lock loop (FLL), which operates independently of the data recovery functions. The maximum value of the 5-ms pulse of the comb filter represents the on-time epoch of the second. When first started, the frequency averaging interval is 8 s to compensate for intrinsic codec clock frequency offsets up to 125 PPM. Under most conditions, the averaging interval doubles in stages from the initial value to 1,024 s, which results in an ultimate frequency resolution of 0.125 PPM or about 11 ms/day.

The predicted propagation delay from the WWV transmitter at Boulder to the receiver at Newark varies over 9.0–9.3 ms due to changing ionospheric layer height and ray geometry over the day and night. In addition, the receiver contributes 4.7 ms and the 600-Hz band-pass filter 0.9 ms. Figure 7.3 shows the measured offsets over a typical day near the bottom of the sunspot cycle ending in October 2006. Conventional wisdom is that manual synchronization using an oscilloscope and calibrate range gate is good only to a millisecond under the best of conditions. The performance of the NTP daemon disciplined by this driver is clearly better than this, even under marginal conditions.

The behavior of the autotune function over a typical day is shown in Figure 7.4. As expected, the lower frequencies prevail when the ray path is in moonlight (0100–1300 UTC) and the higher frequencies when the path is in sunlight (1300–0100 UTC). Note that three periods in the figure show zero frequency when signals are below the minimum for all frequencies and stations.

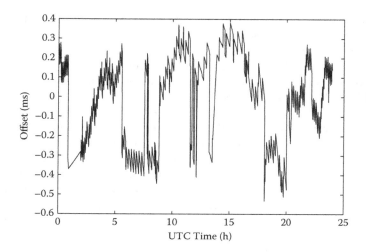

FIGURE 7.3
WWV time offsets over a 24-h period.

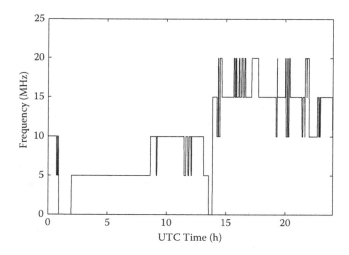

FIGURE 7.4
Autotune frequency over a 24-h period.

7.6.3 CHU Driver

The CHU driver synchronizes the computer time using shortwave radio transmissions from Canadian time/frequency station CHU in Ottawa, Ontario. CHU transmissions are made continuously on 3.330, 7.850, and 14.670 MHz in the upper sideband, compatible AM (amplitude modulation) mode. An ordinary shortwave receiver can be tuned manually to one of these frequencies, or, in the case of ICOM receivers, the receiver can be tuned automatically as propagation conditions change throughout the day and season. It is interesting to note that this driver is used at the station to provide synchronization for the NRC public time servers.

The driver can be compiled to use either a sound card or a Bell 103-compatible 300-b/s modem and a serial port. If compiled for a serial port, the driver uses it to receive the demodulated radio signal and then decodes the data. If compiled for a sound card, it emulates the modem in software. In general and without calibration, the driver is accurate within 1 ms relative to the broadcast time when tracking a station. However, variations up to 0.3 ms can be expected due to diurnal variations in ionospheric layer height and ray geometry. In Newark, 625 km from the transmitter, the predicted one-hop propagation delay varies from 2.8 ms in sunlight to 2.6 ms in moonlight. After calibration relative to the PPS signal from a GPS receiver, the mean offset with a 2.4-GHz P4 running FreeBSD 6.1 is generally within 0.2 ms short term with 0.4 ms jitter. The long-term mean offset varies up to 0.3 ms due to propagation path geometry variations. The processor load due to the driver is 0.4 percent on the P4.

The CHU broadcast format consists of nine bursts of ten 8-bit characters transmitted at 300 b/s during each minute. The driver exploits the considerable degree of redundancy available in this format. Every character in every burst is sent twice, and all but one burst are redundant. Every character in every burst provides an independent timestamp on arrival with a potential total of 60 timestamps for each minute.

The program consists of four major parts: software modem, software UART, burst assembler, and majority decoder. The software modem demodulates Bell 103 modem answer-frequency tones of 2,225 Hz (mark) and 2,025 Hz (space). It consists of a 500-Hz band-pass filter followed by a limiter/discriminator and raised-cosine low-pass filter optimized for the 300-b/s data rate. The software UART uses maximum likelihood techniques for optimum decoding.

The burst assembler processes characters either from the software UART or directly from the serial port as configured. A burst begins when a character is received and is processed after a time-out when no characters are received. A valid burst consists of 10 characters in two replicated 5-character blocks, each block representing ten 4-bit BCD digits. The format B blocks sent in second 31 contain the year and other information in 10 digits. The eight format A blocks sent in seconds 32–39 contain the timecode in 10 digits, the first of which is a framing code. The majority decoder uses a decoding matrix of 10 rows, one for each digit position in the timecode, and 16 columns, one for each 4-bit code combination that might be decoded at that position. To use the character timestamps, it is necessary to reliably determine the second number of each burst. In a valid format A burst, the last digit of the two timecodes in the burst must match, and the value must be in the range 2–9 and greater than in the previous burst.

As each digit of a valid burst is processed, the value at the row corresponding to the digit position in the timecode and column corresponding to the code found at that position is incremented. At the end of the minute, each row of the decoding matrix encodes the number of occurrences of each code found at the corresponding position. The maximum over all occurrences at each digit position is the distance for that position, and the corresponding code is the maximum likelihood digit. If the distance is not more than half the total number of occurrences, the decoder assumes a soft error and discards all information collected during the minute. The *decoding distance* is defined as the sum of the distances over the first nine digits; the tenth digit varies over the seconds and is uncounted.

The result of the majority decoder is a nine-digit timecode representing the maximum likelihood candidate for the transmitted timecode in that minute. Note that the second and fraction within the minute are always zero and that the actual reference point to calculate timestamp offsets is backdated to the first second of the minute. At this point, the timecode block is reformatted and the year, days, hours, and minutes extracted along with other information from the format B burst, including DST state, DUT1 correction, and leap warning. The reformatting operation checks the timecode for invalid code combinations that might have been left by the majority decoder and rejects the entire timecode if found.

If the timecode is valid, it is passed to the driver interface along with the backdated timestamps accumulated over the minute. A perfect set of eight bursts could generate as many as 80 timestamps, but the maximum the interface can handle is 60. These are processed using the core algorithms, so the resulting system clock correction is usually much better than would otherwise be the case with radio noise, UART jitter, and occasional burst errors.

References

1. Mogul, J., D. Mills, J. Brittenson, J. Stone, and U. Windl. *Pulse-per-Second API for Unix-like Operating Systems, Version 1*. Request for Comments RFC-2783, Internet Engineering Task Force, March 2000, 31 pp.
2. *IRIG Standard 200-98 IRIG Serial Timecode Formats*. Range Commanders Council, Telecommunications and Timing Group, May 1998, 52 pp.
3. Mills, D.L. *A Precision Radio Clock for WWV Transmissions*. Electrical Engineering Report 97-8-1, University of Delaware, Newark, August 1997, 25 pp.

8

Kernel Timekeeping Support

"Or else it doesn't you know. The name of the song is called 'Haddocks' Eyes'." [the Knight said]

"Oh, that's the name of the song, is it?" Alice said, trying to look interested.

"No, you don't understand," the Knight said, looking a little vexed. That's what the name is called. The name really is 'The Aged Aged Man'."

"Then I ought to have said 'That's what the song is called'?" Alice corrected herself.

"No, you oughtn't; that's quite another thing!" The song is called 'Ways and Means'; but that's only what it's called, you know!"

"Well, what is the song, then?" said Alice, who was by this time completely bewildered.

"I was coming to that," the Knight said. "The song really is 'A-Sitting On A Gate'; and the tune's my own invention."

Lewis Carroll
Through the Looking Glass

This chapter discusses generic Unix kernel modifications designed to improve the system clock accuracy ultimately to the order of nanoseconds when a sufficiently accurate reference clock is available. Relative to a previous version described in Mills [1], it provides about 10 times smaller time and frequency errors and 1,000 times better time resolution. The modifications include a set of subroutines to be incorporated in the Unix kernels of various architectures, including Digital (RISC, Alpha), Hewlett Packard (Alpha and PA2), Sun Microsystems (SPARC, UltraSPARC), and Intel (x386, Pentium). The new design has been implemented for testing in Tru64 5.1 and SunOS 4.1.3 and is a standard feature of current FreeBSD and an add-on feature of current Linux.

The primary purpose of the modifications, called the *kernel discipline*, is to improve timekeeping accuracy to the order less than 1 µs and ultimately to 1 ns. The kernel discipline replaces the daemon discipline described in Chapter 4 with equivalent functionality in the kernel. While clock corrections are executed once per second in the NTP discipline, they are executed at every tick interrupt in the kernel discipline. This avoids sawtooth errors that accumulate between daemon executions. The greatest benefit is when the clock oscillator frequency error is large (above 100 PPM) and when the NTP subnet path to the reference clock includes only servers with these modifications. However, in cases involving long Internet paths and congested paths with large network jitter, when the interval between synchronization updates is large (greater than 1,024 s), or when the step threshold is large (greater than 0.5 s), the benefits are reduced. The primary reason for the reduction is that the errors inherent in the time measurement process greatly exceed those inherent in the discipline algorithm, whether implemented in the daemon or the kernel.

The kernel software described in this chapter is suitable for 64-bit machines, in which some variables occupy the full 64-bit word, or for 32-bit machines, in which these variables are implemented using a macro package for double-precision arithmetic. Following current kernel implementation practices, floating point arithmetic is forbidden and multiply/divide instructions minimized. If possible, multiply/divide operations are replaced by shifts.

The software is suitable for kernels where the time variable is represented in seconds and nanoseconds and for kernels in which this variable is represented in seconds and microseconds. In either case, and when the requisite hardware supports are available, the system clock resolution is to the nanosecond. Even if the resolution of the hardware clock is only to the microsecond, the software provides extensive signal grooming and averaging to minimize reading and round-off errors.

The extremely intricate nature of the kernel modifications requires a high level of rigor in the design and implementation. Following current practice, the routines have been embedded in a special-purpose, discrete event simulator. In this context, it is possible not only to verify correct operation over the wide range of tolerances likely to be found in current and future computer architectures and operating systems but also to verify that resolution and accuracy specifications can be met with precision synchronization sources. The simulator can measure the response to time and frequency transients, monitor for unexpected interactions between the clock oscillator and pulse-per-second (PPS) signal, and verify correct monotonic behavior as the oscillator counters overflow and underflow due to small time and frequency variations. The simulator can also read data files produced during regular operation to determine the behavior of the modifications under actual conditions.

It is important to note that the actual code used in the kernel discipline is nearly identical to the code used in the simulator. The only differences in fact have to do with the particular calling and argument passing conventions of each system. This is important to preserve correctness assertions, accuracy claims, and performance evaluation.

The kernel discipline can adjust the system clock in nanoseconds in time and nanoseconds per second in frequency, regardless of the timer tick increment. The NTP daemon itself includes an extensive suite of data-grooming algorithms that filter, select, cluster, and combine time values before presenting them to either the daemon or the kernel discipline. At each processing step in both the kernel and NTP daemon, limit clamps are imposed to avoid overflow and prevent runaway time or frequency excursions. In particular, the kernel response is clamped over a time and frequency range consistent with NTP correctness principles. In addition, the PPS offset is clamped over a narrow time and frequency range to resolve ambiguity and suppress signal noise.

The kernel design supports symmetric multiple processor (SMP) systems with common or separate processor clocks of the same or different frequencies. The system clock can be read by any processor at any time without compromising monotonicity or jitter. When a PPS signal is connected, the PPS interrupt can be vectored to any processor. The tick interrupt must always be vectored to a single processor, but it does not matter which one.

The chapter begins with an architecture overview of the kernel algorithms and the principles of operation. The chapter continues with analysis and modeling of the disciplined clock and concludes with a proof-of-performance assessment using the actual kernel implementations for selected hardware and software operating systems.

8.1 System Clock Reading Algorithm

The ubiquitous Unix kernel implements the system clock as a 64-bit logical clock that increments at each hardware interrupt or tick. The frequency is disciplined by increasing or decreasing the tick by some value producing a slew of 500 PPM and then computing the number of ticks to continue the slew to complete the requested adjustment. Where available, an auxiliary counter called the processor cycle counter (PCC) is used to interpolate between tick interrupts. For multiprocessor systems, the increment and interpolate functions are protected as an atomic operation by any of several techniques.

For a truly precise nanosecond clock, the discipline algorithm must maintain time to within 1 ns and frequency within 1 ns per second and do this in both single and multiprocessor systems. In multiprocessor systems, the PCC used to interpolate between tick interrupts might be integrated with the processor and might run at a slightly different frequency in each. Finally, it is usually assumed that a system call to read the clock might be serviced by different processors on successive calls. Obviously, the Unix model described is not up to this level of performance.

It is tempting to adopt a simplistic approach that returns the system time as the sum of the PCC scaled to nanoseconds plus a logical clock value updated at the beginning of each second. However, this results in small errors as the PCCs, logical clock, and tick interrupt are not syntonic. In fact, there are $n + 1$ clocks, where n is the number of processors, so the herd is more properly described as wrangled rather than disciplined.

In the design described here, each processor is associated with a set of state variables used to discipline its PCC time and frequency with respect to one of the processors arbitrarily designated the master. The PCC values are scaled to nanoseconds (1 GHz), called the *nanosecond counter*, by means described in this chapter. At intervals of about 1 s, but at staggered tick interrupts, the master saves its nanosecond counter in a global variable and interrupts each processor in round-robin fashion. When a processor is interrupted, it computes the logical time and number of nanoseconds since the last inter-rupt, then saves the current logical time and nanosecond counter for the next interrupt in its state variables. It also saves a correction factor computed as the master nanosecond counter less the processor nanosecond counter for use later.

The ratio of the logical time difference to the nanoseconds difference since the last interrupt represents the scaling factor used to produce the nanosecond counter for each processor. This is used by the clock read rou-tine to interpolate within the second. However, both the numerator and denominator must be saved separately and used in a multiply/divide oper-ation both to preserve resolution and to support PCC frequencies below and above 1 GHz. As each processor services a request to read the clock, it adds the correction factor to be consistent with the master processor nano-second counter.

Put another way, each processor measures the rate of its nanosecond counter and offset from the master nanosecond counter in 1 s as a predictor for the next. However, the devil is in the details. Consider the diagram in Figure 8.1 (not to scale), where the staircase *ABC* represents the logical clock as it increments by a fixed value Δ at each tick. The dark rectangles represent the additional clock adjustment δ determined by the discipline algorithm, which can range to 5 μs for a 100-Hz clock. The nanosecond counter is rep-resented by the trace *XYZ*. Due to little wiggles δ in the discipline process or slight errors in the nanosecond counter rate, the nanosecond counter value

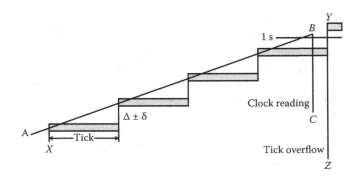

FIGURE 8.1
Logical clock and nanosecond counter.

at a tick interrupt might not coincide with the adjusted tick value. If less than the adjusted tick value, the counter is increased to that value. Near the end of a tick interval, the counter can exceed the projected tick value, so it is clamped to that value until the next tick interrupt.

Note the behavior at the end of the second where the logical clock and nanosecond counter overflow the second. When this happens, 1 s in nanoseconds is subtracted from the current value in the nanosecond field of the time value, and 1 s is added to the seconds field. As the result of normal operation, the rollover *BC* of the nanosecond counter precesses around the rollover *YZ* of the logical clock. Finally, note that the overflow of the nanosecond counter is detected only when the clock is read, so the clock must be read at least once per second. This is ensured since the clock is read during the processor interrupt described previously.

Under some conditions, such as during a large frequency correction, the time may appear to run backward, which would be a violation of the happens-before principle. The design ensures that the clock reading is always monotone, increasing by rounding up the value to at least 1 ns greater than the last reading. An exception allows the clock to be adjusted backward if the adjustment is 1 s or more. With the NTP daemon, this would happen only if the clock was stepped, and in that case only if the step was greater than 1 s.

8.2 Kernel Discipline Algorithms

Figure 8.2 shows the general organization of the kernel discipline algorithm. Updates produced by the NTP daemon are provided at intervals ranging from 16 to 1,024 s. When available, PPS updates are produced as the result of PPS signal transitions on an input/output (I/O) pin at intervals of 1 s. The phase and frequency predictions computed by either or both updates

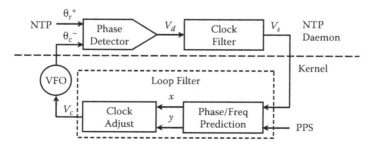

FIGURE 8.2
Kernel discipline algorithm.

are selected by the kernel application program interface (API) and NTP daemon. The system clock corrections are redetermined at the end of each second and new phase adjustments x and frequency adjustments y determined. The clock adjust routine amortizes these adjustments over the next second at each hardware tick interrupt. The adjustment increment is calculated using extended precision arithmetic to preserve nanosecond resolution and avoid overflows over the range of tick frequencies from below 50 Hz to above 1,000 Hz.

As in the NTP discipline, the kernel discipline operates as a hybrid of phase-locked (PLL) and frequency-locked (FLL) feedback loops. As shown in the figure, the phase difference V_d between the reference clock θ_r and system clock θ_c is determined by the synchronization protocol to produce a raw offset and delay measurement. These values are then groomed by the mitigation algorithms as described in Chapter 3 and then passed to the discipline algorithm described in Chapter 4. If the kernel discipline is enabled, the system clock is not disciplined by the NTP daemon but is passed to the kernel discipline instead. However, the clock state machine remains operative and in effect shields the kernel discipline from adjustments greater than the step threshold, usually 128 ms. The offset update V_s passed to the kernel is processed by the prediction filters to produce the phase prediction x and frequency prediction y. Once each second, these predictions are scaled and amortized at each tick interrupt during the second to produce a correction term V_c. This value adjusts the clock oscillator frequency so that the clock displays the correct time.

The kernel discipline includes two separate but interlocking feedback loops. The PLL/FLL discipline operates with updates produced by the NTP daemon, while the PPS discipline operates with an external PPS signal and modified serial or parallel port driver. The heart of the kernel discipline is the prediction filters shown in Figure 8.3. Each delivers phase and frequency adjustments once each second. The switch shown in the figure is controlled by the application program, in this case the NTP daemon. If PPSFREQ is lit, the frequency adjustment is determined by the PPS discipline; otherwise, it is determined by the PLL/FLL discipline. If PPSTIME is

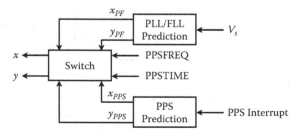

FIGURE 8.3
Kernel loop filter.

lit, the phase adjustment is determined by the PPS discipline; otherwise, it is determined by the PLL/FLL discipline. Strategies for manipulating these bits are described in this chapter.

8.3 Kernel PLL/FLL Discipline

The PLL/FLL discipline is similar to the discipline algorithm described in Chapter 4, which is specially tailored for typical network jitter and oscillator wander. However, the kernel discipline provides better accuracy and stability than the NTP discipline as well as a more precise adjustment. The x_{PF} and y_{PF} predictions are developed from the phase update V_s shown in Figure 8.4. As in the NTP algorithm, the phase and frequency are disciplined separately in PLL and FLL modes. In both modes, x_{PF} starts at the value V_s and then decays exponentially in the same fashion as the NTP discipline. However, the actual phase adjustment decays at each tick interrupt rather than 1-s intervals as in the NTP discipline. The kernel parameters are scaled such that, using the time constant determined by the NTP discipline, the kernel discipline response is identical to the NTP discipline response.

The frequency is disciplined quite differently in PLL and FLL modes. In PLL mode, y_{PLL} is computed using a type II feedback loop, as described in Chapter 4. In PLL mode, y_{FLL} is computed directly using an exponential average of offset differences with weight 0.25. This value, which was determined from simulation with real and synthetic data, is a compromise between rapid frequency adaptation and adequate glitch suppression.

Either the PLL or the FLL mode can be selected by a switch controlled by the NTP daemon. As described in Chapter 12, extensive experience with simulation and practice has developed reliable models for timekeeping in

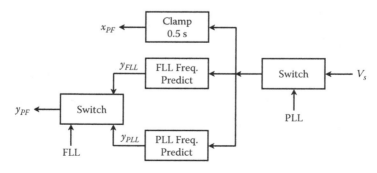

FIGURE 8.4
PLL/FLL discipline.

the typical Internet and workstation environment. At relatively small update intervals, white-phase noise dominates the error budget, and the PLL discipline performs best. At relatively large update intervals, random-walk frequency noise dominates, and the FLL discipline performs best. The optimum crossover point between the PLL and FLL disciplines, as determined by simulation and analysis, is the Allan intercept discussed in Chapter 12. In the current design, the PLL discipline is selected with poll intervals less than 256 s and in FLL mode for intervals greater than 2,048 s. Between these two extremes, the discipline can be selected by the NTP daemon using the FLL switch. This design is not as sophisticated as the NTP discipline, which uses a gradual transition between PLL mode and FLL mode.

Notwithstanding this careful design, there are diminishing returns when operating at update intervals of 1,024 s and larger since the errors introduced by oscillator wander almost always exceed the sawtooth errors. In addition, the Allan intercept is often greater than 2,048 s. In spite of the careful attention to detail here, future designs will probably not include the FLL discipline.

8.4 Kernel PPS Discipline

PPS signals produced by an external source can be interfaced to the kernel using a serial or parallel port and modified port driver. The on-time signal transitions cause a driver interrupt, which in turn calls the PPS discipline, which is functionally separate from the PLL/FLL discipline. The two disciplines have interlocking control functions designed to provide seamless switching between them when either the synchronization daemon fails to provide NTP updates or the PPS signal fails or operates outside nominal tolerances.

The PPS discipline shown in Figure 8.5 is called at each PPS on-time signal transition. The latches capture the system clock time and nanosecond counter

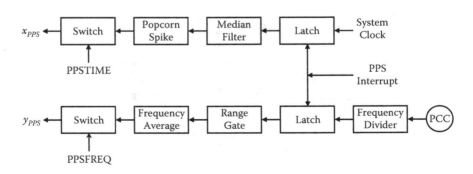

FIGURE 8.5
PPS discipline.

at the on-time epoch. The nanosecond counter can be implemented using the PCC in modern computer architectures or the application-specific integrated circuit (ASIC) counter in older architectures. In either case, the actual counter frequency is scaled to 1 GHz (nanoseconds). The intent of the design is to discipline the clock phase using the timestamp and to discipline the clock frequency using the nanosecond counter. This makes it possible, for example, to stabilize the system clock frequency using a precision PPS source, such as a cesium or rubidium oscillator, while using an external time source, such as a reference clock or even another time server, to discipline the phase. With frequency reliably disciplined, the interval between updates from the external source can be greatly increased. Also, should the external source fail, the system clock will continue to provide accurate time limited only by the accuracy of the precision PPS source.

The range gate is designed to reject noise and improper signal format. It rejects noise interrupts less than 0.999500 s since the previous interrupt and frequency deviations are more than 500 PPM relative to the system clock. The counter samples are processed by an ambiguity resolver that corrects for counter rollover and anomalies when a tick interrupt occurs in the vicinity of the second rollover or when the PPS interrupt occurs while processing a tick interrupt. The latter appears to be a feature of at least some Unix kernels, which rank the serial port interrupt priority above the tick interrupt priority.

PPS signals are vulnerable to large spikes when connecting cables pick up electrical transients due to light switches, air conditioners, and water pumps, for example. These turn out to be the principle hazard to PPS synchronization performance. To reduce jitter, the system timestamps are processed by a three-stage shift register operating as a median filter. The median value of these samples is the phase estimate, and the maximum difference between them is the jitter estimate. The kernel jitter statistic is computed as the exponential average of these estimates with weight 0.25 and is reported in the kernel API. A popcorn spike suppressor rejects phase outliers with amplitude greater than four times the jitter statistic. This value, as well as the jitter-averaging weight, was determined by simulation with real and synthetic PPS signals.

The PPS frequency y_{PPS} is computed as the exponential average of the nanosecond counter difference between the beginning and end of the calibration interval. When the system is first started, the clock oscillator frequency error can be quite large, in some cases 100 PPM or more. To avoid ambiguities throughout the performance envelope, the counter differences must not exceed the tick interval, which can be less than a millisecond for some systems. Therefore, the calibration interval starts at 4 s to ensure that the frequency estimate remains valid for frequency errors up to 250 PPM with a 1-ms tick interval. Gradually, as the frequency estimate improves, the calibration interval increases to a target of 256 s or more, as specified by the kernel API.

The actual PPS frequency is calculated by dividing the counter difference by the calibration interval. To avoid integer divide instructions, which in some systems are implemented in software, and intricate residuals management, the length is always a power of 2 so that division reduces to a shift. However, if due to signal dropouts or noise spikes this is not the case, the adjustment is avoided, and a new calibration interval is started. The oscillator wander statistic is calculated as the exponential average of frequency adjustments with weight 0.25 and reported along with error counters to the kernel API.

It is important at this point to observe that the PPS frequency determination is independent of any other means to discipline the system clock frequency and operates continuously, even if the system clock is being disciplined by the NTP daemon or PLL/FLL algorithm. The intended control strategy is to initialize the PPS discipline state variables, including PPS frequency, median filter, and related values during the interval the synchronization daemon is grooming the initial protocol values to set the clock. When the NTP daemon recognizes from the kernel API that the PPS frequency has settled down, it switches the clock frequency discipline to the PPS signal but continues to discipline the clock phase with either the NTP discipline or the kernel PLL/ FLL discipline. When the phase offset is reduced well below 0.5 s, to ensure unambiguous seconds numbering, the daemon switches the clock phase discipline to the PPS signal. Should the synchronization source or daemon malfunction, the PPS signal continues to discipline the clock phase and frequency until the malfunction has been corrected.

8.5 Clock Adjust Algorithm

Figure 8.6 shows how the x and y predictions are used to discipline the system clock and interpolate between tick interrupts. In this example for the Digital Alpha, the system clock runs at 1,024 Hz, creating a tick interrupt for every cycle. The tick interrupt advances the phase φ by the value z, which was calculated at the last second rollover, and reduces the value of x by the same amount. When the accumulated phase exceeds 1 s in nanoseconds, the phase is reduced by 1 s in nanoseconds and a new value of z computed as the sum of the x and y predictions divided by the frequency in hertz. These operations are similar to the clock adjust process in the NTP discipline but scaled to match the tick interval.

While the operations described here are straightforward, the implementation is complicated by overflow and precision issues, and the adjustment quantities can be very tiny. For instance, a 1-PPM frequency offset results in a z adjustment of about 1 ns, and every nanosecond must be carefully taken into account. Also, at 1,024 Hz the tick interval does not divide the second, so the second overflow precesses the actual second over a 1,024-s cycle.

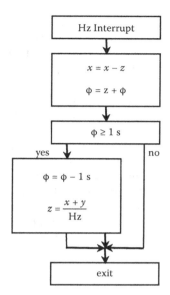

FIGURE 8.6
Tick interrupt.

8.6 Proof of Performance

In this section, the performance of the kernel discipline is assessed with a set of experiments designed to measure time and frequency errors and associated statistics. There were three computer systems involved: (1) Sun Microsystems UltraSPARC 5_10 running Solaris 10 (Pogo), (2) Pentium II 200 MHz running FreeBSD 5.3 (Rackety), and (3) Hewlett-Packard Alphastation 433au running Tru64 5.1 (Churchy). Pogo and Churchy function as moderately busy NTP time servers for the campus and public at large. Rackety is dedicated to NTP service with well over 700 clients in the public Internet. Pogo is an NTP server for the entire campus as well as an NFS and NIS server for a modest collection of laboratory clients used by students and faculty. Both machines are connected to dual-redundant GPS receivers via a PPS signal—Rackety via a parallel port ACK (acknowledge) pin and Pogo and Churchy via a serial port data carrier detect (DCD) pin. All three machines have the PPSAPI interface, and all support the kernel discipline described in this chapter. Rackety and Churchy have the latest version supporting full-nanosecond resolution; Pogo uses an older version capable only of microsecond resolution. Other than this fact, all three disciplines behave in the same way.

The PPSAPI interface operates near the highest hardware priority. At a selected PPS signal pulse edge, it captures a timestamp from the system clock and saves it and a serial number in a kernel structure. An application program can read the latest values using an operating system call. Alternatively or at the same time, the timestamp and associated nanosecond counter can be passed directly to the kernel PPS discipline. This design avoids latencies in device management, processor scheduling, memory management, and the application program itself.

Rackety and Pogo are connected to the GPS receivers with specified accuracy of 130 ns at the PPS output. Churchy is connected to a cesium oscillator calibrated to the GPS receivers with comparable accuracy. From previous experiments, the ACK and DCD signal jitter is expected to be about 1–2 μs and the interrupt latency generally less than 5 μs in Rackety and less than 1 μs in Pogo and Churchy. Other sources of error are identified as the discussion continues. It is important to understand that the true time and frequency offsets of the system clock relative to the PPS signal cannot be measured directly; however, the kernel jitter and oscillator wander can be measured and bounds determined for the time and frequency offsets.

8.7 Kernel PLL/FLL Discipline Performance

There are two experimental configurations used in this chapter. The first was designed to evaluate the PLL/FLL discipline performance using the configuration shown in Figure 8.7. The other configuration is described in the next section. PPS signals from the GPS receiver are processed by the PPSAPI interface and delivered to the PPS driver, a component of the NTP daemon. Once each second, the driver reads the PPSAPI timestamp and shifts this value into a 15-stage shift register used as a median filter. At intervals of 15 s, the shift register is copied to a temporary list and the results sorted. Then, the first and last third of the sorted list are discarded and the remainder averaged to obtain a filtered offset value for the NTP mitigation algorithms. This removes most high-frequency noise and "grass" typical of the PPSAPI interface.

The PPS driver does not provide the seconds portion of the timestamp, only the fraction within the second. The seconds portion is normally provided by another driver synchronized to a radio, satellite, or telephone source. When the NTP daemon is first started, it synchronizes to one of these sources in

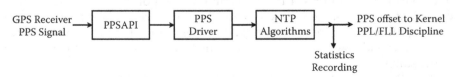

FIGURE 8.7
Experimental setup.

the ordinary way using the NTP mitigation algorithms and either the NTP or kernel discipline. When the PPS signal is present and the system clock offset is within 0.5 s of the correct time, the PPS driver assumes sole control of the discipline algorithm. The filtered offset is passed to the kernel discipline and the statistics monitoring function, which records each update in a data file for offline processing. Note that, while the clock filter, select, cluster, and combine algorithms are all active, the mitigation rules result that only the PPS driver data are used and unaffected by other drivers and servers that might be included in the NTP configuration. Data were collected in this way for several experiments lasting from a day to 2 months using both Pogo and Rackety.

The first set of experiments is designed to establish a baseline time and frequency error statistics typical of a multiapplication server. Figure 8.8 shows the offsets measured by Pogo over a typical week (168 h). Note that the measurements are made at point V_s on Figure 8.2 and, while useful for comparison purposes, do not represent the actual clock accuracy statistic represented at point V_c. For later comparison, the mean offset is 0.14 µs, which suggests this as the long-term systematic offset error. In general, this is not a useful statistic, and the maximum error 47 µs and standard deviation 18 µs may be more revealing. The standard deviation is rather higher than expected, probably influenced by the spikes.

There are two interesting features shown in the figure, including an apparent diurnal wiggle over the 7 days and the effect of infrequent, relatively large spikes. It is difficult to explain the nominal 5-µs diurnal variations; they could be due to small fluctuations in room temperature or main voltage over the day. The spikes, although relatively infrequent, ranged from 20 to 30 µs and one near the center of the figure to over 40 µs. Figure 8.9 is an expanded

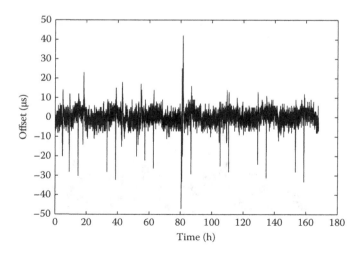

FIGURE 8.8
Kernel time offset.

view of this spike over a 2.5-h interval; the figure shows that the spike is more properly a series of surges lasting well beyond the 15-stage median filter aperture that reduces only the high-frequency noise. The fact that this surge happened only once in the 2-month experiment run from which this week was extracted suggests that something violent, like a temporary loss of satellite signals, was involved.

Figure 8.10 shows the peer jitter measured by the clock filter algorithm during the week. The mean value of this characteristic is 1.6 μs, somewhat lower

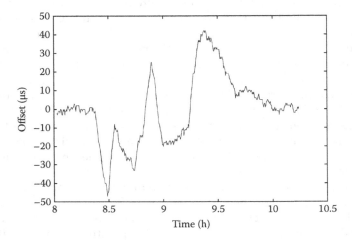

FIGURE 8.9
Kernel expanded time offset.

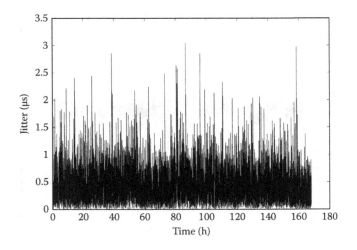

FIGURE 8.10
Kernel time jitter.

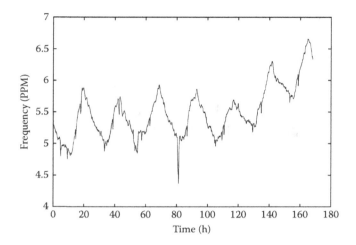

FIGURE 8.11
Kernel frequency offset.

than the standard deviation of the offset data itself but still a good predictor of expected error. The fact that the peer jitter is relatively small compared to the spikes shown in Figure 8.8 suggests that the spikes, like the one shown in Figure 8.9, are rare and rather more characterized as surges; as such, they are not readily removed by the median filter in the driver or popcorn spike suppressor in the clock filter algorithm.

Figure 8.11 shows the measured frequency during the week. The diurnal variation is clearly evident, suggesting that the offset variation is indeed due to frequency variation. Pogo is located in an air-conditioned machine room and ordinarily uninhabited. As the temperature coefficient of a typical uncompensated quartz oscillator is about 1 PPM per degree celsius, the machine room temperature would have to vary about 1 degree over the day to account for the frequency variation. Note the glitch near hour 80, which corresponds to the spike noted in Figure 8.9.

Figure 8.12 shows the oscillator wander computed as the exponential average of root-mean-square (RMS) frequency differences during the week. The mean value 0.0036 PPM of this characteristic can be a useful quality metric for the system clock oscillator. The fact that the apparent spikes shown in the figure correspond closely to the spikes shown in Figure 8.9 suggests that the causative disturbance was indeed frequency surges. Note especially the spike near hour 80, which corresponds to the spike shown in Figure 8.9.

All things considered, the statistical characterization of the kernel discipline algorithm in this experiment is best evaluated in Figure 8.13, which shows the cumulative distribution function of the absolute offset data. From the figure, 50 percent of the samples had error less than 11 µs, 90 percent less than 33 µs,

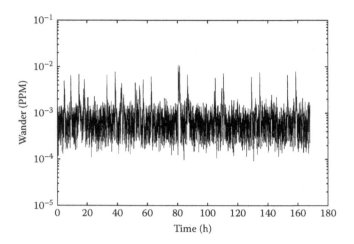

FIGURE 8.12
Kernel oscillator wander.

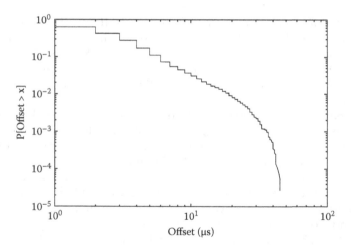

FIGURE 8.13
Kernel time offset CDF.

and all less than 47 µs. Additional insight can be gained from Figure 8.14, which shows the autocorrelation function of the offset data from Figure 8.8.

An interesting conclusion evident from these graphs is that the disruptions, small as they may be, were not affected by high-frequency spikes, which have been removed by the various filters in the NTP mitigation algorithms. On the other hand, low-frequency surges are due to oscillator flicker (1/f) noise, which is common in unstabilized quartz oscillators. The autocorrelation function shows very low dependency for lags greater than

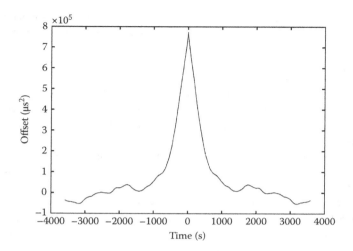

FIGURE 8.14
Kernel time offset autocorrelation function.

1,000 s, which would be expected with a time constant of about the same value. The inescapable conclusion is that, for performance in the submicrosecond region, something better than an ordinary computer clock oscillator is necessary. Even without them, performance in the low microseconds can be expected most of the time.

There are several observations that can be made as the result of these experiments using Pogo and Rackety with the PLL/FLL discipline. The first is that, under typical conditions, offset variations on the order of a few microseconds can be expected with typical Unix kernels, but occasional spikes of tens of microseconds must be expected with modern computers and up to a millisecond with older ones. Second, as far as precision timekeeping is concerned, system clock resolution better than 1 μs is probably not a showstopper. Third, while the NTP mitigation algorithms are quite effective in suppressing high-frequency noise, the dominant characteristic appears to be low-frequency flicker (1/f) noise.

8.8 Kernel PPS Discipline

All the performance data described to this point relate to the kernel PLL/FLL discipline; we now turn to the PPS discipline. Performance data were collected using a Digital Alphastation 433au running the Tru64 5.1 operating system over a typical day. The PPS signal from a cesium oscillator was connected via the DCD pin and a serial port. The PPSAPI interface was used but was connected directly to the PPS discipline as shown in Figure 8.2. Data were collected at approximately 2-s intervals.

It is important to note that, in contrast to the PLL/FLL discipline in which the measurement point is at the phase detector V_s in Figure 8.2, the measurement point for the PPS discipline is at the variable-frequency oscillator (VFO) point V_c. There is a subtle reason for this choice. The V_s samples represent the raw time series offset data but not the actual VFO adjustments, which are attenuated by the loop filter. The loop filter has an inherent low-pass characteristic dependent on the time constant, which itself depends on the poll interval. At the poll interval of 16 s used in the experiment, the raw offsets were reduced by at least an order of magnitude. Thus, the V_c time series represents the actual error inherent in the discipline algorithm.

Figure 8.15 shows the time offset for Churchy over a typical day. The mean kernel offset was −754 ns, absolute maximum 371 ns, and standard deviation 53 ns. The mean kernel jitter was 353 ns and mean oscillator wander 0.0013 PPM. To the trained eye, the data look more regular than the PLL/FLL discipline, and the diurnal variation is not apparent. Churchy is in a small laboratory and may not be subject to diurnal temperature variations. The PPS discipline peaks shown at the V_s point in Figure 8.15 are generally in the range 100–300 ns, while the PLL/FLL discipline showed peaks at the V_c point in Figure 8.8 are in the range 20–30 µs.

Figure 8.16 shows the frequency offset over the same day. The characteristic has rather more high-frequency noise compared with the PLL/FLL discipline shown in Figure 8.11. This is due to the frequency calculation used in the PPS discipline, which computes the frequency directly from

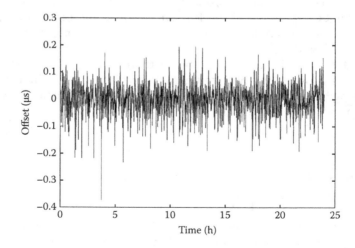

FIGURE 8.15
Kernel PPS time offsets.

offset differences over fixed 256-s intervals rather than as an exponential average with a relatively long time constant. Note that a diurnal frequency variation is not apparent, but there is a noticeable low-frequency flicker noise component.

These statistical effects are summarized in Figure 8.17, which shows the cumulative distribution function of the PPS discipline loop. The cumulative statistics show 50 percent of the samples within 32 ns, 90 percent within

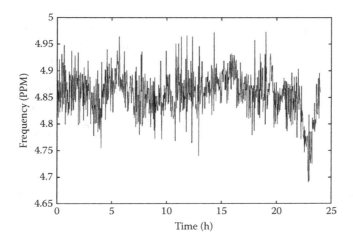

FIGURE 8.16
Kernel PPS frequency offset.

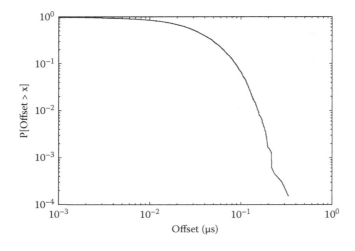

FIGURE 8.17
Kernel PPS time offset CDF.

89 ns, and all within 370 ns. The bottom line is that a fast modern machine can keep the system clock to better than 300 ns relative to a good PPS source and in the same order as the GPS source itself.

8.9 Parting Shots

The kernel discipline code, especially the most recent version, is probably the most intricate in the NTP algorithm suite, mainly because of the tiny residuals resulting from the wandering herd of multiple oscillators, including the tick interrupt and PCC oscillators. The problem is especially acute in SMP systems with per-processor tick interrupt and PCC oscillators likely to be found in highly reliable duplexed processors. Multiple-CPU IBM mainframes use a single timing signal generated by an expensive wrangler, the 9037–2 Sysplex Timer, but this costs over $100,000 and does not even speak NTP.

References

1. Mills, D.L. *Unix Kernel Modifications for Precision Time Synchronization.* Electrical Engineering Department Report 94-10-1, University of Delaware, Newark, October 1994, 24 pp.

Further Reading

Mills, D.L. Adaptive hybrid clock discipline algorithm for the Network Time Protocol. *IEEE/ACM Trans. Networking 6, 5* (October 1998), 505–514.

Mills, D.L. *Network Time Protocol (Version 3) Specification, Implementation and Analysis.* Network Working Group Report RFC-1305, University of Delaware, Newark, March 1992, 113 pp.

9

Cryptographic Authentication

One of the most salient features in our culture is that there is so much bullshit. Everyone knows this. Each of us contributes his share. But we tend to take the situation for granted. Most people are rather confident of their ability to recognize bullshit and to avoid being taken in by it. So the phenomenon has not aroused much deliberate concern, nor attracted much sustained inquiry.

H. G. Frankurt
On Bullshit (Princeton University Press, 2005)

A distributed network service requires authentic, ubiquitous, and survivable provisions to prevent accidental or malicious attacks on the secondary servers and clients in the network or the values they exchange. *Authentic* means that clients can determine whether received packets are authentic; that is, they were actually sent by the intended server and not manufactured or modified by an intruder. *Ubiquitous* means that any client can verify the authenticity of any server using public credentials augmented by a private identification scheme, if necessary. *Survivable* means protection from lost, misordered, or duplicate packets and protocol errors these might provoke. These requirements are especially stringent with widely distributed, public network services like the NTP since damage due to failures and intrusions can propagate quickly throughout the network, devastating archives, databases, and monitoring systems and even bring down major portions of the network.

Over the last decade, the Internet Engineering Task Force (IETF) has defined and evolved the IPSEC infrastructure for privacy protection and source authentication in the Internet. The infrastructure includes the Encapsulating Security Payload (ESP) [1] and Authentication Header (AH) [2] for the Internet Protocol Version 4 (IPv4) and Version 6 (IPv6), as well as cryptographic algorithms such as MD5 and SHA message digests, RSA and DSA digital signature, and several variations of DH key agreement. However, as demonstrated in the reports and briefings cited in the references at the end of this chapter, none of these schemes alone satisfies the requirements of the NTP security model. The various key agreement schemes [3–5] proposed by the IETF require per-association state variables, which contradicts the principles of the remote procedure call (RPC) paradigm in which servers keep no state for a possibly large client population. An evaluation of the PKI model and algorithms as implemented in the OpenSSL library leads to the conclusion that any scheme requiring every NTP packet to carry a PKI digital signature would result in unacceptably poor timekeeping performance.

A digital signature scheme using public certificates and a certificate trail provides secure server authentication, but it does not provide protection against masquerade unless the server identity is verified by other means. The PKI security model assumes each client is able to verify the certificate trail to a root certificate authority (CA) [6,7] by which each client must prove identity to a server by independent means before the server will sign the client certificate and forge the next link on the trail. While the NTP security model uses a certificate trail by default, any server along the trail will sign a client certificate on request and without proof; however, a separate identity scheme is used to prove authenticity with respect to a trusted host (TH) acting as a root CA.

The security model and protocol described in this chapter and the identity schemes described in Chapter 10 might seem at first as really heavy machinery in view of the lightweight nature of the NTP protocol itself. The fact is that NTP is sometimes required to thrive in Internet deserts, tundra, and rainforests where accidental tourists bumble and skilled terrorists plot. The schemes are intended for hardball scenarios with national time dissemination services and as the basis for secure timestamping services. Having made this point, please note that security features are not a necessary component of the NTP protocol specification, and some implementers may choose to cheerfully ignore this chapter.

The cryptographic means in NTP Version 4 (NTPv4) are based on the OpenSSL cryptographic software library available at http://www.openssl. org, but other libraries with equivalent functionality could be used as well. It is important for distribution and export purposes that the way in which these algorithms are used precludes encryption of any data other than incidental to the operation of the authentication function. With this caveat, NTP without OpenSSL can be exported and reexported anywhere in the world.

9.1 NTP Security Model

The current and previous reference implementations of NTP include provisions to cryptographically authenticate individual servers using symmetric key cryptography, as described in the most recent protocol NTPv3 specification [8]. However, that specification does not provide a security model to bound the extents of a cryptographic compartment or provide for the exchange of cryptographic media that reliably bind the host identification credentials to the associated private keys and related public values.

NTP security requirements are even more stringent than most other distributed services. First, the operation of the authentication mechanism and the time synchronization mechanism are inextricably intertwined. Reliable time synchronization requires certificates that are valid only over designated time intervals, but time intervals can be enforced only when participating servers and clients are reliably synchronized to UTC. Second, the NTP subnet is hierarchical by nature, so time and trust flow from the primary servers at the root through secondary servers to the clients at the leaves. Typical clients use multiple redundant servers and diverse network paths for reliability and intruder detection. Third, trust is not universal, and there may be multiple interlocking security groups, each with distinct security policies and procedures.

The NTP security model assumes the possible limitations listed next. Further discussion is in Mills [9] and in the briefings at the NTP project page but is beyond the scope of this chapter.

- The running times for public key algorithms are relatively long and highly variable. In general, the performance of the time synchronization function is badly degraded if these algorithms must be used for every NTP packet.

- In some NTP modes of operation, it is not feasible for a server to retain state variables for every client. It is, however, feasible to regenerate them for a client on arrival of a packet from that client.

- The lifetime of cryptographic values must be strictly enforced, which requires a reliable system clock. However, the sources that synchronize the system clock must be cryptographically authenticated. This interdependence of the timekeeping and authentication functions requires special handling.

- The only encrypted data sent over the net are digital signatures and cookies. The NTP payload, including the entire contents of the header and extension fields, is never encrypted.

- Cryptographic media involving private values, such as host, sign, and group keys, are ordinarily generated only by the host that uses them. Media derived from these values, such as certificates, are ordinarily generated only by the host with the associated private values. This is to ensure that private values are never disclosed to other hosts by any means. The only exception is when a trusted agent is involved and secure means are available to disseminate private values to other hosts in the same secure group.

- Public certificates must be retrievable directly from servers without necessarily involving DNS (domain name system) services or resources outside the secure group.

9.1.1 On the Provenance of Filestamps

A fundamental requirement of the NTP security model is that a host can claim authentic to dependent applications only if all servers on the path to the trusted primary servers are bona fide authentic. Note that the path in this case applies only to the servers along the path; the network links and routers themselves play no part in the security model. To emphasize this requirement, in this chapter the notion of authentic is replaced by *proventic*, a noun new to English and derived from provenance, as in the provenance of a painting. Having abused the language this far, the suffixes fixable to the various noun and verb derivatives of authentic are adopted for proventic as well. In NTP, each server authenticates the next-lower stratum servers and proventicates (authenticates by induction) the lowest-stratum (primary) servers. Serious computer linguists would correctly interpret the proventic relation as the transitive closure of the authentic relation.

It is important to note that the notion of proventic does not necessarily imply that the time is correct. An NTP client mobilizes a number of concurrent associations with different servers and uses a crafted agreement algorithm to pluck a truechimer from the population possibly including falsetickers. A particular association is proventic if the server certificate and identity have been verified by the means described in this chapter, but this does not require that the system clock be synchronized. However, the statement "the client is synchronized to proventic sources" means that the system clock has been set using the time values of one or more proventic associations and according to the NTP mitigation algorithms. While a CA must satisfy this requirement when signing a certificate request, the certificate itself can be stored in public directories and retrieved over unsecured network paths.

We have to ask what it is that is so important and worth protecting. The simple answer is that it is the time a file is created or modified; in other words, its *filestamp*. It is important that filestamps be proventic data; thus, files cannot be created and filestamps cannot be produced unless the host is synchronized to a proventic source. As such, the filestamps throughout the entire NTP subnet represent a partial ordering of all creation epochs and serve as means to expunge old data and ensure that new data are always consistent. As the data are forwarded from server to client, the filestamps are preserved, including those for certificates. Packets with older filestamps are discarded before spending cycles to verify the signature.

The proventic relation is at the heart of the NTP security model. What this means is that the timestamps conform to Lamport's "happens-before" relation described in Chapter 3. As required by the security model and protocol, a host can be synchronized to a proventic source only if all servers on the path to a TH are so synchronized as well. It is a depressing exercise to speculate a cosmic bang when all cryptographic media in the network are erased by the same ionospheric storm, and the NTP subnet has to reformulate itself from scratch.

9.1.2 On the Naming of Things

Unlike the secure shell (ssh) security model, in which the client must be securely authenticated to the server, in NTP the server must be securely authenticated to the client. In typical security models, each different interface address can be bound to a different name, as returned by a reverse-DNS query. In this design, a distinct key may be required for each interface address with a distinct name. A perceived advantage of this design is that the security compartment can be different for each interface. This allows a firewall, for instance, to require some interfaces to perform security functions and others to operate in the clear. As discussed in this chapter, NTP secure groups function as security compartments independently of interface address.

For ssh to operate correctly, there must be a functional DNS to verify name-address mapping. However, such cannot be assumed in the NTP security model since DNS uses caching, which is time sensitive. In principle, DNS as a system cannot operate reliably unless the DNS server clocks are synchronized, and that can happen only if the clocks have been synchronized to proventic sources. Therefore, the NTP security model assumes DNS is not available, secure or not, and that the NTP security host name is an arbitrary ASCII (American Standard Code for Information Interchange) string with no particular relevance to the DNS name or address. For convenience, in NTPv4, the default NTP host name is the string returned by the gethostname() library function but can be changed by a configuration command. This string becomes part of the file names used for cryptographic keys and certificates and also the distinguished names used on certificates.

9.1.3 On Threats and Countermeasures

There are a number of defense mechanisms already built in the NTP architecture, protocol, and algorithms. The fundamental timestamp exchange scheme is inherently resistant to spoof and replay attacks. The engineered clock filter, select, and cluster algorithms are designed to defend against evil cliques of Byzantine traitors. While not necessarily designed to defeat determined intruders, these algorithms and accompanying sanity checks have functioned well over the years to deflect improperly operating but presumably friendly scenarios. However, these mechanisms do not securely identify and authenticate servers to clients.

The fundamental assumption in the security model is that packets transmitted over the Internet can be intercepted by other than the intended receiver, remanufactured in various ways, and replayed in whole or part. These packets can cause the server or client to believe or produce incorrect information, cause protocol operations to fail, interrupt network service, or consume precious network and processor resources. In the case of NTP, the assumed goal of the intruder is to inject false time values; disrupt the protocol or clog the network, servers, or clients with spurious packets that exhaust resources; and deny service to legitimate applications.

A threat can be instigated by an intruder with capabilities ranging from accidental tourist to talented terrorist. The intruder can also be a program bug, unstable protocol,* or operator blunder. The threats can be classified according to the following taxonomy:

- For a cryptanalysis attack, the intruder can intercept and archive packets forever, as well as all the public values ever generated and transmitted over the net.

- For a clogging attack, the intruder can generate packets faster than the server, network, or client can process them, especially if they require expensive cryptographic computations.†

- For a wiretap attack, the intruder can intercept, modify, and replay a packet. However, it cannot permanently prevent onward transmission of the original packet; that is, it cannot break the wire, only tell lies and congest it. We assume that the modified packet cannot arrive at the victim before the original packet.

- For a middleman attack, the intruder is positioned between the server and client, so it can intercept, modify, and send a packet and prevent onward transmission of the original packet.

These threats suggest a security model design approach that minimizes exposure. For instance, cryptanalytic attacks can be minimized by frequent refreshment of cryptographic keys, parameters, and certificates. Clogging attacks can be minimized by avoiding cryptographic computations on data known to be invalid or old. Wiretap attacks can be avoided by using unpredictable nonces in cryptographic protocols. Middleman attacks can be avoided by using digital signatures and identity schemes. However, throughout this chapter we assume that the intruder has no access to private cryptographic media, such as the host key, sign key, or group key, and that cryptanalysis of these media is not practical over the lifetime of the media.

---

* An example is the program bug that brought down the entire AT&T telephone network for 9 h on 15 January 1990. I learned firsthand that the ultimate cause was a program bug exposed when a switch in Manhattan became overloaded. But, the really scary thing was that when first learning how widespread the problem had become, the system operators concluded that it was a terrorist attack.

† Several incidents involving clogging attacks on the national time servers operated by the National Institute of Standards and Technology (NIST) and the U.S. Naval Observatory (USNO) are documented in Reference 10.

9.2 NTP Secure Groups

The NTP security model provides a hierarchical network of secure compartments or groups in which hosts can authenticate each other using defined cryptographic media and algorithms. Think of an NTP secure group as an upside-down tree with roots one or more THs and with network paths leading downward via secondary servers to the clients at the leaves. The THs must all operate at the same stratum and are often, but not necessarily, primary servers. In this security model, secure groups might be operated by a national or corporate time service with customers represented by large corporations.

We assume every member of a secure group is associated with a secret group key, although the key itself may be obscured in some intricate way and known only to the TH that generated it. A TH (but not other group hosts) may belong to more than one group and will have the keys for each group. Furthermore, we assume that there are some clever protocol and algorithm that allow a client to verify that its servers belong to the same group as the TH. The protocol and algorithm together are called the *identity scheme*, several of which are described in Chapter 10.

As in the PKI model, NTP relies on certificate trails to verify proventicity. Each host in the group has a self-signed certificate, usually generated by that host. THs generate trusted certificates; other hosts generate ordinary ones. In the Autokey protocol described further in this chapter, each host in the tree asks the next host closer to the TH to sign its certificate and verify identity, thereby creating a certificate trail for every group host to the THs. It is important to note that group keys carry the NTP name of the host that generates them. When generating the certificate trail, the client caches all certificates for all servers along the trail ending at the TH. By design, the NTP name of the group is the name of the TH as used in the subject and issuer fields of the TH certificate. The NTP name of hosts other than the TH is arbitrary, but unless specified otherwise by a configuration command, the names default to the string returned by the Unix gethostname() function.

The secure group model is surprisingly flexible but requires a little ingenuity to construct useful scenarios. Figure 9.1 shows for each host its certificates, which are identified by subject name and issuer (signer) name. Notice that the self-signed certificate generated by each host is near the bottom, while the self-signed certificate of the server is next, and the server-signed client certificate is near the top. The order of search is from top to bottom, so a server-signed certificate will be found before the self-signed one.

The Alice group consists of THs Alice and Carol. Dependent servers Brenda and Denise have configured Alice and Carol, respectively, as their time sources. Stratum 3 server Eileen has configured both Brenda and Denise as her time sources. The certificates are identified by the subject and signed by the issuer. Note that the group key has previously been generated by Alice and deployed by secure means to all group members.

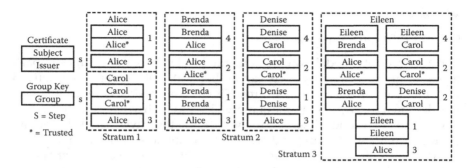

FIGURE 9.1
NTP secure group.

The steps in hiking the certificate trails and verifying identity are listed next. Note that the step number in the description matches the step number in the figure.

1. At startup, each server loads its self-signed certificate from a local file. By convention, the lowest-stratum server certificates are marked trusted in an X.509 extension field. As Alice and Carol have trusted certificates, they need do nothing further to validate the time. It could be that the THs depend on servers in other groups; this scenario is discussed later in this chapter.

2. Brenda, Denise, and Eileen run the Autokey protocol to retrieve the server name, digital signature scheme, and identity scheme for each configured server. The protocol continues to load server certificates recursively until a self-signed trusted certificate is found. Brenda and Denise immediately find self-signed trusted certificates for Alice, but Eileen will loop because neither Brenda nor Denise has her own certificate signed by either Alice or Carol.

3. Brenda and Denise continue with one of the identity schemes to verify that each has the group key previously deployed by Alice. If this succeeds, each continues to the next step. Eileen continues to loop.

4. Brenda and Denise present their certificates to Alice for signature. If this succeeds, either or both Brenda and Denise can now provide these signed certificates to Eileen, who may still be looping. When Eileen receives them, she can now follow the trails via Brenda and Denise to the trusted certificates for Alice and Carol. Once this is done, Eileen can execute the identity scheme and present her certificate to both Brenda and Denise for signature.

The example illustrates how a secure group with more than one TH can be constructed in which each group host has the same group key. As long as the group key is secured and only the group hosts know it, no intruder can masquerade as a group host. However, many applications require multiple overlapping secure groups, each with its own group key and THs. To preserve security between the groups, the identity scheme must obscure the group key in such a way that no host in one group can learn the key of another group. The IFF (identity friendly or foe) and MV (Mu-Varadharajan) identity schemes described in Chapter 10 are specifically designed to preserve the group key in this way. In these schemes, there is a private key known only to the servers and a matching public key known to the clients.

Obviously, group security requires some discipline in obtaining and saving group keys. In the scheme used now by the NTP Public Services Project at the Internet Systems Consortium (http://www.isc.org), an encrypted Web application serves as an agent for the THs. The public and private group keys have previously been provided to the agent in a secure transaction. Group hosts can retrieve public or private keys over the net. Public keys are unencrypted; private keys are encrypted by a secret password known only to previously designated servers.

Figure 9.2 shows three secure groups: Alice, Helen, and Carol. Hosts A, B, C, and D belong to the Alice group with THs A and B. Hosts R and S belong to the Helen group with TH R. Hosts X, Y, and Z belong to the Carol group with TH X, which is a client of both the Alice and Helen groups. Each of these groups can use a different identity scheme or identity group key. Note that all hosts in a group other than the THs do not configure certificate trails outside the group as such would not be a good security practice.

Assume for example that Alice and Helen belong to national standards laboratories and that their group keys are used to confirm identity within the group. Carol is a prominent corporation receiving standards products via broadcast satellite and operating as a third group. As the lowest-stratum servers in the group, THs A, B, R, and X are trusted. By implication in the figure, but not strictly necessary, hosts A, B, and R operate at stratum 1, while TH X operates at stratum 3. Note that the certificate trails for Y and Z lead to X, but the trail for X can lead to R or via C to either A or B, depending on the order of certificates in the certificate caches.

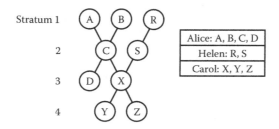

FIGURE 9.2
Multiple secure groups.

9.3 Autokey Security Protocol

The Autokey protocol is based on the PKI and the algorithms of the OpenSSL library, which includes an assortment of the message digest, digital signature, and encryption schemes. As in NTPv3, NTPv4 supports symmetric key cryptography using keyed MD5 message digests to detect message modification and sequence numbers (actually timestamps) to avoid replay. In addition, NTPv4 supports timestamped digital signatures and X.509 certificates to verify the source as per common industry practices. It also supports several optional identity schemes based on cryptographic challenge-response algorithms.

What makes the Autokey protocol special is the way in which these algorithms are used to deflect intruder attacks while maintaining the integrity and accuracy of the time synchronization function. The detailed design is complicated by the need to provisionally authenticate under conditions when reliable time values have not yet been verified. Only when the server identities have been confirmed, signatures verified, and accurate time values obtained does the Autokey protocol declare success.

In NTPv4, one or more extension fields can be inserted after the NTP header and before the message authentication code (MAC), which is always present when an extension field is present. The extension field shown in Figure 9.3 includes 16-bit Type and Length fields, a 32-bit Association ID, and two 32-bit timestamp fields. These are followed by an optional variable-length Data field and a variable-length Signature field. The Type field contains the operation code together with the response bit R and error bit E. The Association ID field is used to match a response to the association of the request.

If the system clock is synchronized to a proventic source, extension fields carry a digital signature and timestamp, which is the NTP seconds at the time of signature. Otherwise, the Timestamp and Signature Length fields are 0. The filestamp is the NTP seconds when the file associated with the

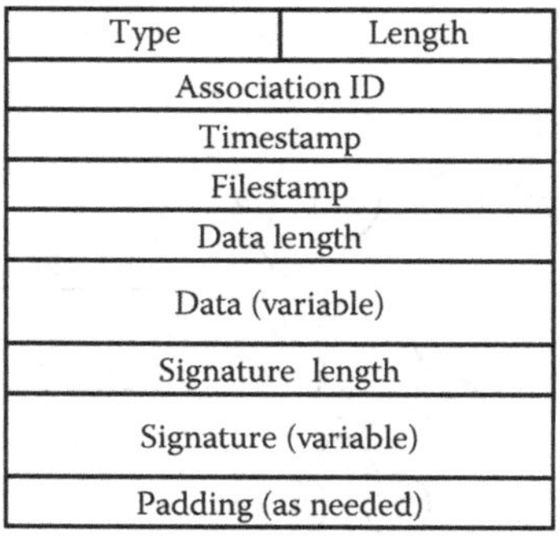

Type	Length
Association ID	
Timestamp	
Filestamp	
Data length	
Data (variable)	
Signature length	
Signature (variable)	
Padding (as needed)	

FIGURE 9.3
Extension field format.

data was created. The protocol detects and discards replayed extension fields with old or duplicate timestamps, as well as fabricated extension fields with bogus timestamps, before any values are used or signatures verified.

In the most common protocol operations, a client sends a request to a server with an operation code specified in the Type field, and the R bit is dim. Ordinarily, the client sets the E bit to 0 as well but may in the future set it to 1 for some purpose. The server returns a response with the same operation code in the Type field, and the R bit is lit. The server can also light the E bit to 1 in case of error. However, it is not necessarily a protocol error to send an unsolicited response with no matching request.

9.3.1 Session Key Operations

The Autokey protocol exchanges cryptographic values in a manner designed to resist clogging and replay attacks. It uses timestamped digital signatures to sign a session key and then a pseudorandom sequence to bind each session key to the preceding one and eventually to the signature. In this way, the expensive signature computations are greatly reduced and removed from the critical code path for constructing accurate time values. In fact, once a source has been proventicated, extension field baggage is not used, leaving the intruder to wonder why the key ID in the MAC changes for every packet.

There are three Autokey protocol variants, called *dances*, corresponding to each of the three NTP modes: client/server, symmetric, and broadcast. All three dances make use of specially contrived session keys, called *autokeys*, and a precomputed pseudorandom sequence of autokeys with the key IDs saved in a key list. As in the original NTPv3 authentication scheme, the Autokey protocol operates separately for each association, so there may be several autokey dances operating independently at the same time.

Each session key is hashed from the IPv4 or IPv6 source and destination addresses and key ID, which are public values, and a cookie, which can be a public value or hashed from a private value depending on the mode. The pseudorandom sequence is generated by repeated hashes of these values and saved in a key list. The server uses the key list in reverse order, so as a practical matter the next session key cannot be predicted from the previous one, but the client can verify it using the same hash as the server.

NTPv3 and NTPv4 symmetric key cryptography uses keyed MD5 message digests with a 128-bit private key and 32-bit key ID. To retain backward compatibility with NTPv3, the NTPv4 key ID space is partitioned in two subspaces at a pivot point of 65536. Symmetric key IDs have values less than the pivot and indefinite lifetime. Autokey protocol key IDs have pseudorandom values equal to or greater than the pivot and are expunged immediately after use. Both symmetric key and public key cryptography authenticate as shown in Figure 9.4. The server looks up the key associated with the key ID and calculates the message digest from the NTP header and extension fields together with the key value. The key ID and message digest form the

MAC included in the message. The client does the same computation using its local copy of the key and compares the result with the message digest in the MAC. If the values agree, the message is assumed authentic.

The session key is the hash of the four fields shown in Figure 9.5. IPv4 source and destination addresses are 32-bit fields, while IPv6 addresses are 128-bit fields. The key ID and cookie are 32-bit fields. For packets without extension fields, the cookie is a shared private value conveyed in encrypted form. For packets with extension fields, the cookie has a default public value of 0 since these packets can be validated independently using digital signatures. The 128-bit hash itself is the secret key, which in the reference implementation is stored along with the key ID in a cache used for symmetric keys as well as autokeys. Keys are retrieved from the cache by key ID using hash tables and a fast lookup algorithm.

Figure 9.6 shows how the autokey list and autokey values are computed. The key list consists of a sequence of key IDs starting with a random 32-bit

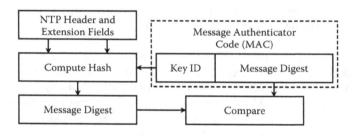

FIGURE 9.4
Receiving messages.

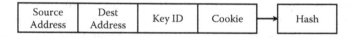

FIGURE 9.5
Autokey session key.

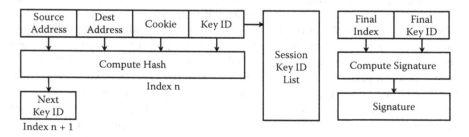

FIGURE 9.6
Constructing the key list.

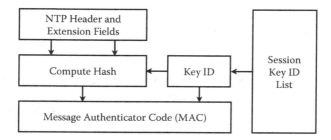

FIGURE 9.7
Sending messages.

nonce (autokey seed) equal to or greater than the pivot value as the first key ID. The first autokey is computed as discussed using the given cookie, and the first 32 bits of the result become the next key ID. Operations continue to generate the entire list, which may contain a hundred or more key IDs. The lifetime of each key is set to expire one poll interval after its scheduled use.

The index of the last key ID in the list is saved along with the next key ID for that entry, collectively called the *autokey values*. The autokey values are then signed using one of several combinations of message digest and signature encryption algorithms. The list is used in reverse order as in Figure 9.7, so that the first autokey used is the last one generated. The Autokey protocol includes a message to retrieve the autokey values and signature, so that subsequent packets can be validated using one or more hashes that eventually match the last key ID (valid) or exceed the index (invalid). This is called the *autokey test* and is done for every packet, including those with and without extension fields. In the reference implementation, the most recent key ID received is saved for comparison with the first 32 bits of the next following key value. This minimizes the number of hash operations should a single packet be lost.

9.3.2 X509 Certificates

Certain certificate fields defined for the IP security infrastructure are used by the identity schemes in ways not anticipated by the specification [7]. X509 Version 3 certificate extension fields are used to convey information used by the identity schemes, such as whether the certificate is private or trusted or contains a public group key. While the semantics of these fields generally conform with conventional usage, there are subtle variations used only by NTP. The fields used by the Autokey protocol include

Basic Constraints

This field defines the basic functions of the certificate. It contains the string `critical,CA:TRUE`, which means the field must be interpreted, and the associated private key can be used to sign other certificates. While included for compatibility, the Autokey protocol makes no use of this field.

Key Usage

This field defines the intended use of the public key contained in the certificate. It contains the string digitalSignature, keyCertSign, which means the contained public key can be used to verify signatures on data and other certificates. While included for compatibility, the Autokey protocol makes no use of this field.

Extended Key Usage

This field further refines the intended use of the public key contained in the certificate and is present only in self-signed certificates. It contains the string Private if the certificate is designated private or the string trustRoot if it is designated trusted. A private certificate is always trusted.

Subject Key Identifier

This field contains the public group key used in the Guillou-Quisquater (GQ) identity scheme described in Section 10.1. It is present only if the GQ scheme is in use.

9.3.3 Protocol Operations

The Autokey protocol state machine is simple but robust. It executes a number of request/response exchanges by which the client obtains cryptographic values or challenges the server to confirm identity. It includes provisions for various kinds of error conditions that can arise due to missing files, corrupted data, protocol violations, and packet loss or misorder, not to mention hostile invasion. There are several programmed request/response exchanges, depending on the protocol mode, and collectively they are called dances.

Autokey protocol choreography includes a dance for each protocol mode, client/server, symmetric, or broadcast, each with specific exchanges that must be completed in order. The server and client provide the host name, digest/signature scheme, and identity scheme in the parameter exchange. The client recursively obtains and verifies certificates on the trail leading to a trusted certificate in the certificate exchange. The trusted certificate provides the group name and thus the name of the client local file containing the client group key. This file is used to verify the server identity in the identity exchange. In the values exchange, the client obtains the cookie or the autokey values, depending on the particular dance. Finally, the client presents its self-signed certificate to the server for signature in the sign exchange.

Once the certificates and identity have been validated, subsequent packets are validated by the autokey sequence. These packets are presumed to contain valid time values; however, unless the system clock has already been set by some other proventic means, it is not known whether these values actually represent a truechime or falsetick source. As the protocol evolves, the NTP associations continue to accumulate time values until a majority clique is available to synchronize the system clock. At this point, the select algorithm culls the falsetickers from the population, and the remaining truechimers are allowed to discipline the clock.

9.4 Parting Shots

To the true believers of the Internet PKI religion, this chapter may be considered heresy. Once time is considered a precious but frangible quantity, many sacred idols are toppled. Perhaps the most sacred of these is the apparent lack of interfaces to the commercial certificate infrastructure community. For reasons mentioned, NTP includes its own certificate infrastructure; however, keen observers should recognize that the certificate data formats are consistent with those used throughout the security community. Having said that, there are a couple of "gotchas" by which certain certificate extension fields have been hijacked for special purpose. Should the Autokey protocol be deployed widely, these uses should be submitted for resolution in the protocol standards process. As a parting-parting shot, there is no reason why the THs could not themselves authenticate using commercial services.

References

1. Kent, S., and R. Atkinson. *IP Encapsulating Security Payload (ESP)*. RFC-2406, November 1998.
2. Kent, S., and R. Atkinson. *IP Authentication Header*. RFC-2402, November 1998.
3. Maughan, D., M. Schertler, M. Schneider, and J. Turner. *Internet Security Association and Key Management Protocol (ISAKMP)*. Network Working Group RFC-2408, November 1998.
4. Orman, H. *The OAKLEY Key Determination Protocol*. RFC-2412, November 1998.
5. Karn, P., and W. Simpson. *Photuris: Session-key Management Protocol*. RFC-2522, March 1999.
6. Adams, C., and S. Farrell. *Internet X.509 Public Key Infrastructure Certificate Management Protocols*. Network Working Group Request for Comments RFC-2510, Entrust Technologies, March 1999, 30 pp.

7. Housley, R., et al. *Internet X.509 Public Key Infrastructure Certificate and Certificate Revocation List (CRL) Profile*. Network Working Group Request for Comments RFC-3280, RSA Laboratories, April 2002, 129 pp.
8. Mills, D.L. *Network Time Protocol (Version 3) Specification, Implementation and Analysis*. Network Working Group RFC-1305, March 1992.
9. Mills, D.L. *Public Key Cryptography for the Network Time Protocol*. Electrical Engineering Report 00-5-1, University of Delaware, Newark, May 2000, 23 pp.
10. Mills, D.L., J. Levine, R. Schmidt, and D. Plonka. Coping with overload on the Network Time Protocol public servers. *Proceedings Precision Time and Time Interval (PTTI) Applications and Planning Meeting* (Washington, DC, December 2004).

Further Reading

Bassham, L., W. Polk, and R. Housley. *Algorithms and Identifiers for the Internet X.509 Public Key Infrastructure Certificate and Certificate Revocation Lists (CRL) Profile*. RFC-3279, April 2002.

Guillou, L.C., and J.-J. Quisquatar. A "paradoxical" identity-based signature scheme resulting from zero-knowledge. In *Proceedings CRYPTO 88 Advanced in Cryptology*, Springer-Verlag, New York, 1990, 216–231.

Mills, D.L. *Proposed Authentication Enhancements for the Network Time Protocol Version 4*. Electrical Engineering Report 96-10-3, University of Delaware, Newark, October 1996, 36 pp.

Mu, Y., and V. Varadharajan. Robust and secure broadcasting. In *Proceedings of INDOCRYPT 2001, LNCS 2247*, Springer Verlag, New York, 2001, 223–231.

Prafullchandra, H., and J. Schaad. *Diffie-Hellman Proof-of-Possession Algorithms*. Network Working Group Request for Comments RFC-2875, Critical Path, Inc., July 2000, 23 pp.

Schnorr, C.P. Efficient signature generation for smart cards. *J. Cryptol. 4, 3* (1991), 161–174.

Stinson, D.R. *Cryptography—Theory and Practice*. CRC Press, Boca Raton, FL, 1995.

10

Identity Schemes

'Twas brillig, and the slithy toves
Did gyre and gimble in the wabe;
All mimsy were the borogroves,
And the mome raths outgrabe.

Lewis Carroll
Through the Looking Glass

This chapter is for mathematicians, specifically number theory enthusiasts. It presents several identity schemes with which Bob can prove to Alice, Brenda, and Carol that he has the secret group key previously instantiated by the trusted authority (TA) or trusted host (TH) acting as TA. We need to be really sneaky; not only is the secret never revealed, but also an interceptor cannot cryptanalyze it by overhearing the protocol interchange, even if overhearing the exchange many times. In the sneakiest schemes, the girls do not even know the group key itself; these schemes are called *zero-knowledge proofs*.

The Network Time Protocol (NTP) security model and Autokey protocol operate in a possibly overlapping system of secure groups as described in Chapter 9. The identity schemes described in this chapter are based on a trusted certificate (TC) and a group key cryptographically bound to that certificate. The certificate is a public value, but depending on the particular scheme, the group key itself may or may not be known to other group hosts. All group hosts use the same identity scheme and predistributed parameters, which, depending on the particular scheme, may or may not be public values.

As in other chapters, we make a distinction among the TA, TH, and certificate authority (CA). Only a TA can generate group keys, server keys, and client keys. Only a TH, which is ordinarily a server, can generate a self-signed TC and may or may not also serve as a TA. Ordinarily, TAs and THs are primary servers, and this much simplifies the NTP subnet configuration, but other configurations are possible. In the NTP security model, every server can act as a CA to sign certificates provided by clients. However, in this case signature requests need not be validated by outside means as this is provided by the identity scheme.

The important issue is the cryptographic strength of the identity scheme since if a middleman could masquerade as a CA, the trail would have a security breach. In ordinary commerce, the identity scheme can be based on handwritten signatures, photographs, fingerprints, and other things hard to counterfeit. As applied to NTP secure groups, the identity scheme must allow a client to securely verify that a server knows the secret that was previously instantiated by the TA but without necessarily revealing the secret itself.

So, why use an identity scheme in the first place? Could this not be done using an agreement exchange or a public/private key pair? The identity scheme described in Request for Comments 2875 (RFC-2875) [1] is based on a ubiquitous Diffie-Hellman key agreement infrastructure, but it requires the server to maintain state for each client and is expensive to generate. There are two reasons for the NTP design. The obvious one is that the identity credentials have to live a long time compared to the lifetime of a typical certificate, and it must be possible to proventicate (see Chapter 9 regarding this term) a source without requiring synchronized time. The second is that the scheme must be rock hard to serious cryptanalysis. Therefore, repeated identity exchanges, even if overheard and archived, never use the same nonces and provide no clue whatsoever to prying eavesdroppers.

The remainder of this chapter consists of a detailed description of the identity schemes implemented in NTP Version 4 (NTPv4) followed by a discussion of how a combination of these schemes, called a *cryptotype*, can be integrated in a functioning NTP secure group. On first reading, the detailed description of each identity scheme can be skipped, but the section on cryptotypes is important for understanding the security model. Save the deliciously intricate mathematics of the Mu-Varadharajan (MV) identity scheme for a long airplane ride.

10.1 Identity Schemes

This section describes five identity schemes implemented in NTPv4: (1) private certificate (PC), (2) TC, (3) a modified Schnorr algorithm (IFF, also known as identify friendly or foe), (4) a modified Guillou-Quisquater algorithm (GQ), and (5) a modified MV algorithm. The modifications are necessary so that each scheme can operate within the Autokey protocol model yet preserve the original mathematical correctness assertions. While all NTPv4 servers and clients support all five schemes, one or more of them are instantiated when the server and client first start, depending on the presence of related parameter and key files. The particular scheme is selected during the Autokey parameter exchange.

Recall from Chapter 9 that the Autokey identity exchange occurs after the certificate exchange and before the values exchange. It operates as shown in Figure 10.1. The IFF, GQ, and MV schemes involve a cryptographically strong challenge-response exchange by which an intruder cannot learn the group key or secret parameters, even after repeated observations of

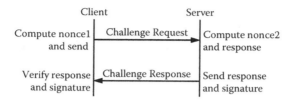

FIGURE 10.1
Identity exchange.

FIGURE 10.2
Private certificate (PC) identity scheme.

multiple exchanges. These schemes begin when the client sends a nonce to the server, which then rolls its own nonce, performs a mathematical operation, and sends the results along with a hash of a secret value to the client. The client performs a second mathematical operation to produce a hash that matches the hash in the message only if the server has the private server group key and the client has the public client group key. To the extent that a server can prove identity to a client without revealing the server group key, these schemes are properly described as zero-knowledge proofs.

10.1.1 Private Certificate Identity Scheme

The PC scheme is not a challenge-response scheme; it is in fact a symmetric key scheme in which the certificate itself is the secret key. It is the only scheme usable for NTP one-way broadcast mode by which clients are unable to calibrate the propagation delay and run the Autokey protocol. The scheme shown in Figure 10.2 uses a PC as the group key. A certificate is designated private if it has an X509 Extended Key Usage field containing the string `Private`. The certificate is distributed to all other group members by secure means and is never revealed outside the group. This scheme is cryptographically strong as long as the PC is protected; however, as in any symmetric key scheme, it can be awkward to refresh the keys or certificate since new values must be securely distributed to a possibly large population and activated simultaneously.

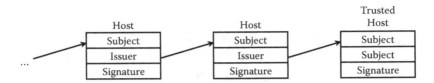

FIGURE 10.3
Trusted certificate (TC) identity scheme.

10.1.2 Trusted Certificate Identity Scheme

All other schemes involve a conventional certificate trail as shown in Figure 10.3. As described in RFC-2510 [2], each certificate is signed by an issuer one step (stratum) closer to the TH, which has a self-signed TC. A certificate is designated trusted if it has an X509 Extended Key Usage field containing the string `trustRoot`. A client obtains the certificates of all servers along the trail leading to a TH by repeated Autokey certificate exchanges, then requests the immediately ascendant host to sign its certificate in a sign exchange. Subsequently, the signed certificate is provided to descendent hosts by the Autokey protocol. In this scheme, certificates can be refreshed at any time, but a masquerade vulnerability remains unless the sign exchange is validated by some means, such as reverse DNS (domain name system). If no specific identity scheme is specified in the Autokey parameter exchange, this is the default scheme.

The TC identification exchange follows the parameter exchange and is actually the Autokey certificate exchange in which the protocol recursively obtains all certificates up to and including the TC by following the Issuer field in each certificate. The TC would normally belong to a primary server but could belong to a secondary server if the security model permits it and the subnet root for all group members is this server.

10.1.3 Schnorr Identity Scheme

The IFF identity scheme is designed for national time servers operated by the U.S. Naval Observatory (USNO), NIST, and other governments, but it can be used in other contexts as well. It is also useful when certificates are generated by means other than the NTPv4 utility routines, such as the OpenSSL utility routines or a public trusted authority like VeriSign. In such cases, an X.509v3 extension field might not be available for Autokey use. The scheme involves two sets of group keys that persist for the life of the scheme, one set for servers and the other set for clients. New generations of server keys must be securely transmitted to all other servers in the group. Client keys are public values and can be retrieved, for example, from a Web site. The scheme is self-contained and independent of new generations of host keys, sign keys, and certificates.

The IFF parameters and keys are generated by OpenSSL routines normally used to generate DSA keys. By happy coincidence, the mathematical principles on which IFF is based are similar to DSA, but only the moduli p, q and generator g are used in identity calculations. The parameters hide in a DSA "cuckoo" structure and use the same members but not in the way originally intended. The values are used by an identity scheme described in Schnorr [3] and Stinson [4, p. 285]. The p is a 512-bit prime, and g is a generator of the multiplicative group Z_p^*. The q is a 160-bit prime that divides $p-1$ and is a qth root of 1 mod p; that is, $g^q = 1$ mod p. The TA rolls a private random group key b ($0 < b < q$), then computes public client key $v = g^{q-b}$ mod p. The TA distributes private (p, q, g, b) to all servers using secure means and public (p, q, g, v) to all clients using insecure means. Note that the difficulty of computing private b from public v is equivalent to the discrete log problem.

Figure 10.4 illustrates the operation of the IFF identity scheme. The TA generates a DSA parameter structure for use as IFF parameters. The IFF server and client parameters are identical to the DSA parameters, so the OpenSSL library DSA parameter generation routine can be used directly. The DSA parameter structure shown in Table 10.1 is written to a file as a DSA private key encoded in PEM and encrypted with DES. The same structure, but with private key b omitted, is encoded in PEM but not encrypted. Unused structure members are set to 1.

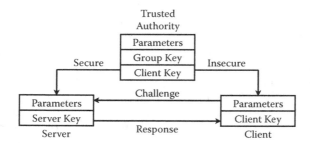

FIGURE 10.4
Schnorr (IFF) identity scheme.

TABLE 10.1

IFF Identity Scheme Parameters

IFF	DSA	Item	Include
p	p	Modulus	All
q	q	Modulus	All
g	g	Generator	All
b	priv_key	Group key	Server
v	pub_key	Client key	All

In this and the following schemes, Alice represents the client and Bob the server. Alice challenges Bob to confirm identity using the following protocol exchange:

1. Alice rolls random r ($0 < r < q$) and sends to Bob.
2. Bob rolls random k ($0 < k < q$), computes $y = k + br \bmod q$ and $x = g^k \bmod p$, then sends (y, hash(x)) to Alice.
3. Alice computes $z = g^y v^r \bmod p$ and verifies that hash(z) equals hash(x).

If the hashes match, Alice knows that Bob has the group key b. Besides making the response message smaller, the hash makes it effectively impossible for an intruder to solve for b by observing a number of these messages. The signed response binds this knowledge to Bob's private key and the public key previously received in his certificate.

10.1.4 Guillou-Quisquater Identity Scheme

While in the IFF identity scheme the parameters and keys persist for the life of the scheme and are difficult to change in a large NTP subnet, the GQ identity scheme obscures the group key each time a new certificate is generated. This makes it less vulnerable to cryptanalysis but does have the disadvantage that the actual group key is known to all group members and if stolen by an intruder would compromise the entire group. This is one of the reasons all private cryptographic files in the reference implementation can be encrypted with a secret password.

In the GQ scheme, certificates are generated by the NTP utility routines using the OpenSSL cryptographic library. These routines convey the GQ public key in the X.509v3 Subject Key Identity extension field. The scheme involves a set of parameters that persist for the life of the scheme and a private/public group key pair that is refreshed each time a new certificate is generated. The public group key is used by the client when verifying the response to a challenge. The TA generates the GQ parameters and keys and distributes them by secure means to all group members. The scheme is self-contained and independent of new generations of host keys, sign keys, and certificates.

The GQ parameters are generated by OpenSSL routines normally used to generate RSA keys. By happy coincidence, the mathematical principles on which GQ is based are similar to RSA, but only the modulus n is used in identity exchanges. The parameters hide in an RSA cuckoo structure and use the same members. The values are used in an identity scheme described in Guillou and Quisquatar [5] and Stinson [4, p. 300 (with errors)]. The 512-bit public modulus $n = pq$, where p and q are secret large primes. The TA rolls private random group key b ($0 < b < n$) and distributes (n, b) to all group

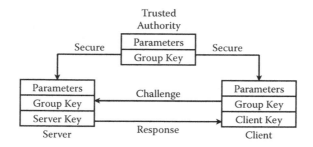

FIGURE 10.5
Guillou-Quisquater (GC) identity scheme.

TABLE 10.2

GQ Identity Scheme Parameters

GQ	RSA	Item	Include
n	n	Modulus	All
b	e	Group key	Server
u	p	Server key	Server
v	q	Client key	Client

members using secure means. The private server key and public client key are constructed later.

Figure 10.5 illustrates the operation of the GQ identity scheme. When generating new certificates, the server rolls new random private key u $(0 < u < n)$ and public key as its inverse obscured by the group key $v = (u^{-1})^b \bmod n$. These values replace the private and public keys normally generated by the RSA scheme. In addition, the public client key is conveyed in an X.509 certificate extension field. The updated GQ structure shown in Table 10.2 is written as an RSA private key encoded in PEM and encrypted with DES. Unused structure members are set to 1.

Alice challenges Bob to confirm identity using the following exchange:

1. Alice rolls random r $(0 < r < n)$ and sends to Bob.
2. Bob rolls random k $(0 < k < n)$ and computes $y = ku^r \bmod n$ and $x = k^b \bmod n$, then sends $(y, \text{hash}(x))$ to Alice.
3. Alice computes $z = v^r y^b \bmod n$ and verifies that $\text{hash}(z)$ equals $\text{hash}(x)$.

If the hashes match, Alice knows that Bob has the same group key b. Besides making the response shorter, the hash makes it effectively impossible for an intruder to solve for b by observing a number of these messages. The signed response binds this knowledge to Bob's private key and the public key previously received in his certificate. Further evidence is the certificate containing the public group key since this is also signed with Bob's private key.

10.1.5 Mu–Varadharajan Identity Scheme

The MV scheme is surely the most interesting, intricate, and flexible of the three challenge-response schemes implemented in NTPv4. It can be used when a small number of servers provide synchronization to a large client population in which there might be considerable risk of compromise between and among the servers and clients. It was originally intended to encrypt broadcast transmissions to receivers that do not transmit. There is one encryption key for the broadcaster and a separate decrypting key for each receiver. It operates something like a pay-per-view satellite broadcasting system in which the session key is encrypted by the broadcaster, and the decryption keys are held in a tamper-proof set-top box. We do not use it this way, but read on. As a disclaimer, the mathematics are truly awesome.

In the MV scheme, the TA generates an intricate cryptosystem involving both public and private media. The TA provides the THs with a private encryption key and public decryption keys. For each client, the TA generates an activation key and associated private client decryption keys. The activation keys are used by the TA to activate and deactivate individual client decryption keys without changing the decryption keys themselves. The THs blind the public decryption keys using a nonce for each plaintext encryption, so the keys appear different on each use. The encrypted ciphertext and public decryption keys are provided to the client. The client computes the decryption key using its private decryption key and public decryption key.

In the MV scheme, the activation keys are known only to the TA and not revealed even to the THs. The TA decides which keys to activate and provides to the THs a private encryption key E and public decryption keys $\bar{g}$ and $\hat{g}$ that depend on the activated keys. The THs have no additional information and, in particular, cannot masquerade as the TA. In addition, the TA provides to each client j individual private decryption keys $\bar{x}_j$ and $\hat{x}_j$, which do not need to be changed if the TA activates or deactivates these keys. The clients have no further information and, in particular, cannot masquerade as a TH or the TA.

The MV values hide in a DSA cuckoo structure, which uses the same parameters but generated in a different way. The values are used in an encryption scheme similar to El Gamal cryptography described in Stinson [4] but using a polynomial formed from the expansion of product terms $\prod_{0<j\leq n} (x-x_j)$, as described in Mu and Varadharajan [6]. However, that article has significant errors and serious omissions.

Figure 10.6 illustrates the operation of the MV identity scheme. The TA writes the server parameters, private encryption key, and public decryption

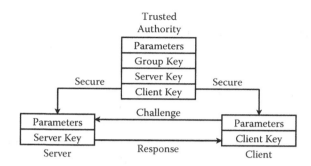

FIGURE 10.6
Mu-Varadharajan (MV) identity scheme.

TABLE 10.3

MV Scheme Server Parameters

MV	DSA	Item	Include
p	p	Modulus	All
q	q	Modulus	Server
E	g	Private encrypt	Server
$\bar{g}$	priv_key	Public decrypt	Server
$\hat{g}$	pub_key	Public decrypt	Server

TABLE 10.4

MV Scheme Client Parameters

MV	DSA	Item	Include
p	p	Modulus	All
$\bar{x}_j$	priv_key	Private decrypt	Client
$\hat{x}_j$	pub_key	Private decrypt	Client

keys for all servers as a DSA private key encoded in PEM and encrypted with DES as shown in Table 10.3.

The TA writes the client parameters and private decryption keys for each client as a DSA private key encoded in PEM and encrypted with DES as shown in Table 10.4. It is used only by the designated recipients, who pay a suitably outrageous fee for its use. Unused structure members are set to 1.

The devil is in the details, and the details are computationally expensive, at least for the TA. Let q be the product of n distinct primes s'_j ($j = 1, ..., n$), where each s'_j, called an *activation key*, has m significant bits. Let prime $p = 2q + 1$, so that q and s'_j each divide $p - 1$ and p has $M = nm + 1$ significant bits. Let g be a generator of the multiplicative group Z_p^*; that is, $\gcd(g, p - 1)$ and $g^q - 1 \bmod p$. We do modular arithmetic over Z_q and then project into Z_p^* as powers of g. Sometimes, we have to compute an inverse b^{-1} of random b in Z_q, but for that purpose we require $\gcd(b, q)$. We expect M to be in the 500-bit range and n relatively small, like 30. The TA uses a nasty probabilistic algorithm to generate the cryptosystem.

1. Generate the m-bit primes $s'_j (0 < j \leq n)$, which may have to be replaced later. As a practical matter, it is tough to find more than 30 distinct primes for $M \approx 512$ or 60 primes for $M \approx 1{,}024$. The latter can take several hundred iterations and several minutes on a Sun Blade 1000.

2. Compute modulus $q = \prod_{0<j\leq n} s'_j$, then modulus $p = 2q + 1$. If p is composite, the TA replaces one of the primes with a new distinct prime and tries again. Note that q will hardly be a secret since p is revealed to servers and clients. However, factoring q to find the primes should be adequately hard as this is the same problem considered hard in RSA.*

3. Associate with each s'_j an element s_j such that $s_j s'_j = s'_j \bmod q$. One way to find an s_j is the quotient $s_j = q + s'_j / s'_j$. The student should prove the remainder is always zero.

4. Compute the generator g of Z_p using a random roll such that $\gcd(g, p - 1)$ and $g^q = 1 \bmod p$. If not, roll again. Rarely, this can be tedious.

Once the cryptosystem parameters have been determined, the TA sets up a specific instance of the scheme as follows:

1. Roll n random roots x_j $(0 < x_j < q)$ for a polynomial of order n. While it may not be strictly necessary, make sure that each root has no factors in common with q.

2. Expand the n product terms $\prod_{0<j\leq n} (x - x_j)$ to form $n + 1$ coefficients a_i mod q $(0 \leq i \leq n)$ in powers of x using a fast method contributed by C. Boncelet (private communication).

3. Generate $g_i = g^{a_i} \bmod p$ for all i and the generator g. Verify that $\prod_{0\leq i\leq n, 0<j\leq n} g_i^{a_i x_j^i} = 1 \bmod p$ for all i, j. Note that the $a_i x_j^i$ exponent is computed mod q, but the g_i is computed mod p. Also note that the expression given in the article cited is incorrect.

4. Make the master encryption key $A = \prod_{0<i\leq n, 0<j<n} g_i^{x_j^i} \bmod p$. Keep it around for a while since it is expensive to compute.

5. Roll the private random group key b $(0 < b < q)$, where $\gcd(b, q) = 1$ to guarantee the inverse exists, then compute $b^{-1} \bmod q$. If b is changed, all keys must be recomputed.

---

* This raises the question, is it as hard to find n small prime factors totaling M bits as it is to find two large prime factors totalling M bits? Remember, the bad guy does not know n.

6. Make private client keys $\bar{x}_j = b^{-1} \sum\limits_{0<i\leq n, i\neq j} x_i^n \bmod q$ and $\hat{x}_j = s_j x_j^n \bmod q$ for all j. Note that the keys for the jth client involve only s_j but not s'_j or s. The TA sends $(p, \bar{x}_j, \hat{x}_j)$ to the jth clients using secure means.

7. The activation key is initially q by construction. The TA deactivates client j by dividing q by s'_j. The quotient becomes the activation key s. Note that we always have to deactivate one key; otherwise, the plaintext and cryptotext would be identical. The TA computes $E = A^s$, $\bar{g} = \bar{x}^s \bmod p$, $\hat{g} = \hat{x}^{sb} \bmod p$, and sends $(p, E, \bar{g}, \hat{g})$ to the THs using secure means.

On completing these labors, Alice challenges Bob to confirm identity using the following exchange:

1. Alice rolls random r ($0 < r < q$) and sends to Bob.

2. Bob rolls random k ($0 < k < q$) and computes the session encryption key $E' = E^k \bmod p$ and public decryption key $\bar{g}' = \bar{g}^k \bmod p$ and $\hat{g}' = \hat{g}^k \bmod p$. He encrypts $x = E'r$ and sends $(\text{hash}(x), \bar{g}, \hat{g})$ to Alice.

3. Alice computes the session decryption key $E'^{-1} = \bar{g}'^{\hat{x}_j} \hat{g}'^{\bar{x}_j} \bmod p$, recovers the encryption key $E' = (E'^{-1})^{-1} \bmod p$, encrypts $z = E'r \bmod p$, then verifies that $\text{hash}(z) = \text{hash}(x)$.

10.2 Cryptotypes

The NTP security model is specifically crafted to provide a smorgasbord of authentication schemes, digest/signature schemes, and identity schemes. A specific selection of one scheme from each of these categories is called a *cryptotype*. An NTPv4 subnet can include multiple secure groups that interact in various ways as described in Chapter 9. Each group can support a different set of cryptotypes, but all hosts in the same group should support the same set. The hosts can be configured in several ways while keeping in mind the principles explained in this chapter. Note, however, that some cryptotype combinations may successfully interoperate with each other but may not represent good security practice.

The cryptotype of an association is determined at the time of mobilization, either at configuration time or some time later when a packet of appropriate cryptotype appears. When a client/server, broadcast, or symmetric active association is mobilized at configuration time, it can be designated nonauthentic, authenticated with symmetric key, or authenticated with the Autokey protocol and selected digest and identity schemes; subsequently, it will send packets with that cryptotype. When a responding server, broadcast client, or symmetric passive association is mobilized, it is assigned the same cryptotype as the received packet.

All clients and servers in a secure group should use the same digest/signature and identity schemes, although a TH in one group can support a different digest/signature and identity scheme with a server in another group. When multiple identity schemes are supported, the parameter exchange determines which one is used. The request message contains bits corresponding to the schemes the requester supports, while the response message contains bits corresponding to the schemes the responder supports. Both requester and responder match the bits and select a compatible identity scheme. When multiple selections are possible, a prescribed order determines the first matching cryptotype.

Servers and clients can support multiple cryptotypes, but not all combinations are interoperable. Note that some cryptotype combinations may successfully interoperate with each other but may not represent good security practice. The server and client cryptotypes are defined by the following codes.

NONE

A client or server is type NONE if authentication is not available or not configured. Packets exchanged between client and server have no MAC.

AUTH

A client or server is type AUTH if the key option is specified with the server configuration command and the client and server keys are compatible. Packets exchanged between clients and servers have an MAC.

PC

A client or server is type PC if the autokey option is specified with the server configuration command and compatible host key and PC files are present. Packets exchanged between clients and servers have an MAC.

TC

A client or server is type TC if the autokey option is specified with the server configuration command and compatible host key and public certificate files are present. Packets exchanged between clients and servers have an MAC.

IDENT

A client or server is type IDENT if the autokey option is specified with the server configuration command and compatible host key, public certificate, and identity scheme files are present. Packets exchanged between clients and servers have an MAC.

The compatible cryptotype combinations for clients (in the first column) and servers (in the top row) are listed in the Table 10.5.

Following the principle that time is a public value, a server responds to any client packet that matches its cryptotype capabilities. Thus, a server receiving a nonauthenticated packet will politely respond with a nonauthenticated packet, while the same server receiving a packet of a cryptotype it supports will respond with a packet of that cryptotype. However, new broadcast or many-cast client associations or symmetric passive associations will not be mobilized unless the server supports a cryptotype compatible with the first packet received. By default, the reference implementation will not mobilize nonauthenticated associations unless overridden in a decidedly dangerous way.

Some examples may help to reduce confusion. Client Alice has no specific cryptotype selected. Server Bob supports both symmetric key and public key cryptography. Alice's nonauthenticated packets arrive at Bob, who replies with nonauthenticated packets. Carol has a copy of Bob's symmetric key file and has selected key ID 4 in packets to Bob. If Bob verifies the packet with key ID 4, he sends Carol a reply with that key. If authentication fails, Bob sends Carol a thing called a crypto-NAK, which tells her something broke. She can see the evidence using the utility programs of the NTP software library.

Symmetric peers Bob and Denise have rolled their own host keys, certificates, and identity parameters and lit the host status bits for the identity schemes they can support. On completion of the parameter exchange, both parties know the digest/signature scheme and available identity schemes of the other party. They do not have to use the same schemes, but each party must use the digest/signature scheme and one of the identity schemes supported by the other party.

It should be clear from this that Bob can support all the girls at the same time as long as he has compatible authentication and identification credentials. Now, Bob can act just like the girls in his own choice of servers; he can run multiple configured associations with multiple different servers (or the same server, although that might not be useful). But, wise security policy might preclude

TABLE 10.5

Cryptotype Combinations

	NONE	AUTH	PC	TC	IDENT
NONE	Yes	Yes*	Yes*	Yes*	Yes*
AUTH	No	Yes	No	No	No
PC	No	No	Yes	No	No
TC	No	No	No	Yes	Yes
IDENT	No	No	No	No	Yes

* These combinations are not valid if the restriction list includes the notrust option.

some cryptotype combinations; for instance, running an identity scheme with one server and no authentication with another might not be wise.

10.3 Parting Shots

These schemes are lots of fun, and the MV scheme is glorious, although probably impractical in all but special cases. The astute reader will quickly realize that the schemes can be used for symmetric key cryptography, by which the group key is used as the symmetric key itself. There are many other combinations of the schemes, providing a rich tapestry of mutations remaining to be explored.

References

1. Prafullchandra, H., and J. Schaad. *Diffie-Hellman Proof-of-Possession Algorithms.* Network Working Group Request for Comments RFC-2875, Critical Path, Inc., July 2000, 23 pp.
2. Adams, C., and S. Farrell. *Internet X.51209 Public Key Infrastructure Certificate Management Protocols.* Network Working Group Request for Comments RFC-2510, Entrust Technologies, March 1999, 30 pp.
3. Schnorr, C.P. Efficient signature generation for smart cards. *J. Cryptol. 4, 3* (1991), 161–174.
4. Stinson, D.R. *Cryptography—Theory and Practice.* CRC Press, Boca Raton, FL, 1995.
5. Guillou, L.C., and J.-J. Quisquatar. A "paradoxical" identity-based signature scheme resulting from zero-knowledge. In *Proceedings CRYPTO 88 Advanced in Cryptology*, Springer-Verlag, New York, 1990, 216–231.
6. Mu, Y., and V. Varadharajan. Robust and secure broadcasting. In *Proceedings INDOCRYPT 2001, LNCS 2247*, Springer Verlag, New York, 2001, 223–231.

Further Reading

Housley, R., et al. *Internet X.509 Public Key Infrastructure Certificate and Certificate Revocation List (CRL) Profile.* Network Working Group Request for Comments RFC-3280, RSA Laboratories, April 2002, 129 pp.
Mills, D.L. *Network Time Protocol (Version 3) Specification, Implementation and Analysis.* Network Working Group Report RFC-1305, University of Delaware, Newark, March 1992, 113 pp.

11

Analysis of Errors

> Then the bowsprit got mixed with the rudder sometimes:
> A thing as the Bellman remarked,
> That frequently happens in tropical climes,
> When a vessel is, so to speak, "snarked."

Lewis Carroll
The Hunting of the Snark

This chapter contains a theoretical and practical analysis of errors incidental to the NTP and its operation on the Internet. It includes material adapted from Mills [1], [2] with several corrections and much additional material. It is intended to quantify the error statistics that might be provided to applications dependent on NTP. These statistics are both deterministic and stochastic, depending on manufacturing tolerances and nominal time and frequency variations. They are essential for constructing strong correctness assertions when managing time-sensitive applications.

Recall from previous chapters that the clock time can be expressed

$$T(t) = T(t_0) + R(t - t_0) + D(t - t_0)^2 + x(t)$$

where t is the current time, t_0 is the time of the last measurement update, T is the time offset, R is the frequency offset, D is the drift due to oscillator resonator aging, and x is a stochastic error term. The first two terms represent systematic errors that can be bounded by the analysis in this chapter. The third term is ordinarily neglected for computer clocks, while the last term represents stochastic errors estimated in a detailed error budget analyzed later in this chapter.

Some creative notation will simplify the development to follow. The notation $x = [u, v]$ describes the closed interval x in which $\lfloor x \rfloor$ is the lower limit and $\lceil x \rceil$ the upper limit and $\lfloor x \rfloor = u \leq v = \lceil x \rceil$. For intervals x and y, $x \cup y = [\min((\lfloor x \rfloor, \lfloor y \rfloor), \max(\lceil x \rceil, \lceil y \rceil)]$ and for scalar a, $a[x] = [a\lfloor x \rfloor, a\lceil x \rceil]$ and $[x] + a = [\lfloor x \rfloor + a, \lceil x \rceil + a]$. For scalar a, $|a|$ means the absolute value; for interval w, $|w| = max(\lfloor w \rfloor, \lceil w \rceil)$ is called the amplitude of w. The notation $\langle x \rangle$ designates the (infinite) average of x, which is usually approximated by an exponential average, and the notation $\hat{x}$ designates an estimator for x. Lowercase Greek letters are used to designate measurement data for the system clock relative to a server clock, while uppercase Greek letters are used to designate measurement data for the system clock relative to the reference clock at the root of the synchronization subnet. Exceptions are noted as they arise.

11.1 Clock Reading Errors

The Bureau International des Poids et Mesures (BIPM) in Paris defines the standard second (s) as "9,192,631,770 periods of the radiation corresponding to the transition between the two hyperfine levels of the ground state of the Cesium-133 atom," which implies a resolution of about 110 ps. In principle, intervals other than integer multiples of the transition period require an interpolation oscillator and phase-lock loop. While the 64-bit NTP timestamp format has a limiting resolution of about 232 ps, most computer clocks have resolutions much coarser than this, so the inherent error in resolving NTP time relative to the standard second can usually be neglected (maybe not for long; the central processing unit [CPU] clock oscillator period in the fastest modern workstations is now creeping downward from 300 ps).

In this analysis, a clock is represented by an oscillator operating at a frequency of f_c and an oscillator counter/divider that increments at intervals of $\rho = 1/f_c$. A timestamp $T(t)$ is determined by reading the clock at an arbitrary time t (the argument t will usually be omitted for conciseness). The clock reading error is represented by the uniformly distributed random variable x bounded by the interval $[-\rho, 0]$, where ρ represents the clock precision. Since the intervals between reading the clock are almost always independent of, and much larger than, ρ, successive readings can be considered independent and identically distributed (iid).

The oscillator fractional frequency error is represented by the random variable f, which is constrained to a defined tolerance specified by the oscillator manufacturer. While f for a particular clock is a random variable with respect to the population of all clocks, for any one clock, it ordinarily changes only slowly with time and over a much smaller range. Therefore, the discipline algorithm computes an adjustment a such that $y = a + f$ and $\langle y \rangle \cong 0$. To make strong correctness assertions, a is clamped to ensure that, given the known frequency tolerance, y is always bounded on the interval $[-\phi, \phi]$, where ϕ represents the clock oscillator frequency tolerance. Thus, the clock error τ seconds after the reading can be approximated by the random variable z,

$$z = x + y\tau, \tag{11.1}$$

where minor approximations inherent in the measurement of τ are neglected.

As a practical matter, the reference implementation assumes that a frequency tolerance $\phi = 15$ PPM is a nominal value for a disciplined clock oscillator under closed-loop conditions. However, the undisciplined oscillator tolerance can be much worse, up to 500 PPM in extreme cases. Thus, while the discipline algorithm can compensate for intrinsic frequency errors of this magnitude, once compensated, the residual errors are assumed bounded by 15 PPM.

Computer science purists might take exception to the 15-PPM assumption. If the manufacturing tolerance can be as large as 500 PPM, why is ϕ assumed any smaller? The answer is found in the art of engineering. Where a tighter specification applies, as in reference clocks and at least one architecture (Digital Alpha), the 15-PPM figure is a conservative value. Where a looser specification or no specification applies, it is in principle possible to trim the oscillator frequency within 15 PPM by adjusting relevant kernel variables. We assume in this presentation that some magic elf has done this before delivery of the machine.

To assess the nature and expected magnitude of clock errors and the calculations based on them, it is useful to examine the characteristics of the probability density functions (pdfs) $p_x(t)$ and $p_y(t)$ for x and y, respectively. As discussed, $p_x(t)$ is uniform over the interval $[-\rho, 0]$. Elsewhere in this book, $p_y(t)$ is approximated by a random-walk distribution computed as the integral of a zero-mean Gaussian distribution with standard deviation σ_y. In general, σ_y is much smaller than the interval $[-\phi, \phi]$, so the characteristic can be assumed zero outside this bound. The pdf for the clock error $p_z(t)$ is thus the sum of the x and y contributions computed as the convolution

$$p_z(t) = \int_{-\infty}^{\infty} p_x(z) p_y\left(\frac{t-z}{\tau}\right) dz \quad (\tau > 0),\tag{11.2}$$

which appears as a bell-shaped curve, symmetric about $\rho/2$, and grows wider as τ increases.

In practice, $p_z(t)$ is not directly computable, and this is not necessary. However, by construction x is bounded on the interval $[-\rho, 0]$, and y is bounded on the interval $[-\phi, \phi]$. In the next section, these relations are used to establish strong assertions about the accuracy of the system clock.

11.2 Timestamp Errors

In NTP, the clock offset and round-trip delay between two clocks A and B are determined by a timestamp exchanged via the network path between them. The exchange involves the four most recent timestamps numbered as shown in Figure 11.1. In the figure, θ_0 represents the true offset of clock B relative to clock A. T_1 and T_4 are determined relative to the A clock, while T_2 and T_3 are determined relative to the B clock. The clock offset θ and round-trip delay δ of B relative to A are given by

$$\theta = \frac{1}{2}[(T_2 - T_1) + (T_3 - T_4)] \text{ and } \delta = (T_4 - T_1) - (T_3 - T_2),\tag{11.3}$$

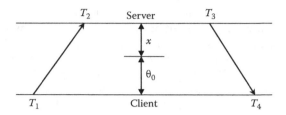

FIGURE 11.1
Timestamp error.

respectively. This formulation demonstrates that the relevant calculations involve sums and differences of timestamp differences. The four terms in parentheses include a systematic bound, as described in this section, plus stochastic error components. Here, we are concerned about the systematic bound; the error components are discussed further in this chapter.

Let f_A and f_B be the fractional frequency errors of A and B, respectively, and assume that each is contained in $[-\phi_A, \phi_A]$ and $[-\phi_B, \phi_B]$, respectively. The errors inherent in determining the timestamps T_1, T_2, T_3, and T_4 are, respectively,

$$\varepsilon_1 = [-\rho_A, 0], \; \varepsilon_2 = [-\rho_B, 0], \; \varepsilon_3 = [-\rho_B, 0] + f_B(T_3 - T_2),$$

$$\varepsilon_4 = [-\rho_A, 0] + f_A(T_4 - T_1)$$

The error in determining θ must be contained in the interval

$$\frac{1}{2}[\lfloor \varepsilon_2 \rfloor - \lceil \varepsilon_1 \rceil + \lfloor \varepsilon_3 \rfloor - \lceil \varepsilon_4 \rceil, \lceil \varepsilon_2 \rceil - \lfloor \varepsilon_1 \rfloor + \lceil \varepsilon_3 \rceil - \lfloor \varepsilon_4 \rfloor],$$

which can be expanded to

$$\frac{1}{2}\{[-\rho_A - \rho_B, \rho_A + \rho_B] + f_B(T_3 - T_2) - f_A(T_4 - T_1)\} \qquad (11.4)$$

The error in determining δ must be contained in the interval

$$[\lfloor \varepsilon_4 \rfloor - \lceil \varepsilon_1 \rceil - \lceil \varepsilon_3 \rceil + \lfloor \varepsilon_2 \rfloor, \lceil \varepsilon_4 \rceil - \lfloor \varepsilon_1 \rfloor - \lfloor \varepsilon_3 \rfloor + \lceil \varepsilon_2 \rceil], \qquad (11.5)$$

which can be expanded to

$$[-\rho_A - \rho_B, \rho_A + \rho_B] + f_A(T_4 - T_1) - f_B(T_3 - T_2). \qquad (11.6)$$

Note that the interval can contain both positive and negative points. In the NTP system clock model, the residual frequency errors f_A and f_B are minimized by the discipline algorithm, which uses a hybrid of phase-lock and frequency-lock feedback loops. Under most conditions, these errors will be small and can be ignored. If $\rho_A = \rho_B = \rho$, that is, both the A and B clocks have the same resolution, the pdf for the remaining errors is symmetric, so that the averages $\hat{\theta} = \langle \theta \rangle$ and $\hat{\delta} = \langle \delta \rangle$ are unbiased maximum likelihood estimators for the true clock offset and round-trip delay, independent of the particular value of ρ. If $\rho_A \neq \rho_B$, $\langle \theta \rangle$ is not an unbiased estimator; however, the bias error is on the order of $\frac{\rho_A - \rho_B}{2}$.

In the following, we assume $\rho = \max(\rho_A, \rho_B)$, $\phi = \max(\phi_A, \phi_B)$, and $T = T_4 - T_1$. To reliably bound the errors throughout the frequency tolerance range, the oscillator frequency errors f_A and f_B, plus the additional frequency trim injected by the discipline algorithm, must not exceed the interval $[-\phi, \phi]$. From Equation 11.4, the maximum absolute error in determining θ is

$$\varepsilon_\phi = \rho + \phi T, \tag{11.7}$$

called the *offset dispersion*, while from Equation 11.6, the maximum absolute error in determining δ is

$$\varepsilon_\delta = 2(\rho + \phi T), \tag{11.8}$$

called the *delay dispersion*.

11.3 Sawtooth Errors

NTP controls the system clock using the discipline algorithm described in Chapter 4. In some operating systems, the algorithm is implemented in the kernel and controls the clock using the kernel application program interface (API) described in Chapter 8, which provides an extremely smooth and precise control. Since the kernel algorithm provides both time and frequency discipline, it needs to be called only when a new clock offset has been determined. If not implemented in the kernel, the discipline is implemented in the NTP daemon using the Unix adjtime() system call. However, this routine provides only a time discipline, so it must be called on a regular basis to provide a frequency discipline. In NTP, the clock adjust process provides both time and frequency discipline by calling adjtime() at intervals of 1 s.

The Unix adjtime() kernel routine amortizes a given time offset at a constant slew rate, typically 500 PPM. The interval during which the slew is

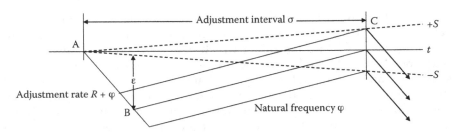

FIGURE 11.2
Sawtooth error.

effective is calculated from the given offset and slew rate. As the routine is called once per second, the slew must be completed within the second. Obviously, if the intrinsic frequency error is greater than the slew rate, the adjtime() routine will not be able to discipline the system clock accurately.

During the interval between adjustments, the actual time error will increase at a rate dependent on the intrinsic oscillator frequency error. When the frequency error is significant, like hundreds of parts per million, the peak error just before the next adjtime() call can reach hundreds of microseconds. Figure 11.2 shows the effects, commonly called *sawtooth error*. In the figure, the line BC shows the time offset while the clock oscillator runs at its natural frequency φ. A correction is introduced by the adjtime() system call, which injects an additional offset AB at rate $R = 500 + \varphi$ PPM until the desired correction ε has been amortized. The ε determines the frequency correction required. The result is the characteristic ABC, which repeats every adjustment interval of σ seconds, which slews the nominal frequency to follow the dotted lines over the range $+S$ or $-S$ as shown.

Sawtooth errors are not incorporated in the error budget since their effects appear in the peer jitter measured by the clock filter algorithm. Obviously, the smaller the natural frequency error, the smaller the sawtooth error. In general, typical natural frequency errors are in the range from a few parts per million to 200 PPM, so that with an adjustment interval of 1 s, the sawtooth error is in the range from a few to 200 μs.

11.4 Peer Error Budget

As mentioned, there are two statistics of concern when characterizing errors: maximum error, which depends mainly on root delay and root dispersion, and expected error, which depends on stochastic delay variations. Here, we are concerned about maximum and expected errors for a path between a server and a client. In Equation 11.2, let $a = T_2 - T_1$ represent the outbound path and $b = T_3 - T_4$ the return path. Then, the clock offset and round-trip delay are

$$\theta = \frac{a+b}{2} \text{ and } \delta = a - b,$$

respectively. Note that a and b represent network delays, a on the outbound path to the server and b on the inbound path to the client. The delays are composed of three parts: a fixed propagation component representing the actual time of travel, a variable transmission component depending on the transmission rate and the packet length, and a stochastic component representing various queuing delays in the switches and routers. Often in the modern Internet, propagation delays have varying differences due to nonreciprocal routing, different network rates, and different timestamping strategies. These issues are discussed in Section 15.3.

It is a simple exercise to calculate bounds on clock offset errors as a function of measured round-trip delay. Let the true offset of B relative to A be called θ_0 as in Figure 11.1. Let x denote the delay between the actual departure of a message from A and its arrival at B. Therefore, $x + \theta_0 = T_2 - T_1 = a$. Since x must be positive in our universe, $a - \theta_0 \geq 0$, which requires $\theta_0 \leq a$. A similar argument requires that $b \leq \theta_0$, so surely $b \leq \theta_0 \leq a$. This inequality can also be expressed as

$$b = \frac{a+b}{2} - \frac{a-b}{2} \leq \theta_0 \leq \frac{a+b}{2} + \frac{a-b}{2} = a,$$

which is equivalent to

$$|\theta_0| \leq |\theta| + \frac{\delta}{2}. \tag{11.9}$$

However, Equation 11.9 does not account for the offset and delay dispersion, which are determined along with the offset and delay at time T_4. Including these factors, Equation 11.9 becomes

$$|\theta_0| \leq |\theta| + \varepsilon_\theta + \frac{\delta + \varepsilon_\delta}{2}. \tag{11.10}$$

Substituting from Equations 11.7 and 11.8 and simplifying yields

$$|\theta_0| \leq |\theta| + \frac{\delta}{2} + 2(\rho + \phi T),$$

where $T = T_4 - T_1$, and $\varepsilon = 2\rho + 2\phi T$ is the peer dispersion. However, the $2\phi T$ term includes both the error due to the B clock as well as the A clock, and we do not need the B clock after T_4. So, at T_4, ε is initialized at 2ρ and then increases at rate ϕ after that.

On a statistical basis, θ is the best estimate of the server clock offset relative to the client clock, and φ is the expected error of this estimate. The maximum error of the client clock relative to the server clock is $\lambda = \delta/2 + \varepsilon + \varphi$, which is called the *peer distance*. The maximum error of the client clock relative to the root of the NTP subnet, called the *root distance*, is defined as

$$\Lambda = \frac{\delta + \Delta}{2} + \varepsilon + E + \varphi \, , \qquad (11.11)$$

where Δ and E are, respectively, the accumulated delay and dispersion from the server to the root of the NTP synchronization subnet represented by the reference clock of the primary (stratum 1) server. This represents the maximum error in the estimate of θ_0 due to all causes in time and frequency error. It is used as a peer selection metric and to organize the NTP subnet as a shortest-path spanning tree.

11.5 System Error Budget

In NTP, the ultimate time reference is UTC as disseminated by national standards means, but in general there is a chain of time servers between the primary server and the client. In the NTP subnet, each secondary server is synchronized to the next server closer to the primary server. The NTP grooming and mitigation algorithms develop a number of error statistics and bounds. These values are inherited by the next server further from the

Name	Description
t	Update time
θ	Clock offset
δ	Roundtrip delay
ε	Dispersion
φ	Jitter

Peer Variables

Name	Description
T_1	Origin timestamp
T_2	Receive timestamp
T_3	Transmit timestamp
T_4	Destination timestamp
x	Clock offset
y	Roundtrip delay
z	Dispersion

Sample Variables

Name	Description
μ	Update interval
Δ	Root delay
E	Root dispersion
Θ	Clock offset
ϑ	System jitter
φ_S	Selection jitter
ρ	Max. reading error
φ	Frequency tolerance

System Variables

Name	Description
ρ_R	Max. reading error
Δ_R	Root delay
E_R	Root dispersion

Server Packet Variables

FIGURE 11.3
Glossary of symbols.

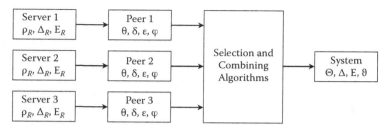

FIGURE 11.4
Error statistics.

primary server. The manner in which they accumulate and the resulting error statistics is the topic of this section.

Figure 11.3 shows a glossary of the variables used in the analysis, while Figure 11.4 shows the principal statistics calculated by the peer and system processes. The variables are classified as packet variables, peer variables, system variables, and server variables. In order to resolve ambiguities when variables in difference classes have the same name, the name will be prefixed by the class name.

Figure 11.5 shows the detailed equations that produce the various statistics described in Chapter 3 and how they contribute to the error budget. The server packet variables include the root delay Δ_R and root dispersion E_R inherited along the path via server R to the primary server, as well as the precision ρ_R of the server clock. The packet variables include the four timestamps T_1, T_2, T_3, and T_4 used to calculate the clock offset x and round-trip delay y as in Equation 11.3. The peer dispersion z is initialized with the precision, then accumulates at rate ϕ over the interval from T_1 to T_4. The peer variables are calculated from recent packet variables as in the clock filter algorithm of Section 3.7. They include the clock offset θ, round-trip delay δ, and peer dispersion ε. In addition, the peer jitter ϕ_p is calculated as the RMS average of the first-order sample offset differences.

The system variables are inherent from the system peer variables determined by the select, cluster, combine, and mitigation algorithms described in Chapter 3. They include the system clock offset θ, root delay Δ, root dispersion E, and select jitter ϕ_s. The system clock offset θ is computed as the weighted average of the survivor clock offsets, and the peer jitter ϕ_p is computed as the weighted average of the survivor jitter components. The select jitter ϕ_s is calculated from the first-order clock differences between the survivors. The system jitter $\vartheta = \sqrt{\phi_p^2 + \phi_s^2}$ is provided to the API as the expected error statistic, and the root distance $\Lambda = \Delta/2 + E$ is provided to the API as the maximum error statistic.

If the kernel includes the precision time features described in Chapter 8, the kernel API can be used to assess current timekeeping quality. The values returned include the residual offset, estimated error, and maximum error.

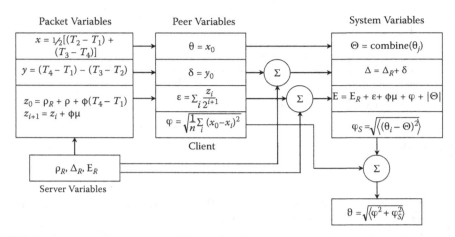

FIGURE 11.5
Error budget calculations.

The residual offset represents the best estimate of the system clock deviation from UTC, while the expected error and maximum error represent the best estimate of the error inherent in the deviation estimate.

It should be understood that the above constructions are only the outline of the actual code in the reference implementation. A number of intricate provisions have to be made in the code to handle special cases, like when the computed round-trip delay goes negative due to large frequency error and to avoid overflow, underflow, and division by zero when working with very small residuals.

11.6 Parting Shots

Many years of experience have proved the worth of this analysis. The root distance, aka maximum error statistic, represents the metric used to organize the NTP subnet, and this has worked well over a very wide range of NTP subnet configurations, intentionally organized and accidental. However, the expected error statistic is the most useful when somebody asks just how well the contraption works.

References

1. Mills, D.L. Modelling and analysis of computer network clocks. Electrical Engineering Department Report 92-5-2, University of Delaware, May 1992, 29 pp.
2. Mills, D.L. Network Time Protocol (Version 3) specification, implementation and analysis. Network Working Group Report RFC-1305, University of Delaware, March 1992, 113 pp.

12

Modeling and Analysis of Computer Clocks

"I sent a message to the fish:
I told them 'This is what I wish.'
The little fishes of the sea,
They sent an answer back to me.
The little fishes' answer was
'We cannot do it, Sir, because—'"

Lewis Carroll
Through the Looking Glass

That typical computer clocks behave in ways quite counterproductive to good timekeeping should come as no surprise. For instance, in a survey of about 20,000 Internet hosts synchronized by the NTP, the median clock oscillator frequency error was 78 PPM, with some oscillators showing errors over 500 PPM [1]. With a 78-PPM frequency error, the time error over 1 day accumulates almost 7 s. Commodity computers have no explicit means to control the ambient temperature, crystal drive level, voltage regulation, or mechanical stability, so the oscillator frequency may vary over a few parts per million in the normal course of the day.

This chapter discusses the mathematical analysis of computer clocks, including the effects of environmental factors on oscillator frequency, as well as the modeling of the feedback loop used to discipline time and frequency. The treatment is quite mathematical, and in some cases additional information is available from the references at the end of this chapter. However, these models should be considered only a guide to the nominal characteristics. The actual discipline algorithm, which is discussed in Chapter 4, has a number of features that allow it to adapt more quickly to ambient temperature variations and to suppress and avoid disruptive spikes.

The chapter begins with a probabilistic model of the computer clock oscillator, including its inherent time and frequency fluctuations. The behavior of the model is first described in terms of experiments, then compared to statistical models. Time fluctuations or *jitter* are primarily due to network and operating system latencies and can be modeled as a random process driven by continuous or exponential distributions. Frequency fluctuations or *wander* are primarily due to temperature variations and can be modeled as a random-walk process driven by the integral of a zero-mean Gaussian distribution.

The chapter continues with an analysis of the clock discipline feedback loop driven by a phase- or frequency-locked oscillator. The phase-locked model applies most closely at the smaller poll intervals, while the frequency-locked model applies most closely at the larger poll intervals. The important thing to learn from this analysis is how to design the various parameters of the discipline for the best transient response.

12.1 Computer Clock Concepts

Recall the key concepts of resolution, precision, and accuracy from Chapter 4. Resolution is the degree to which one clock reading can be distinguished from another, normally equal to the reciprocal of the processor clock frequency. For a modern 3-GHz processor with a processor cycle counter (PCC), the resolution is 0.33 ns or about the time clock pulses travel 4 inches along a wire. A timestamp $T(t)$ is determined by reading the clock at an arbitrary time t (the argument t will usually be omitted for conciseness). However, in most systems the PCC is not read directly as it has to be scaled and combined with other kernel variables. The latency of a kernel system call to read the system clock and return the time to the application program is defined as the *precision*.

The traditional characterization of oscillator stability is a plot of *Allan variance* [2], which is defined using a series of time differences measured between a clock and some external standard. Let x_k be the kth measurement and T be the interval between measurements. Define the *fractional frequency*

$$y_{k+1} \equiv \frac{x_{k-1} - x_k}{T},$$

which is a dimensionless quantity. Now, consider a sequence of N independent fractional frequency samples y_k ($k = 1, 2, \ldots, N$) where the interval τ between samples is some multiple of T. Since τ is the nominal interval over which these samples are averaged, the Allan variance is defined as

$$\sigma_y^2(N,T,\tau) = \left\langle \frac{1}{N-1}\left[\sum_{i=1}^{N} y_i^2 - \frac{1}{N}\left[\sum_{j=1}^{N} y_j\right]^2\right]\right\rangle.$$

A particularly useful formulation is $N = 2$ and $T = \tau$, called the two-sample Allan variance:

$$\sigma_y^2(\tau) \equiv \left\langle \frac{1}{2}(y_{k+1} - y_k)^2 \right\rangle.$$

Let Δ_τ be the first-order differences of y_k taken τ samples apart. Then,

$$\sigma_y^2(\tau) = \frac{1}{2}E(\Delta_\tau^2)$$

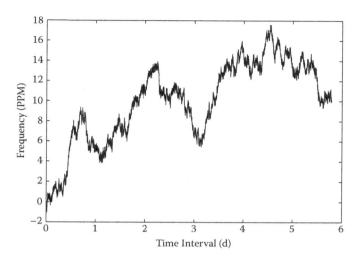

FIGURE 12.1
Typical computer oscillator frequency wander.

and the *Allan deviation* $\sigma_y(\tau)$ is the square root of this quantity. This is a particularly useful formulation since it can be quickly computed using software packages such as MATLAB®.

In principle, the Allan deviation characteristic must be determined for each clock separately since it depends on the prevailing measurement phase noise and clock frequency noise. For the computer clock, phase noise is usually dominated by the interrupt latency jitter of the pulse-per-second (PPS) signal. Frequency noise is due to the intrinsic characteristic of the clock oscillator itself and the environment in which it runs. In typical computer clocks, the oscillator wander depends largely on ambient temperature variations. A plot of frequency versus time for a typical computer clock oscillator is shown in Figure 12.1. The data shown in this figure were collected while the clock discipline loop was disconnected, so the clock oscillator was not adjusted in any way, and it wandered to its own instincts.

Figure 12.2 shows the Allan deviation characteristic $\sigma_y(\tau)$ in log-log coordinates for two typical systems, one with a "good" oscillator and one with a "bad" oscillator. In both cases, the x_k are created from the system clock sampled at input/output (I/O) interrupts generated by a PPS signal. Each characteristic appears as a V-shaped curve, although some curves overlap on the plot. The curve labeled 1 represents a typical good clock but with relatively high interrupt latency jitter, while curve 2 represents a typical bad clock but with reduced latency jitter. Curves 3 and 4 are generated from the addition of samples from two distributions with defined parameters. The white-phase noise is generated from an exponential distribution, while the random-walk frequency noise is generated from the integral of a Gaussian distribution. The parameters of each distribution are adjusted to closely simulate the actual measured data.

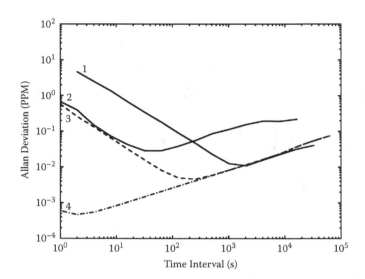

FIGURE 12.2
Allan deviation characteristics for Pentium and Alpha systems.

Curve 3 represents the good clock but with reduced latency jitter. Curve 4 represents the extrapolation of the good clock with projected jitter of 1 ns.

As the figure shows, at the smaller averaging times for both systems the characteristic is dominated by white-phase noise, which appears on the log-log plot as straight lines with slope −1 [3]. At the larger averaging times, the characteristic is dominated by random-walk frequency noise, which appears as straight lines with slope +0.5. Between the two regimes, the characteristic is a blend of both noise sources. In the following, the line with slope −1 is called the phase line, while the line with slope +0.5 is called the frequency line.

The intersection coordinate (x, y) of the phase and frequency lines, called the *Allan intercept*, characterizes each particular timing source and clock oscillator. A useful statistic is the x value, which specifies the optimum averaging time for the particular source and oscillator combination. The x value on Figure 12.1 ranges from about 500 to 2,000 s. Above the intercept, the performance is limited by oscillator wander, while below it the performance is limited by interrupt latency jitter. For comparison, the NTP Version 4 (NTPv4) clock discipline time constant is about 2,000 s at a poll interval of 64 s. The y statistic represents the best stability that can be achieved for the particular source and oscillator combination.

The dashed lines in Figure 12.2 show the Allan deviations determined from a random sequence in which each plotted value consists of the sum of a phase noise sample and a frequency noise sample. The phase noise generator amplitude is set by the σ_p parameter, while the frequency noise generator amplitude is set by the σ_f parameter. Table 12.1 shows the measured σ_p for several sources commonly found on the Internet [4]. Here,

TABLE 12.1

Allan Intercepts for Various Internet Paths

Source	Distribution	$\sigma_p \, \mu s$
MICRO	Uniform	1
PPS	Uniform	28
LAN	Exponential	50
BARN	Exponential	346
PEERS	Exponential	809
USNO	Exponential	1,325
IEN	Exponential	6,324

local-area network (LAN), PPS, and MICRO correspond to curves 1, 2, and 4, respectively, in Figure 12.2. In PPS and MICRO, the source is a PPS signal; in the remaining cases, the source is a primary server reached via some Internet path. BARN is a slow machine on a busy Ethernet. The network path to the U.S. Naval Observatory (USNO) involves a campus network, a lightly loaded T1 circuit, and another campus network. The path to IEN represents probably the most congested of the transatlantic paths considered in Mills [4]. The PEERS case is special; it has several sources, so the system jitter is from not only a single source but also the combined peer jitter of several sources plus the select jitter.

To model the curve 1 (LAN) source in Figure 12.2, phase samples are the first-order differences between samples drawn from an exponential distribution with $\sigma_p = 50 \, \mu s$, while frequency samples are drawn from the integral of a Gaussian distribution with $\sigma_f = 5.0 \times 10^{-10}$. To model the curve 2 (PPS) characteristic, phase samples are the first-order difference between samples drawn from a uniform distribution with $\sigma_p = 19 \, \mu s$, while frequency samples are drawn from the integral of a Gaussian distribution with $\sigma_f = 1.5 \times 10^{-8}$. These particular values were determined by experiment to closely match the measured curves. Over most of the range, the fit is quite good and clearly demonstrates that the phase and frequency contributions are separable and can be accurately characterized by intersecting straight lines defined by the Allan intercept.

It would be useful to display a noise floor, so to speak, at which the phase noise is at the lower limits supported by the operating system and hardware. A useful assumption in modern computers is that this limit is on the order of 1 μs, representing the nominal resolution of the Unix kernel, in which the time is reckoned in seconds and microseconds. In the figure, the MICRO phase noise samples are drawn from a uniform distribution with $\sigma_p = 0.5$ μs representing the precision of this kernel. The gap between the PPS and MICRO characteristics represents improvements that might be achieved in the future.

A brief word of explanation is in order about the particular choice of random distributions to model phase and frequency noise. The PPS, MICRO, and LAN synthetic frequency samples are produced by an integral of a Gaussian distribution, which from these and other experiments is a reliable predictor of real oscillator behavior. This is not a realistic assumption in the wide sense as the autocorrelation function is infinite. As the graphs show, however, the fit is good except at the largest lag, where the number of samples averaged becomes small.

The PPS and MICRO phase samples are produced by uniform distributions over a defined range. This is appropriate when the underlying process is reading a counter at random, irregular times. In the MICRO case, the range is set at 1 μs, recognizing that the system clock counts in microseconds. In the PPS case, the range is set at 38 μs to match the actual measurements, but it is useful to note that this value is close to the jitter of the serial port interrupt routine. On the other hand, the LAN case involves a two-way transit across the Ethernet in the presence of queuing delays for other traffic on the interfaces and cable, so the delays are better modeled as exponential. Having gone to this degree of detail, the choice of distribution does not make a lot of difference; the characteristic slopes are the same, and the parameters differ by only small amounts.

12.2 Mathematical Model of the Generic Feedback Loop

The hybrid phase-/frequency-locked feedback loop discussed in Chapter 4 can be modeled as a disciplined oscillator in which the time and frequency are stabilized by interlocking feedback loops. The NTP disciplined oscillator operates using a hybrid of two interlocking feedback loops, a phase-lock loop (PLL) for relatively small poll intervals well below the Allan intercept and a frequency-lock loop (FLL) for relatively large poll intervals well above the intercept. The behavior for poll intervals near the intercept point is a weighted combination of both loop types, as described in Chapter 4.

A hybrid loop such as used in NTPv4 is a complex, nonlinear algorithm that is difficult to analyze and express in simple mathematical terms. In the NTPv4 discipline algorithm design, the averaging time is determined by the feedback loop time constant, which by design is determined by the poll interval. It is possible to model the hybrid algorithm at the extremes of the poll interval span as the influence of the PLL is suppressed at the larger poll intervals and the influence of the FLL is suppressed at the smaller poll intervals. In the following discussion, the PLL and FLL are analyzed separately to derive the open-loop and closed-loop transient response. While the response to the combined hybrid discipline is not easily predicted near the Allan intercept where both loops contribute to the response, the behavior has been verified using the NTP simulator in the reference implementation software distribution.

The PLL and FLL feedback loop behavior can be described using an extensive body of mathematics developed for the purpose, such as given in Smith [5] and elaborated in this section. Recall in Figure 4.1 that the variable θ_r represents the phase of the reference signal and θ_c the phase of the variable-frequency oscillator (VFO). The phase detector produces a signal V_d representing the phase difference $\theta_r - \theta_o$. The clock filter, select, cluster, and combine algorithms provide the output V_s. The loop filter and clock adjust process, represented by the equations given in this section, produce a VFO correction signal V_c, which controls the oscillator frequency and thus the phase.

For the moment, we can consider that the loop is linear, so the open-loop Laplace transfer function can be constructed by breaking the loop at point V_c on Figure 4.1 and computing the ratio of the VFO phase θ_c to the reference phase θ_r. This function is the product of the individual transfer functions for the phase detector, clock filter, loop filter, and VFO. With appropriate scaling, the phase detector delivers a signal $V_d = \theta_r$, so its transfer function is simply

$F_d(s) = 1$. The VFO delivers a frequency change $\Delta\omega = \dfrac{d\theta_o}{dt} = V_c$ and $\theta_c = \int V_c dt$,

so its transfer function is the Laplace transform of the integral $F_o(s) = 1/s$. The clock filter contributes a statistical delay, but for present purposes, this delay will be assumed a constant T, so its transfer function is the Laplace transform of the delay, $F_s(s) = e^{-Ts}$. The open loop gain is the product of these four transfer functions:

$$G(s) = \frac{\theta_c(s)}{\theta_r(s)} = F_d(s)F_s(s)F_o(s)F(s) = \frac{1}{2}e^{-Ts}F(s), \qquad (12.1)$$

where $F(s)$ is the transfer function of the loop filter. In the NTP design, the time constant is about 32 times the poll interval, so the effects of the clock filter delay T can be neglected, and $e^{-Ts} = 1$. By combining terms, Equation 12.1 can be written as

$$G(s) = \frac{F(s)}{s}.$$

The loop behavior is then completely determined by the transfer function $F(s)$. In the simplest case where $F(s)$ is a constant, the loop behaves as an integrator and can reduce the residual error to zero as long as there is no frequency error. However, to reduce incidental jitter, it is usually desirable to include a low-pass characteristic in $F(s)$, but this does not materially affect the transient response at low frequencies. This design, called a type I feedback control loop, cannot drive the residual error to zero if a frequency error exists. To do this, a type II feedback control loop uses an additional stage of integration. The mathematical analysis is different for each type of loop.

In either type of loop, the closed-loop gain is determined from classic feedback analysis:

$$H(s) = \frac{G(s)}{1+G(s)}.$$

Assuming the output is taken at V_s, the closed-loop I/O transfer function is the ratio of the forward gain to the open loop gain:

$$H_o(s) = \frac{F_d(s)}{1+G(s)} = \frac{1}{1+G(s)}. \tag{12.2}$$

The acquisition and tracking behavior of the loop are determined by the gain and the poles and zeros of the loop filter. The *capture range* is the maximum frequency range over which the loop will achieve phase lock, having previously been not in lock. The *tracking range* is the maximum frequency range over which the loop will remain locked once phase lock has been achieved. The capture and tracking ranges of the loop must be at least as large as the VFO frequency tolerance. In the designs discussed here, the tracking range is typically greater than the capture range, but both are greater than the tolerance.

12.2.1 Type I FLL Feedback Control Loop

The type I feedback control loop used by the FLL is characterized by a single low-pass filter with transfer function

$$F(s) = \left(1 + \frac{s}{\omega_L}\right)^{-1},$$

where ω_L is the corner frequency. Substituting in Equations 12.1 and 12.2 and rearranging yields the closed-loop gain

$$H(s) = \left(\frac{s^2}{\omega_n^2} + \frac{2\zeta}{\omega_n} + 1\right)^{-1},$$

where ω_n and ζ are related to the loop gain α and corner frequency ω_L:

$$\omega_n^2 = \alpha\omega_L \quad \text{and} \quad \zeta = \frac{1}{2\sqrt{\dfrac{\omega_L}{\alpha}}}.$$

For a critically damped (Butterworth) system, $\zeta = \sqrt{2}$, which implies that $\alpha = \omega_L/2$.

The FLL loop filter can be implemented as a sampled data system using an exponential average of frequency offsets. Let y_k ($k = 1, 2, \ldots$) be a sequence of average frequency offsets and x_k be the corresponding sequence of time offsets. Then, the new average frequency offset is

$$\overline{y}_{k+1} = \overline{y}_k + \frac{x_k - x_{k-1}}{\mu \tau_{\text{FLL}}},$$

where $\mu = t_k - t_{k-1}$ is the update interval, and t_k is the epoch of the x_k measurement. The τ_{FLL} is an FLL averaging parameter designed to increase the effectiveness of the FLL as the poll exponent increases to the maximum. An empirical formulation of this parameter is

$$\tau_{\text{FLL}} = 18 - \tau,$$

where τ is the poll exponent. If the poll interval is less than the Allan intercept, the FLL is effectively disabled; if above that, the effectiveness increases from 2^{-7} at $\tau = 11$ (2,048 s) to 2^{-1} at $\tau = 17$ (36 h). This simple formulation was suggested by the observation that the poll exponent is the log of the poll interval, and the frequency line in the Allan deviation plot is a straight line in log-log coordinates.

12.2.2 Type II Feedback Control Loop

The type I feedback control loop does not have the capability to compensate for the intrinsic oscillator frequency error, which can be up to 500 PPM in commodity computers. With a frequency error of this magnitude, it is necessary to provide frequent updates determined by the time synchronization protocol. For instance, if these adjustments were discontinued for a day, the time error could accumulate over 43 s.

To minimize the residual time and frequency errors yet allow relatively large update intervals and averaging times, it is necessary to add another stage of integration, which amounts to the addition of another pole at zero frequency. However, a loop with two poles at zero frequency is unstable since the phase characteristic of the Bode plot approaches 180° as the amplitude characteristic passes through unity gain. Instability can be avoided through the addition of a zero in the transfer function, as shown in the loop filter transfer function:

$$F(s) = \frac{\omega_c^2}{\tau_c^2 s} \left(1 + \frac{\tau_c s}{\omega_z} \right), \tag{12.3}$$

where ω_c is the crossover frequency, ω_z is the corner frequency required for loop stability, and τ_c determines the time constant and thus the bandwidth.

While this is a first-order function and some improvement in phase noise might be gained from a higher-order function, in practice the improvement is lost due to the effects of the clock filter delay. Making the following substitutions:

$$\omega_c = \frac{1}{K_f} \text{ and } \omega_z = \frac{K_g}{K_f^2},$$

and rearranging yields

$$G(s) = \frac{F(s)}{s} = \frac{\alpha}{s}\left(\frac{1}{K_g \tau_c} + \frac{1}{(K_g \tau_c)^2 s}\right), \qquad (12.4)$$

which corresponds to a constant term plus an integrating term scaled by the loop gain α and time constant τ_c. If we set $\alpha = 1$, $\tau = 2^6$, $K_g = 2^4$, and $K_f = 2^6$, the Bode plot of the open-loop transfer function consists of a –12-dB/octave line that intersects the 0-dB baseline at $\omega_c = 2^{-12}$ rad/s, together with a +6-dB/octave line at the corner frequency $\omega_z = 2^{-14}$ rad/s. The damping factor $\zeta = \omega_c/2 \omega_z = 2$ suggests that the loop will be stable and have a large phase margin together with a low overshoot.

Equation 12.4 can be interpreted with respect to Figures 4.1 and 4.2 in Chapter 4. The VFO in Figure 4.1 accounts for the 1/s term; the x prediction in Figure 4.2 accounts for the phase term $\frac{1}{(K_f \tau_c)^2 s}$ which is recomputed by the clock adjust process once per second, while the y prediction accounts for the frequency term $1/(K_g \tau_c)^2 s$, which is recomputed at each clock update. Assuming the output is taken at V_s on Figure 4.1, the closed-loop transfer function can be obtained from Equation 12.3. If only the relative response is needed and the clock filter delay can be neglected, this can be written as

$$H_0(s) = \frac{1}{1+G(s)} = s^2 \left[s^2 + \left(\frac{\omega_c^2}{\omega_z \tau_0 s + \frac{\omega_c^2}{\tau_c^2}} \right) \right]^{-1}.$$

For some input function $I(s)$, the output function $I(s)H(s)$ can be inverted to find the time response. Using a unit step input $I(s) = 1/s$ and the values as determined yields a loop rise time of about 52 min, a maximum overshoot of about 4.8 percent in about 1.7 h. After that, the offset settles to within 1 percent of the initial offset in about 8.7 h. This characteristic is appropriate for most scenarios involving LANs and wide-area networks (WANs); however, for reasons detailed in Chapter 4, it is desirable to increase the poll interval to considerably larger values. This can be done by a proportional change in the time constant τ_c. The scaling has been conveniently chosen so that $\tau_c = 2^{\tau+5}$, where τ is the poll exponent. Note that the frequency term in Equation 12.4 varies as the inverse square, so the PLL contribution to frequency control grows weaker with increasing poll exponent, which is opposite to the FLL behavior. The phase term continues to operate over the full poll interval range.

The time and frequency response of the hybrid PLL/FLL feedback loop is illustrated in Chapter 4. Figure 4.3 shows the phase response and Figure 4.4 the frequency response of a 100-ms time step measured using the reference implementation in simulator mode. The phase and frequency characteristics are very nearly identical to the analytical results and confirm that the implementation behavior is accurately predicted by the analysis here.

12.3 Synthetic Timescales and Clock Wranglers

Almost everywhere in this book, the emphasis is on synchronizing to the UTC timescale as disseminated by radio, satellite, or telephone modem. It may happen that a subnet of NTP time tellers has no access to any such dissemination means, so it may be convenient to designate one or more tellers as primary servers and synchronize all the other clients to them. This is the model for the orphan mode discussed in Section 3.13. In orphan mode, dependent clients are all at the mercy of a single orphan parent clock oscillator.

If more than one orphan parent is available, it might be desirable to combine their offsets in some fashion to achieve a common timescale. The now-retired Fuzzball system implemented a distributed algorithm in which the system clocks of all subnet hosts contribute to a single ensemble timescale more accurate than any clock separately. In this approach, all local servers operate at the same stratum in symmetric mode with all other local servers. corrections needed to follow the ensemble timescale. Each host then runs an algorithm similar to those used by national laboratories to wrangle herds of cesium clocks.

It is the practice in national standards laboratories to construct a synthetic timescale based on an ensemble of at least three contributing cesium clocks. The timescale is produced by an algorithm using periodic measurements of the time offsets between the clocks of the ensemble. The algorithm combines the offsets using computed weights to produce an ensemble timescale more accurate than the timescale of any clock in the ensemble. The algorithm used by USNO is based on autoregressive, integrated, moving-average (ARIMA) models [6], while the algorithm used by the NIST evolved from Kalman filter models [7–9]. These algorithms result in long-term fractional frequency stabilities on the order of 1.5×10^{-14}.

A description of the combine method used by the Fuzzball [10] follows. The method was adapted from the NIST algorithm used to determine the NBS(AT1) synthetic laboratory timescale from an ensemble of Cesium clocks [9]. The NIST method, while not a Kalman filter in the strict sense, can be shown equivalent to that method by suitable choice of gains and time constants. See Weiss, Allan, and Peppler [9] for a discussion of the fine points of these issues, which are not explored further here.

Consider a herd of real clocks connected by real networks, each clock meandering to its own haphazard timescale. Plot the offsets of each clock relative to an arbitrary timescale for many samples. The plot appears as a system of bell-shaped figures slowly precessing relative to each other but with some further away from nominal zero than others. The bells will normally be scattered over the offset space, more or less close to each other, with some overlapping and some not. The problem is to develop the best estimate for the ensemble timescale from periodic offsets between the clocks collected at fixed intervals.

The ensemble timescale can be synthesized from a sequence of offsets measured between a herd of n clocks at nominal intervals τ. Let $T(t_0)$ be the time displayed by a clock at epoch t_0 relative to an arbitrary timescale. Assume the first derivative with respect to time $R(t_0)$ (drift) and second derivative $D(t_0)$ (aging) are known at t_0 and do not change over the interval τ. Then, the time displayed at the end of the interval τ is

$$T(t_0 + \tau) = T(t_0) + R(t_0)\tau + \frac{1}{2}D(t_0)\tau^2 + x(t_0 + \tau),$$

where x is a stochastic error term. For the moment, we neglect the aging and stochastic terms. Let $T_i(t_0)$ be the time and $R_i(t_0)$ be the frequency of the ith clock at epoch t_0 relative to the arbitrary timescale and let "^" designate the associated estimates. The following algorithm wrangles the frequency of each clock so that the time differences between them are minimized.

Given that the ith clock is set correctly at time t_0, the estimated time at epoch $t_0 + \tau$ is

$$\hat{T}_i(t_0 + \tau) = T_i(t_0) + R_i(t_0)\tau,$$

neglecting second-order terms. If the frequencies are correct for all clocks in the ensemble, they will all display the same time at epoch $t_0 + \tau$. If not, the wrangler constructs a set of n independent time offset measurements between each clock and all the others at epoch $t_0 + \tau$. Define the offset between the ith clock and the jth clock at that epoch as

$$T_{ij}(t_0 + \tau) = T_i(t_0 + \tau) - T_j(t_0 + \tau).$$

Note that $T_{ij} = -T_{ji}$ and $T_{ii} = 0$. Let w_j be a previously determined set of weight factors for the nominal interval τ and $\sum_{j=1}^{n} w_j = 1$. These factors represent the fractional contribution of each clock to the ensemble timescale. The new basis value for the time at epoch $t_0 + \tau$ is then

$$T_i(t_0 + \tau) = \sum_{j=1}^{n} w_j [\hat{T}_j(t_0 + \tau) + T_{ij}(t_0 + \tau)].$$

The corrected time displayed by the ith clock at epoch $t_0 + \tau$ is the weighted average of the estimated time for the jth clock plus the offset measured from that clock to the ith clock. Next, the frequency estimate for the ith clock $\hat{R}_i(t_0 + \tau)$ is determined so that corrections are minimized in the future. The average frequency assumed for the ith clock at the end of the interval is the difference between the times at the beginning and end of the interval divided by τ. Thus, the new frequency estimate is

$$\hat{R}_i(t_0 + \tau) = \frac{T_i(t_0 + \tau) - T_i(t_0)}{\tau}.$$

In the following, angle brackets < and > indicate the infinite time average, but in practice the infinite averages are computed as exponential time averages. The new basis value for the frequency at epoch $t_0 + \tau$ is

$$R_i(t_0 + \tau) = \left\langle \hat{R}_i(t_0 + \tau) \right\rangle \equiv R_i(t_0 + \tau) + \frac{\hat{R}_i(t_0 + \tau) - R_i(t_0 + \tau)}{\alpha_i}.$$

In the NIST algorithm, α_i is an averaging parameter whose value is a function of τ and the Allan intercept for the ith clock. In a typical NTP herd where τ is nearly the same as the Allan intercept, the value works out to about eight. This value is also used for the averaging parameter in the remaining functions of this section.

The weight factor w_i for the ith clock is determined from the nominal error φ_i of that clock. The error calculated for each interval τ is

$$\varphi_i = \left| \hat{T}_i(t_0 + \tau) - T_i(t_0 + \tau) \right| + \beta_i.$$

In the NIST algorithm, β_i corrects for the bias due to the fact that the ith clock is included in the ensemble averages. For the much milling about NTP herd, the correction is lost in the noise and so ignored. The accumulated error of the entire ensemble is

$$\left\langle \varphi_e^2 \right\rangle = \left[\sum_{i=1}^{n} \left\langle \varphi_i^2 \right\rangle^{-1} \right]^{-1}.$$

Finally, the weight factor for the ith clock is calculated as

$$w_i = \frac{\langle \varphi_e^2 \rangle}{\langle \varphi_i^2 \rangle}.$$

When all estimates and weight factors have been updated, the origin of the estimation interval is shifted, and the new value of t_0 becomes the old value of $t_0 + \tau$.

These procedures produce the estimated time and frequency offsets for each clock; however, they do not produce the ensemble timescale directly. To do that, one of the clocks, usually the "best" one with the highest weight factor, is chosen as the reference and used to generate the actual laboratory standard. Corrections to this standard either can be incorporated in the form of a hardware microstepper, which adjusts the phase of the standard frequency in fine-grain steps, or can be published and distributed for retroactive corrections.

12.4 Parting Shots

One might ask why the elegant Fuzzball algorithm has not been incorporated in the reference implementation. The short answer is that it is not needed when all cows in the herd are wrangled from a set of external UTC sources. A more interesting case is when no such external source is available. The reference implementation handles this case using orphan mode, in which an orphan parent masquerades as a primary server, and the other cows follow its lead. There is some hazard in this since the loss of the primary cow leaves the herd leaderless.

The Fuzzball algorithm would be an ideal way to provide mutual redundancy for a leaderless herd. In a strawman design, each cow would run symmetric active mode with all of the others in the herd. A new extension field would be used to convey offsets measured between one cow and each of the others to all of the other cows, so that all cows can construct a matrix T of time offsets. At periodic intervals, each cow would ruminate T to produce a new time and frequency adjustment as if disciplined by a UTC source.

References

1. Mills, D.L., A. Thyagarajan, and B.C. Huffman. Internet timekeeping around the globe. *Proceedings of the Precision Time and Time Interval (PTTI) Applications and Planning Meeting* (Long Beach, CA, December 1997).

2. Allan, D.W. Time and frequency (time-domain) estimation and prediction of precision clocks and oscillators. *IEEE Trans. Ultrason. Ferroelectr. Freq. Control UFFC-34, 6* (November 1987), 647–654. Also in Sullivan, D.B., D.W. Allan, D.A. Howe, and F.L. Walls (Eds.), *Characterization of Clocks and Oscillators*. NIST Technical Note 1337, U.S. Department of Commerce, 1990, 121–128.

3. Stein, S.R. Frequency and time—their measurement and characterization (Chapter 12). In E.A. Gerber and A. Ballato (Eds.), *Precision Frequency Control, Vol. 2*, Academic Press, New York, 1985, 191–232, 399–416. Also in Sullivan, D.B., D.W. Allan, D.A. Howe, and F.L. Walls (Eds.), *Characterization of Clocks and Oscillators*. National Institute of Standards and Technology Technical Note 1337, U.S. Government Printing Office, Washington, DC, January 1990, TN61–TN119.

4. Mills, D.L. Improved algorithms for synchronizing computer network clocks. *IEEE/ACM Trans. Networks* (June 1995), 245–254.

5. Smith, J. *Modern Communications Circuits*. McGraw-Hill, New York, 1986.

6. Percival, D.B. The U.S. Naval Observatory clock time scales. *IEEE Trans. Instrum. Meas. IM-27, 4* (December 1978), 376–385.

7. Jones, R.H., and P.V. Tryon. Estimating time from atomic clocks. *J. Res. Natl. Bur. Std. 88, 1* (January–February 1983), 17–24.

8. Tryon, P.V., and R.H. Jones. Estimation of parameters in models for cesium beam atomic clocks. *J. Res. Natl. Bur. Std. 88, 1* (January–February 1983).

9. Weiss, M.A., D.W. Allan, and T.K. Peppler. A study of the NBS time scale algorithm. *IEEE Trans. Instrum. Meas. 38, 2* (April 1989), 631–635.

10. Mills, D.L. The Fuzzball. *Proceedings ACM SIGCOMM 88 Symposium* (Palo Alto, CA, August 1988), 115–122.

Further Reading

Levine, J. An algorithm to synchronize the time of a computer to universal time. *IEEE Trans. Networking 3, 1* (February 1995), 42–50.

Mills, D.L. *Clock Discipline Algorithms for the Network Time Protocol Version 4*. Electrical Engineering Department Report 97-3-3, University of Delaware, Newark, March 1997, 35 pp.

13

Metrology and Chronometry of the NTP Timescale

Is all our life, then, but a dream
Seen faintly in the golden gleam
Athwart Time's dark resistless stream?

Lewis Carroll
Sylvie and Bruno

The ultimate goal of the NTP infrastructure is to synchronize clocks of the network to a common timescale, but it may or may not be the case that the timescale is synchronized by international agreement. For instance, in the early years of the 20th century the most accurate clocks in the land were kept by railroaders. While it took two days to cross the country by passenger rail with a change of trains in Chicago, it was crucial when meeting at a siding that train conductors had the right time. It did not matter if railroad time was tied to the Sun, Moon, or stars, just that railroaders' pocket watches kept the *same* time.

On the other hand, mariners were concerned about the accuracy of their chronometers to establish accurate longitude. Longitude is established by correlating the position of the Sun or stars with chronometer time, so chronometers must be synchronized to Earth rotation, commonly called *solar time*. Accuracy was so important that the British Admiralty established a prize for the first chronometer with which longitude could be calculated to within half a degree after a trans-Atlantic voyage. The prize was eventually collected by John Harrison, whose No. 4 Chronometer was well within that specification after a 1762 voyage to Jamaica.

This chapter* introduces the concepts of *calendar metrology*, which is the determination of civil time and date according to the modern calendar, and *network chronometry*, which is the determination of computer time relative to international standards as disseminated via computer network. It describes the methods conventionally used to establish civil time and date and the various timescales now in use. In particular, it characterizes the NTP timescale relative to the UTC timescale and establishes the precise interpretation of UTC leap seconds in the NTP timescale.

---

* Some of this material was first published in Mills, D.L. *ACM Computer Communications Review, 21*, 5 (October 1991), 8–17 [1], but has been ruthlessly edited, and much new topical material has been added.

In this chapter, the terms *time, timescale, era, clock, oscillator, timestamp, date,* and *epoch* are used in a technical sense. Strictly speaking, *time* is an abstraction that determines the ordering of events in a given reality. A *timescale* is a continuum of monotone-increasing times in some frame of reference. While those timescales useful for computer networks are continuous in the short term, they may have discontinuities in the long term, such as the insertion of leap seconds in UTC and on the adoption of the Gregorian calendar in 1582. Some timescales are cyclic and span an era with designated beginning and span. For instance, the Julian era* timescale began in 4713 before the common era (BCE, also known as BC) and spans 7,980 years. A date in the Classic Maya calendar is represented as a day–number glyph in the 365-day secular year paired with a day–number glyph in the 260-day religious year. Both numbers increment for each new day. The interval of 18,980 days when the same day–number pair recurs is called the Calendar Round. It spans 52 secular years of 365 days and 73 religious years of 260 days.

A *clock* is an oscillator and an oscillator counter that records the number of increments (sometimes called *ticks* or *jiffies*) since initialized with a given value at a given time. Correctness assertions require that the oscillator frequency error relative to the given timescale never exceed a stated bound, typically 0.05 percent or 500 PPM. While the timescale proceeds from the indefinite past to the indefinite future, the counter modulus is finite. In NTP, the timestamp format spans an era of 2^{32} s or about 136 years, so some means are required to number the eras in the datestamp format.

A *date* is a unique value captured as the timescale progresses, while an *epoch* is a static date of some interest, such as the origin of the common era (CE, also known as AD). In general, both dates and epochs are captured in internal system variables of generous proportions, like 128 bits. On the other hand, *timestamps* are derived from dates but are packed in more compact format, like 64 bits, for efficiency in transport. The 64-bit NTP timestamps are associated with era numbers that provide an unambiguous mapping to dates. Often in the literature and even elsewhere in this book, the distinctions blur among timestamp, date, and epoch, but the meanings will be obvious from context.

The conventional civil timescale used in most parts of the world is based on UTC, which replaced Greenwich (UK) mean time (GMT) many years ago. As described in this chapter, UTC is based on International Atomic Time (TAI), which is derived from hundreds of cesium clocks in the national standards laboratories of many countries. Deviations of UTC from TAI are implemented in the form of leap seconds, which occur on average every 18 months; the most recent event at this writing was the last second of 2008. For almost every computer application today, UTC represents the universal timescale extending into the indefinite past and indefinite future. We know of course that the UTC timescale did not exist prior to 1972, nor the Gregorian

---

* Historians speak of the Julian period; we use the term *era* here for consistency.

calendar prior to 1582, the Roman calendar prior to 46 BCE, or the Julian era prior to 4713 BCE, and we cannot predict exactly when the next leap second will occur. Nevertheless, most folks would prefer that, even if we cannot get future seconds numbering right beyond the next leap second, at least we can get the days numbering right until the end of reason.

There are many eclectic timescales that metricate our civilization. We reckon the years and days and record birthdays, ascendancies, and volcanic eruptions according to the Gregorian calendar. Astronomers calibrate the light year and reckon the age of the universe using the Julian calendar.* Physicists split the second and measure atomic decay using an atomic timescale. Space scientists intricate the position of spacecraft using a relativistic timescale corrected to the solar system barycenter (SSB). We set our watches, navigate the sea, and come to work ruled by a timescale geared to the rotation of Earth. However, we timestamp Internet mail, document transactions of all types, and schedule future events using NTP, which has a timescale all its own. Each of these timescales is based on an oscillator of one form or another but not necessarily running at commensurate rates or starting at the same epoch.

13.1 Scientific Timescales Based on Astronomy and Atomic Physics

For many years, the most important use of time and frequency metrology was for worldwide communications, navigation, and space sciences, for which time determination depends on astronomical observations of the Sun, Moon, and stars [2]. However, we must make a careful distinction between Ephemeris Time (ET), which is reckoned in sidereal days with respect to extragalactic objects, and Universal Time (UT), which is reckoned in solar days with respect to the Sun.

The basic unit of ET is the *tropical year,* which is the interval during which Earth completes one complete orbit around the Sun and can be measured to within 50 ms [3]. The *ecliptic plane* is the nominal orbital plane of Earth and planets revolving around the Sun. It is inclined at an angle of about 23.5° relative to the *equatorial plane* of Earth. The intersection of the two planes defines the *line of nodes,* which has a constant orientation relative to distant quasars, as determined by very long baseline interferometry (VLBI). The epoch when a point on the equator of the Earth ascends past the line of nodes in the northerly direction defines the *vernal equinox* and the longitude at the beginning of a sidereal day. As seen by an observer on the surface of Earth, sidereal time is

---

* Strictly speaking, there is no Julian calendar, just a numbering of the days since 4713 BCE, but for this book it is convenient to overlook the distinction.

reckoned as the hour angle of the vernal equinox as it sweeps over the sidereal day. In 1958, the SI (International System of Units) second was defined as 1/31,556,925.9747 of the tropical year with origin 12 h on 0 January 1900 Greenwich [3]. Although it was redefined later, this established the initial correspondence between ET and the UT1 timescale described here.

The reckoning of UT from ET is complicated since the rotation of Earth is not constant. It is slowly spinning down at a rate of about 1.4 ms per day per century [3] with variations due to precession and nutation of the Earth's poles and random effects. Since the Earth rotation periods vary, the basic measurement unit is the *mean solar day*, which extends from one fictional zenith of the arc of the Sun at the prime meridian (Greenwich) until the next but varies about ±30 ms over the year due to polar wandering and orbit variations [3].

As Earth makes an additional rotation once per tropical year, the *sidereal day* is about 23 h 56 min 4.1 s relative to the *mean solar day*. Since the local time of day depends on the latitude and season, the UT timescale is determined from the equation of time used by sundials. In fact, UT designates a family of timescales based on the mean solar day. The UT1 timescale is UT correct for polar motion. UT2 is UT1 corrected for seasonal variations, but it is no longer in widespread use. In these timescales, the *solar second* is defined as 1/86,400 of the mean solar day as reckoned from midnight at Greenwich. The *tropical year* (one complete orbit of Earth around the Sun) in the early 1900s was 365.2421987 mean solar days, and the *lunar month* (one complete revolution of the Moon around Earth) was 29.53059 solar days. The subsequent departure of UT from ET is an important issue that we discuss further in this chapter.

Of the three heavenly oscillators readily apparent to ancient mariners and astronomers—the rotation of Earth about its axis, the revolution of Earth around the Sun, and the revolution of the Moon around Earth—none of the three has the intrinsic stability, relative to modern technology, to serve as a standard reference oscillator. The first cesium atomic clock began operation at the National Physical Laboratory (NPL) in Teddington, United Kingdom, in 1955. In 1967, the SI second was redefined by the BIPM (International Bureau of Weights and Measures, formerly the International Bureau of the Hour [BIH]) as "9,192,631,770 periods of the radiation corresponding to the transition between the two hyperfine levels of the ground state of the Cesium-133 atom." In 1971, the TAI timescale was established in SI seconds with epoch the value of UT1 in 1958, which was ET retarded by 32.184 s. Present-day timescales are based on TAI or some offset from it. For instance, UTC is defined so that the difference between it and UT1 is always less than 0.9 s. While of less importance to the computer timekeeper, the GPS has its own timescale, which is syntonic with TAI but at a fixed time offset TAI − 19 s since that was the UTC offset from TAI in January 1980. GPS receivers typically convert from GPS to UTC for external readings.

Modern timekeeping for space data links and deep-space missions requires even more intricate corrections for relativistic effects due to velocity and gravity in an inertial frame. In 1976, the Terrestrial Dynamic Time

(TDT) timescale was established as the proper time of a clock on the equator of Earth at mean sea level relative to TAI. With base epoch 12 h 1 January 2000 TAI, the TDT, now called TT, timescale was established as TAI + 32.184 s. Astute readers will observe that TT and ET are essentially the same timescale. By 1972, UT1 had decreased by 10 s, and by 2000 it had decreased 22 s more. Thus, the TT base epoch was coincident with UTC at 11:58:55.816 on 1 January 2000 and Julian day number (JDN) 2,451,545. That is about as precise as it gets.

But, since time is not quite the same throughout the solar system, a reference point has been determined at the SSB, which is defined as the center of mass or equivalently the point at which the gravitational potential is zero. This point moves within the ecliptic plane with harmonic variations determined by the Sun and the positions of the planets in their orbits. The time determined at this point defines the Barycentric Dynamic Time (TDB) timescale, which has the same origin and rate as TT. However, due to different orbital velocities and gravitational potentials, it varies with an amplitude of about 1.66 ms over the orbit of Earth. Therefore, intervals measured in TT may not be the same as intervals measured in TDB due to relativistic effects. Additional discussion of relativistic effects is in Section 17.2.

13.2 UTC and the Leap Second

While atomic timescales are useful within the scientific community, most of us reckon time according to the solar day. The International Earth Rotation Service (IERS) at the Paris Observatory uses astronomical observations provided by the U.S. Naval Observatory (USNO) and other observatories to determine the UT1 timescale corrected for irregular variations in Earth rotation. While UT1 defines the mean solar timescale, adopting it directly would require resetting our clocks some fraction of a second every month or two. At 0 h modified Julian date (MJD) 41,317.0 according to the Julian calendar or 0 h 1 January 1972 according to the Gregorian calendar, the UTC timescale was defined as TAI − 10.107 s and syntonic with TAI. While the UTC timescale was within 0.5 s of UT1 at inception, the difference TAI − UT1 has been slowly increasing since then at about 1 s every 18 months. When the difference exceeds 0.5 s, a leap second is inserted in the UTC timescale. The residual difference is called the DUT1 correction in broadcast timecode formats and is represented in deciseconds (0.1 s). Precisions of this order are required for accurate navigation and pointing of telescopes.

For the most precise coordination and timestamping of events since 1972, it is necessary to know when leap seconds were implemented in UTC and how the seconds are numbered. The insertion of leap seconds into UTC is currently the responsibility of the IERS, which publishes periodic bulletins available on

TABLE 13.1

Leap Insertions [a]

NTP Epoch	Offset	Gregorian Date	NTP Epoch	Offset	Gregorian Date
2,272,060,800	10	1 Jan 1972	2,776,982,400	23	1 Jul 1985
2,287,785,600	11	1 Jul 1972	2,776,982,400	24	1 Jan 1988
2,303,683,200	12	1 Jan 1973	2,840,140,800	25	1 Jan 1990
2,335,219,200	13	1 Jan 1974	2,871,676,800	26	1 Jan 1991
2,366,755,200	14	1 Jan 1975	2,918,937,600	27	1 Jul 1992
2,398,291,200	15	1 Jan 1976	2,950,473,600	28	1 Jul 1993
2,429,913,600	16	1 Jan 1977	2,982,009,600	29	1 Jul 1994
2,461,449,600	17	1 Jan 1978	3,029,443,200	30	1 Jan 1996
2,492,985,600	18	1 Jan 1979	3,076,704,000	31	1 Jul 1997
2,524,521,600	19	1 Jan 1980	3,124,137,600	32	1 Jan 1999
2,571,782,400	20	1 Jul 1981	3,313,526,400	33	1 Jan 2006
2,603,318,400	21	1 Jul 1982	3,439,756,800	34	1 Jan 2009
2,634,854,400	22	1 Jul 1983			

[a] The NTP Epoch and Gregorian dates represent the time of insertion; however, the leap second itself belongs to the previous day.

the Internet. As specified in CCIR Report 517, which is reproduced in Blair [4], a leap second is inserted following second 23:59:59 on the last day of June or December and becomes second 23:59:60 of that day.* A leap second would be deleted by omitting second 23:59:59 on one of these days, although this has never happened. As of late 2009, leap seconds have been inserted on the occasions listed in Table 13.1, in which the date reports when the new UTC timescale begins (see http://hpiers.obspm.fr/eop-pc/ for more details).

In other words, the UTC timescale has marched backward relative to the TAI timescale exactly 1 s on scheduled occasions recorded in the institutional memory of our civilization. Note in passing that leap second adjustments affect the number of seconds per day and thus the number of seconds per year. Apparently, should we choose to worry about it, the UTC clock, Gregorian calendar, and various cosmic oscillators will inexorably drift apart with time until rationalized at an atomic epoch by some future papal bull.

13.3 The Leap Second Controversy

There has been considerable debate among the scientific and industrial stakeholders about the merits or demerits of leap seconds. An eloquent and comprehensive discussion and analysis on the issues is in Nelson et al. [3].

---

* Purists will note that the IERS can, when necessary, declare the leap at the end of any month, but occasions when this might be necessary are highly unlikely.

Proponents argue that they are necessary to align the civil day recorded in UT1 for the transportation, legal, and other services that depend on the rising and setting of the Sun. Opponents argue that this complicates telecommunication, commerce, and computer timekeeping systems. Some insight into the issues involved will be apparent in the following discussion.

From astronomical observations, historical documents, and the fossil record, the mean rate of Earth rotation in some year near 1820 was 1 mean solar day in exactly 86,400 s, but the rate has been slowing by about 1.4 ms per day per century since then. A linear decrease in rate translates to a quadratic difference in time, so the characteristic curve representing the difference between ET and UT1 is approximated by a parabola with apex near the year of 1820 and passing through the base epoch of ET in 1900, the epoch of TAI in 1955, the epoch of UTC in 1972, and the epoch of UTC in 2009, which includes the accumulated leap seconds. There is general agreement that the characteristic difference between UT1 and ET can be represented as the solid line in Figure 13.1. In this figure, the solid line corresponds to the equation [3]

$$\Delta T = 31\left(\frac{T-1820}{100}\right)^2 - 20, \qquad (13.1)$$

where for convenience the units on the left side of the equation are in seconds, and the units on the right side are in years. Assuming a leap second is inserted when the difference UT1 − ET exceeds 0.5 s, the interval between leap seconds can be derived as the solid line shown in Figure 13.2.

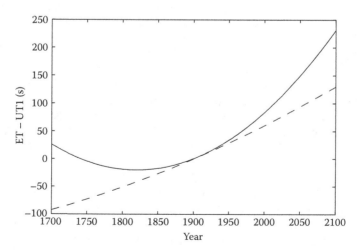

FIGURE 13.1
Difference UT1 − ET in the historical record.

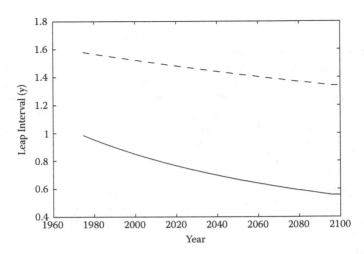

FIGURE 13.2
Interval between leap second insertions.

TABLE 13.2

Interval between Leap Second Insertions

Source	1972	2000	2009	2050	2100
Nelson	1.00	0.85	0.81	0.67	0.56
Quadratic	1.58	1.52	1.50	1.42	1.34

If Earth did spin down as evident in Equation 13.1, we might indeed be in a panic, as in Figure 13.2 leap second insertions would approach twice per year by the end of the century. However, the solid-line characteristics shown in the figures do not fit the facts for the past and current centuries. A best-fit quadratic for the observed UT1 − ET values at 1900, 1958, 1972, and 2009 yields the dashed-line characteristics shown in the figures. The results for the UTC era are tabulated in Table 13.2, which shows the anticipated intervals between leap second insertion predicted by both Equation 13.1 and the quadratic. A similar conclusion was reached in McCarthy and Klepczynski [5]; if we continue the present policy of leap second insertion when the TAI − UTC value exceeds 0.5 s, the insertion interval will not become much less than it is today.

There are several suggestions in Nelson et al. [3] about what to do about this—discontinue leap seconds in the future, increase the step size at each insertion, change the rate of ET, regularize the interval between insertions as in leap days—but none of them satisfies all stakeholders, all of them are expensive and ugly to implement, and all of them probably have unintended consequences.

13.4 How NTP Reckons with UTC Leap Seconds

The NTP timescale is based on the UTC timescale but is not necessarily always coincident with it. On the first tick of UTC at 0 h 1 January 1972, the NTP clock read 2,272,060,800, representing the number of apparent seconds since the first NTP era began at 0 h 1 January 1900. The insertion of leap seconds in UTC and subsequently into NTP does not affect the UTC or NTP oscillator, only the conversion between NTP network time and UTC civil time. However, since the only institutional memory available to NTP is the UTC broadcast services, the NTP timescale is in effect reset to UTC as each broadcast timecode is received. Thus, when a leap second is inserted in UTC and subsequently in NTP, knowledge of all previous leap seconds is lost.

Another way to describe this is to say that there are as many NTP timescales as historic leap seconds. In effect, a new timescale is established after each new leap second. Thus, all previous leap seconds, not to mention the apparent origin of the timescale itself, lurch backward 1 s as each new timescale is established. If a clock synchronized to NTP in 2009 was used to establish the UTC epoch of an event that occurred in early 1972 without correction, the event would appear 24 s late. However, NTP primary time servers resolve the epoch using the broadcast timecode, so that the NTP clock is set to the broadcast value on the current timescale. As a result, for the most precise determination of epoch relative to the historic Gregorian calendar and UTC timescale, the user must subtract from the apparent NTP epoch the offsets shown in Table 13.1 at the relative epochs shown. This is a feature of almost all present-day time distribution mechanisms.

The detailed chronometry involved can be illustrated with the help of Table 13.3, which shows the details of seconds numbering just before, during, and after a leap second insertion at 23:59:59 on 31 December 1998. The NTP leap indicator is set by the protocol on the day of insertion, either directly by a reference clock driver or indirectly by the protocol. The NTP-compliant kernel increments the system clock one additional second following the normal day of 86,400 s, then resets the leap indicator. In the figure, the last second of a normal day is 23:59:59, while the last second of a leap day is 23:59:60. Since this makes the day 1 s longer than usual, the day rollover will not occur

TABLE 13.3

Interval between Leap Second Insertions

Date	Time	TAI Offset	Leap Indicator	NTP Seconds
31 Dec 98	23:59:59	31	1	3,124,137,599
	23:59:60	31	1	3,124,137,600
1 Jan 99	00:00:00	32	0	3,124,137,600
	00:00:01	32	0	3,124,137,601

until the end of the first occurrence of second 600. The UTC time conversion routines must notice the apparent time and the leap indicator and handle the format conversions accordingly. Immediately after the leap insertion, both timescales resume ticking the seconds as if the leap had never happened. The chronometric correspondence between the UTC and NTP timescales continues, but NTP has forgotten about all past leap insertions. Thus, determination of UTC time intervals spanning leap seconds will be in error unless the exact times of insertion are known from Table 13.1 and its successors.

The obvious question raised by this scenario is what happens during the leap second itself when NTP time stops and the clock remains unchanged. If the precision time kernel modifications described in Mills and Kamp [6] and Chapter 8 have been implemented, the kernel includes a state machine that implements the actions required by the scenario. At the first occurrence of second 600, the system clock is stepped backward to second 599. However, the routine that actually reads the clock is constrained never to step backward unless the step is significantly larger than 1 s, which might occur due to explicit operator direction. In this design, time would stand still during the leap second but be correct commencing with the next second.

Figure 13.3 shows the behavior with the modified design used in most kernels. The clock reading is constrained always to increase, so every reading during the leap second increments the least significant bit. In case A, the clock was not read during the leap second and so appears to stand still. In case B, the clock was read one or more times during the leap second, so the value increments beyond the last reading. This will continue until the stepped-back clock catches up to this value.

Note that the NTP seconds column in Figure 13.3 actually shows the epoch of the leap second itself, which is the precise epoch of insertion. The offset column shows the cumulative seconds offset of UTC relative to TAI; that is, the number of seconds to add to the UTC clock to maintain nominal agreement with the TAI clock. Finally, note that the epoch of insertion is relative

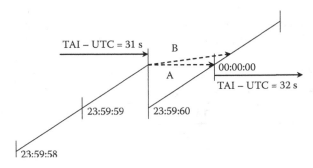

FIGURE 13.3
Epochs of leap second insertion.

to the timescale immediately prior to that epoch; for example, the epoch of the 31 December 1999 insertion is determined on the timescale in effect just prior to this insertion, which means that the actual insertion relative to TAI is 21 s later than the apparent time on the UTC timescale.

Not all historic transmission formats used by the NIST radio broadcast services [7] and not all currently available reference clocks include provisions for year information and leap second warning. In these cases, this information must be determined from other sources. NTP includes provisions to distribute advance warnings of leap seconds using the leap indicator described in Chapter 14. The protocol is designed so that these bits can be set manually or automatically at the primary time servers and then automatically distributed throughout the synchronization subnet to all dependent time servers and clients.

So, why bother with UTC in the first place? It would be much simpler to adopt TAI and avoid leap seconds altogether, as in fact the case with the POSIX specification. However, there is no escaping that synchronization with conventional human activities requires UTC or in case of birth and death certificates UT1. There are many facets of this argument, some based on practical matters like a reliable source of historic and anticipated leap second epochs and suitable provisions in the computer time management software and some based on anecdotal sensibilities. In the end, it seems prudent that the computer clock runs in UTC with leap insertions as described. By agreement between USNO, NIST, and the NTP developer community [8], the NTP Version 4 (NTPv4) Autokey protocol described in Chapter 9 has been modified to automatically download the leap second table from NIST. Assuming the operating system kernel has the required capability, the leap insertion is implemented automatically at the required epoch and the current TAI offset made available via the kernel application program interface (API).

13.5 On Numbering the Calendars and Days

A *calendar* is a mapping from epoch in some timescale to the times and dates used in everyday life. Since multiple calendars are in use today and sometimes these disagree on the dating of the same events in the past, the metrology of past and present events is an art practiced by historians [9]. On the other hand, a computer network metrology must provide a means for precision dating of past, present, and future events in a global networking community. The following history lesson outlines how ancient calendars evolved to the modern Gregorian calendar and day number system [10].

The calendar systems used in the ancient world reflect the agricultural, political, and ritual needs characteristic of the societies in which they flourished. Astronomical observations to establish the winter and summer solstices were in use three to four millennia ago. By the 14th century BCE, the Shang Chinese had established the solar year as 365.25 days and the lunar month as 29.5 days. The lunisolar calendar, in which the ritual month is based on the Moon and the agricultural year on the Sun, was used throughout the ancient Near East (except Egypt) and Greece from the third millennium BCE. Early calendars used either 13 lunar months of 28 days or 12 alternating lunar months of 29 and 30 days and haphazard means to reconcile the 354/364-day lunar year with the 365-day vague solar year.

The ancient Egyptian lunisolar calendar had twelve 30-day lunar months but was guided by the seasonal appearance of the star Sirius (Sothis). To reconcile this calendar with the solar year, a civil calendar was invented by adding five intercalary days for a total of 365 days. However, in time it was observed that the civil year was about one-fourth day shorter than the actual solar year and thus would precess relative to it over a 1,460-year cycle called the Sothic cycle. Along with the Shang Chinese, the ancient Egyptians had thus established the solar year at 365.25 days, or within about 11 min of the present measured value. In 432 BCE, about a century after the Chinese had done so, the Greek astronomer Meton calculated that there were 110 lunar months of 29 days and 125 lunar months of 30 days for a total of 235 lunar months in 6,940 solar days, or just over 19 years. The 19-year cycle, called the *Metonic cycle*, established the lunar month at 29.532 solar days, or within about 2 min of the present measured value.

The Roman republican calendar was based on a lunar year and by 50 BCE was 8 weeks out of step with the solar year. Julius Caesar invited the Alexandrian astronomer Sosigenes to redesign the calendar, which led to the adoption in 46 BCE of the Roman calendar. This calendar is based on a year of 365 days with an intercalary day inserted every 4 years. However, for the first 36 years an intercalary day was mistakenly inserted every 3 years instead of every 4 years. The result was 12 intercalary days instead of 9 and a series of corrections that was not complete until some years later.

The 7-day Sumerian week was introduced only in the fourth century by Emperor Constantine I. During the Roman era, a 15-year census cycle, called the Indiction Cycle, was instituted for taxation purposes. The sequence of day names for consecutive occurrences of a particular day of the year does not recur for 28 years, called the Solar Cycle. Thus, the least-common multiple of the relatively prime 28-year Solar Cycle, 19-year Metonic Cycle, and 15-year Indiction Cycle results in a grand 7,980-year supercycle called the *Julian era*, which began in 4713 BCE. A particular combination of the day of the week, day of the year, phase of the Moon, and round of the census will recur beginning in 3268 CE.

By 1545, the discrepancy in the Roman year relative to the solar year had accumulated to 10 days. In 1582, following suggestions by the astronomers

Christopher Clavius and Luigi Lilio, Pope Gregory XIII issued a papal bull that decreed, among other things, that the solar year would consist of the equivalent of 365.2422 days. To more closely approximate the new value, only those centennial years divisible by 400 would be leap years, while the remaining centennial years would not, making the actual value 365.2425, or within about 26 s of the current measured value. While the Gregorian calendar is in use throughout most of the world today, some countries did not adopt it until early in the 20th century [11].

13.6 On the Julian Day Number System

To measure the span of the universe or the decay of the proton, it is necessary to have a standard day-numbering plan. Accordingly, the International Astronomical Union has adopted the standard (ET) second and JDN to date cosmological events and related phenomena [12]. The standard day consists of 86,400 standard seconds, with time expressed as a fraction of the whole day, and the standard year consists of 365.25 standard days.

In the scheme devised in 1583 by the French scholar Joseph Julius Scaliger and named after his father,* JDN 0.0 corresponds to 12 h (noon) on the first day of the Julian era, 1 January 4713 BCE. In the Gregorian calendar used by historians, the years prior to the CE are reckoned as 365.25 days, while the years of the CE are reckoned according to the Gregorian calendar.† Since there was no year zero or day zero in Roman reckoning, JDN 1,721,426.0 corresponds to 12 h on the first day of the CE, 1 January 1 CE.

The MJD, often used to represent dates near our own era in conventional time and with fewer digits, is defined MJD = JD − 2,400,000.5. In the Gregorian calendar, the second that began 0 h 1 January 1900 (also known as 24h 31 December 1899) corresponds to MJD 15,021.0 and the base of the NTP timescale described in this chapter.

While it remains a fascinating field for time historians, this narrative provides conclusive evidence that conjugating calendar dates of significant events and assigning NTP timestamps to them is approximate at best. In principle, reliable dating of such events requires only an accurate count of the days relative to some globally alarming event, such as a comet passage or supernova explosion; however, only historically persistent and politically stable societies, such as the ancient Chinese and Egyptian and especially the Classic Mayan [13], possessed the means and will to do so.

---

* Scholars sometimes disagree about exactly what Scaliger or others invented and named, but we do not get into that here.
† Strictly speaking, the Gregorian calendar did not exist prior to 15 October 1582, but most historians and Julian calculators do this to avoid Pope Gregory's 10-day hole.

13.7 On Timescales and the Age of Eras

This section contains an intricate description and analysis of the NTP timescale, in particular the issues relative to the conventional civil timescale and when the NTP timescale rolls for the first time in 2036. These issues are also important with the Unix timescale, but that roll will not happen until 2 years later. Among the conclusions, which might be uncomfortable for some, is that the system clock must always be set within 68 years of UTC before NTP is started to preserve correct operation both initially and on the occasion of an era roll.

A universal timescale can be implemented using a binary counter of indefinite width and with the unit seconds bit placed somewhere in the middle. The counter is synchronized to UTC such that it runs at the same rate, and the units increment coincides with the UTC seconds tick. The NTP timescale is defined by 128 bits of this counter, of which the first 64 bits count the seconds and the last 64 bits represent the fraction within the second. The timescale covers well beyond the age of the universe and the smallest times that can be measured. An implementation may choose to limit the size of the fraction field, but not less than 32 bits.

An *NTP date* is a signed, twos-complement integer in which the *prime epoch* (epoch 0) is 0 h 1 January 1900 CE. Positive values represent times after that date; negative values represent times before that date. Conversion between any date format and NTP format is done by computing the seconds and fraction difference between the given date and the prime epoch; the 128-bit signed result is the NTP date. An *NTP timestamp* is a truncated NTP date expressed as an unsigned 64-bit integer that includes the low-order 32 bits of the seconds field concatenated with the high-order 32 bits of the fraction field. This format represents the 136 years from 1900 to 2036 to a precision of 232 ps. Ranges beyond these years require an era number consisting of the high-order 32 bits of the seconds field of the associated date. By convention, a timestamp value of zero is interpreted as undefined; that is, the associated system clock has not been set. There will exist a 232-ps interval, henceforth ignored, every 136 years when the 64-bit field is zero and thus considered undefined.

The counter used to interpolate the time in modern processors operates at rates of 3 GHz or more, but the Unix system clock can resolve times only to the nanosecond. Lamport's correctness assertions require time to be monotone-definite increasing, so the clock must always increment for each reading. The time for an application program to read the clock on a fast modern workstation is currently a few hundred nanoseconds, so the clock cannot be read more than once per nanosecond. However, if future processor speeds increase to the point that the clock can be read more than once per nanosecond, a runaway scenario is possible. When such scenarios become possible, it will be necessary to extend the precision of both the NTP timestamp and the system clock to the full NTP date precision.

The most important thing to observe is that NTP knows nothing about days, years, or centuries, only the seconds and fraction relative to the prime epoch. On 1 January 1970 when Unix life began, the NTP date was 2,208,988,800, and on 1 January 1972 when UTC life began, it was 2,272,060,800. The last second of year 1999 was 3,155,673,599, and the first second of the new century was 3,155,673,600. NTP dates can also be negative. The Julian era began at date −208,657,814,400 in era −49, while the CE began at date −59,926,608,000 in era −14, and the Gregorian calendar began at date −10,010,304,000 in era −3. Other than these observations, the NTP timescale has no knowledge of, or provision for, any of these eclectic epochs.

Table 13.4 illustrates the correspondence between calendar date, MJD, NTP date, NTP era, and NTP timestamp. Note the correspondence between the NTP date on one hand and the equivalent NTP era and timestamp on the other. The era number provides the signed epoch in multiples of 2^{32} s and the unsigned timestamp the offset in the era. Conversion between date and era timestamp formats can be done with cut-and-paste macros requiring no arithmetic operations.

The NTP timescale is almost never used directly by system or application programs. The generic Unix kernel keeps time in seconds since Unix life began in 1970 and microseconds or nanoseconds to provide both time-of-day and interval timer functions. To synchronize the Unix clock, NTP must convert to and from Unix representation. In principle, the Unix seconds counter will change sign on 68-year occasions, the next of which will happen in 2038. How the particular Unix system copes with this is of concern but is beyond the scope of discussion here.

The most probable Unix solution when 2038 comes near is to replace the 32-bit seconds counter with a 64-bit counter. A 64-bit seconds counter can certainly be used internal to the NTP software, but this cannot be done in messages exchanged over the network. The seconds values are exchanged in

TABLE 13.4

Calendar Reckoning

Calendar Date	JDN	NTP Date	NTP Era	NTP Timestamp
1 Jan 4713 BCE	0	−208,657,814,400	−49	1,795,583,104
1 Jan 1 CE	1,721,426	−59,926,608,000	−14	202,934,144
15 Oct 1582	2,299,161	−10,010,304,000	−3	2,874,597,888
1 Jan 1900	2,415,021	0	0	0
1 Jan 1970	2,440,588	2,208,988,800	0	2,208,988,800
1 Jan 1972	2,441,318	2,272,060,800	0	2,272,060,800
7 Feb 2036	2,464,731	4,294,944,000	0	4,294,944,000
8 Feb 2036	2,464,732	4,295,030,400	1	163,104
1 Jan 3000	2,816,788	34,712,668,800	8	352,930,432

32-bit fields that cannot be changed without causing awkward compatibility issues. Fortunately, as described in the next section, we do not need to worry about it if (a) *the clock is first set within 68 years of the correct date* and (b) *clock adjustments are restricted to from 68 years in the past to 68 years in the future.*

13.8 On NTP Era and Timestamp Calculations

The correctness principles on which NTP is based require all clock adjustments to be additive; that is, the only operations permitted are to advance or retard the clock but never to set it directly. NTP timestamp operations conform to this requirement and continue to work even when the era rolls. However, the precise epoch of a roll might not be available when the offset and delay values are determined as these computations are done in real time and involve 64-bit NTP timestamps. This section discusses these issues, particularly how to preserve correctness even near and beyond the epoch of an era roll.

NTP determines the clock offset and round-trip delay using four timestamps T_1, T_2, T_3, and T_4, all of which are 64-bit unsigned integers. T_1 is captured when the client sends a request and T_2 when the server receives it. T_3 is captured when the server sends a response and T_4 when the client receives it. The clock offset of the server relative to the client is

$$\theta = \frac{1}{2}\left[(T_2 - T_1) + (T_3 - T_4)\right],\tag{13.2}$$

and the round-trip delay is

$$\delta = (T_4 - T_1) - (T_3 - T_2).\tag{13.3}$$

Current implementations of the Unix system clock and NTP daemon operate with 64-bit time values. The various arithmetic operations on timestamps are carefully constructed to avoid overflow while preserving precision. The only arithmetic operation permitted on raw timestamps is subtraction, which produces signed 64-bit timestamp differences from 68 years in the past to 68 years in the future. The θ and δ calculations involve addition and subtraction of timestamp differences. To avoid overflow in these calculations, timestamp differences must not exceed from 34 years in the past to 34 years in the future. This is a fundamental limit in 64-bit integer calculations.

However, the limit can be extended from 68 years in the past to 68 years in the future without loss of precision using the following technique: In the reference implementation, all calculations involving offset and delay values are done in floating-double arithmetic, with the exception of timestamp subtraction, which is done in 64-bit integer arithmetic to preserve precision. Since the differences are almost always very small compared to the span of the era, they can in principle be converted to floating double without loss of precision. This is what the reference implementation does.

While it might seem surprising, timestamp subtraction yields the correct result even if the timestamps are in the same or adjacent eras. To see this, let $e = n2^{32}$ be the epoch of era n and let T_1 be in era n and T_2 be in era $n - 1$. Note that, while timestamps are ordinarily considered unsigned integers, the arithmetic unit operates on them as ordinary twos complement integers. Thus,

$$T_1 - T_2 = T_1 - e + e - T_2.$$

This argument also holds if T_1 and T_2 are interchanged. Now, consider addition of a signed number and a timestamp $T_2 = a + T_1$ that crosses an era boundary. If T_1 considered as a twos complement number is negative and both a and T_3 are positive, an overflow from one era to the next higher has occurred, so the era number should be increased by one. If T_1 is positive and both a and T_2 are negative, an underflow from one era to the next lower has occurred, so the era number should be decreased by one.

13.9 Comparison with Other Computer Timescales

Computer time is represented in various ways depending on the hardware capabilities, operating system, and system clock model. The attributes of each model include the size of the fields used to represent time values; whether the timescale is atomic time (TAI) or civil time (UTC); whether to include programmed offsets for local time zone, daylight savings time, and in the case of TAI, UTC. In addition, the method to incorporate some or all of these offsets at programmed times, either automatically or manually, must be specified.

Figure 13.4 shows the time value representations used by Unix, IBM System/390, HP Open VMS, and NTP. Unix time is represented in two formats, seconds and microseconds (timeval) or seconds and nanoseconds (timespec). The values are signed relative to a prime epoch (zero values) 0 h 1 January 1970. When POSIX conformance is required, the TAI timescale is used exclusively, and there is no consideration for leap seconds. The common practice in other Unix environments is to use the UTC timescale with varying degrees of fidelity when a leap second is inserted in the timescale. With a 32-bit signed seconds field, this representation remains unambiguous only from 68 years before to 68 years after the prime epoch. Obviously, something

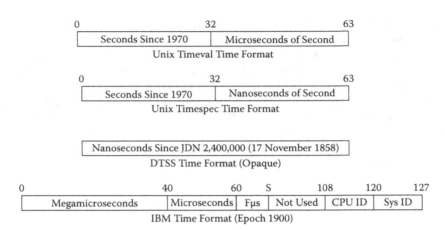

FIGURE 13.4
Computer time value representation.

will have to be done before the era overflows in 2038, most likely extending the seconds field to 64 bits. While the operating system always runs in standard time (TAI or UTC), individual users can specify the rules to incorporate time zone and daylight savings offsets in varying parts of the world.

In the Digital Time Synchronization Service (DTSS), as used in Open VMS and the Distributed Computer Environment (DCE), time is represented in nanoseconds since the base epoch 0 h 17 November 1858 TAI (sic), which coincides (by design) with JDN 2,400,000. It is not clear whether time can be represented prior to that epoch. With a 64-bit word, this representation remains unambiguous for the next 585 centuries. However, the particular operating system realization is opaque. Application programs read the time using a library of language- and locale-dependent format conversion routines that account for the UTC, time zone, and daylight saving offsets.

IBM System/390 time, as provided by the 9037-2 Sysplex Timer, is represented in microseconds and fraction, with the unit microsecond incrementing at bit 59, as shown in Figure 13.4. However, the actual clock hardware uses an oscillator running at some power of two times 1 MHz. For an appropriate power of two, the actual clock increments at what is called the stepping bit S, as shown in the figure. In this design, bit 39 increments at intervals of 1.048576 s, called a *megamicrosecond*, which is assumed "close" to 1 s.

The base epoch is 0 h 1 January 1900 TAI, which in this case is actually TT − 32,184 s; it is not clear whether time can be represented prior to that epoch. With 40 bits of headroom, this representation remains unambiguous for the next 365 centuries. The UTC, time zone, and daylight saving offsets can be programmed automatically or manually to occur at predefined epochs. An interesting feature is that the time of each logical partition acting as a virtual machine can march to its own programmed offset schedule, which is handy for testing.

13.10 Primary Frequency and Time Standards

While there are few NTP primary servers outside national laboratories that derive synchronization from primary frequency and time standards, it is useful to assess the accuracy achievable using these means. A primary frequency standard is an oscillator that can maintain extremely precise frequency relative to a physical phenomenon, such as a transition in the orbital states of an electron or the rotational period of an astronomical body. Existing atomic oscillators are based on the transitions of hydrogen, cesium, rubidium, and mercury atoms, although other means using active and passive masers and lasers of various kinds and even pulsars are available [14]. In addition, there is a wide variety of oscillator types, including oven-stabilized, temperature-compensated, and uncompensated quartz crystal oscillators; rubidium gas cells; and cesium beam oscillators. The best of these may be the hydrogen ion trap oscillator developed by NASA/Jet Propulsion Laboratory (JPL) for use in the Deep Space Network, which has a stability of 1×10^{-15} [15]. Pulsars can be better than this over long averaging times and may be the ultimate cosmic stabilizer since they are self-powered and visible with only a telescope. However, only one of them has been studied so far [16].

For reasons of cost and robustness, cesium oscillators are used worldwide for national primary frequency standards. The characteristics of cesium oscillators have been extensively studied and accurate parametric models developed [17]. The current TAI timescale is maintained by a worldwide ensemble of some 250 cesium oscillators in laboratories throughout the world. Among the best cesium oscillators today is the NIST-F1 Cesium Fountain, which boasts a stability of 2×10^{-15} per day, although future developments are expected to yield stabilities on the order of 1×10^{-18} per day. Achieving this goal requires cryogenic devices and places extreme demands on oscillator and counter technology.

The frequency of crystal oscillators gradually changes over their lifetime, a phenomenon called *aging*. Even if a crystal oscillator is temperature compensated by some means, it must be periodically compared to a primary standard to maintain the highest accuracy. Various means have been developed to discipline precision quartz crystal oscillators using GPS to calibrate parameters specific to each individual crystal, but in general, aging is not a factor in computer clock oscillators.

The telecommunication industry has agreed on a classification of clock oscillators as a function of minimum accuracy, minimum stability, and other factors [18]. There are three factors that determine the stability of a clock: drift, jitter, and wander. *Drift* refers to long-term systematic variations of frequency with time and is synonymous with aging, trends, and the like. *Jitter* (also called *timing jitter*) refers to short-term variations in frequency with components greater than 10 Hz, while *wander* refers to intermediate-term variations

TABLE 13.5

Clock Stratum Assignments

Stratum	Minimum Accuracy (per day)	Minimum Stability (per day)
1	1×10^{-11}	Not specified
2	1.6×10^{-8}	1×10^{-10}
3	4.6×10^{-6}	3.7×10^{-7}
4	3.2×10^{-5}	Not specified

in frequency with components less than 10 Hz. The classification determines the oscillator stratum (not to be confused with the NTP stratum), with the more accurate oscillators assigned the lower strata and less-accurate oscillators the higher strata, as shown in Table 13.5. The construction, operation, and maintenance of stratum 1 oscillators is assumed to be consistent with national standards and often includes cesium oscillators and sometimes precision crystal oscillators synchronized via LORAN-C (Long Range Navigation System C) or GPS to national standards. Stratum 2 oscillators represent the stability required for interexchange toll switches such as the AT&T 4ESS and interexchange digital cross-connect systems, while stratum 3 oscillators represent the stability required for exchange switches such as the AT&T 5ESS and local cross-connect systems. Stratum 4 oscillators represent the stability required for digital channel banks and PBX (private branch exchange) systems.

13.11 Time and Frequency Coordination

A network of clocks that are synchronized (syntonic) at some multiple or submultiple of a common frequency is called *isochronous*. A network of clocks that are not syntonic but operate very close to a multiple or submultiple of a common frequency is called *plesiochronous*. In this context, the cesium clocks at the national laboratories are plesiochronous with each other and with TAI. At NIST, USNO, and some other national laboratories, cesium clocks provide synchronization to one or more NTP servers, which then synchronize the NTP subnet at large. In particular, to *synchronize frequency* means to adjust the subnet clocks to run at the same frequency, to *synchronize time* means to set the clocks so that all agree at a particular epoch, and to *synchronize clocks* means to synchronize them in both frequency and time.

To synchronize clocks, there must be some way to directly or indirectly compare their readings. If two clocks can communicate directly over paths of precisely known delay, then the time difference can be determined directly using algorithms similar to NTP. This is the basis of the two-way satellite time and frequency transfer (TWSTFT) method described in Section

18.1. If they cannot communicate directly but they can communicate with a third clock over paths of precisely known delay, their differences can be determined relative to the third clock and the difference of each clock communicated to the other. Techniques based on this method use the GPS and LORAN-C navigation systems.

Some timescales, including TAI, are generated by an algorithm that combines the relative time differences measured between contributing national and international laboratories. The laboratories themselves usually use an algorithm, not necessarily that used for intralaboratory coordination, to generate a laboratory timescale from an ensemble of cesium clocks. Not all laboratories have a common view of these algorithms, however. In the United States, the national timescale is officially coordinated by both NIST and USNO [14], although both laboratories cling to their own timescales as well. Coordination methods incorporate both Kalman filter and parameter estimation (autoregressive, integrated, moving-average, ARIMA) models [4]. The NIST algorithm that generates NBS(AT1) is described in Weiss, Allan, and Peppler [19], while the USNO algorithm that generates UTC(USNO) is described in Percival [20].

It is important to realize that it is not possible at the present state of the art to establish a permanent time and frequency standard that operates continuously and is completely reliable. A physically realizable standard is an active device that requires power and environmental resources, must occasionally be repaired, and has only a flicker of life compared to the age of the universe. While the TAI timescale in use today is based on a mathematical average of a large ensemble of atomic clocks, which improves the stability and reliability of its institutional memory, it is assumed that there are no subtle atomic conspiracies not yet discovered and that all the clocks in the global ensemble do not burn out at the same instant. The recent discovery of millisecond pulsars may provide a useful sanity check for the timescale as well as a means to detect gravitational waves [16].

13.12 Time and Frequency Dissemination

To improve accuracy and minimize the effects of individual clock variations, it is the practice in national standards laboratories to construct a synthetic timescale based on an ensemble of at least three and possibly very many contributing primary clocks. The timescale is produced by an algorithm using periodic measurements of the time offsets between the various clocks of the ensemble. The algorithm combines the offsets using computed weights to produce an ensemble timescale more accurate than the timescale of any clock in the ensemble. The algorithm used by USNO is based on ARIMA models [20], while the algorithm used by NIST is evolved from Kalman filter models [17,19,21]. These algorithms result in long-term fractional frequency stabilities on the order of 1.5×10^{-14}.

So that atomic and civil time can be coordinated throughout the world, national administrations operate primary time and frequency standards and coordinate them cooperatively using GPS and common-view satellite methods described in Section 18.1. Many seafaring nations of the world operate a broadcast time service for the purpose of calibrating chronometers used in conjunction with ephemeris data to determine navigational position. In many countries, the service is primitive and limited to seconds-pips broadcast by marine communication stations at certain hours. For instance, a chronometer error of one second represents a longitudinal position error of about 0.23 nautical mile at the equator.

13.12.1 Shortwave Radio Services

NIST operates shortwave broadcast services for the dissemination of standard time and frequency information on frequencies of 2.5, 5, 10, 15, and 20 MHz from station WWVH in Fort Collins, Colorado, and on frequencies of 2.5, 5, 10, and 15 MHz from station WWVH in Kauai, Hawaii. The timecode is transmitted over a 60-s interval at a data rate of 1 b/s using pulse-width modulation on a 100-Hz subcarrier. The National Research Council (NRC) of Canada operates a shortwave broadcast service for the dissemination of time and frequency information on frequencies of 3.33, 7.85, and 14.67 MHz from station CHU in Ottawa, Ontario. The timecode is transmitted during seconds 31–39 at 300 b/s using Bell 103-compatible FSK (frequency shift keying) modulation. For all three stations, the timecode format includes UTC time of year in seconds, together with leap second warning, standard/daylight indicator, and DUT1 adjustment. Additional details of the signal design are in Section 7.6.

Signal propagation from shortwave stations is usually by reflection from the upper ionospheric layers. While these transmissions can be received over large areas in North America, reliable frequency comparisons can be made only to the order of 10^{-7}, and time accuracies are limited to the order of a millisecond [4]. As far as is known, only one manufacturer is still producing WWV/H receivers, and these would not ordinarily be considered precision time sources. The current NTPv4 software distribution includes audio drivers for WWV, WWVH, and CHU, as described in Section 7.6. The drivers demodulate and decode the audio signal from a conventional shortwave receiver with accuracies generally to the millisecond or better. Additional details of the signal demodulation and decoding algorithms are in Section 7.6.

13.12.2 Long-Wave Radio Services

NIST also operates a long-wave broadcast service for time and frequency dissemination on a frequency of 60 kHz from station WWVB in Boulder,

TABLE 13.6

Low-Frequency Standard Time Stations

Call Sign and Location	Frequency (kHz)	Power (kW)
WWVB Fort Collins, Colorado, USA	60	50
DCF77 Mainflingen, Germany	77.5	30
MSF Rugby, United Kingdom	60	50
HBG Prangins, Switzerland	75	20
JJY Fukushima, Japan	40	50
JJY Saga, Japan	60	50

Colorado. The timecode is transmitted over a 60-s interval at a rate of 1 b/s using periodic reductions in carrier power. The format is similar to that used by the shortwave stations. The station can be received over the continental United States and adjacent coastal areas. Signal propagation is via the lower ionospheric layers, which are relatively stable and have predictable diurnal variations in height. With appropriate receiving and averaging techniques and corrections for diurnal and seasonal propagation effects, frequency comparisons to within 10^{-11} are possible and accuracies of from a few to 50 µs can be obtained [4].

Table 13.6 lists several other services similar to WWVB and operated by national government agencies in Europe and Japan. A typical long-wave transmitter antenna uses a network of wires connected between two or four towers 100 to 250 m tall and spaced several hundred meters apart. The transmitter powers are in the range 20–50 kW, but the antenna efficiency is low, on the order of 30 percent. These stations can be received at distances of 1,000–3,000 km. In addition to these services, medium-wave stations are operated by BBC Radio 2 on 401 kHz from Droitwich, United Kingdom, and France Inter on 162 kHz from Allouis, France. The transmitter powers are 400–2,000 kW, and signals are usable throughout western Europe. The primary purpose of these stations is for the radio broadcasting service, but the broadcast carrier can be used as a precision frequency reference as well.

13.12.3 Geosynchronous Operational Environmental Satellite Service

NIST also provides a time and frequency dissemination service on about 468 MHz from the Geosynchronous Operational Environmental Satellites (GOES), three of which cover the Western Hemisphere. The timecode is interleaved with messages used to interrogate remote sensors. It consists of 60 four-bit BCD nibbles transmitted over an interval of 30 s. The timecode information is similar to the terrestrial services. There are only a few receivers for this service, which may not be supported in the future.

A distinguishing feature of all the services described so far is that they are one way; that is, they provide no means to measure the propagation delay. The delay must be determined by geographic positions and ray-path geometry. This is complicated by movements of the ionospheric layers during the night and day, changing propagation modes, and orbit station-keeping in the satellite system. Generally, this limits the accuracy with these services to a millisecond.

13.12.4 Telephone Modem Services

NIST also operates the Automated Computer Time Service (ACTS) over the public switched telephone network from Boulder, Colorado. A call to the ACTS modem pool returns about 1 min of timecode data, including time of year, leap warning, and DUT1 value. Calls to ACTS can travel different routes for each call, which can result in significant errors, so ACTS measures the round-trip propagation time if the caller modem echoes received characters. The ACTS driver in the NTP software distribution does this and can realize a reliable error less than a millisecond. The driver can also operate with the telephone format commonly used in Europe, the model for which is the German PTB system, and the format used by the USNO; however, neither of these services can measure and compensate for the propagation time, so the accuracy is degraded, in the case of USNO to the order of 30 ms.

13.12.5 Global Positioning System

The U.S. Department of Defense operates the GPS for precision navigation [22] on land and sea and in the air. This system provides 24-h worldwide coverage using a constellation of satellites in 12-h orbits inclined at 55°. The original constellation of 24 satellites in six equally spaced planes of 4 satellites each has been expanded to 31 satellites in an irregular configuration such that at least 6 satellites are always in view, and 8 or more satellites are in view in most parts of the world. Services similar to GPS are operated or planned by other countries. The Russian service is called GLONASS and has been operating for several years. The European Union service is called Galileo and has completed the design and development phase and is expected to become operational in 2013.

While navigation is not the main topic of this section, understanding the navigation function helps to clarify the time transfer function. Each satellite vehicle (SV) transmits a navigation message that includes the time of transmission, an almanac to determine which SVs are in view, and an ephemeris from which the precise position of an SV in view can be determined. Each transmission from an SV appears as an expanding sphere that eventually intercepts the receiver. The locus of intersection of two spheres is a circle, while the locus of intersection of three spheres is two points. The point nearest Earth is the location of the receiver. As the accuracy of this point is critically dependent on the receiver clock, the fourth SV is used to discipline the receiver clock, which then can provide a pulse-per-second timing signal for the computer clock. If the receiver is not moving, once the receiver position

TABLE 13.7

Global Navigation Frequency Assignments

Channel	Frequency (MHz)	Signals
L1	1575.42	C/A, P(Y), M, L1C
L2	1227.60	P(Y), M, L2C
L3	1381.05	Nuclear detection (NUDET)
L4	1379.913	Ionosphere correction (future)
L5	1176.45	Safety of life (aeronautical)

has been accurately determined, only a single SV is necessary to provide accurate time transfer.

The radio-frequency (RF) channel operates using a code division multiple access (CDMA) channel access protocol. Each SV in the constellation is assigned a unique code number and PR sequence. Receivers identify a particular SV by correlating the received signal with the assigned sequence. The sequence is transmitted using BPSK (binary phase shift keying) modulation of the carrier, while the navigation message is modulated on the sequence.

Four L-band frequencies have been assigned for global navigation purposes, as shown in Table 13.7. All but L4 are multiples of the highest chip rate 10.23 Mb/s. Only the L1 and L2 channels are considered here; the others are used for a special purpose or for future systems. The coarse acquisition (C/A) signal is used by military and civilian receivers to quickly acquire as many SVs in view as the receiver supports. The PR has a chip rate of 1.023 Mb/s with period 1,023 chips, so it has a period of 1 ms. It implements the Standard Positioning Service (SPS) with a nominal accuracy of 15 m. The precision (P) signal is encrypted by a secret code (Y) for military receivers. It has a chip rate of 10.23 Mb/s with a period of almost a week. It implements the Precision Positioning Service (PPS) with nominal accuracy of 1 m. The L1C and L2C signals are for future civilian enhancements, while the M signal is for future military enhancements.

The navigation message is modulated on the PR sequence at a rate of 50 b/s in 1,500-bit frames with five 300-bit subframes, so new complete navigation messages are repeated at 30-s intervals. Many GPS navigation receivers can decode the GPS navigation message and produce a serial ASCII (American Standard Code for Information Interchange) message in National Marine Electronics Association (NMEA) formats that can be used by reference drivers in the NTP software distribution. However, the timing of the NMEA message precesses over the 1-ms C/A code period. For more precise timing, NMEA receivers also output a PPS signal aligned to the internal receiver clock.

13.12.6 LORAN-C Radio Navigation System

The U.S. Coast Guard, along with agencies of other countries, has operated the LORAN-C radio navigation system for many years [23]. It currently provides time-transfer accuracies of less than a microsecond within the ground-wave coverage area of a few hundred kilometers from the stations. All stations operate at 100 kHz using a pulse code modulation. Beyond the ground-wave area, signal propagation is via the lower ionospheric layers, which decreases accuracies to the order of 50 μs. The current deployment of LORAN-C stations permits almost complete coverage of the continental United States, Alaska, and western Europe.

A few notes about the navigation function will help explain how the system can be used for time transfer. LORAN-C receivers measure the time difference of arrival (TDOA) between pulses received from three or more transmitting stations. The locus of points of a specified TDOA between two stations is a hyperbola with its axis the line connecting the stations and focus the nearest station. The position of the receiver is the intersection of two hyperbolas, one for each station pair. Additional stations can be used to refine the position.

All LORAN-C stations use cesium clock ensembles that are routinely calibrated against the USNO master clock. The U.S. Coast Guard publishes station time differences for each station so that the pulse emission time can be calibrated to less than a microsecond. While the LORAN-C system provides a highly accurate frequency and time reference within the ground-wave area, there is no timecode modulation, so the receiver must be supplied with UTC time from an external source. This can be done in an interesting way. A LORAN-C chain consists of a master station and two or more slaves, all operating with the same pulse code group repetition rate (GRI), which is some multiple of microseconds near 10,000. For instance, the eastern U.S. LORAN-C chain operates with a GRI of 9,960 μs, so the least-common multiple of this interval and 1 s is 249 s. The U.S. Coast Guard publishes a table showing past and future times of coincidence (TOC) when the GRI is coincident with the UTC second. So, if the time can be set from other means within the 249-s interval, the TOC can be used to establish the correct time. For instance, the first TOC after 17 h on 6 December 2009 was at 17:02:49 UTC and repeated every 249 s after that. This detail might seem arcane, but it will pop up again in Section 18.6.

LORAN-C receivers are used to monitor local cesium clocks and other LORAN-C stations. Commercial LORAN-C receivers, such as the Austron 2000 shown in Figure 13.5, are specialized and extremely expensive (up to $20,000). However, a useful LORAN-C receiver for NTP use can be built with a junkbox personal computer (PC) and a handful of inexpensive parts. Figure 13.6 shows an example of one built in our laboratory using an oven-controlled crystal oscillator (OCXO). It is not likely that LORAN-C service will be continued indefinitely as GPS receivers are more accurate and less expensive.

Where the highest availability is required, multiple reference clocks can be operated in tandem and connected to an ensemble of servers. Perhaps one of the more extreme configurations is operated at the University of Delaware in

Newark and shown in Figure 13.7. It consists of dual-redundant primary GPS receivers, dual-redundant secondary WWVB receivers, a primary cesium frequency standard, and a secondary quartz frequency standard. The ensemble of radio and satellite receivers is connected using serial ASCII timecode, Inter-Range Instrumentation Group (IRIG), and PPS signals to four primary time servers for the research laboratory and public at large. Figure 13.7 shows

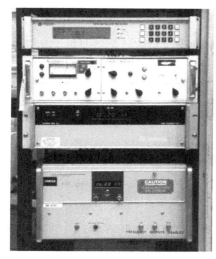

Austron 2201A GPS receiver

Austron 2000 LORAN-C receiver

Spectracom 8170 WWVB receiver

Hewlett Packard 5061A cesium beam frequency standard

FIGURE 13.5
University of Delaware laboratory test equipment.

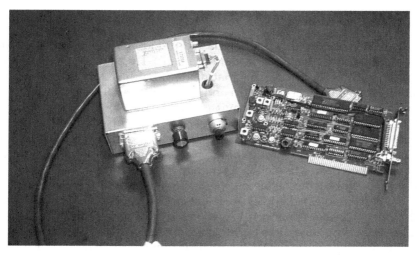

FIGURE 13.6
LORAN-C receiver and OCXO.

Spectracom 8170 WWVB receiver

Spectracom 8170 WWVB
receiver

Spectracom 8183 GPS receiver

Hewlett Packard 105A quartz
frequency standard

Hewlett Packard 5061A cesium beam
frequency standard

FIGURE 13.7
University of Delaware master clock facility.

auxiliary laboratory equipment used in performance experiments and performance evaluation.

13.13 Parting Shots

You may have noticed that nothing has been said in this chapter about local time zone or about daylight or standard time. This is intentional; there is nothing about NTP, or UTC for that matter, that has anything to do with local time or spring leaps forward and fall leaps back. This is the same philosophy practiced by mariners, aviators, and other long-distance runners; UTC is, well, universal. Where local time becomes important, we expect the operating system to include provisions to apply the correct offset. But, there are large corporations running IBM mainframes that insist on local time, at least until they open a branch in Shanghai.

The problem becomes acute on the day of changeover between standard and daylight time. Spring is okay, as the clocks are stepped forward 1 h in each time zone, so it is not just 1 h when message timestamps are inconsistent between time zones, it is four hours as the ripple passes over the United States. It is even worse in the fall because the same time can occur twice. When this happens, says the advice in at least one business computer model, the computer operators are advised to turn the machine off during the repeated hour, which is incomplete advice; it should be 4 h, one for each time zone.

References

1. Mills, D.L. On the chronology and metrology of computer network timescales and their application to the Network Time Protocol. *ACM Computer Commun. Rev. 21, 5* (October 1991), 8–17.
2. Jordan, E.C. (Ed.). *Reference Data for Engineers*, 7th ed. Sams, New York, 1985.
3. Nelson, R.A., et al. The leap second: its history and possible future. *Metrologia 38* (2001), 509–529.
4. Blair, B.E. Time and frequency dissemination: an overview of principles and techniques. In Blair, B.E. (Ed.), *Time and Frequency Theory and Fundamentals*. National Bureau of Standards Monograph 140, U.S. Department of Commerce, 1974, 233–313.
5. McCarthy, D.D., and W.J. Klepczynski. GPS and leap seconds. *GPS World* (November 1999), 50–57.
6. Mills, D.L., and P.-H. Kamp. The nanokernel. *Proceedings Precision Time and Time Interval (PTTI) Applications and Planning Meeting* (Reston, VA, November 2000).
7. *NIST Time and Frequency Dissemination Services*. NBS Special Publication 432 (Revised 1990), National Institute of Science and Technology, U.S. Department of Commerce, 1990.
8. Levine, J., and D. Mills. Using the Network Time Protocol to transmit International Atomic Time (TAI). *Proceedings Precision Time and Time Interval (PTTI) Applications and Planning Meeting* (Reston, VA, November 2000).
9. Dershowitz, N., and E.M. Reingold. Calendrical calculations. *Software Pract. Experience 20, 9* (September 1990), 899–928.
10. Calendar. *Encyclopaedia Britannica Macropaedia*, 15th ed., Vol. 15. Encyclopaedia Britannica, New York, 1986, 460–477.
11. Moyer, G. The Gregorian calendar. *Sci. Am. 246, 5* (May 1982), 144–152.
12. Time. *Encyclopaedia Britannica Macropaedia*, 15th ed., Vol. 28. Encyclopaedia Britannica, New York, 1986, 652–664.
13. Morley, S.G., G.W. Brainerd, and R.J. Sharer. *The Ancient Maya*, 4th ed. Stanford University Press, Stanford, CA, 1983, 598–600.
14. Allan, D.W., J.E. Gray, and H.E. Machlan. The National Bureau of Standards atomic time scale: generation, stability, accuracy and accessibility. In Blair, B.E. (Ed.), *Time and Frequency Theory and Fundamentals*. National Bureau of Standards Monograph 140, U.S. Department of Commerce, 1974, 205–231.
15. Prestage, J.D., et al. Ultra-stable Hg trapped ion frequency standard. *J. Modern Optics 39, 2* (1992), 221–232.
16. Rawley, L.A., J.H. Taylor, M.M. Davis, and D.W. Allan. Millisecond pulsar PSR 1937+21: a highly stable clock. *Science 238* (6 November 1987), 761–765.
17. Tryon, P.V., and R.H. Jones. Estimation of parameters in models for cesium beam atomic clocks. *J. Res. Natl. Bur. Std. 88, 1* (January–February 1983).

18. Bell Communications Research. *Digital Synchronization Network Plan*. Technical Advisory TA-NTSC-000436, 1 November 1986.
19. Weiss, M.A., D.W. Allan, and T.K. Peppler. A study of the NBS time scale algorithm. *IEEE Trans. Instrum. Meas. 38, 2* (April 1989), 631–635.
20. Percival, D.B. The U.S. Naval Observatory Clock time scales. *IEEE Trans. Instrum. Meas. IM-27, 4* (December 1978), 376–385.
21. Jones, R.H., and P.V. Tryon. Continuous time series models for unequally spaced data applied to modelling atomic clocks. *SIAM J. Sci. Stat. Comput. 4, 1* (January 1987), 71–81.
22. Herring, T. The Global Positioning System. *Sci. Am.* (February 1996), 44–50.
23. Frank, R.L. History of LORAN-C. *Navigation 29, 1* (Spring 1982).

Further Reading

Allan, D.W., J.H. Shoaf, and D. Halford. Statistics of time and frequency data analysis. In Blair, B.E. (Ed.), *Time and Frequency Theory and Fundamentals*. National Bureau of Standards Monograph 140, U.S. Department of Commerce, 1974, 151–204.

14

NTP Reference Implementation

For first you write a sentence,
and then you chop it small;
Then mix the bits, and sort them out
Just as they chance to fall:
The order of the phrases makes
No difference at all.

Lewis Carroll
Poeta Fit, Non Nascitur

As mentioned elsewhere in this book, NTP software of one kind or another has been running in the Internet for almost three decades. There have been five NTP versions, the first with no number and the latest is NTP Version 4 (NTPv4). The NTPv4 public software distribution available at http://www. ntp.org has been considered the definitive distribution since 1998. Like all modern software, the code continues to evolve, with old bugs fixed and new features introduced, all while maintaining compatibility with previous versions.

This chapter contains an overview of the current NTPv4 public software distribution for Unix, VMS, and Windows, which is called the reference implementation in this book. The distribution includes the main program ntpd, which is designed to operate as an independent daemon process in a multiple-program operating system such as Unix, VMS, and Windows, along with a suite of monitoring and debugging programs. While the distribution is self-sufficient in most respects, support for public key cryptography requires the OpenSSL cryptographic library, which is available as open source from http://www.openssl.org. Only the ntpd program is described in this chapter.

This chapter begins with an overview of the NTP packet header, which is built on the User Datagram Protocol (UDP) header and in turn on the IP header, as described in the respective standards documents. It continues with a description of the asynchronous processes and the procedures, functions, and variables they contain. The operations of these components are described with the aid of specific functions and procedures, collectively called *routines*. It is not the intent to describe in detail how the actual code operates, only to provide an overview that explains how it works using flowcharts that gather the essence of the code. While the flowcharts closely model the ntpd operation, the actual program is in fact a large, complex, real-time system in its own right. Primarily as an aid in the NTPv4 formal specification project, the flowcharts have been implemented as a skeleton, including the procedures, variables, and parameters described here. The skeleton, which is not intended to be executed in the ordinary way, has been compiled to check for variable conflicts and correct code flow.

14.1 NTP Packet Header

The NTP packet header follows the UDP and IP headers and the physical header specific to the underlying transport network. It consists of a number of 32-bit (four-octet) words, although some fields use multiple words, and others are packed in smaller fields within a word. The NTP packet header shown in Figure 14.1 has 12 words followed by optional extension fields (not shown) and finally an optional message authentication code (MAC) consisting of key identifier and message digest fields. The format of the 64-bit timestamp fields is described in Figure 2.1. The extension fields are used by the Autokey protocol, while the MAC is used by both this scheme and the symmetric key authentication scheme. As is the convention in other Internet protocols, all fields are in network byte order, commonly referred to as *big-endian*.

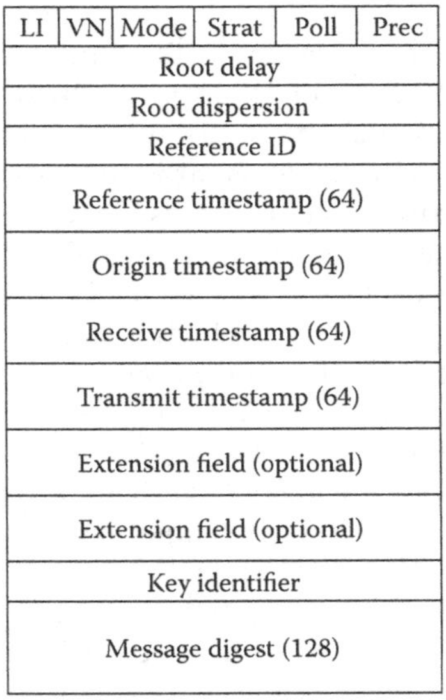

LI	VN	Mode	Strat	Poll	Prec
Root delay					
Root dispersion					
Reference ID					
Reference timestamp (64)					
Origin timestamp (64)					
Receive timestamp (64)					
Transmit timestamp (64)					
Extension field (optional)					
Extension field (optional)					
Key identifier					
Message digest (128)					

FIGURE 14.1
NTP packet header format.

The packet header fields are interpreted as follows:

Leap indicator (LI)

This is a two-bit code warning of an impending leap second to be inserted or deleted in the last minute of the current day, with bit 0 and bit 1, respectively, coded as follows:

00	No warning
01	Last minute of the day has 61 s
10	Last minute of the day has 59 s
11	Alarm condition (clock not synchronized)

Version number (VN)

This is a three-bit integer indicating the NTP version number, currently four (4).

Mode

This is a three-bit integer indicating the mode, with values defined as follows:

0	Reserved
1	Symmetric active
2	Symmetric passive
3	Client
4	Server
5	Broadcast
6	NTP control message
7	Reserved for private use

Stratum

This is an eight-bit integer indicating the stratum level of the system clock, with values defined as follows:

0	Unspecified
1	Reference clock (e.g., radio clock)
2-15	Secondary server (via NTP)
16-255	Unreachable

For convenience, the value 0 in received packets is mapped to 16 as a peer variable, and a peer variable of 16–255 is mapped to 0 in transmitted packets. This allows reference clocks, which normally appear at stratum 0, to be conveniently mitigated using the same algorithms used for external sources.

Poll exponent

This is an eight-bit unsigned integer indicating the maximum interval between successive messages, in seconds to the nearest power of two. In the reference implementation, the values can range from 3 (8 s) through 17 (36 h).

Precision

This is an eight-bit signed integer indicating the precision of the system clock, in seconds to the nearest power of two. For instance, a value of −18 corresponds to a precision of about 1 μs. The precision is normally measured by the daemon at startup and is defined as the minimum of several iterations of the time to read the system clock, which normally is done by a kernel system call. When the clock is not interpolated within the tick, the precision is set at the tick interval.

Root delay

This is a 32-bit, unsigned, fixed-point number indicating the total round-trip delay to the reference clock, in seconds with fraction point between bits 15 and 16. In contrast to the calculated peer round-trip delay, which can take both positive and negative values, this value is always positive.

Root dispersion

This is a 32-bit, unsigned, fixed-point number indicating the maximum error relative to the reference clock, in seconds with fraction point between bits 15 and 16.

Reference identifier

This is a 32-bit code identifying the particular reference clock. The interpretation depends on the value in the stratum field. For stratum 0 (unsynchronized), this is a four-character ASCII (American Standard Code for Information Interchange) string called the kiss code, which is used for debugging and monitoring purposes. For stratum 1 (reference clock) servers, this is a four-octet, left-justified, zero-padded ASCII string. While not enumerated in the NTP specification, the following are suggested ASCII identifiers:

ACTS	National Institute of Standards and Technology (NIST) telephone modem
CHU	HF Radio CHU, Ottawa, Canada
DCF77	LF Radio DCF77, Mainflingen, Germany, 77.5 kHz
GOES	Geosynchronous operational environmental satellite
GPS	Global Positioning System
HBG	LF Radio HBG, Prangins, Switzerland, 75 kHz
IRIG	Inter-Range Instrumentation Group

JJY	LF Radio JJY, Fukushima, Japan, 40 kHz
JJY	LF Radio JJY, Saga, Japan, 60 kHz
LORC	MF Radio LORAN-C, 100 kHz
MSF	LF Radio MSF, Rugby, United Kingdom, 60 kHz
PPS	Generic pulse per second
PTB, etc.	European telephone modem
TDF	MF Radio Allouis, France, 162 kHz
USNO	U.S. Naval Observatory (USNO) telephone modem
WWV	HF Radio WWV, Ft. Collins, Colorado
WWVB	LF Radio WWVB, Ft. Collins, Colorado, 60 kHz
WWVH	HF Radio WWVH, Kauai, Hawaii

For strata 2–15 secondary servers, this is the reference identifier of the system peer. If the system peer is using the IPv4 address family, the identifier is the four-octet IPv4 address. If the system peer is using the IPv6 address family, it is the first four octets of the MD5 hash of the IPv6 address.

Reference timestamp

This is the local time at which the system clock was last set or corrected, in 64-bit NTP timestamp format.

Originate timestamp

This is the local time at which the request departed the client for the server, in 64-bit NTP timestamp format.

Receive timestamp

This is the local time at which the request arrived at the server, in 64-bit NTP timestamp format.

Transmit timestamp

This is the local time at which the reply departed the server for the client, in 64-bit NTP timestamp format.

Message authentication code (MAC)

When the NTP authentication scheme is in use, this contains the 32-bit key identifier followed by the 128-bit MD5 message digest.

14.2 Control Flow

Figure 3.1 shows the general organization of the program. The design is properly described as an adaptive-parameter, hybrid-phase/frequency-locked loop. There is a peer process and poll process for every association mobilized by the program. They exchange packets with a remote server distinguished by IP address, port number, and version number. The system process includes the select, cluster, and combine algorithms, which mitigate among the servers to maximize timekeeping quality. The clock discipline process implements the loop filter necessary for accurate time and frequency corrections. The clock adjust process amortizes the time and frequency corrections to provide smooth, monotonic adjustments for the system clock.

Figure 14.2 shows the various routines and the flow of control among them. The routines are described in detail in following sections. For now, the control flow for received packets is shown on the left with flow along the solid arrows. The control flow for transmitted packets is shown on the right, with flow along the solid arrows. The dashed arrows show the control flow from one routine to a second routine, with return back to the first routine.

In the flowcharts and lists of variables to follow, the variables and parameters in general belong to one of the processes shown in Figure 3.1. Table 14.1 summarizes the naming conventions used in this chapter. Packet variables belong to each arriving and departing packet separately. Peer and poll variables belong to each association separately. Collectively, they define the state variables of the association, as described in other chapters of this book. The

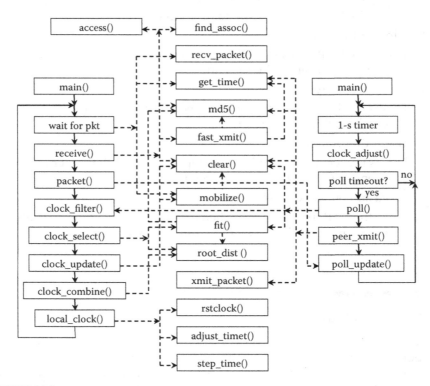

FIGURE 14.2
Control flow.

TABLE 14.1

Naming Conventions

Prefix	Process	Used by
r	Packet	Packet receive routines
x	Packet	Packet transmit routines
p	Peer, poll	Packet processing routines
$p.t$	Peer	Clock filter routine
s	System	System routines
$s.m$	System	Select routine
$s.v$	System	Cluster routine
c	Clock	Clock discipline routines

variables are used by the routines given in the third column and are part of the process given in the second column. When necessary to refer to a particular routine by name, the name will be followed by parentheses ().

To disambiguate between different variables of the same name but implemented in different processes, the following Unix-like structure member naming convention has been adopted, as shown in Table 14.1. Each receive packet variable v is a member of the packet structure r with fully qualified name $r.v$, while each transmit packet variable v is a member of the packet structure x with name $x.v$. Each peer variable v is a member of the peer structure p with name $p.v$. There is a set of peer variables for each association, including one set of clock filter variables, each variable v of which is a member of the peer structure $p.f$ with name $p.f.v$. Each system variable v is a member of the system structure s with name $s.v$, while each local clock variable v is a member of the clock structure c with name $c.v$. The system variables include one set of dynamically allocated chime variables $s.m$ used by the select routine and another set of dynamically allocated survivor variables $s.v$.

The common program parameters used by all routines in this chapter, except the clock discipline routines, are shown in Table 14.2. The mode assignments are shown in Table 14.3, while the authentication code assignments are shown in Table 14.4. The values are for illustration only. Most of the parameter values are arbitrary, such as the version number, maximum stratum, and maximum number of peers. While the precision is shown as a parameter, in actual practice it is measured for each system when the program is first started. Some parameters, such as the minimum and maximum poll exponents, are determined by the limits of the clock discipline loop stability. Others, like the frequency tolerance, involve an assumption about the worst-case behavior of a host once synchronized and then allowed to drift when its sources have become unreachable. The remaining parameter values have been determined by experiment and represent good choices over a wide set of conditions encountered in the Internet brawl.

In the following discussion, it is helpful to summarize the variables and parameters in the form of tables showing the correspondence between the

TABLE 14.2

Program Parameters

Name	Value	Description
VERSION	4	Version number
PRECISION	−18	Precision ($\log_2$ s)
MINDISP	.01	Minimum dispersion (s)
MAXPISP	16	Maximum dispersion (s)
MAXDIST	1.5	Distance threshold (s)
MAXSTRAT	15	Maximum stratum
MINPOLL	3	Minimum poll exponent ($\log_{+2}$ s)
MAXPOLL	17	Maximum poll exponent ($\log_2$ s)
PHI	15e-6	Frequency tolerance (15 PPM)
NSTAGE	8	Clock register stages
NMAX	3	Maximum number of peers
NSANE	1	Minimum intersection truechimers
NMIN	3	Minimum cluster survivors
SGATE	3	Popcorn spike threshold
BDELAY	0.004	Broadcast delay (s)
B_BURST	Flag	Burst enable
B_IBURST	Flag	Initial burst enable
B_COUNT	8	Packet in a burst

TABLE 14.3

Mode Code Assignments

Name	Value	Description
M_SACT	1	Symmetric active
M_PASV	2	Symmetric passive
M_CLNT	3	Client
M_SERV	4	Server
M_BCST	5	Broadcast server
M_BCLN	6	Broadcast client

TABLE 14.4

Authentication Code Assignments

Name	Value	Description
A_NONE	0	Not authenticated
A_OK	1	Authentication OK
A_ERROR	2	Authentication error
A_CRYPTO	3	Crypto-NAK received
A_NKEY	4	Key not trusted

TABLE 14.5

Packet Header Variables (r, x)

Name	Formula	Description
leap	*leap*	Leap indicator (LI)
version	*version*	Version number (VN)
mode	*mode*	Mode
stratum	*stratum*	Stratum
poll	τ	Poll exponent ($\log_2$ s)
precision	ρ	Precision ($\log_2$ s)
rootdelay	Δ	Root delay
rootdisp	E	Root dispersion
refid	*refid*	Reference ID
reftime	*reftime*	Reference timestamp
org	T_1	Origin timestamp
rec	T_2	Receive timestamp
xmt	T_3	Transmit timestamp
keyid	*keyid*	Key ID
MAC	*mac*	Message authentication code

descriptive names used in this narrative and the formula names used in the flowcharts. In this chapter, descriptive names are represented in non-italic serif font, while formula names are represented in Greek symbols or italic sans-serif font. Table 14.5 summarizes the variables used in Figure 14.1, including the descriptive name (first·column), formula name (second column), and a brief explanation (third column). Note that the precision ρ in this and the following tables is in $\log_2$ s units; however, in the figures the precision is interpreted as 2^ρ s to reduce clutter. Also, note the distinction between the terms *poll exponent* τ, which is in $\log_2$ s units, and *poll interval*, which is interpreted as 2^τ s.

14.3 Main Program and Common Routines

The four routines shown in Figure 14.3 stand alone and are not part of any process. The main program main() initializes the program, allocates the persistent associations, and then loops waiting for a received packet. When a packet arrives, the routine captures the receive timestamp and calls the receive() routine. The mobilize() routine allocates and initializes an association and starts the poll timer. The clear() routine resets or demobilizes an association and returns its resources to the system. The md5() routine computes a 128-bit message digest from a given key and message block. For simplicity, the routine shown here is used for both generating and checking. For checking purposes, the routine returns the codes shown in Table 14.4.

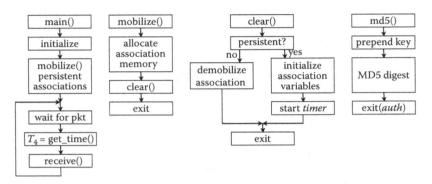

FIGURE 14.3
Main program and common routines.

The md5() routine uses the MD5 algorithm described in Request for Comments (RFC) 1321 [1] but modified to incorporate a symmetric key. The key itself is a 128-bit value held in a special cache where each key is associated with a 32-bit key identifier. The message digest is computed by first prepending the key value to the block and then computing the message digest over the combined key and block.

14.4 Peer Process

Tables 14.6 through 14.9 show the peer variables, routines, and interconnections with other routines There are four sets of variables: configuration, packet, working, and filter. The configuration variables shown in Table 14.6 are initialized when the association is mobilized, either by the main program or as the result of a received broadcast or symmetric active packet. The packet variables shown in Table 14.7 are copied from the most recent received packet header at the time of arrival t. The working variables shown in Table 14.8 represent the data computed by the receive() and packet() routines. The four clock filter variables shown in Table 14.9 represent a vector computed for each arriving packet.

The peer process includes the receive(), packet(), and clock_filter() routines. The receive() routine consists of two parts, the first of which is shown in Figure 14.4. Of the five fragments, the one beginning with receive() accepts a packet from the network and discards those with access control or format violations. It then runs the md5() routine, which returns one of the codes shown in Figure 14.4. Note that a packet without an MAC or with an authentication error is not discarded at this point. The routine then attempts to match the packet IP address, port number, and version number with an association previously mobilized. The switch table shown in Table 14.10 is used to select

TABLE 14.6

Peer Configuration Variables (p)

Name	Formula	Description
srcddr	*IPv4/IPv6*	Source address
srcport	*srcport*	Source port
version	*version*	Version number
hmode	*hmode*	(VN) mode (Table 14.3)
keyid	*keyid*	Key ID
flags		Flags (see Section 5.9)

TABLE 14.7

Peer Packet Variables (p)

Name	Formula	Description
leap	*leap*	Leap indicator (LI)
pmode	*pmode*	Peer mode (Table 14.3)
stratum	*stratum*	Stratum
ppoll	τ	Peer poll exponent ($\log_2$ s)
poll	τ	Poll exponent ($\log_2$ s)
precision	ρ	Precision ($\log_2$ s)
rootdelay	Δ	Root delay (s)
rootdisp	E	Root dispersion
refid	*refid*	Reference ID
reftime	*reftime*	Reference timestamp
org	T_1	Origin timestamp
rec	T_2	Receive timestamp
xmt	T_3	Transmit timestamp
dst	T_4	Destination timestamp

the next code segment as a function of association mode shown in the first column packet mode shown in the first row. The four remaining fragments in Figure 14.4 and the fragment in Figure 14.5 represent the switch targets. If a client packet arrives and there is no matching association, a server packet is sent (FXMIT) without mobilizing an association. While not shown in the figure, if the client packet has an invalid MAC, a special packet called a crypto-NAK is sent instead. This packet consists of a valid server packet header with a single 32-bit word of zeros appended where a MAC would normally be located. What to do if this occurs is up to the client.

If an authentic broadcast server packet arrives matching no existing broadcast client association, the receive() routine mobilizes an ephemeral broadcast client association (NEWBC). If an authentic symmetric active packet arrives matching no existing symmetric association, it mobilizes a symmetric passive association (NEWPS). Otherwise, processing continues to service

TABLE 14.8

Peer Working Variables (*p*)

Name	Formula	Description
dstaddr	*IPv4/IPv6*	Destination address
dstport	*dstport*	Destination port (123)
t	*t*	Update time
filter	*p.f*	Clock filter
offset	θ	Clock offset
delay	δ	Round-trip delay
disp	ε	Dispersion
jitter	φ	Jitter
hpoll	*hpoll*	Host poll exponent ($\log_2$ s)
hmode	*hmode*	Host mode (Table 14.3)
auth	*auth*	Authentication code (Table 14.4)
count	*count*	Burst counter
timer	*timer*	Poll timer
reach	*reach*	Reach register
unreach	*unreach*	Unreach counter

TABLE 14.9

Clock Filter Variables (*p.f*)

Name	Formula	Description
t	*t*	Update time
offset	θ	Clock offset
delay	δ	Round-trip delay
disp	ε	Dispersion

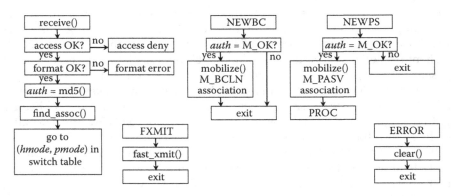

FIGURE 14.4
Routine receive(), part 1 of 2.

TABLE 14.10

Switch Table

Mode	Active	Passive	Client	Server	Broadcast
No peer	NEWPS		FXMIT		
Active	PROC	PROC			
Passive	PROC	ERROR			
Client					
Server					
Broadcast server					
Broadcast client					PROC

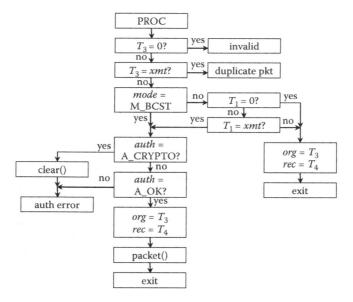

FIGURE 14.5
Routine receive(), part 2 of 2.

the packet (PROC) using the previously mobilized association. Where empty cells appear in Table 14.10, this indicates an invalid mode combination or possibly a broken protocol implementation. The default behavior in this case is to discard the packet, except in the case ERROR when a symmetric passive packet arrives for a symmetric passive association, which indicates either an implementation error or an intruder intending harm. In this case, the best defense is to demobilize the passive association and discard the packet.

Packets that match an existing association are ruthlessly checked for errors, as described in Table 3.1. In particular, the timestamps are checked to be sure they are valid and that the original timestamp T_1 in an arriving packet matches the last transmitted timestamp *xmt*. If it does and the authentication code is for a crypto-NAK, an authentication error is verified and not some

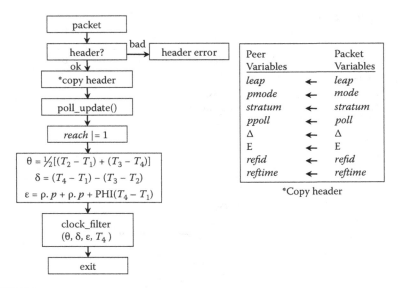

FIGURE 14.6
Routine packet().

rascal attempting to cause a denial of service attack. If not a crypto-NAK, control passes to the packet() routine.

The packet() routine shown in Figure 14.6 performs additional checks as described in Table 3.2. If the header is valid, the header values are copied to the corresponding peer variables, as shown in the figure. Since the packet poll exponent may have changed since the last packet, it calls the poll_update() routine in the poll process to redetermine the poll interval. At this point, the packet is considered valid and the server reachable and is so marked. Next, the offset, delay, dispersion, jitter, and time of arrival (T_4) sample values are calculated from the packet timestamps. The clock_filter() routine shown in Figure 14.7 saves the data from the eight most recent packets to select the best sample as the peer values. It implements the algorithm described in Section 3.7 by choosing the sample values associated with the minimum delay sample, but only if the current packet is later than the last packet. This conforms to the rule to always use only new samples. A popcorn spike suppressor compares the selected sample offset with previous peer jitter values and discards the sample (but updates the jitter value) if it exceeds three times the jitter.

14.5 System Process

Tables 14.11 through 14.13 show the system process variables, which are permanently allocated, except the chime list and survivor list, which are

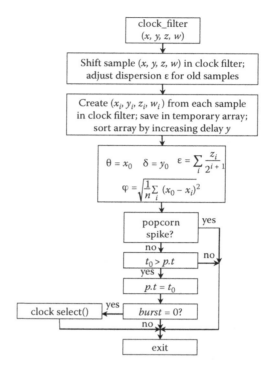

FIGURE 14.7
Routine clock_filter().

dynamically allocated by the clock_select() routine. They include the system variables shown in Table 14.11. The chime list variables shown in Table 14.12 are used by the select algorithm; the survivor list variables shown in Table 14.13 are used by the cluster algorithm.

The system process routines closely implement the mitigation algorithms described in Chapter 3. The clock_select() routine shown in Figure 14.8 first scans the associations to collect just those that are valid sources, as determined by fit() routine, described later in this chapter. Then, the select algorithm cleaves the falsetickers from the population, leaving the truechimers as the majority clique. Finally, the cluster algorithm trims the outliers until the best three survivors are left. The survivors are combined in the combine() algorithm shown in Figure 14.9. The individual peer offset and peer jitter measurements are averaged with a factor depending on the reciprocal of the root distance normalized so that the sum of the factors is unity.

The combined offset is processed by the clock_update() routine shown in Figure 14.10. The routine first compares the age of the most recent update with the age of the current update and discards the current update, if older. This can happen when switching from one system peer to another. Next, the

TABLE 14.11

System Variables (s)

Name	Formula	Description
t	t	Update time
leap	*leap*	Leap indicator (LI)
stratum	*stratum*	Stratum
poll	τ	Poll interval ($\log_2$ s)
precision	ρ	Precision ($\log_2$ s)
refid	*refid*	Reference ID
reftime	*reftime*	Reference timestamp
chime	s.m	Chime list
survivor	s.v	Survivor list (s.v)
peer	p	System peer
offset	θ	Combined offset
rootdelay	Δ	Root delay
rootdisp	E	Root dispersion
sysjitter	ϑ	Combined jitter
jitter	φ_p	Peer jitter
seljitter	φ_s	Select jitter
flags		Option flags

TABLE 14.12

Chime List Variables (s.m)

Name	Formula	Description
p	p	Association ID
type	t	Edge type
edge	*edge*	Edge offset

TABLE 14.13

Survivor List Variables (s.v)

Name	Formula	Description
p	p	Association ID
metric	λ	Survivor metric

local_clock() routine in the clock discipline process is called, which returns PANIC if the update is considered bogus, STEP if it resulted in a step over 128 ms, IGNOR if the update was discarded, and ADJ if it resulted in an ordinary adjustment. If PANIC, the program exits with a message to the operator to set the time manually within 10 min; if STEP, the associations now contain inconsistent data, so are all reset as if for the first time. Along with the initial start procedures, this is the only place the poll exponent is reset to the minimum.

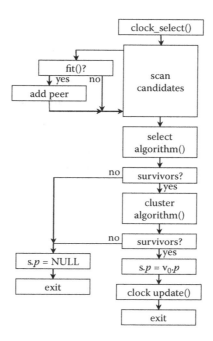

FIGURE 14.8
Routine clock_select().

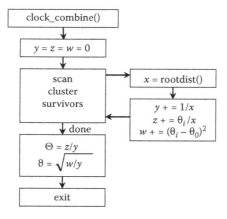

FIGURE 14.9
Routine clock_combine().

There are two functions remaining in the system process. The fit() function shown in Figure 14.11 determines whether the association is viable as required by Table 3.2. The root_dist() function shown in Figure 14.12 calculates the root distance.

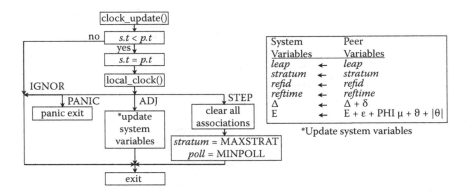

FIGURE 14.10
Routine clock_update().

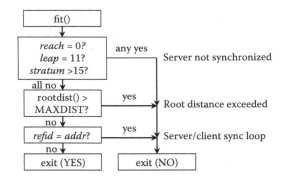

FIGURE 14.11
Routine fit().

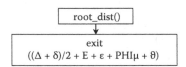

FIGURE 14.12
Routine root_dist().

14.6 Clock Discipline Process

Tables 14.14 and 14.15 show the clock discipline process variables, parameters, and routines. These include the local_clock() routine, which processes offset samples and calculates the system clock time and frequency corrections, and a utility routine rstclock() that does bookkeeping for the clock state machine. Table 14.14 shows the clock discipline variables. Table 14.15 shows a number of critical parameters in this design, including the step, stepout, and panic thresholds discussed in Chapter 4. The Allan intercept parameter is a compromise value appropriate for typical computer oscillators and is not critical. The frequency tolerance parameter is on the high side but consistent with old and new computer oscillators observed in the general population. The loop gain parameters are determined following the principles of Chapter 4. The values of the remaining parameters were determined by experiment under actual operating conditions.

The local_clock() routine is shown in Figures 14.13 and 14.14, while the clock state transition matrix is shown in Table 14.16. The main function of the state machine is to react to bogus time, handle relatively large time steps, suppress outliers, and directly compute frequency corrections at

TABLE 14.14

Clock Discipline Process Variables (c)

Name	Formula	Description
t	t	Update time
state	$state$	Current state
offset	θ	Offset
roffset	θ_R	Residual offset
count	$count$	Jiggle counter
freq	ϕ	Frequency
jitter	φ	Offset jitter
wander	η	Frequency wander

TABLE 14.15

Clock Discipline Process Parameters

Name	Value	Description
STEPT	0.128	Step threshold (s)
WATCH	900	Stepout threshold (s)
PANICT	1,000	Panic threshold (s)
PLL	16	PLL (phase-lock loop) gain
FLL	4	FLL (frequency-lock loop) gain
AVG	4	Averaging constant
ALLAN	11	Allan intercept ($\log_2$ s)
LIMIT	30	Jiggle counter threshold
MAXFREQ	500	Frequency tolerance (PPM)
PGATE	4	Poll adjust gate

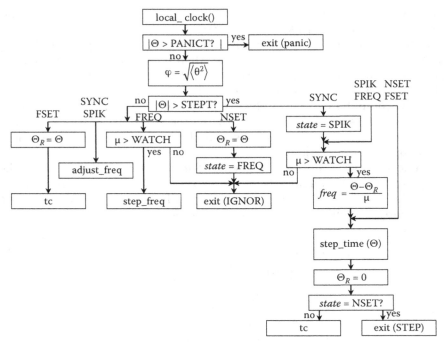

FIGURE 14.13
Routine local_clock(), part 1 of 2.

initial startup. A bogus time step is any over PANIC (1,000 s), which causes the program to exit with a message sent to the system log requesting the time be set manually within 1.000 s. A time step over STEPT (128 ms) is not believed unless the step has continued for WATCH (900 s) or more. Otherwise, the time and frequency adjustments are determined by the feedback loop.

Figure 14.14 shows how time and frequency adjustments are determined and how the poll interval is managed. The adjust_freq entry uses the adaptive parameter hybrid algorithm described in Chapter 4, while the step_freq entry computes the frequency directly. This is done in a manner such that the correction due to the time offset and frequency offset can be separated and each determined individually. The system jitter statistic φ is computed as the exponential average of root-mean-square (RMS) time differences, while the oscillator wander statistic η is computed as the exponential average of RMS frequency differences.

The code following the tc entry is in effect a bang-bang controller that increases the poll exponent if the time correction is less than some fraction times the system jitter and otherwise decreases it. This simple algorithm has proved superior to several more complicated algorithms used previously. In the default configuration, the default poll exponent range is from MINPOLL

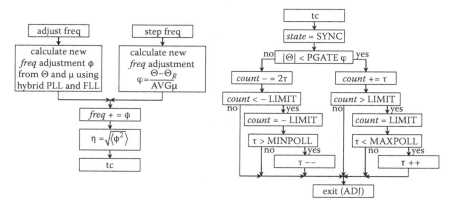

FIGURE 14.14
Routine local_clock(), part 2 of 2.

TABLE 14.16

Clock State Transition Matrix

State	$|\Theta| <$ STEPT	$|\Theta| \geq$ STEPT	Comments
NSET	Adjust time, $\rightarrow$ FREQ	Step time, $\rightarrow$ FREQ	No frequency file
FSET	Adjust time, $\rightarrow$ SYNC	Step time, $\rightarrow$ SYNC	Frequency file present
SPIK	Adjust freq, adjust time, $\rightarrow$ SYNC	Step frequency; step time, $\rightarrow$ SYNC	Outlier detected
FREQ	If (<WATCH) $\rightarrow$ FREQ else step frequency, adjust time, $\rightarrow$ SYNC	If (<WATCH) $\rightarrow$ FREQ else step frequency, step time, $\rightarrow$ SYNC	Initial frequency
SYNC	Adjust frequency; adjust time, $\rightarrow$ SYNC	If (<WATCH) $\rightarrow$ SYNC else $\rightarrow$ SPIK	Normal operation

(6) to MAXPOLL (10), which corresponds to the poll interval range 64–1,024 s. However, the lower limit can be configured as low as 3 (8 s) and the upper limit as high as 17 (36 h).

14.7 Clock Adjust Process

The clock adjust process runs at regular intervals of 1 s. Figure 14.15 shows a flowchart for the clock_adjust() routine in this process. At each update, the local_clock() routine initializes the frequency *freq* and phase Θ_R. Once each second, the local clock is increased by *freq* plus the fraction *tmp* and the value of Θ_R reduced by *tmp*. At the same time, the maximum error represented by the root dispersion E is increased by the frequency tolerance Φ representing the dispersion increase for 1 s. While not shown on the flowchart, the clock

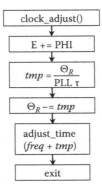

FIGURE 14.15
Clock adjust process.

adjust process scans the associations each second to update the association timer and calls the poll() routine when the timer expires.

14.8 Poll Process

The poll process sends packets to the server at designated intervals τ and updates the reach register, which establishes whether the server is reachable. The poll() routine is shown in Figure 14.16. Each time the poll() routine is called, the *reach* variable is shifted left by one bit. When a packet is accepted by the packet() routine in the peer process, the rightmost bit is set to one. As long as *reach* is nonzero, the server is considered reachable. However, if the rightmost three bits become zero, indicating that packets from the server have not been received for at least three poll intervals, a sample with MAXDIST dispersion is shifted in the clock filter. This causes the dispersion to increase and the server to be devalued in the mitigation process. The *unreach* counter increments at each poll interval; it is reset to zero if the reach register is nonzero. If the counter exceeds the UNREACH parameter, the poll exponent is incremented for each succeeding poll. This reduces useless network load in case of server failure.

The poll() routine can operate in three modes. Ordinarily, polls are sent at the interval selected by *hpoll* and *ppoll* poll exponents assigned. However, if the iburst option in Section 5.9 is enabled and the server is not reachable, a burst of eight polls is sent at 2-s intervals. Alternatively or in addition, if the burst option is enabled and the server is reachable, a burst of eight polls is sent as with iburst. This is especially useful at very large poll intervals of many hours.

The remaining routines are straightforward. The poll() routine calls the peer_xmit() routine when an association has been mobilized. The receive()

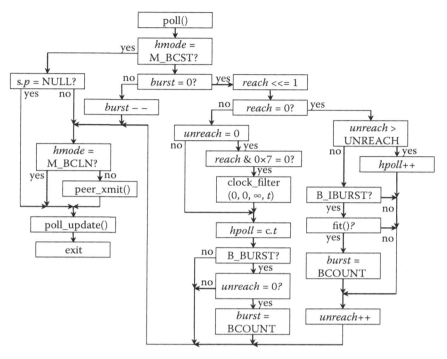

FIGURE 14.16
Routine poll().

routine calls fast_xmit() when a client mode packet is received. Both cases are shown in Figure 14.17. These routines copy values from the association (peer_xmit()) or from the arriving packet (fast_xmit()), as shown in the accompanying tables. The poll_update() routine shown in Figure 14.18 determines the next poll interval or burst interval.

14.9 Parting Shots

An issue worth mentioning is the relationship between the published standard and the reference implementation. It is tempting to construct a standard from first principles, submit it for formal verification, then tell somebody to build it. Of the four generations of NTP, it did not work that way. Both the standard and the reference implementation were evolved from an earlier version, then carefully and methodically cross-checked to make sure that the implementation did what the standard said and vice versa. Along the way, many minor tweaks were needed in both the specification and implementation to ensure that was the case. In the most recent

peer_xmit() fast_xmit()
↓
*copy header
↓
T_1, T_2
↓
$T_3 = clock$
↓
$mac = $ md5()
↓
xmit_packet()
↓
exit

Packet Variable		Desig. Variable	Packet Packet		Desig. Variable
leap	←	s*.leap*	*leap*	←	s*.leap*
version	←	p*.version*	*version*	←	r*.version*
mode	←	p*.hmode*	*mode*	←	M_SERV
stratum	←	s*.stratum*	*stratum*	←	s*.stratum*
poll	←	p*.hpoll*	*poll*	←	r*.poll*
ρ	←	s*.r*	ρ	←	s*.r*
Δ	←	s*.*Δ	Δ	←	s*.*Δ
E	←	s*.E*	E	←	s*.E*
refid	←	s*.refid*	*refid*	←	s*.refid*
reftime	←	s*.reftime*	*reftime*	←	s*.reftime*
T_1	←	p*.org*	T_1	←	r*.*T_3
T_2	←	p*.rec*	T_2	←	r*.*T_4
T_3	←	*clock*	T_3	←	*clock*
keyid	←	p*.keyid*	*keyid*	←	r*.keyid*
mac	←	md5	*mac*	←	md5

*Routine peer_xmit()   *Routine fast_xmit()

FIGURE 14.17
Routines peer_xmit() and fast_xmit().

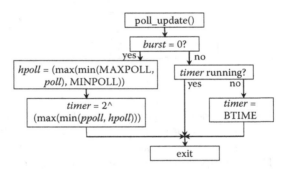

FIGURE 14.18
Routine poll_update().

versions, a simulation tool, properly described as a *skeleton*, was used as a verification tool.

On several occasions during construction of the flowcharts and descriptions in this chapter, some little thing or other suggested a specific test. For example, two symmetric peers cannot ever get in symmetric passive mode with each other. That might even be true in practice, but what would happen if they did? Testing confirmed unsuspected errors in the code and were quickly corrected. Some little errors like this have persisted for many years before rigorous testing exposed them.

References

1. Revisit, R. *The MD5 Message-Digest Algorithm*. Network Working Group Report RFC-1321, MIT Laboratory for Computer Science and RSA Data Security, Inc., April 1992.

Further Reading

Mills, D.L. *The Autokey Security Architecture, Protocol and Algorithms*. Electrical Engineering Report 03-2-20, University of Delaware, Newark, February 2003.

Mills, D.L. *Network Time Protocol (Version 3) Specification, Implementation and Analysis*. Network Working Group Report RFC-1305, University of Delaware, Newark, March 1992.

15

Precision System Clock Architecture

> Time iz like money, the less we hav ov it teu spare the further we
> make it go.
>
> **Josh Billing**
> _Encyclopedia and Proverbial Philosophy of Wit and Humor,_ 1874

Over the almost three decades that the NTP has evolved, accuracy expectations have increased from 100 ms to less than 1 ms on fast local-area
networks (LANs) with multiple segments interconnected by switches and
less than a few milliseconds on most campus and corporate networks with
multiple subnets interconnected by routers. Today, the practical expectation with a GPS receiver, PPS signal, and precision kernel support is a few
microseconds. In principle, the ultimate expectation is limited only by the
232-ps resolution of the NTP timestamp format or about the time light
travels 3 inches.

In this chapter, we turn to the most ambitious means available to minimize
errors in the face of hardware and software not designed for extraordinary
timekeeping. First, we examine the hardware and software components for
a precision system clock and evolve an effective design for future systems.
Next, we survey timestamping techniques using hardware, driver, and software methods to minimize errors due to media, device, and operating system latencies. Finally, we explore the Institute of Electrical and Electronics
Engineers (IEEE) 1588 Precision Time Protocol (PTP), how it is used in a
high-speed LAN, and how it and NTP can interoperate. The Parting Shots
section proposes a hardware-assisted design that provides performance
equivalent to PTP with only minimal modifications to the Unix operating
system kernel.

15.1 Limitations of the Art

Computer timekeepers live in a world of commodity clock oscillators vulnerable to temperature surges and operating systems vulnerable to scheduling and queuing latencies. Once upon a time, it took 42 μs to read the system
clock on a Sun SPARC IPC and up to 22 ms jitter on the Streams driver stack.
Now, the nominal latency to read the system clock on a modern computer is

only half a microsecond. With proper choice of operating system parameters and scheduling priority, the latency variations can be reduced to this order.

Recall the typical Allan deviation characteristic exhibited in Figure 12.2. Note that the apex of the V-shaped characteristic, the Allan intersection, moves to the left as the phase noise is reduced, given the same frequency noise characteristic. In the MICRO characteristic the apex is about 250 s, representing the ideal averaging time. Improvements since that figure was determined suggest that the phase noise can be reduced by an order of magnitude using the system clock design suggested in Section 15.2. To the extent that the phase noise can be reduced, the time constant can be reduced as well, which reduces the effects of frequency noise. As demonstrated in this chapter, this is advisable only with hardware- or driver-assisted timestamps.

A useful benchmark for the current art is an experiment using a PPS signal from a cesium oscillator or GPS receiver hooked up to the kernel PPS discipline. With the poll interval strapped to 8 s, the time constant is about 256 s, which puts a reasonably tight reign on oscillator wander. The results of this experiment with several machines, both old and new, show typical offset and jitter of a few microseconds contributed by the hardware and operating system driver. However, incidental jitter is reduced by three orders of magnitude by the discipline algorithm. While not rigorously justified by statistics, the experiment does suggest a performance bound not likely to be exceeded with commodity computer hardware and operating systems.

Even with the kernel discipline, it is necessary to closely examine the hardware and software components of the system clock to sustain the highest performance without expensive dedicated hardware components. We next explore how this can be done using relatively inexpensive components and closely engineered discipline algorithms. While designs such as this might not appear in commodity computers, they might well be adapted to embedded computers used in spacecraft and measurement applications.

15.2 Precision System Clock

In the simplest form, a computer clock consists of an oscillator and counter/ divider that deliver repetitive pulses at intervals in the range from 1 to 10 ms, called the *tick* (sometimes called the *jiffy*). Each pulse triggers a hardware interrupt that increments the system clock variable such that the rate of the system clock in seconds per second matches the rate of the real clock. This is true even if the tick does not exactly divide the second. The timer interrupt routine serves two functions: one as the source for various kernel and user housekeeping timers and the other to maintain the time of day. Housekeeping timers are based on the number of ticks and are not disciplined in time or frequency. The precision kernel disciplines the system clock in time and frequency to match the real clock by adding or subtracting a small increment to the system clock variable at each timer interrupt.

In modern computers, there are three sources that can be used to implement the system clock: the timer oscillator that drives the counter/divider, the real-time clock (RTC) that maintains the time when the power is off (or even on for that matter), and what in some architectures is called the processor cycle counter (PCC) and in others is called the timestamp counter (TSC). We use the latter acronym in the following discussion. Any of these sources can in principle be used as the clock source. However, the engineering issues with these sources are quite intricate and need to be explored in some detail.

15.2.1 Timer Oscillator

The typical system clock uses a timer interrupt rate in the 100- to 1,000-Hz range. It is derived from a crystal oscillator operating in the 1- to 10-MHz range. For reasons that may be obscure, the oscillator frequency is often some multiple or submultiple of 3.579545 MHz. The reason for this rather bizarre choice is that this is the frequency of the NTSC analog TV color burst signal, and crystals for this frequency are widely available and inexpensive. Now that digital TV is here, expect the new gold standard at 19.39 MHz or some submultiple as this is the bit rate for ATSC.

In some systems, the counter/divider is implemented in an application-specific integrated circuit (ASIC) producing timer frequencies of 100, 256, 1,000, and 1,024 Hz. The ubiquitous Intel 8253/8254 programmable interval timer (PIT) chip includes three 16-bit counters that count down from a preprogrammed value and produce a pulse when the counter reaches zero, then repeat the cycle endlessly. Operated at one-third the color burst frequency or 1.1931816 MHz and preloaded with the value 11932, the PIT produces 100 Hz to within 15 PPM. The resulting systematic error is probably dominated by the inherent crystal frequency error.

15.2.2 Timestamp Counter

The TSC is a counter derived from the processor clock, which in modern processors operates above 1 GHz. The counter provides exquisite resolution, but there are several potential downsides using it directly as the clock source. To provide synchronous data transfers, the TSC is divided to some multiple of the bus clock where it can be synchronized to a quartz or surface acoustic wave (SAW) resonator using a phase-lock loop (PLL). The resonator is physically close to the central processing unit (CPU) chip, so heat from the chip can affect its frequency. Modern processors show wide temperature variations due to various workloads on the arithmetic and logical instruction units, and this can affect the TSC frequency.

In multiprocessor CPU chips, there is a separate TSC for every processor, and they might not increment in step or even operate at the same frequency. In systems like Windows, the timekeeping functions are directed to a single processor. This may result in unnecessary latency should that processor be occupied while another is free. Alternatively, some means must be available to discipline each TSC separately and provide individual time and frequency corrections. A method to do this is described in Section 15.2.5.

In early processors, the TSC rate depended on the processor clock frequency, which is not necessarily the same at all times. In sleep mode, for example, the processor clock frequency is much lower to conserve power. In the most modern Intel processors, the TSC always runs at the highest rate determined at boot time. In other words, the PLL runs all the time. Further complicating the issues is that modern processor technology can support out-of-order execution, which means that the TSC may appear earlier or later relative to a monotonic counter. This can be avoided by either serializing the instruction stream or using a serialized form of the instruction to read the TSC.

The ultimate complication is that, to reduce radio-frequency interference (RFI), a technique called spread-spectrum clocking can be utilized. This is done by modulating the PLL control loop with a triangular signal, causing the oscillator frequency to sweep over a small range of about 2 percent. The maximum frequency is the rated frequency of the clock, while the minimum in this case is 2 percent less. As the triangular wave is symmetric and the sweep frequency is in the kilohertz range, the frequency error is uniformly distributed between zero and 2 percent with mean 1 percent. Whether this is acceptable depends on the application. On some motherboards, the spread-spectrum feature can be disabled, and this would be the preferred workaround.

Considering these observations, the TSC may not be the ideal choice as the primary time base for the system clock. However, as explained in this chapter, it may make an ideal interpolation means.

15.2.3 Real-Time Clock

The RTC function, often implemented in a multifunction chip, provides a battery backup clock when the computer power is off as well as certain additional functions in some chips. In the STMicroelectronics M41ST85W RTC chip, for example, an internal 32.768-kHz crystal oscillator drives a BCD counter that reckons the time of century (TOC) to a precision of 10 ms. It includes a square-wave generator that can be programmed from 1 to 32,768 Hz in powers of two. The oscillator frequency is guaranteed within 35 PPM (at 25°C) and can be digitally steered within 3 PPM. This is much better than most commodity oscillators and suggests a design in which the PIT is replaced by the RTC generator.

The RTC is read and written over a two-wire serial interface, presumably by a BIOS (Basic Input/Output System) routine. The data are read and written bit by bit for the entire contents. The BCD counter is latched on the first read, so reading the TOC is an atomic operation. The counter is also latched on power down, so it can be read at power-up to determine how long the power has been absent.

For laptops in power-down or sleep mode, it is important that the clock oscillator be as stable and as temperature insensitive as possible. The crystal used in RTC devices is usually AT-cut with the zero-coefficient slope as close to room temperature as possible. The characteristic slope is a parabola in which the highest frequency is near motherboard temperature and drops off at both higher and lower temperatures. For the M41ST85W chip, the characteristic frequency dependence is given by

$$\nabla f = k(T - T_0)^2 \, \text{PPM},$$

where $k = 0.036 \pm 0.006$ PPM/C², and T_0 is 25°C. This is an excellent characteristic compared to a typical commodity crystal and would be the much preferred clock source, if available.

There is some art when incorporating an RTC in the system design, especially with laptops, for which the power can be off for a considerable time. First, it is necessary to correct the RTC from time to time to track the system time when it is disciplined by an external source. This is usually done simply by setting the system clock at the current time, which in most operating systems sets the RTC as well. In Unix systems, this is done with the settimeofday() system call about once per hour. Second, in a disciplined shutdown, the RTC and system clock time can be saved in nonvolatile memory and retrieved along with the current RTC time at a subsequent startup. From these data, the system clock can be set precisely within a range resulting from the RTC frequency error and the time since shutdown. Finally, the frequency of the RTC itself can be measured and used to further refine the time at startup.

15.2.4 Precision System Clock Implementation

In this section, we examine software implementation issues for a precision system clock with time resolution less than 1 ns and frequency resolution less than 1 ns/s. The issues involve how to represent precision time values, how to convert between different representations. Most current operating systems represent time as two 32-bit or 64-bit words, one in seconds and the other in microseconds or nanoseconds of the second. Arithmetic operations using this representation are awkward and nonatomic.* Modern computer

---

* Digital/HP VAX systems and the IEEE 1588 clock increment the clock in nanoseconds, while IBM systems increment the clock in microseconds at bit 52 of a 64-bit word. In the IBM design, bit 31 rolls over at something close to but not exactly 1 s. Apparently believing in time dilation, IBM calls this a megamicrosecond.

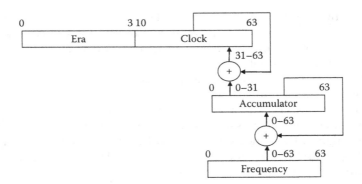

FIGURE 15.1
Precision system clock format.

architectures support 64-bit arithmetic, so it is natural to use this word size for the precision system clock shown in Figure 15.1. The clock variable is one 64-bit word in seconds and fraction with the decimal point to the left of bit 32 in big-endian order. Arithmetic operations are atomic, and no synchronization primitive, such as a spin-lock, is needed, even on a multiple-processor system.

The clock variable is updated at each timer interrupt, which adds an increment of $2^{32}/Hz$ to the clock variable, where Hz is the timer interrupt frequency. The increment is modulated by the control signal produced by the precision kernel discipline described in Chapter 8. This format is identical to NTP unsigned timestamp format, which of course is not accidental. It is convenient to extend this format to the full 128-bit NTP signed date format and include an era field in the clock format. The absence of the low-order 32 bits of the fraction is not significant since the 32-bit fraction provides resolution to less than 1 ns.

In general, the disciplined clock frequency does not divide the second, so an accumulator and frequency register are necessary. The frequency register contains the tick value plus the frequency correction supplied by the precision kernel discipline. At each tick interrupt, its contents are added to the accumulator. The high-order 32 bits of the accumulator are added to the low-order 32 bits of the clock variable as an atomic operation, then the high-order 32 bits of the accumulator are set to zero.

As mentioned in Chapter 1, the clock variable must be set within 68 years of the correct time before timekeeping operations begin. Furthermore, clock adjustments must be less than 68 years in the past or future. Adjustments beyond this range require the era field to be set by other means, such as the RTC. This model simplifies the discipline algorithm since timestamp differences can span only one era boundary. Therefore, given that the era field is set properly, arithmetic operations consist simply of adding a 64-bit signed quantity to the clock variable and propagating a carry or borrow in the era field if the clock variable overflows or underflows. If the high-order bit of the clock variable changes from a one to a zero and the sign bit of the adjustment is positive (0), an overflow has occurred, and the era field is incremented by one. If the high-order bit changes from a zero to a one and the sign bit is negative (1), an underflow has occurred, and the era field is decremented by one.

If a clock adjustment does span an era boundary, there will be a tiny interval while the carry or borrow is propagated and where a reader could see an inconsistent value. This is easily circumvented using Lamport's rule in three steps: (1) read the era value, (2) read the system clock variable, and (3) read the era value again. If the two era values are different, do the steps again. This assumes that the time between clock readings is long compared to the carry or borrow propagate time.

The 64-bit clock variable represented in seconds and fraction can easily be converted to other representations in seconds and some modulus m, such as microseconds or nanoseconds. To convert from seconds-fraction to modulus m, multiply the fraction by m and right shift 32 bits. To convert from modulus m to seconds-fraction, multiply by $2^{64}/m$ and right shift 32 bits.

15.2.5 Precision System Clock Operations

The precision system clock design presented in this section is based on an earlier design for the Digital Alpha running the 64-bit OSF/1 kernel. The OSF/1 kernel uses a 1,024-Hz timer frequency, so the amount to add at each tick interrupt is $2^{32}/1,024 = 2^{22} = 4,194,304$. The frequency gain is $2^{-32} = 2.343 \times 10^{-10}$ s/s; that is, a change in the low-order bit of the fraction yields a frequency change of 2.343×10^{-10} s/s. While omitting the details here, the remaining parameters can be calculated for a given time constant as in Chapter 4.

Without interpolation, this design has a resolution limited to $2^{-10} = 977$ μs, which may be sufficient for some applications, including software timer management. Further refinement requires the PCC to interpolate between timer interrupts. However, modern computers can have more than one processor (up to 14 on the Alpha), each with its own PCC, so some means are needed to wrangle each PCC to a common timescale.

The design now suggested by Intel to strap all clock functions to one processor is rejected as that processor could be occupied with another thread while another processor is available. Instead, any available processor can be used for the clock reading function. In this design, one of the processors is selected as the master to service the timer interrupt and update the system clock variable $c(t)$. Note that the interpolated system clock time $s(t)$ is equal to $c(t)$ at interrupt time; otherwise, it must be interpolated.

A data structure is associated with each processor, including the master. For convenience in the following, sequential updates for each structure are indexed by the variable i. At nominal intervals less than 1 s (staggered over all processors), the timer interrupt routine issues an interprocessor interrupt to each processor, including the master. At the ith timer interrupt, the interprocessor interrupt routine sets structure member $C_i = c(t)$, structure member $P_i = PCC(t)$, and updates a structure member K_i as described in the following discussion.

During the boot process, i is set to 0, and the structure for each processor is initialized as discussed. For each structure, a scaling factor $K_0 = 2^{64}/f_c$, where f_c is the measured processor clock frequency, is initialized. The f_c can be determined from the difference of the PCC over 1 s measured by a kernel timer. As the system clock is set from the RTC at initialization and not yet disciplined to an external source, there may be a small error in K_0, but this is not a problem at boot time.

The system clock is interpolated in a special way using 64-bit arithmetic but avoiding divide instructions, which are considered evil in some kernels. Let $s(t)$ be the interpolated system clock at arbitrary time t and i be the index of the most recent structure for the processor reading the clock. Then,

$$s(t) = C_i + \left[K_i \left(PCC(t) - P_i \right) \right] >> 32 .$$

Note that to avoid overflow, the interval between updates must be less than 1 s.

The scaling factor K is adjusted in response to small variations in the apparent PCC frequency, adjustments produced by the discipline algorithm, and jitter due to thread scheduling and context switching. During the $i + 1$ interprocessor interrupt, but before the C_i and P_i are updated, K is updated:

$$K_{i+1} = \frac{\left[c(t) - C_i \right] << 32}{p(t) - P_i} .$$

Note that the calculation shown here uses a divide instruction, but this is done infrequently. For instance, if the interval spans just under 1 s and if $f_c = 2.4$ GHz, $K = 7.686 \times 10^9$.

Note that only small adjustments in K will be required, which suggests that the adjustment can be approximated with sufficient accuracy while avoiding the divide instruction. If we observe that for small t, $dt/dk = 1/K$ and $Kf_c = 2^{64}$,

$$K_{i+1} = K_i + K \left[f_c \left(s(t) - c(t) \right) \right] >> 32 .$$

The value of f_c was first measured when K_0 was computed so is not known exactly. However, small inaccuracies will not lead to significant error.

Notwithstanding the careful management of residuals in this design, there may be small discontinuities due to PCC frequency variations or discipline operations. These may result in tiny jumps forward or backward. To conform to required correctness assertions, the clock must never jump backward or stand still. For this purpose, the actual clock reading code remembers the last reading and guarantees the clock readings to be monotone-definite increasing by not less than the least-significant bit in the 64-bit clock value.

However, to avoid lockup if the clock is unintentionally set far in the future, the clock will be stepped backward only if more than 2 s. Ordinarily, this would be done only in response to an explicit system call. The threshold of 2 s allows leap seconds to be implemented as in Chapter 13.

15.3 Principles of Precision Timestamping

As shown elsewhere in this book, stochastic errors are generally minimized by the NTP mitigation and discipline algorithms. In general, these errors can be further reduced using some kind of timestamping assist in the form of special provisions in the network interface card (NIC) or device driver. Means to exploit these provisions are discussed in this section.

To better understand the issues, consider the common case by which the server and client implement precision clocks that can be read with exquisite accuracy. The object is to measure the time offset of a server B relative to a client A. As shown in Figure 15.2, the NTP on-wire protocol uses the reference timestamps T_1, T_2, T_3, and T_4, respectively called the origin, receive, transmit, and destination timestamps. In the context of this discussion, reference timestamps are captured just before the first octet of the packet. T_1 and T_4 are captured by client A from its clock, while T_2 and T_3 are captured by server B from its clock. The object of the protocol is to determine the time offset θ of B relative to A and the round-trip delay δ on the path *ABA*:

$$\theta = \frac{1}{2}\left[(T_2 - T_1) + (T_3 - T_4)\right] \tag{15.1}$$

and

$$\delta = (T_4 - T_1) - (T_3 - T_2). \tag{15.2}$$

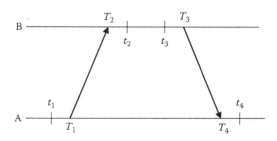

FIGURE 15.2
NTP on-wire protocol/timestamps.

However, the actual timestamps available to the protocol are t_1, t_2, t_3, and t_4. The differences between the actual timestamps and reference timestamps are due to queuing and buffering latencies in the operating system, device driver, and NIC. These issues are discussed in this section.

The precision to which the offset and delay can be calculated depends on the precision with which the timestamps can be captured. In general, it is best to capture the timestamps as close to the physical media as possible to avoid various queuing and buffering latencies. There are three general categories of timestamps to consider: those captured in the application software, called *softstamps*; those captured by the device driver at interrupt time, called *drivestamps*; and those captured by special hardware from the media, called *hardstamps*.

Example 15.1

The timestamping scheme used in the NTP reference implementation attempts to approximate the reference timestamp as follows: The t_1 and t_3 are softstamps captured by the output packet routine just before the message digest (if used) is calculated and the buffer is passed to the operating system. Applicable latencies include digest overhead, output queuing, operating system scheduling, NIC buffering, and possibly NIC retransmissions. These latencies can be largely avoided using the interleaved modes described in Chapter 16. The t_2 and t_4 are drivestamps captured just after the input packet interrupt routine and before the buffer is queued for the input packet routine. Applicable latencies include NIC buffering, interrupt processing, and operating system scheduling but not input queuing.

If these latencies can be avoided, the remaining latencies are due only to propagation time, packet transmission time, and network queues. Inspection of Equation 15.1 shows that the best accuracy is obtained when the delays on the outbound path $T_1 \rightarrow T_2$ and inbound path $T_3 \rightarrow T_4$ are statistically equivalent; in this case, we say that the paths are *reciprocal*. Further refinement demonstrated further in this section shows that, if the reciprocal delays differ by x seconds, the resulting offset error is $x/2$ s.

There are many workable schemes to implement timestamp capture. Using a different scheme at each end of the link is likely to result in a lack of reciprocity. The following provisions apply:

1. A software timestamp is captured as close to the system input/output (I/O) call as possible.

2. A preamble timestamp is captured as near to the start of the packet as possible. The preferred point follows the start-of-frame (SOF) octet and before the first octet of the data.

3. A trailer timestamp is captured as near to the end of the packet as possible. On transmit, the preferred point follows the last octet

of the data and before the frame check sequence (FCS); on receive, the preferred point follows the last octet of the FCS. The reason the capture locations necessarily differ is due to the Ethernet hardware and protocol design. (Note: A sufficiently large and complex field-programmable gate array (FPGA) might be able to deliver the trailer timestamp at the same point as the transmitter, but this does not seem worth the trouble.)

4. In addition to the timestamps, the NIC or driver must provide both the nominal transmission rate and number of octets between the preamble and trailer timestamps. This can be used by the driver or application to transpose between the preamble and trailer timestamps without significant loss of accuracy. The transposition error with acceptable frequency tolerance of 300 PPM for 100-Mb/s Ethernets and a nominal 1,000-bit NTP packet is less than 3 ns.

Except as mentioned in further discussion here, a drivestamp is always a trailer timestamp, and a hardstamp is a preamble timestamp. On transmit, a softstamp is a preamble timestamp; on receive, it is a trailer timestamp. As shown further in this section, the best way to preserve accuracy when single or multiple network segments are involved, some possibly operating at different rates, is the following:

1. The propagation delay measured from the first bit sent in a packet to the first bit received in each direction of transmission must be the same.

2. T_1 and T_3 must be captured from the preamble timestamp.

3. T_2 and T_4 must be captured from the trailer timestamp.

Whatever timestamping strategy is deployed, it should allow interworking between schemes so that every combination of strategies used by the server and client results in the highest accuracy possible. As will be shown, this can be achieved only using the above rules.

15.3.1 Timestamp Transposition

With these requirements in mind, it is possible to select either the preamble or the trailer timestamp at either the transmitter or the receiver and to transpose so that both represent the same reference point in the packet. The natural choice is the preamble timestamp as this is considered the reference timestamp in this document and is consistent with IEEE 1588 and likely to be supported by available hardware.

According to the rules given, a transmitter must transpose trailer timestamps to preamble timestamps, and a receiver must transpose preamble timestamps to trailer timestamps. Transposition must take into account the transmission rate and packet length on the transmit and receive LAN or subnet separately. An NTP packet (about 1,000 bits) is 1 μs on a 1,000-Mb/s LAN, 10 μs on a 100-Mb/s LAN, and 650 μs on a T1 line at 1.544 Mb/s. As will be shown, to drive the residual NTP offsets down to PPS levels, typically within 10 μs, the reciprocal delays must match within 10 μs. If the reciprocal transmission rates and packet lengths are the same to within 10 μs, or one packet time on a 100-Mb/s LAN, the accuracy goal can be met.

In Unix with older NICs, the user-space buffer is copied to a kernel-space buffer chain (mbufs), which then is passed to the driver. The driver waits until the medium becomes idle, then transmits the mbufs using DMA. At completion of the last transfer, the driver captures a drivestamp. However, modern NICs of the PCNET family use a chain of hardware descriptors, one for each buffer, and DMAs directly from user space to an internal 16K first in, first out (FIFO), shared between the transmit and receive sides, and separate frame buffers for each side. The NIC signals an interrupt on completion of the DMA transfer, but one or more frames can be in the FIFO pending transmission, so a more relevant interpretation of the interrupt might be a preamble timestamp.

Example 15.2

NTP servers Macabre and Mort are identical Intel Pentium clones running FreeBSD and operating in symmetric modes. They are synchronized to a GPS receiver via a lightly loaded 100-Mb/s LAN and share the same switch. Each server shows nominal offset and jitter of about 25 μs relative to the GPS receiver and a few microseconds relative to each other. Offsets of this order normally would be considered reciprocal. Both machines have been configured to use drivestamps for both transmit and receive, so the transmitters should transpose to preamble timestamps.

However, both machines use NICs of the PCNET family, so what the driver thinks is a trailer timestamp is actually a preamble timestamp. Each peer shows a round-trip delay of about 140 μs with the other. Since 40 μs (four LAN hops) is due to packet transmission time, the remaining 100 μs is shared equally by each server due to buffering in the operating systems and NICs. The measured delay from the transmit softstamp to the transmit drivestamp is about 15 μs, so the transmit NIC delay is about 5 μs. This leaves 35 μs for the receive NIC delay. These measurements were made in a temperature-stabilized, lightly loaded LAN; performance in working LANs will vary.

The example shows the importance that the drivers know the characteristics of the NIC and compensate accordingly. Further improvement in accuracy to the order of the PPS signal requires hardware or driver assist as described later.

15.3.2 Error Analysis

In Figures 15.2 and the following, uppercase variables represent the reference timestamps used in Equations 15.1 and 15.2; lowercase variables represent the actual timestamps captured by the hardware, driver, or software. The on-wire protocol uses the actual timestamps in the same fashion as the reference timestamps but corrected for systematic errors as described in this and following sections. The object is to explore the possible errors that might result from different timestamp strategies.

In the NTP reference implementation, the t_1 and t_3 transmit softstamps are captured from the system clock just before handing the buffer to the kernel output queue. They are delayed by various latencies represented by the random variable ε_t. Thus, we assume $T_1 = t_2 + \varepsilon_t$ and $T_3 = t_3 + \varepsilon_t$. In anticipation of a packet arrival, the NTP reference implementation allocates an input buffer in user space. When a complete packet (chain of mbufs) arrives, the driver copies them to the buffer. The t_2 and t_4 receive drivestamps are captured from the system clock and copied to a reserved field in the buffer just before handing it to the user input queue. They are delayed by various latencies represented by the random variable ε_r. Thus, $T_2 = t_2 - \varepsilon_r$, and $T_4 = t_4 - \varepsilon_r$.

As shown in Figure 15.2, the NTP on-wire protocol performs the same calculations as Equations 15.1 and 15.2 but using the actual timestamps. After substitution, we have

$$\theta = \frac{1}{2}\{[(T_2 - \varepsilon_r) - (T_1 + \varepsilon_t)] + [(T_3 + \varepsilon_t) - (T_4 - \varepsilon_r)]\},$$

which after simplification is the same as Equation 15.1 on average. On the other hand,

$$\theta = [(T_4 - \varepsilon_r) - (T_1 + \varepsilon_t)] - [(T_3 + \varepsilon_t) - (T_2 - \varepsilon_r)],$$

which results in an additional delay of $2(\varepsilon_t + \varepsilon_r)$ on average.

While these equations involve random variables, we can make strong statements about the resulting accuracy if we assume that the probability distributions of ε_t and ε_r are substantially the same for both client A and server B. We conclude that, as long as the delays on the reciprocal paths are the same and the packet lengths are the same, the offset is as in Equation 15.1 without dilution of accuracy. There is a small increase in round-trip delay relative to Equation 15.2, but this is not ordinarily a significant problem.

The principal remaining terms in the error budget are nonreciprocal delays due to different data rates and nonuniform transposition between the preamble and trailer timestamps. The errors due to such causes are summarized in following sections.

15.3.2.1 Reciprocity Errors

The previous analysis assumes that the delays on the outbound and inbound paths are the same; that is, the paths are reciprocal. This is ensured if the propagation delays are the same, the transmission rates are the same, and the packet lengths are the same. In the NTP on-wire protocol, all packets have the same length. If we assume that the transmission rates are the same, the only difference in path delays must be due to nonreciprocal transmission paths. This often occurs if one way is via landline and the other via satellite. It can also occur when the paths traverse tag-switched core networks.

The magnitude of the errors introduced by nonreciprocal delays can be determined with the aid of Figure 15.3, in which we assume that the reference timestamps represent network paths with zero delay, then add outbound delay d_{AB} and inbound delay d_{BA}. The NTP on-wire protocol performs the same calculations as Equations 15.1 and 15.2 using the reference timestamps but ignoring the latencies discussed in the preceding section. After substitution, we have

$$\theta = \frac{1}{2}\{[(T_2 + d_{AB}) - T_1] + [T_3 - (T_4 + d_{BA})]\}, \tag{15.3}$$

which after simplification results in an error of $(d_{AB} - d_{BA})/2$. On the other hand,

$$\delta = [(T_4 + d_{BA}) - T_1] - [T_3 - (T_2 + d_{AB})], \tag{15.4}$$

which results in a round-trip delay of $d_{AB} + d_{BA}$, as expected.

Example 15.3

Sun Ultra Pogo and Intel Pentium Deacon are synchronized to PPS sources showing typical offset and jitter less than 5 μs. Both are clients of each other via bridged 100-Mb/s LAN segments, so the round-trip delay between the NICs is 40 μs for

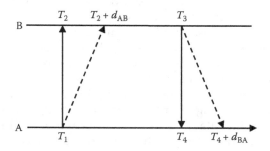

FIGURE 15.3
Nonreciprocal delay error.

1,000-bit packets and four hops. The round-trip delay measured by either machine is about 400 µs, and the jitter is estimated at 25 µs. The measured offset of Pogo relative to Rackety is 89 µs, while the measured offset of Rackety relative to Pogo is −97 µs.

The fact that the two machines are synchronized closely to the PPS signal and the measured offsets are almost equal and with opposite sign suggest that the two paths are nonreciprocal. Of the measured round-trip delay, 40 µs is packet transmission times; the remaining 360 µs must be due to buffering in the operating system and NICs. From the analysis, the offset error is consistent with one path having about 200 µs more overall delay than the other. Of the 360-µs round-trip delay, this suggests Rackety accounts for 80 µs, leaving 280 µs for Pogo.

15.3.2.2 Transposition Errors

With drivestamps, a trailer timestamp is captured for each packet sent or received. The timestamp is available only at driver interrupt time; that is, at the end of the packet and before the FCS on transmit and after the FCS on receive. However, for NICs with a hardstamping capability, the receive hardstamp is actually a preamble timestamp. Assuming that the timestamps can be passed up the protocol stack as in hardstamping, this requires the preamble timestamp to be transposed to a trailer timestamp.

Without transposing, there could be an error due to the packet transmission time d. However, if this is the case for the reciprocal paths, $T_1 = t_1 + d$, $T_2 = t_2$, $T_3 = t_3 + d$, and $T_4 = t_4$. In this case, we neglect the time to transmit the FCS, which is 32 ns for 1,000-Mb/s LANs and 320 ns for 100-Mb/s LANs. Then,

$$\theta = \frac{1}{2}\{[T_2 - (T_1 + d)] + [(T_3 + d) - T_4]\},$$

which after simplification is the same as Equation 15.1. On the other hand,

$$\delta = [T_4 - (T_1 + d)] - [(T_3 + d) - T_2],$$

which after simplification is the same as Equation 15.2. We conclude that, as long as the transmission rates on the reciprocal paths are the same and the packet lengths are the same, the offset and delay can be computed as in Equations 15.1 and 15.2 without dilution of accuracy.

15.3.2.3 Interworking Errors

If the outbound and inbound reciprocal paths use the same timestamping strategy, for example, preamble timestamps or trailer timestamps, and have the same transmission rates and packet length, the offset and delay are invariant to the actual packet length and rate. However, if the reciprocal paths use different strategies, errors will result depending on the transmission rate and packet length. Let the delay between the reference and trailer timestamps be d. Then, consider what happens when interworking between various combinations of software, hardware, and driver timestamps without proper transposition.

Let A use hardstamps and B drivestamps. Then,

$$\theta = \frac{1}{2}\{[T_2 - (T_1 + d)] + [(T_3 - (T_4 + d)]\}$$

which results in an offset error of $-2d$, while

$$\delta = [(T_4 + d) - (T_1 + d)] - [T_3 - T_2]$$

results in no error. Many other combinations are possible.

15.3.2.4 Store-and-Forward Errors

Consider a network with two subnets connected by a router where one subnet operates at 10 Mb/s and the other at 100 Mb/s. Even with hardstamps, store-and-forward errors can occur due to the different packet transmission times. In Figure 15.4, let d_A be the packet time for A and d_B be the packet time for B. The router sends the packet to B only after the packet has been received from A, assuming the router is not capable of cut-through switching.

If the timestamping strategy is preamble timestamps,

$$\theta = \frac{1}{2}\{[(T_2 + d_A) - T_1] + [T_3 - (T_4 + d_B)]\}$$

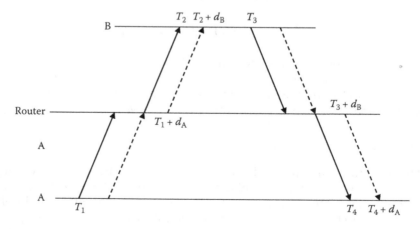

FIGURE 15.4
Two-subnet LAN.

results in an offset error of $(d_A - d_B)/2$. If $d_A = d_B$, there is no offset error. On the other hand,

$$\delta = [(T_4 + d_B) - T_1] - [T_3 - (T_2 + d_A)]$$

results in a delay increase of $d_A + d_B$.

Now, consider the case using preamble transmit timestamps and trailer receive timestamps. In this case, the reciprocal delays are the same, and no offset errors result. This justifies the rules stated at the beginning of Section 15.3. From this, we can conclude that it is not only the timestamping strategies at A and B that must match; some consideration must also be given to the forwarding behavior of the routers in Figure 15.4 that connect A and B when the link speeds differ. Using the preamble timestamp as the transmit timestamp and the trailer timestamp as the receive timestamp solves this problem.

15.3.2.5 Nonreciprocal Rate Errors

A transmission path can include two or more concatenated network segments that might operate at different rates. The previous analysis assumes that the transmit and receive rates are the same for each network segment, even if different on different segments. The problem considered here is when the transmit and receive rates are different on some segments. This is a common condition on space data links. Assume the total packet transmission time is $d = \pi + L/\rho$, where π is the propagation time, L is the packet length in bits, and ρ is the transmission rate in bits per second. Now, consider the concatenated path delay

$$D = \pi_1 + \frac{L}{\rho_1} + \pi_2 + \frac{L}{\rho_2} + \ldots + \pi_N + \frac{L}{\rho_N}, \tag{15.5}$$

where N is the number of segments. If we assume that the outbound and return paths traverse the same segments in reverse order, the total transmission time will be the same in either direction. If the timestamps are taken as described, the delays are reciprocal, and accuracy is not diluted.

Equation 15.5 can be written

$$D = \sum_{i=1}^{N} \pi_i + L \sum_{i=1}^{N} \frac{1}{\rho_i} = \Pi + \frac{L}{R}, \tag{15.6}$$

where the R in the second term on the right represents the overall transmission rate, which in the example is considered the same in both directions. Now, consider where the overall transmission rates are not the same in both directions. Let R_{AB} be the overall outbound transmission rate, let R_{BA} be the overall inbound transmission rate, and compute d_{AB} and d_{BA} as in Equation 15.6. The apparent offset and delay can be obtained from Equations 15.3 and 15.4, which yields the offset error

$$\varepsilon = \frac{L}{2} \left(\frac{1}{R_{AB}} - \frac{1}{R_{BA}} \right). \qquad (15.7)$$

Subtracting this value from the apparent offset yields the correct offset.

One of the most useful applications of Equation 15.7 is with the Proximity-1 space data link protocol used with Mars orbiters and landers. Compared to typical LANs on Earth, space data links operate at low rates, so the delays can be significant. Typically, the uplink from a surface vehicle to an orbiter carries instrument data at a relatively high rate, while the downlink carries telemetry and ACKs (acknowledgments) at a relatively low rate, so rate correction is important. Since the downlink and uplink rates are selected by mission control and known by the spacecraft computer, Equation 15.7 can be used to correct the apparent offset.

15.4 IEEE 1588 Precision Time Protocol

The IEEE 1588 PTP is designed to synchronize real-time clocks in LANs used for telecommunications, industrial automation, and test and measurement applications. It is most commonly used in Ethernet LANs supporting multicast communications but can be used in other network technologies as well. Typical accuracies achieved on a high-speed, multiple-segment LAN are within 100 ns and in some cases much less. Version 1 of the PTP was published in 2002 [1], but it is not described in this chapter. Version 2, published in 2008 [2], is the topic of this section. A number of related publications, including Garner [3] and Subrahmanyan [4], as well as a book by John C. Eidson [5], have been published about the protocol and its applications. This section contains an overview of PTP and a comparison with NTP.

15.4.1 Timestamp Capture

A 1588 clock is an oscillator, usually a temperature-compensated crystal oscillator (TCXO), and a counter that represents time in seconds and nanoseconds since 0 h 1 January 1970. The intended timescale is International Atomic Time (TAI) with provisions for the UTC offset and advance notice of leap seconds. The time representation is similar to POSIX, except the PTP seconds field has 48 bits, making the timestamp 10 octets long. A PTP timestamp is latched from the counter when an Ethernet SOF octet is detected on the wire. This requires an NIC that can provide these timestamps to upper protocol layers.

Figure 15.5 shows the block diagram for a typical 1588 NIC. It includes a media access (MAC) layer, which contains the FIFO and frame buffers together with an embedded state machine that assembles a frame, including the Ethernet header, user data, and FCS. The frame is then sent in four-bit nibbles over the media independent interface (MII) bus to the physical (PHY) layer, where it is coded for transmission over the wire. To support a timestamping function, the MII nibbles are passed through an FPGA, where the necessary 1588 operations are performed without affecting other MAC or PHY operations. The purpose of the FPGA is to latch the 1588 clock when a SOF octet shows up,.

For 10-Mb/s Ethernets, the PHY inserts the Ethernet preamble, then the rest of the frame in Manchester encoding. For 100-Mb/s Ethernets, the PHY first encodes an MII nibble to a five-bit symbol, where each symbol represents either one of the 16 nibble bit combinations or additional special symbols for idle sequence and frame delimiting. The resulting symbol stream is first processed by a scrambler, then encoded in a multilevel transport (MLT-3) stream. The reason for these steps is to reduce RFI by spreading and lowering the signal spectrum, but these are otherwise not important here.

At the present state of the art, it is possible that the entire PTP stack can be implemented onboard the NIC. This is possible using the Intel IXP465 network processor [6] chip, which contains an embedded RISC microprocessor and encryption engine. The PTP specification includes an addendum that defines the Ethernet-specific encapsulation assigned to PTP. Used in this way, PTP operations can be completely transparent to other protocols using the same NIC.

In many cases, some PTP functions are offloaded from the NIC to an associated driver or application program and provisions made to discipline the 1588 clock and retrieve timestamps. This involves encapsulating the PTP

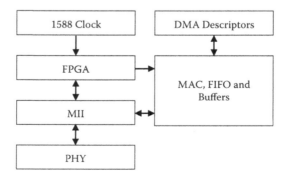

FIGURE 15.5
1588 NIC architecture.

header in some other protocol, typically Internet Protocol/User Datagram Protocol (IP/UDP). The problem remains how to retrieve the transmit and receive timestamps for use by the higher-level protocol. PTP event messages contain a single timestamp field that can be overwritten by the FPGA with a PTP timestamp. If this is done, provisions must be made either to ignore the FCS and UDP checksums or to recalculate them. The PTP specification includes an addendum that defines the UDP-specific encapsulation assigned to PTP.

15.4.2 PTP Clock Architecture

Figure 15.6 shows the block diagram of a PTP ordinary clock (OC) containing a 1588 clock, a discipline loop, and a protocol state machine. It has a universally unique clock identifier (UUID) assigned much the same way as Ethernet MAC addresses. In addition, the OC has one or more physical ports that connect to different LAN segments. Each physical port has two logical ports, one used for timestamped event messages and the other for general messages. The concatenation of UUIC and port number is called the port identifier (portID).

A PTP subnet consists of a number of OCs operating on one or more LAN segments interconnected by bridges. More than one subnet can be deployed on the same network, each distinguished by a unique domain number. One or more OCs acting as grandmaster (GM) clocks provide timing to other OCs operating as masters or slaves. One or more OCs operating as masters provide timing to other OCs operating as masters or slaves.

A PTP bridge operates in either of two modes for PTP messages. For all other messages, it operates as an ordinary bridge. A PTP bridge operating as a transparent clock (TC) calculates a correction due to the ingress PTP message transmission time and the residence time in the bridge itself. It then adds this value to the corrections field in the egress message header. This is a tricky maneuver as it requires correcting or recalculating whatever

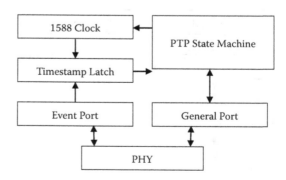

FIGURE 15.6
PTP ordinary clock.

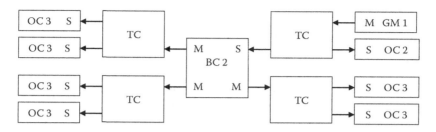

FIGURE 15.7
Typical PTP subnet.

checksums are involved. The LAN segments joined by a TC are considered the same logical LAN segment. A bridge operating as a boundary clock (BC) operates as a slave for an upstream master on one segment and as a master for downstream slaves on all other segments. In particular, it does not repeat PTP broadcast messages from one segment to another. In a very real sense, a BC is like an NTP secondary server.

Figure 15.7 shows a typical PTP subnet including a GM, four TCs, seven OCs, and a BC. The best master clock (BMC) algorithm discussed in Section 15.4.4 constructs a spanning tree designated by the arrows, which show the flow of synchronization from the GM master port M to the slave ports S and from the BC master port M to the slave ports S. The number following the GM, BC, and OC designator is the stratum, called the steps removed in the specification, constructed by the BMC algorithm.

15.4.3 PTP Messages

It will be helpful in the following discussion to briefly describe the message types and formats used in PTP. There are two message classes: event messages and general messages. Event messages and most general messages include a single timestamp field beyond the header. Event messages use this field for the receive timestamp provided by the 1588 NIC; general messages use this field to return requested timestamps.

Table 15.1 shows the PTP message types. Those with type codes less than 8 are event messages; those with other codes are general messages. Only the Sync, Follow_Up, Delay_Req, Delay_Resp, and Announce messages are used in the basic protocol described here. The Sync, Follow_Up, and Announce messages are sent using broadcast means by a master to all slaves on the LAN segment. The other messages are sent using unicast means. The remaining message types are used for special cases and management functions beyond the scope of this discussion.

All PTP messages include a common header shown in Table 15.2. All the messages discussed here have only a single 10-octet timestamp, except the Announce message, which has the payload shown in Table 15.3. Not all the fields are relevant to this discussion.

TABLE 15.1

PTP Message Types

Type	Name	Use
0	Sync	Master broadcasts timestamp T_2
1	Delay_Req	Slave requests timestamp T_3
2	Path_Delay_Req	Not applicable
3	Path_Delay_Resp	Not applicable
8	Follow_Up	Master broadcasts timestamp T_1
9	Delay_Resp	Slave receives timestamp T_4
A	Pedaled	Not applicable
B	Announce	Topology management
C	Signalling	Utility
D	Management	Network management

TABLE 15.2

Message Header Format

Length	Offset	Name	Use
0	1	Type	Message type
1	1	Version	PTP version (2)
2	2	Length	Message length
1	4	Domain	PTP domain
1	5	Reserved	Not used
2	6	Flags	Protocol flag bits
8	8	Correction	Timestamp correction
4	16	Reserved	Not used
10	20	SourcePortID	Port ID of sender
2	30	SequenceID	Message sequence number
1	32	Control	Used for version compatibility
1	33	MessageInterval	log2 of message interval

15.4.4 Best Master Clock Algorithm

An important feature of PTP is its ability to generate an acyclic spanning tree that determines the timing flow from a GM via BCs to the slaves. This is done by the BMC algorithm using a transitive ">" relation determined from the elements of the data sets maintained for each clock and each port of the clock. The > relation defines a partial ordering of the ports, which in turn determines the spanning tree and establishes the state of each port. The composition of the > relation is discussed in the next section.

Assume a particular clock C_0 has a data set D_0 and has N ports. The object of the algorithm is to assign to each port one of three states: MASTER, SLAVE, or PASSIVE. A port in MASTER state broadcasts periodic Announce messages, including data set D_0, to all other ports sharing the same LAN

TABLE 15.3

Announce Message Format

Length	Offset	Name	Use
34	0	Header	Message header
10	34	UTCOffset	Current UTC offset from Posix
2	44	TimescaleInUse	TAI or arbitrary
4	46	AnnounceFlags	Protocol flag bits
2	50	StepsRemoved	Stratum
10	52	GMPortID	GM UUID [7], port number [5]
4	62	GMClockQuality	Class [9], source [9], variance [5]
1	66	GMPriority1	Arbitrary
1	67	GMPriority2	Arbitrary
10	68	ParentPortID	Master port ID
4	78	LocalClockQuality	Class [9], source [9], variance [5]
4	82	ClockChangeRate	Master change rate
2	86	ParentVariance	Master variance

segment. Initially, all ports are in MASTER state. As the result of the BMC algorithm, all but one of them will become slaves.

Announce messages arriving at a port in any state are collected and the latest one from each different clock saved on a list. At periodic intervals, clock C_0 saves the best data set D_i from the ith port, then selects the best data set D_B from among the D_i data sets. Here, "best" is determined by pairwise data set comparisons using the > relation.

The BMC algorithm then uses the data sets D_0, D_i, and D_B to determine the state of each port. This depends on the class of C_0 that determines whether the clock is a GM or not. If C_0 is a GM and $D_0 > D_i$, the state of port i is MASTER; otherwise, it is PASSIVE. If not a GM, the following rules apply to all ports of all clocks:

1. If $D_0 > D_i$, the state of port i is MASTER; otherwise,
2. If $D_i = D_B$, the state of port i is SLAVE; otherwise,
3. The state of port i is PASSIVE.

15.4.5 Data Set Comparison Algorithm

The composition of the > relation is developed from the specification that includes an intricate and sometimes confusing set of flow diagrams. Consider two data sets to be compared. We wish to select the highest (or lowest) value of a data set member as data set A and the other as B, then A > B. However, if the values are identical, the comparison falls through to the next step. The data set member is determined from the fields of the most recent Announce message received (see Table 15.3).

1. Select the highest GMpriority1.
2. Select the lowest class in GMClockQuality.
3. If A and B have the same GM UUID, go to step 8.
4. Select the best source in GMClockQuality (GPS, NTP, etc.).
5. If the variances differ significantly, select the lowest variance in GMClockQuality.
6. Select the highest GMpriority2.
7. Select the lowest GMPortID, which is guaranteed to be unique.

The data sets have the same GM UUID.

8. If stratum is not equal, select the lowest GMStepsRemoved (stratum).

The GM stratum of A is the same as B. There is a potential loop.

9. If the receiving port UUID of B is less than sending port UUID of B, select A and set the state of B to PASSIVE. If the receiving port UUID of A is less than sending port UUID of A, select B and set the state of A to PASSIVE.

15.4.6 PTP Time Transfer

The key to understanding how PTP works is this observation: For event messages (only), the timestamp field in the message is overwritten by the receive timestamp on arrival, and the transmit timestamp is available only in the timestamp field of the next message sent. Note that for a broadcast message sent to many recipients, the receive timestamp may be different.

Figure 15.8 shows the two-step variant normally used by the protocol. The Sync event message and Follow_Up general message are sent from master ports using broadcast means to slave ports on the LAN segment. These messages are sent frequently, typically at intervals of 2 s. On the other hand, the Delay_Req event message and Delay_Resp general messages are sent using unicast means. These message are sent much less frequently as they must be sent for every slave on the LAN segment.

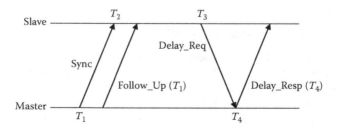

FIGURE 15.8
PTP protocol operations.

The protocol requires four messages to determine four timestamps T_1, T_2, T_3, and T_4, as shown in Figure 15.8. On receipt of the Sync message, the timestamp field contains the receive timestamp (T_2). The master saves the transmit timestamp (T_1) of the Sync message and sends it in the time-stamp field of the Follow_up message. When the highest accuracy is not required, the quantity $T_1 - T_2$ represents the offset of the master relative to the slave.

In the one-step protocol variant, the Sync message timestamp field is overwritten by the transmit timestamp as the message is sent. When the message is received, this field along with the receive timestamp are passed to upper protocol layers for processing, and the Follow_Up message is not used. While this is efficient, it requires that the receive timestamp be saved somewhere in the receive buffer structure without affecting the message itself.

The Delay_Req and Delay_Resp messages are ordinarily interpreted to measure the delay from the master port to each individual slave port, but there is a simpler way to interpret the measurements consistent with the NTP on-wire protocol. At relatively infrequent intervals, the slave sends a Delay_Req event message to the master and saves the transmit timestamp (T_3) for use later. The master immediately replies with a Delay_Resp general message, including the receive timestamp (T_4) in the timestamp field. Finally, the slave calculates its offset and delay relative to the master as in Equations 15.1 and 15.2 but notes that the sign of the offset is inverted relative to the usual NTP conventions.

15.4.7 PTP and NTP Compared

In comparing PTP and NTP, we start with the observation that NTP is engi-neered to synchronize computer clocks in an extended network, while PTP is engineered to synchronize device clocks in a segmented LAN. Device clocks in telecommunications, test, and measurement equipment use rela-tively high-quality oscillators disciplined directly by PTP since in general there is no operating system with competing programs, buffers, and queues that might get in the way. Computer clocks use commodity-quality oscilla-tors disciplined indirectly over a network in which application programs and packets can get in each other's way.

Setting aside the accuracy issue for the moment, PTP and NTP have many aspects in common. In both protocols, synchronization flows from the primary servers (GMs) via secondary servers (BCs) to clients (OCs). An embedded algo-rithm constructs a shortest-path spanning tree, although with quite different metrics. Both NTP and PTP assume each member clock is disciplined by some means in time and frequency, and both have means to detect faults and esti-mate timekeeping quality. Both can measure clock offset and round-trip delay, but neither can detect nonreciprocal delays. Both can operate in broadcast or unicast mode, and both use the same offset and delay calculations, although expressed in different ways. While not discussed here, both have similar authentication provisions based on cryptographic message digests.

One difference between NTP and PTP is expressed in the NTP operating modes, which can be client/server (master-slave in PTP), broadcast/multicast (multicast in PTP), and symmetric modes that have no equivalent in PTP. This is reflected in the NTP service model, in which either of two peers can back up the other should one of them lose all synchronization sources. This can also be the case in PTP with multiple GMs, but the subnet has to reconfigure in case of failure.

The most striking difference between PTP and NTP, at least in some subnet configurations, is that PTP has the intrinsic capability to construct the spanning tree with no specific prior configuration, while in NTP the servers or peers are explicitly configured. However, this is not always the case. An NTP Ethernet including broadcast servers and clients will automatically self-assemble as in PTP with prior configuration only to provide the subnet broadcast address, and this would be necessary in PTP as well. An NTP subnet using manycast mode, in which each NTP segment operates with a distinct group address, would also self-assemble as in PTP.

Recall from Chapter 12 that clock errors are dominated by white-phase noise at shorter update intervals and by random-walk frequency noise at longer update intervals. This applies to both NTP and PTP; however, the fact that PTP uses timestamps captured at the NIC means that the phase noise is much less than with NTP. On the other hand, NTP uses softstamps and drivestamps, which are vulnerable to buffering and queuing latencies in the operating system and network. A fundamental distinction between NTP and PTP is that NTP is normally utilized where relatively long update intervals are required to minimize network load. On the other hand, PTP is normally utilized on high-speed LANs with no such requirement and operates with update intervals on the order of 2 s. On a LAN with reduced phase noise and shorter update intervals, PTP can provide far better performance than NTP, even if using the same commodity oscillator.

An important feature of NTP is the suite of algorithms that groom and mitigate between and among a number of servers when more than one is available. PTP has no need for these algorithms as only the best GM is included in the spanning tree. In NTP, the best source is represented by the system peer at each stratum level. A significant difference between the NTP and PTP specifications is that in NTP the secondary server discipline algorithm must have a defined transient response to control overshoot and avoid instability in long timing chains. The PTP specification leaves this as an implementation choice. This would be most important in the BC discipline loop.

Finally, there is the issue of how many timestamps can be included in the packet header. With PTP, there is only one, which constrains the flexibility in the protocol design. With NTP, there are three operative timestamps that support all NTP modes, including the interleaved modes described in the next chapter. This provides not only flexibility but also strong duplicate and replay protection without needing serial numbers.

There are a number of scenarios in which NTP and PTP can be exploited in a combined system. In principle, a software implementation of PTP with softstamps or drivestamps is possible and should perform as well as NTP, at least without the grooming and mitigation algorithms. Perhaps the most useful scenario would be a server that runs NTP with one or more PTP NICs operating as masters or slaves on the PTP subnet. The PTP NIC could launch NTP packets while running PTP. Some NICs, in particular the Network Instruments NI1588, provide a PPS signal synchronized to the 1588 clock via a connector on the NIC chassis. This signal could be used by the PPS driver included in the NTP software distribution. This is probably the easiest, quickest way to import PTP time to NTP and the operating system.

Importing and exporting PTP time to and from the computer itself is straightforward. It is possible that application programs could read the 1588 clock using an I/O command, but probably it is not a good idea as the overhead to perform I/O instructions is much higher than to read the system clock, which involves queuing, buffering, and scheduling latencies. It would be more efficient to read the 1588 clock infrequently, like once per minute, and treat it as an NTP reference clock. In this design, the computer clock itself is used as a flywheel between 1588 clock updates.

It does not seem practical to translate PTP performance variables to the NTP error budget, other than the various variance statistics carried in the PTP Announce message. If the computer system clock is to be used for the GM function, the 1588 clock adjustment function could be used in a feedback loop much the way the computer clock itself is disciplined by NTP. Some way is needed to pass on components of the NTP error budget that might be useful for PTP statistics or that might be explored in the future, as is the role of management and signaling functions.

15.5 Have Quick, STANAG 4330, and Precise Time and Time Interval Have Quick Interfaces

The modern military battlefield and infrastructure support have become extraordinarily dependent on precise time and frequency distribution for radio communication and long-haul fiber and satellite communication systems. Precise synchronization is necessary for SINCGARS frequency-hopping radios and Synchronous Optical Networks (SONETs) and satellite links. Previously, provisions for precision time and frequency sources was on a system-by-system basis with no urgent need for standardization. However, recent efforts in the U.S. military and NATO (North Atlantic

Treaty Organization) allies [7] have identified a number of standard time and frequency issues so that the various domestic and international military units can interoperate with equipment from different suppliers in different countries. The standards issues have evolved over many years in the precise time and time interval (PTTI) community [7].

There are currently two families of standard interfaces, the MIL-STD 188-125 standard [8] used by the U.S. Have Quick radio system and the STANAG 4330 standard [9] used by the United States and its NATO allies. Certain versions of these standards can interoperate. Both include a frequency interface at 5 MHz or some multiple, which is not of further interest here. Both include a precision time code that might be a useful source to discipline a computer clock, such as might be found on an air force aircraft or navy vessel. The timecode is usually transmitted using Manchester encoding with a pulse width of 60 µs, resulting in a bit rate of about 16.7 kb/s. The on-time epoch is defined by a PPS signal transmitted on a dedicated wire. The current time at the on-time epoch is transmitted as a string of octets, where each octet consists of a four-bit BCD digit preceded by a four-bit checksum of the octet. Each octet represents a code word from a Hamming 8,4 code, which has distance 4 and thus can correct a single-bit error and detect two-bit errors.

The timecode formats used by in Have Quick and STANAG 4330 are shown in Figure 15.9. The timecode is preceded by a start-of-message (SOM) octet and followed in some formats by an end-of-message (EOM) octet. The Have Quick I format includes the hours, minutes, and seconds, each in two octets each in that order. The Have Quick II format appends the day of the year in three octets followed by the year in two octets. The STANAG 4330 and Extended Have Quick (XHQ) format appends a time figure of merit (FOM) in one octet plus seven additional octets, including a control command and leap second warning.

Have Quick I

SOM	Hour	Minute	Second
16	16	16	16

Have Quick II

SOM	Hour	Minute	Second	DOY	Year
16	16	16	16	24	16

STANAG 4330 Extended Have Quick (XHQ)

SOM	Hour	Minute	Second	DOY	Year	FOM	...	EOM
16	16	16	16	24	16	8	56	16

FIGURE 15.9
Have Quick and STANAG 4330 timecode formats.

15.6 Parting Shots

It may be interesting to speculate on how NTP could make use of hard-stamps, perhaps in a way very similar to IEEE 1588, in which an event such as the passage of the Ethernet SOF octet latches an internal NIC counter. In the scheme proposed in this chapter, the NTP NIC is much simpler than the PTP NIC; the counter need not be disciplined and need not run at any particular rate. A timestamp is captured for every transmitted and received packet and buffered in an FIFO until the driver can read them.

Since timestamps are captured for every packet transmitted and received, there is no need to parse the packet itself or change it in any way. The timestamps are conveyed to the NTP program by one means or another. Receive timestamps could be appended to the packet data mbuf chain and eventually placed in the receiver buffer or socket storage. Transmit timestamps could be inserted in the transmit buffer to be returned to the NTP program as the buffer storage is reclaimed.

The transmit case is not as easy as it might seem. In PCNET NICs, the transmit buffer is ordinarily reclaimed when the last bit is DMAed to the FIFO, but it has to hang around until the associated timestamp is captured. However, there might be other Ethernet frames in the FIFO ahead of this frame. Therefore, the driver has to keep track of the number of frames in the FIFO and match them with the entries in the timestamp FIFO.

Note that the NTP NIC counter is not necessarily syntonic with the system clock or even other NTP NIC counters, and the need exists to convert the NIC time to system clock time format. But, this is the same issue studied in Section 15.2, and the same techniques apply. At intervals something less than 1 s, the NIC driver updates the structure holding the last NIC clock and system clock and trims the K multiplier. The NIC clock is read and converted to system format as the driver extracts the entries from the timestamp FIFO.

In principle, this scheme could deliver timestamps as precise as PTP, assuming the NIC clock is fast enough. However, the weakest link in this scheme is that the master reference source is the commodity compute clock oscillator and operating system. A good guess is that this scheme could do as well as the PPS discipline, which has a nominal jitter on the order of a few microseconds.

References

1. *IEEE 1588 Standard for a Precision Clock Synchronization Protocol for Networked Measurement and Control Systems.* IEEE Instrumentation and Measurement Society, November 2002.
2. *IEEE 1588 Precision Time Protocol (PTP)*, Version 2 Specification. IEEE, March 2008.

3. Garner, G.M. *Description of Use of IEEE 1588 Peer-to-Peer Transparent Clocks in A/V Bridging Networks*, Revision 2.0, May 12, 2006.
4. Subrahmanyan, R. Implementation considerations for IEEE 1588v2 applications in telecommunications. *Proceedings IEEE International Symposium on Precision Clock Synchronization or Measurement, Control and Communication* (October 2007), 148–154.
5. Eidson, J.C. *Measurement, Control and Communication Using IEEE 1588*. Springer, New York, 2006.
6. Micheel, J., I. Graham, and S. Donnelly. Precision timestamping of network packets. *Proceedings SIGCOMM IMW* (November 2001).
7. Murray, J.A., and J.D. White. MIL-STDs and PTTI, what's available and what needs to be done. *Proceedings 24th Precise Time and Time Interval Meeting* (December 1992), 123–135.
8. *MIL-STD-188 Interoperability and Performance Standards for Communications Timing and Synchronization Subsystems*. Department of Defense, Washington, DC, March 1986.
9. Bishop, J. Report on NATO PTTI. *Proceedings 25th Precise Time and Time Interval Meeting* (December 1993), 93–100.

16

NTP Interleaved Modes

Something unknown is doing we don't know what.

Sir Arthur Eddington
Comment on the Uncertainty Principle in Quantum Physics, 1927

The Network Time Protocol (NTP) operations in basic client/server, symmetric, and broadcast modes have been described in previous chapters. As pointed out in the previous chapter, the highest accuracy obtainable requires the use of driver or hardware timestamps; however, this requires intervention in the kernel driver or network interface. This chapter describes two new modes, interleaved symmetric and interleaved broadcast, that can improve accuracy without modifying these components. As in previous NTP versions, NTP Version 4 (NTPv4) with interleaved capability is compatible with NTPv4 without this capability and with all previous NTP versions.

In the reference implementation, the receive timestamp is captured shortly after the input device interrupt to avoid input latencies due to buffering and input queuing operations. According to the nomenclature adopted in the previous chapter, this would be described as a drivestamp. The transmit timestamp is ordinarily captured just before computing the message digest and then adding the buffer to the output queue. In this method, the output latencies due to queuing and buffering operations can become significant. In this chapter, the transmit timestamp is captured shortly after the output device interrupt, so it would properly be described as a drivestamp. However, in this case the transmit drivestamp is not available when the packet header fields are determined, so it is sent in the transmit timestamp field of the following packet. This is basically how the interleaved modes work and is the topic of this chapter.

To distinguish between timestamps captured in various ways, timestamps determined when an input packet removed from the input queue or when an output packet is added to the output queue are called *softstamps*, while timestamps determined at interrupt time are called *drivestamps*. While the choice of receive softstamp or drivestamp affects accuracy, it does not affect the protocol operations. On the other hand, while the choice of transmit softstamp or drivestamp affects accuracy, the choice does affect the protocol operations. To emphasize the difference in the diagrams in this chapter, softstamps appear with an asterisk (*), while drivestamps do not. Since all timestamps used in this chapter are drivestamps, it will lesson clutter if we avoid the distinction and simply call them timestamps.

Interleaved symmetric mode is an extension of basic symmetric mode, while interleaved broadcast mode is an extension of the basic broadcast mode described in Chapter 2 The interleaved modes require servers and peers to retain state, so there is no interleaved client/server mode. Mode selection for configured symmetric peers and broadcast servers is determined by a configuration option; mode selection for passive peers and broadcast clients is determined automatically by the protocol. Interleaved broadcast mode is compatible with basic broadcast mode; a server configured for interleaved broadcast mode can support both interleaved and basic broadcast clients at the same time and on the same wire.

The plan for this chapter is first to describe the protocol state machines, including the packet header variables, state variables, and flowcharts. As the protocol state machine must also support both the basic mode operations, all the modes are described in an integrated way. This description is followed by a detailed description of each mode along with examples of operation. Finally, an example is presented that shows how the protocol automatically reverts to basic mode when confronted with an NTP implementation that does not support interleaved modes.

16.1 Basic/Interleaved Protocol State Machines and Flowcharts

The integrated modes require two protocol state machines: one for the transmit process, which runs for each transmit packet, and the other for the receive process, which runs for each receive packet. The processes can run in one of four modes: basic symmetric and basic broadcast modes and interleaved symmetric and interleaved broadcast modes. The state machines described in this section support all of these modes depending on a configuration option. Ordinarily, the transmit and receive state machines run in the same mode; however, as described in this chapter, a transmit process configured for interleaved symmetric mode will automatically switch to basic symmetric mode if confronted by a peer incapable of interleaved operation.

Figure 16.1 shows three packet header variables, t_{org}, t_{rec}, and t_{xmt}; eight state variables *rec*, *dst*, *aorg*, *borg*, *xmt*, *x*, *b*, and *h*; and three peer variables θ, δ, and β used in the flowcharts to follow. The state variables persist from packet to packet; the packet variables, which have subscripts for clarity, persist for the life of the packet only. All the state variables except *x*, *b*, and *h* and all the packet variables carry timestamp values; *b* takes values 0 and 1; *x* takes values 0, +1, and −1; and *h* is a counter used during error recovery in some modes. Some state variables are not used in some modes. By convention in the following, the pseudostate variable *clock* designates the system clock at

Name	State Variable
rec	Receive timestamp
dst	Destination timestamp
$aorg$	A origin timestamp
$borg$	B origin timestamp
x	Transmit interleave switch
h	Hold-off counter

Name	Packet Variable
t_{org}	Orgin timestamp
t_{rec}	Receive timestamp
t_{xmt}	Transmit timestamp

Name	Peer Variable
θ	Clock offset
δ	Roundtrip delay
β	Unicast/broadcast offset

FIGURE 16.1
State, packet, and peer variables.

Transmit Process–Basic and Interleaved

```
t_org = rec
t_rec = dst
If (x == 0) {/* basic mode */
    aorg = clock
    t_xmt = aorg
} else { /* interleaved mode */
    if (x > 0) {
        aorg = clock
        t_xmt = borg
    } else {
        borg = clock
        t_xmt = aorg
    }
    x = -x
}
```

Transmit Process–Broadcast

```
if (x == 0) { /* basic mode */
    txmt = clock
    torg = 0
} else { /* interleaved mode */
    if (x > 0) {
        aorg = clock
        t_xmt = aorg
        t_org = borg
    } else {
        borg = clock
        t_xmt = borg
        t_org = aorg
    }
}
t_rec = 0
```

FIGURE 16.2
Transmit flowcharts.

the time of reading. The peer variables represent the product of the protocol, θ is the clock offset, δ is the round-trip delay, and β is the unicast/broadcast offset, as described in this chapter.

The flowcharts in Figure 16.2 show the transmit operations in all modes. Note that x serves both as a switch to indicate basic modes or interleaved modes and as a means in interleaved modes to alternate the transmit time-stamp between *aorg* and *borg*. It is set at configuration time to 0 for basic mode or +1 for interleaved mode. Note also that in interleaved broadcast mode t_{org}, ordinarily zero in basic broadcast mode, it is hijacked to hold the previous

Receive Process

```
if (t_xmt != 0 && t_xmt == xmt) {
    DUPE
} else if (x == 0) {
    rec = t_xmt
    dst = clock
    If (mode == BROADCAST)
        Broadcast
    else
        Basic Symmetric
} else {
    Interleaved Symmetric
    rec = t_rec
    dst = clock
}
if (h > 0)
    h--
xmt = t_xmt
```

Basic Symmetric Mode

```
T_1 = t_org
T_2 = t_rec
T_3 = t_xmt
T_4 = dst
If (T_1 == 0 || T_2 == 0 || T_3 == 0)
    SYNC
else if (T_1 != aorg)
    BOGUS
} else {
    θ = [(T_2 - T_1) + (T_3 - T_4)] / 2
    δ = (T_4 - T_1) - (T_3 - T_2)
}
```

FIGURE 16.3
Basic receive flowcharts.

Interleaved Symmetric Mode

```
If (x > 0)
    T_1 = aorg
else
    T_1 = borg
T_2 = rec
T_3 = t_xmt
T_4 = dst
if (t_org == 0 || T_1 == 0 || T_2 == 0
    || T_3 == 0) {
    SYNC
} else if (t_org != 0 && t_org ! =T_4){
    h = 2
    BOGUS
} else if (h == 0) {
    θ = [(T_2 - T_1) + (T_3 - T_4)] / 2
    δ = (T_4 - T_1) - (T_3 - T_2)
}
```

Broadcast Mode

```
if (t_org == 0) {    /* basic mode */
    θ = t_xmt - dst + d / 2
} else { /* interleaved mode */
    T_1 = t_org - borg
    T_2 = t_org - aorg
    aorg = t_xmt
    borg = dst
    if (T_2 > 1)
        BOGUS
    else
        θ = T_1 + d / 2
}
```

FIGURE 16.4
Interleaved receive flowcharts.

transmit timestamp. This is how a broadcast client recognizes whether interleaved mode is available. Clients conforming to NTPv4 and previous specifications ignore t_{org} and t_{rec}.

The flowcharts in Figure 16.3 show the receive operations in the basic modes, while the flowcharts in Figure 16.4 show the receive operations in interleaved modes. In this and further flowcharts, labels with capitals are error stubs. DUPE indicates a duplicate packet, SYNC indicates an unsynchronized packet, BOGUS indicates a bogus or misordered packet, and

HOLD indicates a temporary hold-off condition. The underlined actions represent calls to one of the remaining three routines: basic symmetric, interleaved symmetric, or interleaved broadcast. The b state variable (not shown) is a switch used in the calibration phase when the broadcast client first starts. It is discussed in a following section. Note that the basic symmetric flowchart can also be used for the client in basic client/server mode, so the same code can be used for both basic and interleaved operations.

16.2 Basic Symmetric Mode

The basic symmetric modes conform to the current NTPv4 specification and reference implementation. Following is an example illustrating typical operation in this mode, starting from an unsynchronized condition. Figure 16.5 illustrates the most general case in which peers A and B independently measure the offset and delay relative to each other. Note that this is basically the same as shown in Figure 3.2, but it includes much additional information on the interaction with the interleaved modes and emphasizes the use of softstamps. Each packet transmitted is shown as an arrow with the receive timestamp at the head and the transmit timestamp at the tail. The gray boxes hold timestamps captured from the system clock; the other boxes hold values copied from them, other state variables, or packet variables.

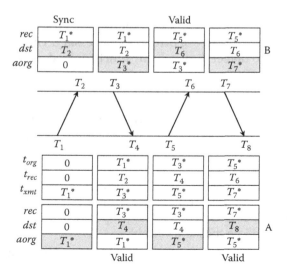

FIGURE 16.5
NTP basic mode protocol.

The labels shown are after arrival or departure of a packet. Keep in mind that, on arrival of a packet, a state variable might be needed before update from a packet variable.

- When a packet is received, t_{xmt} is copied to *rec* and the receive time-stamp to *dst*.

- When a packet is transmitted, *rec* is copied to t_{org}, *dst* to t_{rec} and the transmit timestamp to *aorg* and t_{xmt}.

After the state variables have been updated, the timestamps are $T_1 = t_{org}$, $T_2 = t_{rec}$, $T_3 = t_{xmt}$, and $T_4 = dst$. As in Chapter 2, these timestamps can be used to calculate the clock offset and round-trip delay.

It is important to note that the protocol operations are symmetric, in that A can determine the offset and delay of B relative to A; at the same time, B can determine the offset and delay of A relative to B. In Figure 16.5, A first sends $T_1 \rightarrow T_2$ (0, 0, T_1) to B. Later, B sends $T_3 \rightarrow T_4$ (T_1, T_2, T_3) to A. At T_4, the timestamps T_1, T_2, and T_3 and *dst* variable T_4 are available to compute the offset and delay of B relative to A. Later, A sends $T_5 \rightarrow T_6$ (T_3, T_4, T_5) to B. In a similar fashion, at T_6 the timestamps T_3, T_4, and T_5 and *dst* variable T_6 are available to compute the offset and delay of A relative to B. The protocol is said to be synchronized when both A and B have computed the offset and delay; that is, at T_6.

In symmetric modes, each peer independently polls the other peer but not necessarily at identical intervals. Thus, one or the other peer might receive none, one, or more than one packet between polls. This can result in lost or duplicate packets and even cases where packets cross each other in flight, resulting in out-of-sequence or bogus packets. In addition, provisions must be made to reset and restart the protocol if necessary. There are three sanity checks designed to detect duplicate, unsynchronized, or bogus packets.

1. The packet is a duplicate if t_{xmt} matches *xmt* saved from the last packet received. This might occur due to a retransmission in the network or a malicious replay without modification. The proper response is to ignore the packet without modifying the state variables. Thus, if the network or an intruder replays the $T_3 \rightarrow T_4$ packet, this test would discard it.

2. The packet is unsynchronized if t_{org} is zero, t_{rec} is zero, or t_{xmt} is zero. This could result if the transmitter has not yet synchronized or if the implementation is defective. The proper response is to ignore the packet but update the state variables.

3. The packet is bogus if t_{org} does not match *org*. This might occur due to packet loss, reorder, or a malicious replay with modification. The proper response is to ignore the packet but update the state variables.

The bogus test is actually a strong nonce that binds a previously transmitted packet to the reply. For this reason, every t_{org} should be different. As the resolution of this variable is less than 1 ns and, in principle, packets cannot be sent that fast, this is feasible. However, in many cases the resolution of the system clock is insufficient. In these cases, the low-order insignificant bits of the timestamp should be filled with a random bit string. Not only does this ensure that every timestamp will be different, but also it helps to avoid averaging bias.

Although not shown in Figure 16.5, *org* is set to zero after the bogus test to deflect a replay of the first packet in client/server mode. Thus, if the network or an intruder were to replay the $T_1 \rightarrow T_2$ packet causing B to generate a spurious $T_3 \rightarrow T_4$ packet, the bogus test would discard it. Thus, in client/server mode the protocol is protected against replays of either the $T_1 \rightarrow T_2$ or $T_3 \rightarrow T_4$ packets. In symmetric modes, replay of the $T_1 \rightarrow T_2$ packet would be caught as a duplicate by B. The protocol is inherently resistant to lost packets and overlapped packets. For instance, if the $T_3 \rightarrow T_4$ packet is lost, the next set of timestamps T_5, T_6, T_7, and T_8 is available to compute offset and delay. If packets $T_3 \rightarrow T_4$ and $T_5 \rightarrow T_6$ overlap, A will discard the latter as bogus and use the next set of timestamps as before.

16.3 Interleaved Symmetric Mode

In interleaved symmetric modes, the transmit timestamp is captured after the packet has been sent, so it is sent in the next following packet. This can be done using the two-step or interleaved protocol described in this section. The trick, however, is to implement the interleaved protocol without changing the NTP packet header format, without compromising backward compatibility, and without compromising the error recovery properties. Following is a typical example of operation, starting from an unsynchronized condition.

Figure 16.6 illustrates the most general case in which interleaved symmetric peers A and B independently measure the offset and delay relative to each other. Note that the receive (even-numbered) timestamp is available immediately after the packet has been received, but the transmit (odd-numbered) timestamp is available only after the packet has been transmitted. In contrast to the basic protocol, which requires one complete round to calculate offset and delay, the interleaved round requires two basic rounds. The interleaved round that begins at t_1 is not complete until t_8, while the interleaved round that begins at t_5 is not complete until t_{12}. However, the rate of offset/delay calculations is the same as the basic protocol. The NTP packet header fields are the same in the interleaved protocol as in the basic protocol but carry different values.

Each peer requires the state variables defined in Figure 16.1. The transmit state machine operates as in Figure 16.2, while the receive state machine operates as in Figure 16.4.

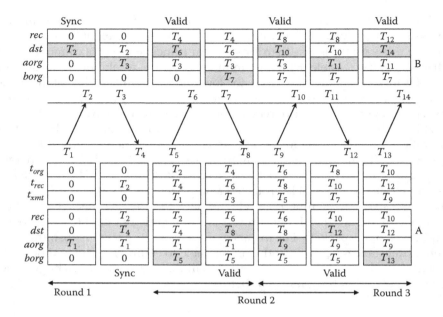

FIGURE 16.6
NTP interleaved symmetric protocol.

- When a packet is received, t_{rec} is copied to *rec* and the receive timestamp to *dst*.
- When a packet is transmitted, *rec* is copied to t_{org} and *dst* to t_{rec}. If $x > 0$, *aorg* is copied to t_{xmt}. After transmission of the packet, the transmit timestamp is copied to *borg*, and x is set to -1. If $x < 0$, *borg* is copied to t_{xmt}. After transmission of the packet, the transmit timestamp is copied to *aorg*, and x is set to $+1$.

On receipt and before the state variables have been updated, the timestamps are $T_2 = rec$, $T_3 = t_{xmt}$, and $T_4 = dst$. If $x > 0$, $T_1 = aorg$; if $x < 0$, $T_1 = borg$. After this, t_{rec} is copied to *rec* and the receive timestamp to *dst*.

As in the basic interleaved mode, there are three tests to detect duplicate, unsynchronized, or bogus packets.

1. The packet is a duplicate if t_{xmt} matches *xmt* saved from the last packet received. This is the same test as in basic interleaved mode. The proper response is to discard the packet without modifying the state variables.
2. The packet is unsynchronized if t_{org} is zero, T_1 is zero, T_2 is zero, or T_3 is zero. This test is slightly different due to the requirement that

old state variables be expunged when a peer restarts the protocol. The proper response is to ignore the packet but update the state variables.

3. The packet is bogus if t_{org} does not match T_4. This test is slightly different due to the different placement of the state variables. The proper response is to ignore the packet and the next one received but update the state variables.

A bogus packet in interleaved symmetric mode is much more expensive than in basic symmetric mode. It can happen during startup when the timestamps for previous packets are not yet available or when packets are dropped or cross in flight. The protocol state machine extends over two basic rounds, which means that recovery will last that long. The strategy chosen is to update the state variables but otherwise ignore the timestamps for the bogus packet and the next one as well. By that time, the old state variables have been flushed and replaced with fresh ones. This is the purpose of the h state variable. It is set to 2 when a bogus packet is found and is decremented by 1 for each received packet, but not below zero. The state variables are updated, but timestamps are not used if $h > 0$.

A refinement that minimizes occasions when packets cross in flight is to measure the interval from the time of arrival of a packet until the next poll event. If the interval is less than half the poll interval, increase the poll timeout by one; otherwise, reduce it by one. This operates as a servo that adjusts packet departures from one peer near the center of the poll interval used by the other.

16.4 Interleaved Broadcast Mode

In NTP basic broadcast mode, the client responds to the first broadcast received by executing a number of client/server mode protocol rounds to calibrate the offset difference between the broadcast spanning tree topology and the unicast spanning tree topology. In the reference implementation, the rounds are continued several times to refine the measurements and complete the security protocol, if required. In client/server mode, the protocol is inherently resistant to lost, duplicate, or misordered packets, but in interleaved broadcast mode special considerations apply to avoid disruptions due to these causes.

Recall from Section 15.4 that, in Institute of Electrical and Electronics Engineers (IEEE) 1588 Precision Time Protocol (PTP), the master broadcasts a Sync message to the slaves, which capture the receive timestamp T_2. Immediately thereafter, the master broadcasts a Follow_up message, including the transmit timestamp of the Sync message T_1. Some time later, each client separately sends a Delay_req message to the master and captures the transmit timestamp T_3. The master returns a Delay_resp message containing the receive timestamp T_4 for the Delay_req message. The client collects these timestamps to calculate the offset and delay, as in the NTP protocol with the offset sign inverted. Subsequently, the master broadcasts a Sync/Follow_up pair of messages from time to time, and the slaves apply a correction equal to one-half the measured delay to determine the true offset.

The problem with IEEE PTP applied to large networks is that the packet routing for broadcast packets and unicast packets can be far different. Unicast packets are usually routed via a shortest-path spanning tree, while broadcast packets can be routed either by distance vector multicast (DVM) protocol or by protocol-independent multicast (PIM) protocol; each has different subgraph aggregation rules. In PTP, T_1 and T_2 are determined via the broadcast subgraph, while T_3 and T_4 are determined via the unicast subgraph. While the delays on the outbound and inbound paths of the unicast subgraph are often substantially the same, the delays between the same two points on the broadcast subgraph can be substantially different.

The NTP interleaved broadcast protocol faces this problem in a fundamentally different way. The actual transmit timestamp T_1 for one broadcast packet is sent in the following broadcast packet. The client saves the receive timestamp T_2 for the previous packet and uses the associated transmit timestamp T_1 in the current packet. The client applies a correction measured during the client/server calibration phase and determines the current clock offset.

Figure 16.7 shows a typical scenario in which the clock is updated as each broadcast packet arrives. In basic broadcast mode, the transmit softstamp t_{xmt} is used to determine the clock offset. On the other hand, the transmit timestamps *aorg* and *borg*, which alternate with each packet, are captured at output device interrupt time, so they do not have output queuing and buffering latencies. The interleaved broadcast mode uses the same packet header format as the basic mode but includes in t_{org} the transmit timestamp for the previous broadcast packet. As each packet is received, t_{org} contains the transmit timestamp for the previous packet, *borg* the corresponding receive timestamp, and *aorg* the corresponding transmit softstamp. While transmit softstamps are not used directly in interleaved broadcast mode, they are included to support both basic and interleaved modes with the same packet stream and to detect lost packets in interleaved mode. In the current NTP specification and NTP versions implemented prior to the interleaved protocol support, the t_{org} and t_{rec} packet variables are unused in broadcast mode and are ordinarily set to zero.

In Figure 16.7, B is the broadcast server, and A is the broadcast client. Packets sent at T_1, T_3, T_{11}, and T_{13} use broadcast mode (5), while the packet

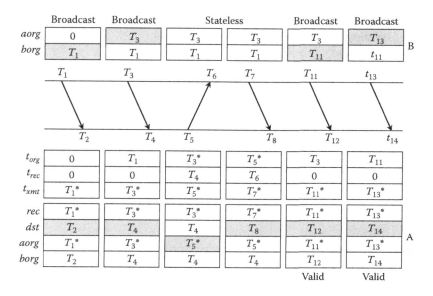

	Broadcast	Broadcast	Stateless		Broadcast	Broadcast	
$aorg$	0	T_3	T_3	T_3	T_3	T_{13}	B
$borg$	T_1	T_1	T_1	T_1	T_{11}	t_{11}	
	T_1	T_3	T_6	T_7	T_{11}	t_{13}	
	T_2	T_4	T_5	T_8	T_{12}	t_{14}	
t_{org}	0	T_1	T_3^*	T_5^*	T_3	T_{11}	
t_{rec}	0	0	T_4	T_6	0	0	
t_{xmt}	T_1^*	T_3^*	T_5^*	T_7^*	T_{11}^*	T_{13}^*	
rec	T_1^*	T_3^*	T_3^*	T_7^*	T_{11}^*	T_{13}^*	
dst	T_2	T_4	T_4	T_8	T_{12}	T_{14}	A
$aorg$	T_1^*	T_3^*	T_5^*	T_5^*	T_{11}^*	T_{13}^*	
$borg$	T_2	T_4	T_4	T_4	T_{12}	T_{14}	
					Valid	Valid	

FIGURE 16.7
NTP interleaved broadcast protocol.

sent at T_5 uses client mode (3), and the packet sent at T_7 uses server mode (4). As in basic broadcast mode, the stateless calibration round T_5 to T_8 uses no server state variables, and the timestamps T_6 and T_7 are essentially coincident. While only one stateless round is shown, there can be a number of them to refine the measurements using the NTP data-grooming algorithms as well as the optional Autokey security protocol. During the calibration phase, broadcast packets are ignored.

For simplicity in presentation, assume that the first broadcast is not received by the client. Clients that support interleaved broadcast mode will note that t_{org} is nonzero in later broadcasts; in that case, set state variable b to 1. The broadcast client now executes one or more ordinary stateless client/server mode rounds, which in this example results in a unicast clock offset θ_U at T_8. In the reference implementation, stateless rounds continue until the root distance drops below the select threshold, normally in about four rounds.

If on the arrival of the next broadcast at T_{12} b is nonzero, the broadcast clock offset is $\theta_B = t_{org} - dst$. The difference between the unicast offset and the broadcast offset represents the bias of the unicast subgraph delay relative to the broadcast subgraph delay. The peer bias variable $\beta = \theta_U - \theta_B$, and b is set to zero. To simplify the calculations in the various modes of operation, the delay computed in the unicast rounds is replaced by $\delta = 2\beta$. In interleaved broadcast mode, this packet calculates the delay and initializes the state variables but is not otherwise used to calculate other peer variables. For packets arriving at T_{14} and later, the peer offset is

$$\theta = \theta_B + \frac{\delta}{2}.$$

By construction, the difference between the transmit timestamp t_{org} and the corresponding softstamp *aorg* represents the message digest and queuing and buffering latencies in the broadcast server, $\varepsilon = t_{org} - aorg$. If ε is less than zero or greater than the largest expected latency, a packet has been lost or replayed. In such cases, the state variables are updated but not the peer variables.

16.5 Error Detection and Recovery

When a packet is lost or appears unsynchronized, bogus, or crossed in basic symmetric mode, the strategic response is simply to drop it. In interleaved symmetric mode, duplicate packets are ignored; unsynchronized and bogus packets update the state variables only. While not shown in the flowcharts, a hold-off counter h is used to avoid updating the peer variables for this and the next packet, even if it appears valid. It is set to 2 for bogus packets and decrements by 1 for subsequent packets. This causes the bogus packet and the next packet received to update only the state variables, but otherwise be ignored.

As previously, the interleaved modes have been implemented and tested in the reference implementation. However, a code surveyor might find it difficult to follow the code flow as it is intertwined with the authentication and rate management subsystems. The implementation is based on a simple test program used to verify correct behavior under normal and abnormal conditions with errors of various types. As an aside, this program was used to generate the packet traces of Figure 16.8. Here, peer A starts in basic symmetric mode, while peer B starts in interleaved symmetric mode. To make the example more interesting, both peers start at the same time, but B hears A at T_2 before A hears B at T_4. By rule and the state machine in Figure 16.4, packets received at T_2, T_4, and T_6 are unsynchronized, and only the state variables are updated. However, the packets received at T_8 and T_{12} are declared bogus by A since t_{org} does not match *aorg* as required by the basic symmetric state machine. Likewise, the packet received at T_{10} is declared bogus by B since t_{org} does not match *rec*. However, t_{org} matches *aorg*, so B knows that A is in basic symmetric mode. B switches to that mode, and both A and B continue in that mode.

This is not the only error/recovery scenario, of course, but it does verify that the state machines can settle their arguments without producing an

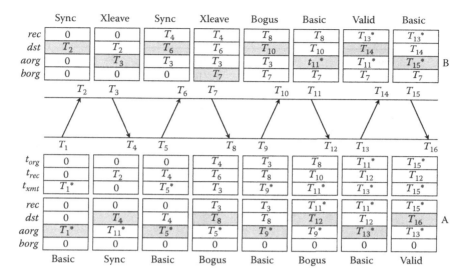

FIGURE 16.8
Interleaved mode error recovery.

undetected error. In fact, correct protocol behavior has been demonstrated in all cases involving no mode switch, even under an artificial dropped packet error rate of 10 percent.

16.6 Measured Performance with the Interleaved Modes

As mentioned, the interleaved modes have been implemented and tested in the reference implementation. This section contains a performance analysis using seven test and production machines on test and production local-area networks (LANs). The synchronization paths operate in basic, symmetric, interleaved symmetric, and interleaved broadcast modes and with various combinations of symmetric key and Autokey cryptographic means. The goal of the testing program is to quantify the accuracy and evaluate the latencies due to various causes.

There are two networks available for testing: the Backroom LAN, a 100-Mb/s switched Ethernet with very little traffic other than the test traffic, and the Campus LAN, a 100-Mb/s switched Ethernet with two very busy servers and an NTP traffic volume of well over 1,000 packets per second. The test and production machines used on the LANs are summarized in Table 16.1. The Backroom LAN shown in Figure 16.9 includes three switches (one not shown) interconnected by 100-Mb/s fiber repeaters. As

TABLE 16.1

Test and Production Machines

Name	CPU	Ethernet NIC	OS
Baldwin	Sun UltraSPARC III	10/100/1000 Mb/s	Solaris 5.10
Bridgeport	Sun UltraSPARC III	10/100/1000 Mb/s	Solaris 5.10
Howland	Intel P II, 1.0 GHz	RealTek 8139 10/100 Mb/s	FreeBSD 6.1
Macabre	Intel P 4x2, 2.8 GHz	Broadcom BCM5751 10/100/1000 Mb/s	FreeBSD 6.1
Mort	Intel P 4x2, 2.8 GHz	Broadcom BCM5751 10/100/1000 Mb/s	FreeBSD 6.1
Pogo	Sun Ultra 5.1	10/100 Mb/s	Solaris 5.10
Rackety	Intel P II, 500 MHz	3COM 3C905B 10/100 Mb/s	FreeBSD 6.1

CPU, central processing unit; OS, operating system.

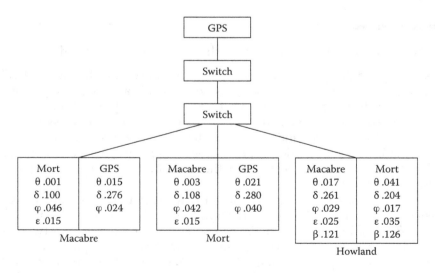

FIGURE 16.9
Backroom LAN.

the lengths of the fiber segments are less than 30 m, the propagation delays are well below the microsecond and so are neglected. The GPS server is a Meinberg LANtime M600, which includes an integrated NTP server and Ethernet port. This network is used for program development and testing only, so it carries little production traffic other than NTP.

The Backroom LAN includes three hosts: Macabre, Mort, and Howland. Macabre and Mort hosts are identical Pentium machines operating in interleaved symmetric mode with each other as well as client/server mode with the GPS server. Each includes an interleaved broadcast server in the configuration. Howland operates as an interleaved broadcast client. Each of the three hosts uses two associations as shown in the figure. Each association includes as peer variables the measured offset θ, delay δ, root mean square (RMS) jitter (offset differences) φ, and output queuing delay ε, all in milliseconds. In addition, interleaved broadcast client Howland includes the bias β calculated in Section 16.4. The interleaved associations are all operated using Autokey cryptography. The delays reported in this case are calculated in the calibration rounds.

Inspection of the results suggests that Macabre and Mort can maintain the system clock within a few microseconds of each other and within low tens of microseconds with the GPS server. Slower Howland can maintain the system clock relative to the servers within low tens of microseconds. Further inspection suggests that the jitter measured over the network (two or three LAN segments) is in the low tens of microseconds.

One interesting result of the experiment is the output queuing delay, about 15 μs for Macabre and Mort and about twice that for Howland. The experiment included Autokey, so the measured delays include the message digest computation. For the interleaved broadcast client, the value of β is roughly one-half the round-trip delay δ, as expected. From these results, the input queuing delays can be calculated from the measured round-trip delay and the calculated LAN delays. Note that the output queuing delays do not contribute to the calculations. For Macabre and Mort, the round-trip path between them includes four LAN hops, with each LAN hop about 8 μs plus 2 μs for the switch, for a total of 40 μs round-trip transmission delay. For a round-trip delay of roughly 100 μs, this leaves 60 μs for the input queuing delay split between two network interface cards (NICs). These measurements are typical of lightly loaded backwater LANs in which the performance improvement using the interleaved modes is only a few tens of microseconds.

The scenario can be quite different with slower machines, heavily loaded LANs, and large Ethernet switches contributing modest-to-large delay variations. The Campus LAN shown in Figure 16.10 includes one large Ethernet switch serving about two dozen subnets with several hundred production servers and clients and a few test hosts. The particular LAN referred to here is one of these subnets. It includes two busy NTP servers (Pogo and Rackety) and two test hosts (Bridgeport and Baldwin) dedicated to the experiment.

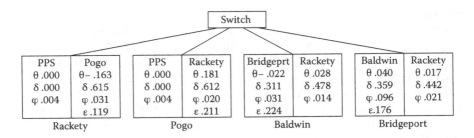

PPS	Pogo		PPS	Rackety		Bridgeprt	Rackety		Baldwin	Rackety
θ .000	θ– .163		θ .000	θ .181		θ– .022	θ .028		θ .040	θ .017
δ .000	δ .615		δ .000	δ .612		δ .311	δ .478		δ .359	δ .442
φ .004	φ .031		φ .004	φ .020		φ .031	φ .014		φ .096	φ .021
	ε .119			ε .211		ε .224			ε.176	
Rackety			Pogo			Baldwin			Bridgeport	

FIGURE 16.10
Campus LAN.

Collectively, the NTP servers support over a thousand clients in the global Internet with a traffic level of several hundred packets per second. In the figure, Pogo and Rackety operate with each other in interleaved symmetric mode, while Bridgeport and Baldwin operate with each other in interleaved symmetric mode. Both Bridgeport and Baldwin operate in client/server mode with Rackety. As in the Backroom LAN experiment, Autokey is used for all interleaved associations.

In addition to the interleaved associations shown, both Pogo and Rackety are configured for individual Spectracom 8183 GPS receivers, which produce both a serial timecode and a pulse-per-second (PPS) signal. The serial timecode is processed by a reference clock driver, while the PPS signal is processed by the kernel PPS discipline described in Chapter 8. This produces an exceptionally clean reference offset that hovers near zero as shown but occasionally surges up to 3 µs. The round-trip delay for reference clock drivers is by design zero, and the jitter is at the minimum, limited by the machine precision.

While Baldwin and Bridgeport have identical architecture and operating systems, they share a busy switch with a core throughput of several gigabytes per second, so the jitter and delay variations are somewhat higher than the Backroom LAN. However, note that the round-trip delay is three times higher than the Backroom LAN, and the output queuing delay is twice as high, suggesting that the Ethernet NICs or the NIC driver may be aggregating interrupts to reduce the interrupt load. The round-trip delays measured by both Pogo and Rackety are roughly 600 µs, while the jitter and output queuing delays are about the same as Baldwin and Bridgeport.

The interesting thing about these data is that the offsets of Pogo and Rackety are about the same but of opposite sign, which reveals an asymmetric path between the machines, most certainly due to the Ethernet NIC or driver structure. The results show Rackety offset roughly –180 µs relative to Pogo and Pogo offset roughly +180 µs relative to Rackety, which can only be accounted for if the difference in delay from Rackety to Pogo is 360 µs larger than the delay from Pogo to Rackety. By calculation, the input queuing plus transmission delays from Pogo to Rackety are 120 µs, while the delays in the reciprocal direction are 480 µs. This highlights the extreme case for which differences in NIC hardware and driver design can have significant effect on overall network accuracies.

16.7 Parting Shots

It is tempting to speculate on an interleaved symmetric design for the Proximity-1 space link protocol described in the next chapter. In the current hardware design, the timestamps are captured in a way very similar to IEEE 1588; that is, they are captured on passage of a designated octet at the hardware frame level. As in IEEE 1588, this requires intricate hardware and software provisions that may not be justified if the expected accuracy is at the millisecond level.

A Proximity-1 frame can have up to 2,048 octets and is transmitted at rates from 1 to 128 kb/s. Frames are first processed by a Reed-Solomon encoder, then by a convolutional encoder that operates at one-half rate. We can assume that, once the transmission rate and frame length are known, the transmission delay can be calculated. However, the transmission rates and frame lengths are often far different in the reciprocal directions. Assuming a Unix-like design for the spacecraft computer system, the timestamp capture techniques described in the previous chapter, and the interleaved symmetric protocol described in this chapter, accuracies less than a millisecond should be achievable, even with whopping output queuing delays of several minutes.

17

Time Transfer for Space Data Links

If one writes well and has the patience, someone will come from among the runners and read what one has written quickly, and go away quickly, and write out as much as he can remember in the language of the highway.

William Butler Yeats
quoted in Essays on Poetry, J. C. Squire, 1977

While the NTP has been deployed on the seabed, onboard ships, and on every continent, it is probably not widely known that it has been deployed in space. NTP first flew on an AMSAT satellite in the early 1980s and on another AMSAT satellite in 2000 [1]. It flew on at least two NASA Shuttle missions and in simulation experiments for future Moon missions. This and the next chapter discuss issues of time synchronization for space vehicles and space missions. In this chapter, the emphasis is on methods for time transfer between spacecraft in orbit around a planet or between spacecraft and surface vehicles.

In this book, we have discussed principles familiar, in one degree or another, to a computer scientist or electrical engineer. This chapter discusses principles of physics and astronomy, including general relativity and astro-dynamics—the mechanics of bodies rotating about their axis or revolving around a planet or the Sun. There is a certain amount of vector calculus, spacecraft navigation, and communications engineering included to facili-tate the discussion but not nearly enough for a definitive treatment. Further information is available in the citations at the end of this chapter.

Time transfer is usually determined using packets exchanged over space data links, but there are other methods based on the navigation function. It is vital to understand that spacecraft navigation and timekeeping are intimately entwined. Spacecraft navigation requires many sets of precision position and velocity measurements to accurately determine orbital param-eters and surface position. For instance, navigation accuracies to the tens of meters for Mars landers can only be achieved by refining repeated observa-tions over several days [2]. As explored in the next chapter, it may be possible to piggyback a precision time transfer function on the navigation function, or as explored in this chapter, it might be possible to piggyback a coarse navi-gation function on the time transfer function.

The NASA/Jet Propulsion Laboratory (JPL) space community has estab-lished three regimes of time synchronization accuracy requirements: *precision*

(1 ns to 1 µs), *fine* (1 µs to 1 ms), and *coarse* (1 ms to 1 s). In space, all three regimes require some form of hardware assist as the errors due to packet transmission times can be relatively large compared to the current Internet deployment on Earth. But, it is important to understand that these regimes are relative. For instance, precise navigation requires measurements of range to the order of 10 ns but does not require synchronization to a common timescale. Spacecraft clocks, such as those onboard Mars orbiters, have a granularity of about 4 ms, so they cannot schedule events more closely than this. However, for the purposes of the following discussion, the spacecraft clock is assumed to be interpolated as described in Section 15.2, so the clock resolution should be near the lower limit of the fine regime.

By far the most important consideration in space timekeeping is that distance, measured by round-trip light time (RTLT), can become huge. An RTLT to the Moon takes over 2 s, while an RTLT to Mars takes up to 40 min, and an RTLT to Voyager 2 at Uranus takes over 8 h. In principle, NTP can work well in the fine and coarse regimes within the Earth-Moon system and within other planetary systems, but something quite different might be required for missions between planets. Nevertheless, many of the fundamental algorithms intrinsic to the NTP architecture and protocol are well suited for planetary and deep-space missions but are packaged in a different way.

The discourse begins with several topics necessary to understand the principles of time transfer in space. It includes an overview of the principles of orbit mechanics and state vectors that determined the position and velocity of a spacecraft relative to an inertial frame. It continues with an overview of general relativity and its effects on clocks moving in a gravitational field. Following this is a description of current spacecraft clocks and then a description of the Proximity-1 protocol used to communicate between spacecraft in the vicinity of Mars and, in the future, in the vicinity of the Moon. Application of these principles to specific deep-space missions is presented in the next chapter.

Before we lift off, please note that, as in most space science, the units are in kilometers, kilograms, and seconds.

17.1 Orbit Mechanics

One of the first things to learn about space navigation is that everything orbits something else. The Moon and Earth satellites orbit Earth, the Earth and other planets orbit the Sun, and the solar system orbits the Milky Way. Even a deep-space mission to Pluto is in orbit about the Sun, although its motion is perturbed by everything, including the mass of Jupiter and even leaking propellant. In most cases considered here, the mass of a primary body such as the Sun or its planets is large compared to the mass of its satellites, so this presents a two-body problem that can be analyzed with the mathematics of

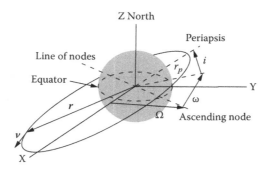

FIGURE 17.1
Earth-centered rectangular coordinate system.

astrodynamics as told in Bate [3], a widely cited textbook used by the U.S. Air Force Academy.

Figure 17.1 shows a three-dimensional rectangular coordinate system with origin the center of the Earth, but it does not rotate with it or as it proceeds along the heliocentric orbit. In further discussion, we will interpret this as an inertial frame. The X-Y plane coincides with the mean equator plane of Earth. The line of nodes is formed by the intersection of this plane and the plane of the Earth orbit, called the *plane of the ecliptic,* inclined at an angle of about 23.5°. The positive X axis is aligned to the vernal equinox as described in Section 13.1. The Z axis coincides with the Earth spin axis and points north, and the Y axis completes a right-hand coordinate system. The node where a point on the equator passes the line of nodes going north is called the *ascending node;* the opposite point is called the *descending node.* The time of the ascending node at the vernal equinox (i.e., when the line of nodes coincides with the X axis) can be determined with exquisite accuracy. Astrodynamicists call this the Earth-centered inertial (ECI) frame and coordinate system. Astronomers might find rectangular ECI coordinates rather cumbersome as they are used to right ascension, declination, and hour angle. Geographers are used to latitude, longitude, and altitude above mean sea level. Transformations between these systems are readily possible, but we will not need them here.

Figure 17.1 also shows a typical satellite orbit defined by a plane that intersects the equator along the orbit line of nodes, one ascending, the other descending. The orbit geometry is defined by a set of six parameters called *Keplerian* or *osculating elements*; these are defined in Table 17.1. The periapsis distance r_p is defined as the lowest point in the orbit. The orientation of the orbit plane is defined by the longitude of the ascending node Ω, argument of periapsis ω, and inclination i with respect to the equator plane. The shape of the orbit is defined by the eccentricity e. The epoch t of the orbit is defined as the time of periapsis passage.

Figure 17.2 shows a typical satellite orbit defined by two foci, apofocus F_a and perifocus F_p, for a major body such as Earth. The orbit itself is defined as

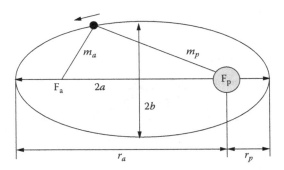

FIGURE 17.2
Orbit parameters.

TABLE 17.1

Keplerian Elements

Symbol	Units	Parameter
Ω	rad	Longitude of ascending node
i	rad	Inclination
e	dimless	Eccentricity
r_p	km	Periapsis distance
ω	rad	Argument of periapsis
t	s	Epoch of periapsis

the locus of points such that the sum of the line lengths $m_a + m_p$ is constant. In the figure, a is the semimajor axis, b is the semiminor axis, r_a is the apoapsis (apogee for Earth), and r_p is the periapsis (perigee for Earth). The eccentricity is defined as

$$e = \frac{r_a - r_p}{r_a + r_p}.$$

An eccentricity near zero implies a near-circular orbit, while an eccentricity near one implies a highly eccentric orbit. While not of interest here, $e = 1$ implies a parabolic orbit, and $e > 1$ implies a hyperbolic orbit. Thus, the orbit is completely defined by the six parameters in Table 17.1; however, other formulations are possible. Orbits defined in this are called conic sections.

In the following, vectors are indicated in boldface. The position and velocity of a satellite in orbit is defined by a state vector consisting of a three-element position vector r and a three-element velocity vector v at a defined epoch t. While the state vector changes over the course of the orbit, the orbit is completely defined by the planet gravity-mass (GM) product and state vector sampled at any point in the orbit. For Earth, GM is in cubic kilometers per second squared (km^3/s^2). State vectors can be determined from Earth or a spacecraft by radiometric observations of range and range rate (Doppler) at three or more different times in the orbit.

A state vector defines and also is defined by the six Keplerian elements in Table 17.1 at a particular epoch t. That is, a set of elements for a particular epoch t defines a state vector for that epoch, while a state vector at a particular epoch t defines a set of elements for that epoch. Transformations between state vector and element representation are a straightforward exeresis using trigonometry and matrix transformations as described in Bate et al. [3, Chapter 2].

Equatorial orbits have inclinations near 0°; polar orbits have inclinations near 90°. Most satellites have circular orbits with eccentricity near zero; some have highly eccentric orbits with perigee near 800 km and apogee near 58,000 km. Satellites used for planet mapping and weather observation usually operate in circular, polar, low-Earth orbit (LEO; altitude 800 km) with period about 1.7 h. GPS satellites operate in circular, medium-inclination (55°), medium-Earth orbit (MEO; altitude 20,000 km) with period 12 h. Communications and broadcast satellites operate in circular, equatorial, geosynchronous orbit (GEO; altitude 42,000 km) with period 24 h. Similar orbits are possible at Mars and other planets. For example, two Mars orbiters are now in circular, polar orbits at 300–400 km altitude and period about 2 h, while a third is in a highly eccentric, medium-inclination, orbit and period about 7 h. Additional examples are presented in the next chapter.

In principle, then, if we know the state vectors for the planets at a particular time and know the GM of the Sun, we can calculate the planetary positions at some future time and thus the geometry of the ray paths between them. Knowing the distances along a path and the velocity of light, we can determine the time delay, called *light time*, and thus set the planetary clocks to a common timescale.

Not so fast ... let us examine more closely.

17.2 Clock Comparisons and the Effects of General Relativity

Time transfer between vehicles in space and on the surface of planets is complicated by the effects of general relativity, including *time dilation* and *redshift*, relative to an inertial reference frame. A comprehensive tutorial on general relativity is in Petit and Wolf [4], while its application to time transfer in the solar system is in Nelson [5]. A full treatment requires the use of tensor mathematics and space-time variables, but this is beyond the scope of this book. This section contains an overview of general relativity phenomena and practical applications to space missions.

The purpose of the time synchronization function on Earth is to align clocks to a common timescale, such as UTC (Coordinated Universal Time).

This assumes that the clocks all run at a common rate; that is, 1 s on one clock is the same as 1 s on any other clock. In planetary systems, things are not that simple. Precision timekeeping in space must account for relativistic effects as well as planetary motion during measurements. In extreme cases, timekeeping must account for the effects of the Earth's ionosphere, solar wind, and the influence of other objects in the solar system. Due to relativity effects, moving clocks in a gravitational field are not syntonic; that is, over an orbit, they may gain or lose nanoseconds or even microseconds in a day. It is even more complicated because the degree of gain or loss can vary as the velocity or gravitational potential varies over the orbit.

Before launching the mathematics, you should be aware that comparing clocks between solar system objects is a tricky business. The bad news is that time transfer from one object to another might require integration from an eclectic epoch at which by magic all clocks in the universe were set to the same time. The good news is that subsequent effects can be accurately determined using simple models, including a secular (constant) term, plus cyclic contributions from a small number of other objects. We leave this as an exercise for the reader actually to do the messy integrations.

An *inertial reference frame* is a rectangular coordinate system that is nonrotating and free falling and with origin at the barycenter (zero gravity) of a planet or the solar system. In such a frame, Newton's laws are valid, and objects are unaffected by outside forces such as other planets or rotations. The major advantages of using inertial frames are that most include a single massive object, such as the Earth or the Sun, and the other objects of interest either have small mass or are too far away to have much influence. Thus, an ECI frame, such as shown in Figure 17.1, is handy for Earth satellites but ignores the Moon and the Sun, while an inertial frame at the solar system barycenter (SSB) is handy for interplanetary missions. Inertial frames exist for other planets as well.

Transforming a geographic position on the surface of Earth (Earth-centered, Earth-fixed frame) to position and velocity in the ECI frame is complicated by polar motion due to precession, by which the equinoxes circle the equator over a period of 25.8 thousand years, and nutation, by which the North Pole oscillates over an 18-year period with amplitude about 1 s [6]. In the extreme, Earth is very slowly spinning down and the day becoming longer. As Earth revolves around the Sun, the ECI frame is not inertial for interplanetary missions. For these missions, the position and velocity of the ECI frame itself must be determined in the inertial frame at the SSB, which must take into account the orbit of Earth and eccentricity. Thus, any transformation must specify the epoch of Ephemeris Time (ET) so that these effects can be determined.

Armed with position and velocity, we now consider general relativity effects. For an object A at position r_A moving at velocity v_A in an inertial frame, the clock rate of A relative to a clock at rest at the barycenter is

$$R_A = 1 - \frac{v_A{}^2}{2c^2} - \frac{U(r_A)}{c^2},$$

(17.1)

TABLE 17.2

Body-Fixed and Inertial Frames

Abbreviation	IAU Name	Reference Frame
TCB	Barycentric Coordinate Time	SSB
TDB	Barycentric Dynamic Time	J2000
TAI	International Atomic Time	Earth centered, Earth fixed
UTC	Coordinated Universal Time	Earth centered, Earth fixed
TT	Terrestrial Dynamic Time	Earth centered, Earth fixed
TCG	Geocentric Coordinate Time	Earth centered inertial (ECI)
LT	Lunar Dynamic Time	Moon centered, Moon fixed
TCS	Selenocentric Coordinate Time	Moon centered inertial (LCI)
MT	Mars Dynamic Time	Mars centered, Mars fixed
TCA	Aerocentric Coordinate Time	Mars centered inertial (MCI)

where $U(r_A)$ is the gravitational potential at position r_A. Note that for a vector v, $v^2 = |v|^2$, where $|v|$ is the norm of v and is a scalar independent of direction. The second term on the right is the time dilation effect; the higher the velocity of an object is, the slower its clock appears relative to a clock at rest in the frame. The third term on the right is the gravitational redshift; the higher the gravitational potential at an object is, the slower its clock appears relative to a barycentric clock. Acute observers will note the similarity to nonrelativistic Newtonian mechanics by simply replacing the c^2 term in the denominators by unity.

The gravitational potential energy at point r_A is

$$U(r_A) = \frac{GM}{c^2 |r_A|},$$

where GM is the gravity-mass product for the primary (orbited) body.

Table 17.2 shows the nomenclature used by the astrodynamics community for the various timescales and inertial frames used in the rest of this chapter. *Proper time* is the time displayed by a clock on the surface of a planet or the body of a spacecraft. *Coordinate time* is the time displayed in an inertial frame such as the ECI frame. Proper time on Earth is called Terrestrial Dynamic Time (TT), while the time in the ECI frame is called Geocentric Coordinate Time (TCG). Strictly speaking, TT is not dynamic unless the clock is moving on the surface or in the air. An atomic clock on the equator of Earth at sea level moving at 0.463 km/s at a mean altitude of 0.047 km runs slower than TCG by 60.0 µs/day due to time dilation and by 0.1 µs/day due to redshift for a total of 60.1 µs/day.* However, the TT clock runs faster at the peak of Mt. Everest and faster at the poles, so in this sense TT is indeed a dynamic timescale. Similar features apply to the other planets orbiting the Sun.

---

* The time dilation and redshift values for Earth and its satellites were calculated using the space fleet simulator described in Section 18.4; the values for Mars are from Nelson [5].

A GPS clock moving at 3.882 km/s at an altitude of 20,135 km runs slower than TCG by 7.2 µs/day due to time dilation and by 14.5 µs/day due to redshift. Since proper time comparisons can only be done in a coordinate frame,

$$(GPS - TCG)_{ECI} - (TT - TCG)_{ECI} = GPS - TT$$

is the time of the GPS clock relative to the TT clock. Thus, the GPS clock runs $(14.5 + 7.2) - (60.0 + 0.1) = -38.4$ µs/day slower than the TT clock. The net rate 38 µs/day "blueshift" is programmed in the spacecraft before launch.*

For the most precise timekeeping and navigation, additional effects need to be included. With a GPS orbital eccentricity of 0.02, there is a relativistic sinusoidal variation in the apparent clock time of 46 ns at the orbital period of 12 h. Also, as described in the next chapter, a Sagnac correction up to 133 ns must be included, depending on the satellite and receiver positions. Additional corrections are due to ionospheric effects. These corrections must be calculated in the receiver.

Proper time transfer from the Moon to Earth is subject to the same relativistic effects, but the effects of lunar gravity must be included. The procedure is to transfer proper time LT on the lunar surface to coordinate time TCS at the lunar barycenter in the LCI (moon-centered inertial) frame, then to TCG in the ECI frame, and finally to proper time TT on the surface of Earth. The times can then be compared in the ECI frame, as shown in Figure 17.3. Thus,

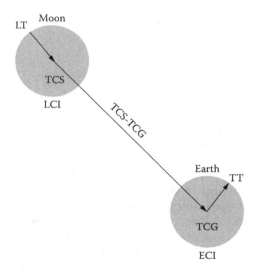

FIGURE 17.3
Compare times on Moon and Earth.

---

* This raises interesting issues should GPS be used for navigation other than on or near the surface of Earth.

$$(LT - TCS)_{LCI} + (TCS - TCG)_{ECI} - (TT - TCG)_{ECI} = LT - TT$$

is the time of the LT clock relative to the TT clock. Since the Moon is rotating only slowly, transfer from LT to TCS includes only the effects of lunar gravity, while transfer from TCS to TCG is like any other Earth satellite. Considering all relativistic effects, the LT clock runs slow in the ECI frame by 1.5 μs/day with variations of 0.96 μs over the lunar orbit of 27.3 day. The net effect is that LT runs fast by $60.1 - 1.5 = 58.6$ μs/day relative to TT.

A clock at the SSB runs faster than the TCG clock due to the gravity of the Sun and the velocity of Earth around the Sun. This timescale is called Barycentric Coordinate Time (TCB); it has a secular rate of about 0.5 s/year faster than the TCG clock. If the secular rate is removed, say by adjusting the TCB clock frequency, the result is Barycentric Dynamic Time (TDB), which is much more useful for precision time comparisons.

Proper time comparisons between Mars and Earth can be determined in a similar way, except that relativistic effects must be determined in the J2000 inertial frame. The procedure is to compute the relativistic effects for proper time transfer from Mars Dynamic Time (MT) on the surface of Mars to Ares Coordinate Time (TCA) in Mars inertial coordinates and then transfer TCA to TDB in J2000 inertial coordinates. In a similar manner shown in Figure 17.4, transfer proper time TT on the surface of Earth to TCG in ECI coordinates and then to TDB in J2000 coordinates. The time difference between a clock on the surface of Mars and a clock on the surface of Earth is

$$((MT - ATC)_{MCI} - TDB)_{J2000} - ((TT - TCG)_{ECI} - TDB)_{J2000} = MT - TT.$$

Considering all relativistic effects, the Mars clock runs slower relative to the Earth clock by 0.49 ms/day with irregular variations up to 13.1 ms.

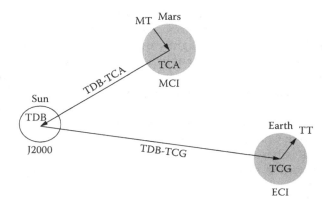

FIGURE 17.4
Compare times on Mars and Earth.

17.3 Time Transfer from a Planet to the Solar System Barycenter

A clock on the surface of Earth or Mars runs slower than at the barycenter of the associated planetocentric inertial frame due to the gravity and velocity in that frame. But, the planetocentric frame itself is moving in the gravitational field of the Sun, so it runs slower than the SSB clock. The two effects are additive and can be accounted for separately. For Earth, this is the approach taken in the tau-DTDB program using the principles of Fairhead and Bretagnon [7].* When given the Earth geodetic position and UT1 time, this program can compute TDB − TT to within 3 ns. The result has a main (annual) sinusoidal amplitude term approximately 1.66 ms, plus planetary terms up to about 20 μs, and lunar and diurnal terms up to 2 μs. However, using UT1 requires the user to compute it using external leap second and DUT1 information, which might become awkward beyond the next predicted leap second. However, this program is not for the fainthearted; it requires about 800 calls to the double-precision sin routine in the mathematics library.

If precisions adequate for navigation to 3 feet are not required, the following procedure based on orbital parameters can be used: First, to understand the principles involved, consider a *gedanken* experiment involving three clocks, one on the surface of Earth at the equator (TT), one dropped down a hole bored to the center of Earth (TCG), and the third hovering in J2000 (TDB). We know that the TCG clock runs faster than the TT clock by a constant rate of 60.1 μs/day, so we fiddle with the escapement to slow it to apparent TT and set its hands to agree with TT. We know that the TCB clock runs faster than the TCG clock, so we do the same thing to the TCB clock, which then becomes a TDB clock. If we set each of the three clocks to the same time at the same instant by cosmic thunderclap, they should read the same at any future time.

The problem with the TDB clock relative to the TCG clock is that it does not run at constant rate due to variations in Earth's velocity and the Sun's gravitational potential over the slightly eccentric orbit. We could fix this by integration of the Earth state vector as in Section 17.4, but this would be expensive and can be replaced with methods based entirely on celestial mechanics. A detailed explanation of how to transfer proper time on Earth TT to ET (also known as TDB) is given in Moyer [8, 9]. The method is encapsulated in the set of files in the JPL SPICE Toolkit documentation.

As explained in Chapter 13, the fundamental timescale for astronomy and space missions is based on International Atomic Time (TAI), which is disciplined by a herd of as many as 250 cesium clocks in national laboratories

---

* The tau-DTDB program is a FORTRAN subroutine included in the International Astronomical Union (IAU) Standards of Fundamental Astronomy (SOFA) software collection available from http://www.iau-sofa.rl.ac.uk/2001_0331/Timescales.html.

all over the world. Proper time TT on Earth is defined as the time of a clock at sea level TT = TAI + 32.184 s, for which the additive term accounts for the offset from ET at a prior epoch. For historical reasons [6], JPL mission times are reckoned in UTC, which makes time transfer awkward. First, the offset L = TAI − UTC is determined using a table of historic leap seconds derived from data provided by the International Earth Rotation Service (IERS). Finally, the ET is determined from relativistic effects as

$$ET = TT + L + K\sin(e),$$

where K = 1.657* ms is a constant, and e is the eccentric anomaly of the helio-centric orbit of Earth. Note the close agreement of K with the tau-DTDB program.

The eccentric anomaly is given by

$$e = M + E_B \sin(M)$$

where E_B = 0.0671 is a constant, and M is the mean anomaly

$$M = M_0 + M_1 t,$$

where M_0 = 6.239996 and M_1 = 1.990687 × 10^{-7} are constants, and t is the number of ET seconds past J2000. The procedure for planets other than Earth is similar but with different constants. This equation, which ignores short-term fluctuations, is accurate to within 30 μs (as stated in the mro.lsk kernel file for the Mars Reconnaissance Rover [MRO]), which is expected since the procedure does not model the planetary or diurnal terms.

17.4 Time Comparisons between Clocks in Space

At this point in the narrative, we have the tools to construct a common timescale for a number of orbiting spacecraft in an inertial frame. If we have the gravity–mass constant GM for a planet and the state vector for each spacecraft in orbit at a common epoch t_0 in coordinate time, we can determine the orbit parameters and calculate the new state vector at any other coordinate time t using the prop2b_c() routine of the SPICE Toolkit (available at http://naif.jpl.nasa.gov/naif/toolkit.html). Consider two spacecraft X and Y orbiting a planet in an inertial frame. Let $S_X(t, r, v)$ be the state vector for X and $S_Y(t, r, v)$ be the state vector for Y, both at coordinate time t. Here, r is

---

* The constants given are from the JPL Navigation and Astronomy Information Facility (NAIF).

the position vector, v is the velocity vector in the inertial frame, and the time dependence in both vectors is implicit.

If x is the position vector of one spacecraft and y is the position vector of another spacecraft, the light time for a ray from transmitter X to a moving receiver Y is approximately

$$\Delta \approx \frac{|y - x|}{c} + \frac{(y - x) \cdot v_y}{c^2} ,$$

where the first term on the right accounts for the geometry and the second the velocity of the receiver. Let t_x be the coordinate time of transmission at X and t_y be the coordinate time of reception at Y. In a naïve analysis, $t_y = t_x + \Delta$; however, Y is moving as time flies along the ray, so an iterative light time procedure such as shown in Figure 17.5 is required. In the procedure, the conic() routine is an abstraction of the prob2b_c() SPICE routine that propagates the position y at t_y to the position at $t_y + \delta$. In practice and as demonstrated in Section 18.4, with $K = 100$ ns and $M = 0.95$, the procedure converges in five iterations or less.

From the GM and state vector for each spacecraft, we can calculate the time dilation and redshift using Equation 17.1 at any point in its orbit. Note that all the operations done so far are in coordinate time t. However, the spacecraft clock runs in proper time τ relative to that spacecraft. Let p_t be the orbital period of a spacecraft measured in coordinate time and p_τ be the period measured in proper time. Then, the secular rate of the proper clock relative to the coordinate clock is

$$R = \frac{p_\tau}{p_t} , \qquad (17.2)$$

which is always less than one. A spacecraft can measure its own orbit period in proper time by noting the proper times at the point of maximum velocity,

$$\Delta = |y - x| / c + [(y - x) \cdot v_y] / c^2$$

$$d = ty - tx + \Delta$$

while $(|d| > K)\{$

$$t_y = t_y + \delta$$

$$y = conic(y, \delta)$$

$$\Delta = |y - x| / c$$

$$\delta = (t_x + \Delta - t)M$$

$\}$

FIGURE 17.5
Iterative light time procedure.

which is the epoch of periapsis, but it does not have the coordinate time unless provided by external means. However, the proper clock rate is not the same over the entire orbit. We can interpret Equation 17.1 as the rate of the proper clock relative to the coordinate clock at coordinate time t,

$$R(t) = 1 - \frac{1}{c^2}\left(\frac{v(t)^2}{2} + \frac{GM}{c^2|r(t)|}\right). \tag{17.3}$$

Let τ_0 be the proper time from the spacecraft clock at the coordinate time produced by the iterated procedure. At some other coordinate time t, the proper time is

$$\tau(t) = \tau_0 \mp \int_{t_0}^{t} R(t)dt. \tag{17.4}$$

Note that this expression remains valid whether the upper limit of integration is earlier or later than t_0. As a practical matter, the integral is most easily determined by numerical integration, as in Section 18.4. In principle, then, if t_x can be determined accurately at X, t_0 and τ_0 can be determined within 100 ns at Y.

Finding accurate coordinate time when only proper time is known from the spacecraft clock requires careful consideration. Ordinarily, the time transfer techniques considered in this book require periodic transmission of time values. With respect to time transfer over space data links, this means propagating state vectors and computing the proper time-coordinate time correspondence on every transmitted update. In the scenarios considered in this book, this occurs at intervals of about 1 min in coordinate time. However, the time between received updates can be relatively long since a particular pair of spacecraft might not see each other for up to a day. During 1 min, which is a small fraction of the orbit period for planetary orbiters, the proper clock rate can be considered a constant given by Equation 17.3.

Let $\varepsilon = t_0 - \tau_0$ be the initial offset of coordinate time relative to proper time at the last received update. At regular transmitted update intervals ΔT, which correspond to proper time intervals ΔTR, compute $R(t)$ as in Equation 17.3 and add $\Delta TR(t)$ to ε. Then, at proper time intervals of $\Delta TR(t)$, the transmitter sets $t_x = \varepsilon + \tau$, where τ is read directly from the system clock. In principle, t_x can be determined in this way to less than 100 ns over an orbit period in which the nonsecular rate terms can vary up to several microseconds.* The ε can be used by application programs needing coordinate time to synchronize experiments between spacecraft. Its value changes very slowly over the minute and need not be interpolated.

---

* See Table 18.1 for a tabulation of secular and nonsecular terms for a number of Earth-orbiting satellites.

These techniques can be used to transfer time from X to Y with precision less than 1 μs, but they can also be used to transfer time from Y to X. An exchange of one message from X to Y and another from Y to X generates the four timestamps necessary to calculate clock offset and round-trip delay as in Equation 15.1. Assuming that the hardstamps described in Section 15.3 are available, the interleaved symmetric mode described in Section 16.3 is used, and the spacecraft clock is constructed according to the principles of Section 15.2, time transfer over space data links should be accurate to within a few microseconds. However, there may be small differences between the proper time τ_0 determined from a received update and the value integrated from the last received update. Without further analysis in each specific case, it is not clear whether this error might be due to spacecraft clock frequency fluctuations, orbit perturbations, or navigation errors.

17.5 Spacecraft Electronics

With few exceptions, no two spacecraft are alike. Some have a frightfully expensive ultrastable oscillator (USO), with stability in parts per 10^{12}, while others have a sufficiently stable oscillator (SSO) with stability in parts per 10^{11}. Some are powered by photovoltaics with battery backup, others by radioisotope thermal generators (RTGs), which use thermocouples and heat generated by the decay of a plutonium isotope. NASA spacecraft use one kind of spacecraft data bus; European Space Agency (ESA) spacecraft use another. The spacecraft we are interest in carry a Proximity-1 capable transceiver, which is the means for communications in the vicinity of Mars.

This section describes typical spacecraft electronics used for science data and telemetry communication. The emphasis is on those components important to maintain the spacecraft time. Figure 17.6 shows a spacecraft computer (SC), a number of science instruments, communications/navigation transceivers, and a mission-elapsed time counter space sailors call the SCLK

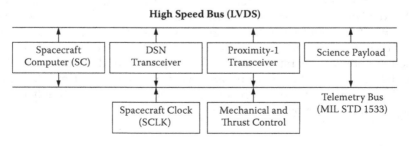

FIGURE 17.6
Spacecraft components.

(pronounced "essclock," spacecraft clock). These devices are interconnected by the MIL STD 1553 low-speed telemetry bus [10] and a low-voltage, differential-signaling (LVDS) high-speed data bus. In the case of Mars orbiters and some landers, the Deep Space Network (DSN) transceiver is used for navigation and communications with Earth, while the Proximity-1 transceiver is used for navigation and communications with other vehicles in Mars orbits or on the surface. Some landers carry X-band transceivers for direct-to-Earth (DTE) communications, but recent landers carried only Proximity-1 transceivers and can communicate with Earth only via the orbiters.

The Consulting Committee on Space Data Systems (CCSDS) has produced a set of recommendations on bus protocols, interfaces, and formats. A description of ongoing CCSDS standards work to adapt the OSI (Open System Interconnection) reference model to the 1553, SpaceWire, and CAN buses is in Plummer et al. [11]. A detailed discussion on the 1553 bus and its influence on spacecraft engineering and standards development is in Killough [12].

The 1553 bus operates at 1 Mb/s with Manchester encoding, by which each device derives bit timing independently. The bus controller (BC) function is implemented by the SC. The remaining devices function as remote terminals (RTs). The BC initiates all transfers and polls for responses. It can read from an RT, write to an RT, or instruct one RT to write to another RT. RTs neither initiate transfers on their own nor interrupt the BC. Commands and data messages consist of up to thirty-two 16-bit words at 1 Mb/s, so a message cannot be longer than 0.5 ms. Each message is addressed to a single RT or broadcast to all RTs. In this design, the accuracy for time transfers to or from science instruments via the bus will be limited to the order of 1 ms.

The SCLK is implemented in various ways depending on the particular spacecraft architecture. The most common design consistent with CCSDS time format [13] uses two counters: one for the seconds and the other for the fraction of the second. For instance, the Mars landers count only the seconds and have no provision for the fraction. The NASA Mars orbiters implement a 256-Hz clock, so they have eight bits for the fraction. If the SCLK fails for some reason, the mission is probably lost. In the Mars landers, it is implemented as a separate, ruggedized device accessed via the telemetry bus and runs even when the rest of the spacecraft is shut down during the Martian night. While not clear from available documents, the SCLK for the orbiters is most likely the SC time-of-day clock driven by a counter/divider with battery backup real-time clock (RTC) as described in Section 15.2.

For practical and historical reasons, the SCLK counts the elapsed seconds and fraction since some time before launch, so each SCLK in the fleet will have a notionally constant frequency but different offset with respect to any other spacecraft or to Earth. During the mission, the SCLK is not reset or adjusted and runs at its intrinsic frequency. However, the SCLK is subject to the whims of relativity and environmental effects, especially temperature changes [14]. JPL mission databases include what is called the *SCLK kernel file*, which characterizes the clock type, tick interval, and a table of clock time offsets from UTC, together with corresponding frequency offsets. These are in the form of segmented intervals that may or may not be concurrent or continuous due to differences between mission phases or extended shutdowns during Mars winters. These segments allow scheduling software on Earth to interpolate and adjust telemetry commands and data events with acceptable accuracy.

At least some NASA and ESA spacecraft generate a pulse-per-second (PPS) signal that is sent to all devices as necessary. If a device needs time resolution less than 1 s, it implements an interpolation counter phase locked to the PPS signal. The PPS signal can be generated by a numeric-controlled oscillator (NCO), such as the Analog Devices AD 9854 chip shown in Figure 17.7. It consists of an accumulator, phase increment, lookup table, and digital-analog converter (D/A). The device produces a sine wave output equal to the clock frequency, in this case 300 MHz, divided by the factor $2^{48}/N$. Thus, the device can produce any frequency from 0 to 75 MHz with resolution of 1 μHz. While useful for demonstration purposes, this particular device runs rather hot and is probably overkill for most space applications.

For the Electra transceiver described in Section 17.8, the NCO is implemented in the FPGA and driven from the USO at approximately 76 MHz. The NCO can be programmed to generate a PPS signal by adjusting the phase increment in much the same way as in Section 15.2. Of particular interest, the phase of the PPS signal can be adjusted by temporarily changing the phase increment, perhaps by a telecommand from Earth. The SCLK kernel files for the Mars orbiters show extremely low frequency offsets, suggesting that the PPS signal disciplines the SCLK, probably in much the same way as the current NTPv4 implementation.

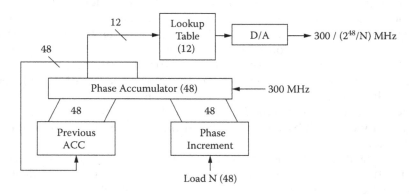

FIGURE 17.7
Numeric-controlled oscillator (NCO).

17.6 Proximity-1 Protocol

The CCSDS has defined several protocols for communication over space data links. In general, these protocols are designed for use where distances, and thus delays, are very large. On the other hand, our interest here is where distances are relatively small, as with Mars orbiters and landers. The CCSDS has designated the Proximity-1 architecture and protocol [15] for the transmission of commands, telemetry, and science data between spacecraft on and near Mars (or the Moon for that matter).

The Proximity-1 specification includes six sublayers: I/O (Input/Output), Data Services, Frame, Coding and Synchronization (C&S), Physical (PHY), and Medium Access (MAC), as shown in Figure 17.8. All but the C&S and PHY layers are implemented in the SC. The C&S is implemented in dedicated chips and FPGAs, while the PHY is the radio-frequency (RF) modem itself.

The MAC is the main point of interaction for the time transfer function. It has means to instruct the C&S sublayer to intercept a 24-bit ASM marker that is used to delimit C&S frames and capture a time tag from the SCLK or NCO, depending on the detailed design. Time tag capture in this way is important since buffering and queuing functions can take many seconds. The MAC can also send and receive supervisory frames to and from the remote MAC for the space link.

User data units (U frames) are sent and received over the space link along with supervisory data units (P frames). There are two kinds of U frames: sequenced and expedited. Sequenced frames carry sequence numbers modulo 256, while expedited frames carry sequence numbers modulo 8. Frame numbers are visible to the C&S at both ends of the space link. The SC includes separate queues for each of these and a SPDU (P frame) queue, which has no sequence numbers. The priority of these queues (leaving out some special cases) is SPDU, UPDU expedited, and UPDU sequenced. A maximum frame of 2,048 octets transmitted at the lowest channel rate of 1,000 bps takes 32 s

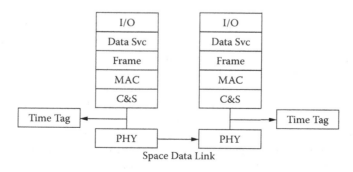

FIGURE 17.8
Proximity-1 protocol stack.

in transmission, so an SPDU or expedited frame might have to wait that long. Thus, it is imperative that time tags be captured at the C&S layer. The C&S time tag and associated sequence number can be captured and retained for later retrieval. Note that the MAC does not have direct access to the data stream and can only inject or capture SPDU frames and enable or disable C&S time tag capture. In particular, the MAC cannot inspect or overwrite sequenced or expedited frames.

17.7 Proximity-1 Time Service

The Proximity-1 specification includes a transmit parameters SPDU to enable the remote MAC to capture a specified number of transmit time tags and a receive parameters SPDU to capture a specified number of receive time tags. These are retained in buffers for later transmission in the telemetry stream. In addition, there is a time distribution SPDU to convey time tags from one MAC to another and to broadcast the time. SPDU frames carry no sequence numbers, so time tags associated with these frames are not useful in the present design other than to broadcast the time. The specification expects that the time tags and associated sequence numbers are captured only for UPDU expedited frames. To capture for both sequenced and expedited frames would create an ambiguity as the sequence numbers are from different spaces. The C&S determines the frame type and sequence number from the five-octet frame header.

What would seem to be a prudent procedure is for the MAC to enable the local C&S to capture a number of transmit and receive time tags and send SPDUs to enable the remote C&S to do the same. Then, each end sends a number of expedited frames to the other. Several cases ensue, depending on whether frames are already in the expedited queue at either end of the link. In the current design, the time tags and sequence numbers collected are returned to Earth for processing.

While not in the specification, it is the intent that captured time tags are correlated by sequence numbers to select the transmit and receive time tags for the same expedited frame in one direction and then in the other. Each frame results in two time tags, which then have to be converted to UTC timestamps using the SCLK kernel file. For the highest accuracy, the correlation must take into account the motion of each spacecraft between frames. This could be determined from state vectors using methods described in Section 18.4. The resulting four timestamps can be used as in the on-wire protocol of Section 3.6 to calculate clock offset and round-trip delay of each vehicle relative to the other. While probably a bug in the Proximity-1 specification, the format specified in CCSDS 301.0-B3 [13] has no provision for the sequence number.

17.8 Time Transfer Using the Electra Transceiver

This section considers the accuracy expectations using the Electra transceiver described in Hamkins and Simon [16]. It is used for communication and navigation by Mars orbiters and landers. There are ingenious features of this radio that can provide time tag resolution limited only by the onboard USO used by the Mars orbiters. The USO operates at a frequency f_0 of about 76 MHz and provides the master reference for all signals used by the radio. The resolution of a counter/divider driven by the USO is about $1/f_0 \approx 15$ ns. The analysis presented in this section suggests that, at least at moderate-to-high data rates, time tag accuracies to this order can be achieved without averaging. Accuracy in this context means the precision to which the ASM marker can be captured relative to the USO phase. The Parting Shots section of this chapter suggests modifications to the Proximity-1 protocol with which this can be achieved. Note that some discussion in this section reeks of high geek speak and might be skipped by a casual reader.

The Electra transceiver represents the first generation of JPL software-defined radios (SDRs). The radio has been built in three versions: the original Electra transceiver flown in recent Mars missions [17]; a smaller, lighter version called Electra Lite intended for landers; and an even smaller, lighter version intended for balloons and aerobots [18]. These radios operate at UHF (ultrahigh frequency) frequencies (390–415 and 435–450 MHz) using low-power transmitters and simple antennas. One model is equipped with an X-band to UHF-band downconverter to receive signals directly from Earth. With SDR technology, the radio can be reconfigured in flight in response to commands issued from Earth. In the future, an even more sophisticated SDR may become available that can recognize each transmitted signal design and automatically reconfigure without instructions from Earth. The technology is being continuously improved for the Electra UHF band and Advanced Transponder for the X- and Ka-bands [19].

Our concern here is with the Electra receiver and the various design features that affect time tag accuracy. A block diagram of the receiver is shown in Figure 17.9. All components except the low-noise amplifier (LNA), downconverter, and A/D converter are implemented in an FPGA. The downconverter

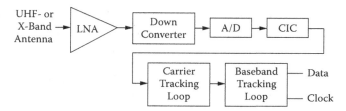

FIGURE 17.9
Electra transceiver receiver.

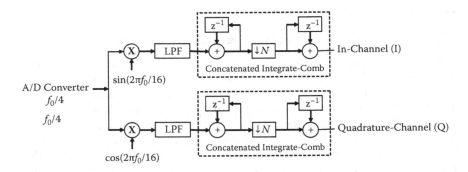

FIGURE 17.10
Concatenated integrate-comb (CIC). LPF, low-pass filter.

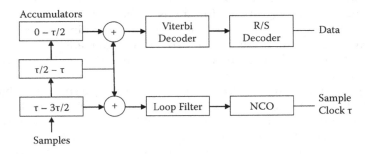

FIGURE 17.11
Digital transition tracking loop (DTTL).

produces the intermediate frequency (IF) at about 76 MHz. The A/D converter samples the IF at about $f_0/4 \approx 19$ Ms/s, resulting in at least four samples per symbol at the highest data rate of 4,096 kb/s.

The FPGA circuitry shown in Figure 17.9 first multiplies the digital samples by quadrature sinusoids at a frequency of $f_0/16 \approx 4.25$ Ms/s to produce in-phase (I) and quadrature-phase (Q) signals. Each phase is passed through a low-pass filter to remove aliases above 8.5 MHz. To reduce power as much as possible at rates below 1,024 kb/s, a concatenated integrate-comb (CIC) filter [20] is used to decimate the symbol stream by a factor of N. This allows the IF bandwidth to be optimized over a large range of symbol rates simply by varying N. The CIC requires no multipliers and thus very little power. Below 8 kb/s, the decimation is a constant 128 to allow enough bandwidth for the carrier tracking loop to track the Doppler signal component.

The carrier tracking loop is a phase-lock loop (PLL) or a suppressed carrier (Costas) loop that produces the baseband data and phase signals. The baseband tracking loop is a digital transition tracking loop (DTTL) [21] shown in Figure 17.11. It accumulates symbols of period τ in three accumulators to produce the data and clock signals. The Viterbi decoder and Reed-Solomon decoder and interleaver contribute substantial delays, as do their counterparts in the transmitter signal chain, but the delays are constant. The time tags are captured after the decoders at the passage of the ASM, as described in Section 17.6. With this design, the resolution of the DTTL depends on symbol rate and the number of samples per symbol. The resolution is better than 60 ns above 512 kb/s, rising to 1 μs at 64 kb/s and then rising to about 8 μs below 16 kb/s. The loop filter can provide substantial averaging to improve sample clock accuracy by several hundred times. So, at least at moderate-to-high data rates, the accuracy should be in the tens of nanoseconds.

17.9 Parting Shots

The current method for time synchronization in the Mars space fleet requires the time tag correlation function for each spacecraft to be performed on Earth and time synchronization to be done offline. As the fleet grows, this can put an onerous burden on the DSN and mission operating procedures. Time synchronization should be an intrinsic, distributed, and ubiquitous service for the fleet. This requires means to accurately measure and exchange coordinate timestamps between the vehicles. A strong case is made in Stadter et al. [22] for integrated communication, navigation, and control functions in a space fleet. This section extends this concept to include the time transfer function as well.

The proposed Proximity-1 Interleaved Time Service (PITS) described in this section does this using the Proximity-1 data link protocol with certain minor modifications. PITS is applicable in NTP-like configurations involving multiple spacecraft and space data links. In this design, the Earth-disciplined vehicles operate as PITS primary servers and the others as PITS secondary servers and clients as in NTP. However, servers can come and go relatively frequently, depending on Earth telemetry schedules and orbit crosslink communications opportunities.

To avoid conflict with the existing Proximity-1 provisions, PITS defines a new Timestamp SPDU (type 3) frame format as in Figure 17.12 with two 8-octet data fields in NTP or CCSDS format. These fields can be used to convey timestamps from one vehicle to another. For those spacecraft equipped with a USO or SSO and NCO, we assume the SCLK is disciplined by the PPS signal and that the 4-ms tick interval is interpolated as described in Section 17.5. The resolution of the SCLK timestamp is a few nanoseconds, while the resolution of the NCO time tag is a few tens of nanoseconds relative to the ASM passage. While these data can be used for a simple time transfer application, they do not take into account relativistic effects or spacecraft motion. These effects are handled by the PITS protocol described in this section.

SPDU Header (5)	Transmit Time Tag (8)	Receive Time Tag (8)

FIGURE 17.12
Timestamp SPDU format.

In this proposal, the C&S sublayer sniffs the transmit and receive data stream for a timestamp SPDU and captures a time tag at the ASM passage. The transmit and receive time tags are saved in separate buffers for later retrieval by the SC. Capture does not need to be enabled; it is always enabled for the timestamp SPDU. Only a single buffer is necessary for the transmit time tag and another for the receive time tag since timestamp SPDUs are never sent back to back.

At present, the Mars fleet does not need time synchronized to a coordinate timescale such as ET since scheduling functions are done on Earth and the SCLK kernel used to translate UTC to and from SCLK time. However, if the Mars fleet is to evolve an in-flight timekeeping capability, some means must be available to run the fleet on a coordinate timescale. In this proposal, the uplink telemetry from Earth at spacecraft time τ_0 includes a timestamp that specifies the ET time in seconds and fraction on arrival at the spacecraft, as described in the next chapter. In the nomenclature of Section 17.4, SCLK is considered proper time τ_0 and ET is considered coordinate time t, so the correspondence between coordinate and proper time is $\varepsilon = t - \tau_0$. Subsequently, relativistic effects can be included as in Section 17.4.

Within the space fleet, the protocol suggested in Section 17.4 is used. For the purpose of illustration only, the interleaved symmetric NTP protocol described in Section 16.3 is suggested as encapsulated in Proximity-1 expedited frames. Operations go something like this:

1. At intervals ΔTR, spacecraft X sends an ordinary NTP interleaved symmetric mode packet to Y followed by a timestamp SPDU and captures a time tag τ from SCLK. Next, it adds the current ε to τ to form a transmit timestamp t_x and propagates its state vector to this time. It will use the timestamp and state vector in the following NTP packet. The state vector and possible ancillary information are sent in an NTP extension field.

2. On receiving the NTP packet, spacecraft Y waits for the following timestamp SPDU, which captures a time tag τ_0 from SCLK. It determines the receive timestamp t_y using the iterated procedure of Section 17.4.

3. Spacecraft Y now performs an identical procedure to complete the round. As required by the interleaved protocol, two rounds must be exchanged to determine the relative clock offset and one-way delays. The one-way delays might be useful as a crude navigation function.

This method requires that both spacecraft X and Y have accurate state vectors and the GM of the primary planet. In principle, these data for Y could be included as an extension field in packets sent by X to Y, possibly relayed from Earth or another spacecraft. In addition to the sanity checks available in the interleaved symmetric protocol, an additional check is needed to be sure that the timestamp SPDU received is the same SPDU transmitted; that is, the loss or duplicate of an SPDU can be detected. This is easily done using a sequence number in the SPDU data field.

The accuracy using this method is limited by the accuracy of navigation and the precision of the iterated procedure, which is less than 100 ns. However, the precision of the PPS signal used to discipline the spacecraft clock via hardware interrupt is probably limited to the SC interrupt latency, estimated at less than 3 µs in modern computers.

References

1. Rash, J. *Internet Access to Spacecraft.* Technical Report SSC00-IX-1, NASA Goddard Space Flight Center, April 2000.
2. Guinn, J., and T. Ely. Preliminary results of Mars exploration rover in-situ radio navigation. *Proceedings of the 14th AAS/AIAA Spaceflight Mechanics Meeting* (February 2004).
3. Bate, R.R., et al. *Fundamentals of Astrodynamics.* Dover, 1971.
4. Petit, G., and P. Wolf. Relativistic theory for time comparisons: a review. *IOP Metrologia 42* (June 2005), 138–144.
5. Nelson, R.A. Relativistic time transfer in the Solar System. *Proceedings of IEEE 2007 International Frequency Control Symposium, 2007 Joint with the 21st European Frequency and Time Forum* (May 2007), 1278–1283.
6. Nelson, R.A., et al. The leap second: its history and possible future. *Metrologia 38* (2001), 509–529.
7. Fairhead, L., and P. Bretagnon. *Astron. Astrophys. 229* (1990), 240–247.
8. Moyer, T.D. Transformation from proper time on Earth to coordinate time in Solar System barycentric space-time frame of reference—Part 1. *Celestial Mech. 23* (1981), 33–56.
9. Moyer, T.D. Transformation from proper time on Earth to coordinate time in Solar System barycentric space-time frame of reference—part 2. *Celestial Mech. 23* (1981), 57–68.
10. Military Standard. *Aircraft Internal Time Division Command/Response Multiplex Data Bus MIL STD 1553.* Department of Defense, Washington, DC, September 1978.
11. Plummer, C., et al. Standardising spacecraft onboard interfaces—the CCSDS SOIF activity. August 2002, 1–10.
12. Killough, R. Integrating CCSDS and MIL-STD-1553: what you should know. *Proceedings of the IEEE 2002 Conference on Aerospace*, Vol. 4, 1917–1926.

13. *CCSDS 301.0-B-3 Time Code Formats.* Blue Book. Issue 3. January 2002.
14. Tugnawat, Y., and W. Kuhn. Low temperature performance of COTS electronic components for Martian surface applications. *Proceedings of the IEEE 2006 Aerospace Conference* (July 2006).
15. *CCSDS 210.0-G-1 Proximity-1 Space Link Protocol-Rationale, Architecture, and Scenarios.* Green Book. Issue 1. August 2007.
16. Hamkins, J., and M.K. Simon, Eds. *Autonomous Software-Defined Radio Receivers for Deep Space Applications, Chapter 2: The Electra Radio.* JPL Deep-Space Communications and Navigation Series, 2006.
17. Edwards, C.D., et al. The Electra Proximity link payload for Mars relay telecommunications and navigation and Bretagnon, P. *Astron. Astrophys. 229,* 240–247.
18. Kuhn, W. A low-volume, low-mass, low-power UHF Proximity micro-transceiver for Mars exploration. *Proceedings of the 12th NASA Symposium on VLSI Design* (October 2005), 1–5.
19. Cook, B., et al. *Development of the Advanced Deep Space Transponder.* IPN Progress Report 42-156, Jet Propulsion Laboratory, February 2004.
20. Meyer-Baese, U., et al. Cost-effective Hogenauer cascaded integrator comb decimator filter design for custom ICs. *Electron. Lett. 41, 3* (February 3, 2005).
21. Mileant, A., et al. The performance of the all-digital data transition tracking loop using nonlinear analysis. *Proc. IEEE Trans. Commun. 43, 2/3/4* (February/March/April 1995), 1202–1215.
22. Stadter, P.A., et al. Confluence of navigation, communication, and control in distributed spacecraft systems. *Proc. IEEE Aerospace Conf., 2* (March 2001), 563–578.

Further Reading

Jet Propulsion Laboratory. Basics of space flight. http://www2.jpl.nasa.gov/basics/index.html Basics of Space Flight.
Braeunig, R.A. Rocket and space technology: orbital mechanics. http://www.braeunig.us/space/orbmech.htm.

18

Time Transfer for Deep-Space Missions

> Learned men are the cisterns of knowledge, not the fountainheads.
>
> **William Hazlett**
> *Conversations of James Northcote, Esq. R. A.,* 1830

This chapter discusses several time transfer scenarios involving planetary orbiters, landers, and deep-space probes on science and exploration missions. While the objective is to synchronize the spacecraft clock in these vehicles to Earth, this function is often integrated with the navigation function [1,2]. This chapter relies heavily on the material of the Chapter 17 and on general knowledge of mathematics and physics principles. While the general relativistic effects described in the Chapter 17 are always present to some degree, they are neglected in most of this chapter.

The first scenario is not really a space mission at all since it describes time transfer between national laboratories on Earth via a geosynchronous satellite. However, the means described could be used for time transfer on the Moon or on other planets where distances are relatively small and signal-to-noise ratios (SNRs) are moderate to large. The second scenario describes time transfer from Earth to Earth orbiters like the Space Shuttle. This involves the services of the Tracking and Data Relay Satellite (TDRS) system, which uses a network of geosynchronous satellites to relay data between Earth and Earth orbiters. A similar system could be used for other objects in a planetary system, such as the Moon and Mars.

The third scenario involves time transfer to the Moon and satellites of the Moon. This raises special issues as the Moon stubbornly faces the Earth, so communicating with landers on the far side requires relay of some kind. The fourth scenario involves time transfer for Mars orbiters, landers, and aeroprobes. The means described use the internationally standardized Proximity-1 protocol described in Chapter 17. Jet Propulsion Laboratory (JPL) operational procedures now provide navigation and time transfer direct from Earth via the NASA Deep Space Network (DSN). As the number of vehicles near and on Mars grows over time, DSN resources may become prohibitively expensive. We discuss an alternative by which one or more Mars vehicles are synchronized from Earth, and then they provide time transfer for the other Mars vehicles.

The fifth scenario involves navigation and time transfer from Earth to deep-space vehicles. The DSN has transitioned from a multiple-subcarrier ranging system to a system based on a pseudorandom (PR) ranging signal. The technique requires considerable resources that may be impractical for space vehicles but does not provide precision time to the space vehicle. The Parting Shots section describes a method with which this might be achieved.

18.1 Time Transfer between Earth Stations

Early in the history of time transfer between national laboratories, the only way to synchronize the laboratory cesium clock ensemble was to fly a portable cesium clock from one laboratory to another. While cesium clocks typically have batteries, the battery charge lasts only a few minutes, long enough for the backup generator to kick in. For transport over intercontinental distances, they required a first-class seat and a heavy-duty, deep-discharge battery. It is unlikely that airlines would permit that today. In recent times, the OMEGA and LORAN-C (Long Range Navigation System C) long-wave radio navigation systems and later the GPS satellite navigation system have became available for time transfer, and the flying clocks have been grounded. These means provide accuracies to the microsecond for LORAN-C and to the nanosecond for GPS. However, GPS is only a common-view system and does not provide a two-way capability. In particular, a method is needed for time transfer between stations that does not involve a flywheel clock in the satellite.

The solution developed by the National Institute of Standards and Technology (NIST) [3] and later refined by the U.S. Naval Observatory (USNO) [4] is called two-way satellite time and frequency transfer (TWSTFT) [5]. It uses a common-view geosynchronous satellite capable of two-way operation with very small antenna terminal (VSAT) Earth stations and a digital modem specially designed for time transfer service. In operation, each station sends an on-time pulse together with ancillary information via the satellite to the other station. After compensation for various propagation effects, the time of each station relative to the other can be determined within 100 ps or better.

The VSAT terminals and geosynchronous satellite operate at Ku band, at 14 GHz Earth to satellite and 12-GHz satellite to Earth. The high frequency relative to C band (6/4 GHz) allows much smaller antennas to be used. The transmitter power is typically 10 W and the antenna diameter 1–2 m. The radio-frequency (RF) upconverter and downconverter operate with a 70-MHz intermediate frequency (IF) and a digital modem. Equipment with these characteristics is common in the satellite communications community.

What makes the TWSTFT application unique is a specially designed digital modem first implemented as the Hartl/Mitrex modem [3] and later refined by USNO [4]. It uses the 1-Hz (pulse-per-second, PPS) and 5-MHz signals generated by a cesium clock. The PPS signal is used as a precision time tag for transmissions of one station to the other, while the 5-MHz signal is multiplied to 25 MHz and used to drive the analog-to-digital and digital-to-analog (A/D and D/A, respectively) converters and timing signals used in the modem.

The heart of the modem is a PR sequence generated by a linear feedback shift register (LFSR). Devices like these are widely employed in digital communications systems. The USNO modem uses a 12-stage LFSR that generates a sequence of $2^{12} - 1 = 4,095$ bits (more properly called *chips*) with a uniquely powerful autocorrelation function together with a very low cross-correlation function with other codes and noise. This makes the LFSR ideally suited for time transfer applications.

In the USNO design, each 4,095-chip PR sequence is interpreted as 1 bit in a word of 32 bits. Nineteen words per second are biphase modulated on a carrier frequency of $4,095 \times 32 \times 19 = 2.489760$ Mb/s, which is appropriate for a commercial TV satellite transponder. A binary one is transmitted in the upright phase, while a binary zero is transmitted in the inverted phase. The resulting BPSK signal consists of a $32 \times 19 = 608$ b/s data stream. The data stream begins with the on-time tag followed by the time of day, station identifier, and ancillary data. The on-time tag consists of a word of 16 zeros followed by 16 ones, which cannot be duplicated by legitimate data.

As shown in Figure 18.1, each station includes a time interval counter that is initialized at zero when a station transmits the on-time tag to the other station. On receiving the on-time tag, a station stops its counter and sends the counter value to the other station in the next second. On completion of two rounds, each station subtracts the value received from the other station from its own value. As shown in the figure, the offset between the stations can be easily computed; in fact, this method is a variation of that used by the Network Time Protocol (NTP).

The success of this method depends on accurate calibration of residual delays. In Figure 18.2 at station A, the delays d_{TA} and d_{RA} include components due to cables, modem, and RF equipment. The d_{AS} includes the free-space

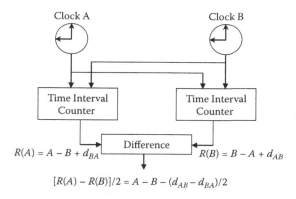

FIGURE 18.1
Two-way satellite time and frequency transfer.

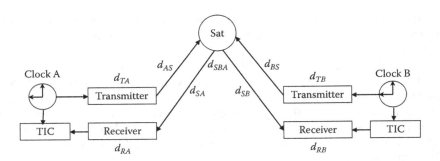

FIGURE 18.2
Space and equipment delays. TIC, tick interval counter.

propagation delay plus components due to the ionosphere and troposphere, while d_{SAB} includes the satellite transponder and related RF equipment delays. Similar effects occur at station B. In practice, every attempt is made to keep the signal paths symmetric so that these delays cancel out. The two stations should use the same satellite transponder and the same uplink channel and down-link channel. Since the uplink and downlink channel frequencies are differ-ent, differential ionospheric and tropospheric corrections may be necessary.

In addition, an adjustment called the Sagnac effect is necessary to com-pensate for the motion of Earth during the time of passage between one sta-tion and the other. Let ω be the angular velocity of Earth rotation and r a position vector in the Earth-centered inertial (ECI) frame, so $v_r = \omega \times r$ is the velocity at r. If Δr is an incremental change in r, then the light time to travel over Δr is $\dfrac{1}{c^2}\Delta r \cdot v_r$ where c is the velocity of light in kilometers per second. Integrating over the path from A via S to B,

$$d = \frac{1}{c^2}\int_A^B (\omega \times \mathbf{r})\cdot d\mathbf{r} = \frac{2A\omega}{c^2},$$

where A is an area to be computed, is the Sagnac effect. Figure 18.3 shows how A is computed geometrically. Consider the geometrical figure formed by the line segments connecting the satellite, each Earth station, and the center of the Earth geoid as the path SACBS. Then, form the projection of this figure on the Earth equator SA′CB′S, if S is not already in the equatorial plane, and compute the area A of the projection in square kilometers. If the direction of propagation is to the east, the correction is positive; if to the west, the correction is negative.

In practice, a number of rounds are made over some minutes and the counter values averaged to refine the measurements. In this way, the offsets between stations can be determined to within 100 ps. A number of stations can participate; one of them polls the others in turn so that all stations can

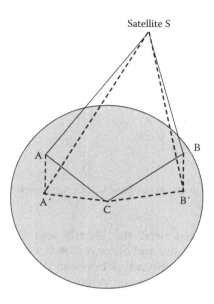

FIGURE 18.3
Sagnac effect.

measure their laboratory offsets relative to the others in one session. At one time, NIST and USNO participated in these measurements three times a week.

In principle, the TWSTFT method would work on any planet or moon with a stationary equatorial satellite relay. However, the most useful technology to come from this method is the use of long PR codes to improve the SNR and the ability to encode data by modulating the codes. This shows up in the discussion of time transfer for deep-space missions.

18.2 Time Transfer to Earth Satellites

This section describes a method for time transfer from Earth to a satellite in low-Earth orbit (LEO) or medium-Earth orbit (MEO). Accuracies within 5 μs were demonstrated in a NASA Space Shuttle mission using the TDRS [6]. This method has been extended to other Earth orbiters as well. TDRS supports multiple, simultaneous, near-Earth space missions using several geosynchronous orbit (GEO) satellites operating at S (2–4 GHz) and Ku (11–18 GHz) bands. The satellites use wideband, quasilinear transponders, often called *bent pipes*. These transponders translate a 10-MHz band of signals from 14 to 2.3 GHz and vice versa without demodulation.

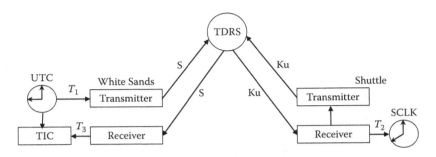

FIGURE 18.4
Time transfer from Earth to the Space Shuttle. SCLK, spacecraft clock; TIC, tick interval counter.

The NASA experiment used the Shuttle and the White Sands, New Mexico, communications site and other remotely controlled sites. The TDRS was used as the communications link between White Sands and the Shuttle. Figure 18.4 shows the paths between White Sands, a TDRS satellite, and the Shuttle. Uplink S-band signals from White Sands are translated by TDRS to Ku band and downlinked to the Shuttle. These signals are immediately remodulated to another Ku-band frequency, uplinked to TDRS, translated to another S-band frequency, and downlinked to White Sands. As in the TWSTFT method, the propagation paths and translations are reciprocal, so the delays nearly cancel out.

For time transfer purposes, the White Sands uplink signal is modulated by a PR ranging signal similar to the TWSTFT signal. At regular intervals, the uplink equipment inserts a pulse in the ranging signal and captures the pulse time T_1 according to the station clock. The pulse is synchronized by precision means to UTC. Equipment onboard the Shuttle captures the pulse time T_2 according to the spacecraft clock. When the pulse is received at White Sands, the pulse time is captured T_3 according to the station clock. White Sands now calculates the round-trip delay

$$d = T_3 - T_1 + d_S,$$

where d_S is the Sagnac effect due to the rotation of Earth during the round-trip time. Unlike the TWSTFT technique in which the satellite is stationary at GEO, the Shuttle is moving along its orbit. However, the time while the pulse is turned around at the Shuttle is short, so the Sagnac effect can be calculated as in TWSTFT.

The time the pulse arrived at the Shuttle according to the White Sands station clock is

$$T_4 = T_1 + \frac{d}{2},$$

with accuracy limited primarily by the station clock. Finally, T_4 is uplinked to the Shuttle in the telemetry stream, where it is used to correct the spacecraft clock

$$\theta = T_4 - T_2.$$

In this design, the time for the pulse to leave White Sands and return requires two round trips between on and near Earth and GEO, which is about 540 ms. An additional round trip is required to uplink T_4.

While this example shows time transfer from Earth to a satellite using a two-way transfer, it is also possible to use a one-way transfer if the light time is known from other means. For instance, time transfer to the Moon is possible using a TWSTFT signal in which the light time is determined by laser pulse and Moon retroreflector and transmitted as data in the signal.

An experiment similar to the Space Shuttle was reported in Feltham, Gonzalez, and Puech [7]. It used a pair of cesium clocks and a hydrogen maser onboard the International Space Station (ISS). In the low-gravity environment, the clocks have stabilities on the order of 10^{-16}. The experiment used modulated laser pulses and existing laser stations on Earth. Modulated laser pulses were sent to the ISS, where a set of retroreflectors returned them to Earth. The pulses were also captured at the ISS and used to latch a counter. The transmit and receive times were recorded on Earth and exchanged by microwave data link. The Earth clock and ISS clock were compared using the same means as the Space Shuttle experiment, with claimed results to the level of 50 ps.

18.3 Time Transfer to the Moon and Satellites of Other Planets

A good deal has been written about navigation, communication, and time transfer to planetary systems, including the Moon and its satellites [8], Mars and its satellites [9,10], and deep space [2,11]. In general, there is a clear distinction between vehicles with navigation as the primary purpose and other vehicles with the primary purpose of science data collection and data relay. Navigation vehicles need to precisely measure range and range rate to determine state vectors for other vehicles. For this purpose, they need ultrastable oscillators (USOs) in the 10^{-12} class, which are frightfully expensive. While these vehicles do not need precise time transfer from a coordinated timescale such as J2000, it is natural to embed a time transfer capability in the navigation signal, as described in Section 18.6. In other vehicles not intended for precise navigation, time transfer can be embedded in the communications protocols such as Proximity-1 and NTP. However, while Proximity-1 ultra–high frequencies (UHF) are available for the Moon and other planetary systems, they are not available for Earth-Moon missions as they are allocated for other purposes on Earth.

We first consider time transfer to satellites of the Moon, which might involve a space fleet of communication, navigation, and science vehicles. A scenario for developing a lunar navigation and communications network has been proposed in Guilford et al. [2]. It starts with a constellation of three polar orbiters approximately 120° apart, which would support lunar polar missions on a continuous basis, depending on the altitude of the orbit. These orbiters would need a navigation capability to locate landers, as well as navigation signals that enable landers to determine surface position and surface topography. Time transfer could be provided either using the Proximity-1 protocol, as described in Chapter 17, or by embedding a time tag in the ranging signal, as in the Space Shuttle experiment.

Polar orbiters would be in view of the DSN for at least half the orbit period. With three orbiters in a 2-h orbit, a lander near the poles will see a pass every 40 min, but it will last only 10 min or so. However, a three-orbiter polar constellation cannot support lunar missions at lower latitudes on a continuous basis. To do this, Guilford and coworkers [2] proposed a three-orbiter constellation of equatorial satellites again spaced 120° apart. In the evolved six-orbiter network, there would be frequent crosslink opportunities between the polar orbiters and equatorial orbiters. A constellation like this could be used for Mars and the other planets as well.

An orbiter with a 2-h period, for example, will see the same surface point twice each day, once on the ascending pass and once on the descending pass. However, each pass advances 30° from the last, so a surface point might not see more than two passes per day per orbiter. In any case, a pass is not likely to last very long—a few to 10 min at Mars, for example. A constellation involving Moon orbiters and landers is a special case as the Moon seen from Earth always shows the same face. As seen from a lunar polar orbiter, the Moon appears to rotate with a period of 27.3 days.

If multiple polar orbiters are deployed to improve the communications and navigation coverage, they might not be able to communicate with each other all the time. Some authors have proposed one or more equatorial orbiters at medium to high altitudes to provide a relay capability between orbiters and landers, especially on the far side of the Moon, which cannot be reached directly from Earth. Such a scenario is explored in the next section of this chapter.

Some authors have suggested a relay/navigation satellite placed at the L1 Lagrange point, that is, at the Earth–Moon barycenter located about 62,000 km from the Moon and about 322,000 km from Earth. As shown in Figure 18.5, there are five Lagrange points for the Earth–Moon system, with Earth at the center of the orbit. In fact, the geopotential at all five points is zero, so they are each at a barycenter. All but L4 and L5 (Trojans) are unstable, so the position must be actively managed using spacecraft propellants. While not

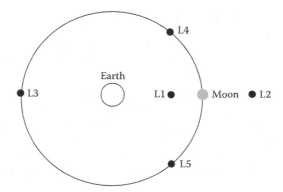

FIGURE 18.5
Lagrange points for the Earth–Moon system.

discussed in the available briefings, the L2, L4, and L5 points might be useful for relay between Earth and the far side of the Moon without using polar orbiters. An additional opportunity, a so-called halo orbit at the L1 point, is possible where the orbit plane is perpendicular to the line joining the Earth and Moon centers and the center of the orbit is at L1. A halo orbiter could be used to relay between Earth and L2 without occultation by the Moon.

Some authors have suggested using Earth orbit resources as a navigation and time transfer augmentation, including TDRS and GPS. There are problems perhaps not foreseen by the authors using these resources. First, the Earth satellite antennas are optimized for the Earth and Earth orbit communication, so they are useful only shortly before loss of signal (LOS) and shortly after acquisition of signal (AOS), as seen from the Moon. This issue is discussed in the next section. Second, the Earth-orbiting spacecraft antenna boresight and link budget is optimized for near-Earth communication and may not be sufficient for 300,000-km links to the Moon. To some extent, this can be mitigated by a high-gain antenna at L1. If so, time transfer to L1 might be possible using TDRS and the method described previously. It might also be possible to use GPS in a similar manner, but only at times when the link budget permits, which might not result in continuous operation.

18.4 Time Transfer for a Planetary Space Fleet

This section discusses scenarios for time transfer from one spacecraft to another, perhaps on or near Mars using the PITS (Proximity-1 Interleaved Time Service) protocol described in Section 17.9. The primary interest is on how and when the spacecraft can communicate with each other to exchange data packets. While the scenario is applicable for the Mars space fleet, the methods could be extended to any planetary space fleet supporting a communications protocol similar to PITS.

In mid-2009, NASA and the European Space Agency (ESA) had a number of orbiters and landers in the vicinity of Mars, including three orbiters: Mars Express (MEX), Mars Reconnaissance Orbiter (MRO), and Odyssey (ODY). At present, there are two Mars rovers (MER), *Opportunity* and *Spirit*, but these might not live much longer. The recent *Phoenix* lander (PHY) died of frostbite in the Martian winter. The Mars Science Laboratory (MSL) rover is planned for launch in 2011. All but PHY and MSL can communicate at X band directly to Earth via the DSN but only at very low data rates. In addition, the Mars vehicles can communicate with each other using UHF transceivers with the Proximity-1 protocol.

This section contains a strawman proposal that could be used with any planetary body, including Earth, the Moon, and Mars. It involves a scheduling algorithm that utilizes available communications crosslink opportunities between the vehicles. The scheduling algorithm can be implemented in a flexible manner with some components on Earth and some others on space vehicles. It can evolve by gradually moving some components from Earth to the space vehicles, retaining Earth components for backup. Eventually, the vehicles would be able to determine the pass opportunities and transfer time and data from one vehicle to another, possibly via a third or even a fourth vehicle. It is understood that this can become rather intricate as the vehicles move in different orbits, and crosslink opportunities may conflict.

To determine the feasibility of such an approach, an experiment has been implemented to simulate a projected Mars space fleet using a constellation of satellites orbiting Earth. The reason for using Earth rather than Mars for this simulation is that Earth satellite orbit data are readily available but not Mars satellite orbit data. The experiment involves six Earth orbiters, including the Moon, and one Earth lander (see Table 18.1). This constellation was chosen to explore the forwarding delays and throughput of the various crosslinks between the vehicles. Vehicles 2 and 5 are typical satellites at LEO

TABLE 18.1

Earth-Orbiting Spacecraft

Spacetrack Name	Altitude (km)	Incline (°)	Eccentricity	Period (h)	Rate (µs/d)	Variation (µs)
OSCAR 40	800–58,000	7.9	0.79	19.11	15.8	4.2
AMSAT ECHO	800	98.1	0.008	1.67	80.6	0.019
NAVSTAR 62	20,000	55.3	0.002	11.97	21.6	0.007
INTELSAT 1002	36,000	0.0	0.0002	23.93	13.6	0.001
NOAA 18	870	98.0	0.001	1.70	79.5	0.002
Moon	392,719	25.6	0.049	655.7	1.4	0.65
W3HCF	Surface	39.7N 75.8W	0	24	60.1	0

but seldom, if ever, see each other. Vehicle 3 is a GPS satellite at MEO, while vehicle 4 is an INTELSAT communications satellite at GEO. Vehicle 5 is the Moon, while Vehicle 6 is on the surface in Newark, Delaware. The interesting case is vehicle 1, which has a highly eccentric orbit with apogee beyond GEO. This satellite spends most of its time loitering near apogee and zips around Earth near perigee. While not used in the simulator, the rate column shows the secular rate of the proper clock due to relativistic effects, and the variation column indicates the deviation along the orbit. From these data, only the OSCAR 40 satellite would justify nonsecular corrections described in Section 17.4.

The simulator itself uses a software library available from JPL called the SPICE Toolkit (available from http://naif.jpl.nasa.gov/naif/toolkit.html). It includes an extensive set of routines to perform vector calculus, time metrology, geometric transformations, and state vector processing. The library is used by JPL mission planners and scientific investigators from several institutions. In the simulation experiment described in this section, the planetary orbits of all seven vehicles were explored over a period of 2 days.

The simulator first initializes all six orbiters using the Keplerian elements from the NORAD (North American Air Defense Command) Spacetrack database (available from http://www.space-track.org), which catalogs radar tracking data for almost all objects in Earth orbit. This establishes the initial state vector for each vehicle at a given time. Subsequently, at intervals of 1 min, the state vector for each vehicle is updated by integrating along the orbit. Next, a pass list is constructed that shows each pass when one vehicle can see another, that is, only if the ray path is not occulted by Earth or by components on the spacecraft itself, as shown in Figure 18.6. Note that the spacecraft antennas always point directly to Earth, so a crosslink is possible

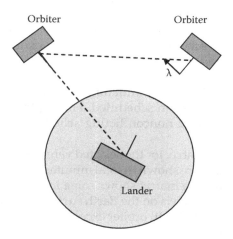

FIGURE 18.6
Space vehicle crosstrack geometry.

only if the nadir angle λ is less than 90°. A pass list entry includes the send vehicle number, receive vehicle number, pass begin time, and pass duration. For the set of seven vehicles selected, the simulator found 986 passes during the simulation run of about 2 days.

Reasonable assumptions are that each vehicle has a single full-duplex transceiver, and that each receiver operates at a different frequency. Thus, the transmitters must be tuned to the particular receiver frequency for each pass. Even with this assumption, it is quite likely that on some passes two transmitters might target the same receiver, causing collisions. Thus, some sort of discipline is required.

Periodically, perhaps during a pass between two vehicles and without obstructing science data or telemetry, the current state vector and coordinate time for each vehicle are exchanged over the space link. The receiver determines its current state vector and coordinate time, then runs the iterated procedure described in Section 17.4 to obtain the coordinate clock offset and round-trip delay, although the delay might not be useful other than to adjust the state vectors in response to orbit perturbations.

In a typical simulation run, pass durations vary from a few minutes to almost 6 h. Passes less than 10 min are discarded as the time to acquire and lock on the signals can be significant. The most valuable passes are the longest, so for each pass the simulator assigns a score equal to the pass duration in seconds. It then scans the pass list for all other passes to see if one or more collide, that is, overlap on the same frequency, and if so, saves the collided pass on a knockout list. At the same time, it subtracts the duration of the collided pass from the score. The resulting data structure, including the pass list along with the knockout lists for each pass, can become moderately large.

Next, the simulator enters a scheduling loop looking for the pass with the highest score that has not yet been scheduled and has an overlapping reciprocal pass so that full-duplex operation is possible. It then scans the knockout lists for all scheduled passes. If a knockout is found, the new pass is marked as disabled. If no knockout is found, the pass is scheduled. In this case, the simulator scans the knockout list and disables all other passes on the list. The simulator continues in this way until all nondisabled passes have been scheduled. Finally, the disabled passes are removed, leaving the final nonconflicting schedule of 142 passes during the simulation run.

The aggregate traffic matrix for the selected vehicles is shown in Table 18.2, in which pass durations are shown in total minutes for all passes between the vehicles in the matrix. The matrix shows some interesting results. Vehicle 3 (Moon) sees Vehicle 7, which is on the Earth surface, over 10 h a day, which is not surprising, but sees no Earth orbiter except vehicle 1, which is in a highly eccentric, near-equatorial orbit. This reinforces the conjecture in Section 17.3 that Earth orbiters might make poor relays to the Moon. Vehicles 3 and 5 never see each other; the same is true for vehicles 1 and 3, 2 and 6, and 4

TABLE 18.2

Crosslink Traffic Matrix

Vehicle	1	2	3	4	5	6	7
1	0	164	0	22	507	23	126
2	164	0	117	251	433	0	0
3	0	118	0	397	0	0	698
4	22	249	397	0	119	0	0
5	508	430	0	120	0	200	22
6	23	0	0	0	201	0	602
7	125	0	698	0	22	602	0

TABLE 18.3

Crosslink Incidence Matrix

Vehicle	1	2	3	4	5	6	7
1	0	6	0	1	17	1	1
2	6	0	7	9	12	0	0
3	0	7	0	1	0	0	2
4	1	9	1	0	5	0	0
5	17	12	0	5	0	6	2
6	1	0	0	0	6	0	1
7	1	0	2	0	2	1	0

and 6. Obviously, if the space fleet is to enjoy total connectivity, some vehicles will have to relay for others. This might even be worse at the Moon or Mars. Table 18.3 shows the aggregate incidence matrix, which tallies the number of passes between one spacecraft and another over the 2-day period. Some spacecraft see each other for only one pass per day, but that pass is quite long. Others see each other several times per day, but the pass is relatively short. However, as the minimum pass duration is 10 min, the five-packet exchange required by the interleaved symmetric protocol of Section 16.3 and the iterated algorithm of Section 17.4, each pass is guaranteed to produce a valid clock comparison.

Recall that the intended scenario is for the DSN to upload time and state vectors to one or more of the space vehicles and have them distribute the data to the others directly or via relay. The next step for the simulator is to construct a spanning tree so that when data arrive at a vehicle, it knows when and where to relay it. This can be a messy problem as it depends on whether to optimize for maximum throughput over a given period or whether to minimize the time to deliver to all vehicles. For this preliminary study, we chose the latter.

The simulator next does a recursive, breadth-first search of the pass list, which at this point is interpreted as a tree, in which each entry identifies the source and destination vehicles. In general, there will be two entries on the list, one for each of the reciprocal directions, and this makes the algorithm much more interesting. The algorithm is in fact a variant of the Dijkstra routing algorithm often used in computer networks.

An important feature of the pass list is that the entries are in order of the begin time. The algorithm starts by scanning the pass list for the first entry with source matching a vehicle selected as the target of a DSN upload. It then executes an embedded recursive algorithm to construct a shortest-path spanning tree with this pass as root. The embedded algorithm first creates a node on the tree, then scans the pass list starting at the given time for entries with the given vehicle as the source but skips passes that overlap the given pass or where the source and destination match the given pass as these must always be later. If none is found, the embedded algorithm recurses to add the new node and construct the shortest-path spanning tree from that point. The algorithm terminates when no new nodes are found, and the spanning tree is complete. Table 18.4 shows a typical spanning tree. Starting at minute 0 of the day, the data have arrived at all nodes by minute 855. All but nodes 1 and 6 can be reached in two hops or less; node 1 is reached via the path $4 \rightarrow 3 \rightarrow 2 \rightarrow 1$ by minute 996, but the Moon has to wait almost a day later.

Running this program is not trivial; the unoptimized simulation here took 41 s on a Sun Blade 1500, but it only has to be done once a day or so. These are several ways this might be implemented for the Mars fleet, depending on how much of the burden is assigned to Earth and how much is assigned to Mars vehicles. At one extreme, all the burden could be assigned to Earth and only the spanning tree uploaded to a Mars vehicle that would distribute it one hop at a time. At the other extreme, state vectors could be determined via the DSN and uploaded to a Mars vehicle, which would propagate the state vectors, construct the pass list and spanning tree, then forward it to the remaining vehicles.

There are other practical issues, like how things get started, how possible disruptions are found and repaired, and how the time transfer scheduling functions can be integrated with the science data relay functions in a comprehensive way.

TABLE 18.4

Shortest Path Spanning Tree Schedule

Pass	Begin (m)	Duration (m)	Score
$4 \rightarrow 3$	0	397	8,820
$3 \rightarrow 2$	420	39	−180
$3 \rightarrow 7$	514	349	20,940
$2 \rightarrow 1$	749	11	−71,760
$4 \rightarrow 5$	996	38	540
$1 \rightarrow 6$	2,411	23	1,380

18.5 Time Transfer for Deep-Space Missions

This section discusses scenarios for time transfer from Earth to planetary and deep-space missions by piggybacking the time transfer function on the navigation function. NASA has compiled a list of radiometric measurement requirements for various space missions. Some highlights are summarized in Table 18.5 (from Nelson et al. [12]). Current DSN navigation functions use radiometric signals that can provide range measurements to the low nanoseconds. Since the SNR is low, on the order of less than 0 dB, this requires great ingenuity in signal design and processing methods. With the methods discussed in this and the next section, it should be possible to discipline the spacecraft clock within 100 ns, which is about 10 times better than the methods described in Chapter 17. The same methods can be used for an orbiter to navigate relative to another orbiter or lander, but the SNR is typically much higher, enabling methods such as the TWSTFT-modulated PR codes to be practical. However, an important point to make here is that the goal is not to navigate the spacecraft but to set its logical clock to coordinate time.

In general, radiometric means are used to determine range and range rate for an orbiter relative to a DSN station, and this is used to establish a state vector relative to an inertial frame such as J2000. Using the Electra transceiver, an orbiter can measure the range and range rate (Doppler) of another vehicle and report these data to Earth, where the vehicle state vector is determined. Once the state vectors are available, the time can be transferred using iterated methods similar to those of Section 17.4. Using ordinary telemetry and spacecraft bus designs, time transfer accuracies should meet the current requirements for better than 1 ms. However, with a little more effort, it should be possible to achieve accuracies to the order of 100 ns. To explore this issue further, it is necessary to go into more detail about how the DSN navigation function operates, how ranging codes are designed and used, and how the correlation function is performed.

TABLE 18.5

Navigation Requirements for Space Missions

Function	3-D Position	ΔT
Nonprecision landing	5 km	15 μs
Docking and berthing, in-space servicing	1 km	3 μs
Constellations	100 m (absolute)	300 ns
Relay spacecraft	10–100 m	<300 ns
Surface operations (navigation)	30 m	100 ns
Surface operations	30 m	100 ns
Surface rendezvous, landing, ascent	10 m	30 ns
Formation flying	3 cm to 10 m (relative)	<30 ns

There are three DSN complexes: Goldstone, California; Canberra, Australia; and Madrid, Spain. They provide continuous coverage for deep-space missions. Each station includes a farm of huge antennas capable of precise orientation, high-power transmitters, and low-noise receivers. In addition, each station is equipped with an extraordinarily stable master clock traceable to UTC. At the present state of the art, navigation and time transfer functions are performed using several RF bands allocated by the International Telecommunication Union Radiocommunication Sector (ITU-R). In the future, this might be done using optical frequencies [13]. Table 18.6 shows the frequency bands allocated for space communication. The UHF band is used with Proximity-1 space links in the vicinity of Mars, while the S band is typically used in the vicinity of Earth. Most deep-space navigation, telemetry, and science data transport use X band. Recent missions have experimented at Ka band as the antenna gains are higher, and the available bandwidth is larger.

Past and present DSN navigation operations provide precise range and range rate measurements for each spacecraft separately. Past DSN missions performed these functions using a sequence of tone subcarriers transmitted along with the telemetry subcarrier on the same RF carrier [14]. Current DSN missions use a PR code and correlators similar to the TWSTFT method. A comparison between the past and present operations is given in Berner and Bryant [15]. The general technique is described in great detail in Thornton and Border [16]. It is important in the following discussion to note that the DSN transmitter carrier frequency is derived from the extremely stable station clock, and that all ranging and telemetry signals are coherent with the carrier frequency. The spacecraft locks on the uplink carrier frequency and synthesizes a coherent downlink carrier frequency at a defined ratio. In principle, this allows precise measurement of range to within a fraction of a carrier cycle, which is about 10 mm at Ka band.

The navigation function is typically performed using X-band uplinks modulated with a command subcarrier at 128 kb/s and a ranging subcarrier at some fraction of the RF carrier frequency, typically in the range 250–1,000 kHz. Both subcarriers are phase modulated on the RF carrier with the ranging subcarrier modulation index on the order of 0.2 rad, which leaves most of the signal power for uplink telemetry. In this design, the navigation and telemetry functions are simultaneous and noninterfering with each other.

TABLE 18.6

Space Communication Frequency Bands

	Band (MHz)	Uplink (MHz)	Downlink (MHz)	Downlink Ratio
UHF	15	435–450	390–405	Not used
S	10	2,110–2,120	2,290–2,300	221/240
X	50	7,145–7,190	8,400–8,450	749/880
Ka	500	34,200–34,700	31,800–32,300	3,557/3,344

Tracking by one station alone can be done in noncoherent or coherent mode, but for satellites in deep space with round-trip light times of many hours, coherent handover mode is required. In this mode, the next DSN station locks to the downlink carrier resulting from the previous station uplink and synthesizes its own uplink carrier from this signal. In this case, the navigation and telecommand functions can be continued for many hours as the orbit and state vector are refined.

A block diagram of a typical spacecraft transceiver is shown in Figure 18.7. The diplexor allows the transmitter and receiver to share the same antenna. The low-noise amplifier (LNA), single-sideband (SSB) mixer, and numeric-controlled oscillator (NCO1) downconverter translate the RF signal at frequency f_u to an IF at about 70 MHz. This signal is filtered and converted to digital form as in the Electra transceiver described in Section 17.8. The carrier tracking loop, loop filter, and NCO1 form a phase-lock loop that tracks the RF carrier phase and frequency (Doppler). The upconverter oscillator (NCO2) RF frequency is synthesized from the NCO1 at the required ratio shown in Table 18.6. The IF signal is translated to the downlink frequency f_d for the power amplifier (PA).

At the spacecraft, the uplink signal can be processed in either of two ways. In the *turnaround* mode shown in Figure 18.7, the uplink IF ranging subcarrier is demodulated, filtered, and remodulated on the downlink IF carrier. It is the presumed intent that the uplink telemetry subcarrier is demodulated, filtered out, and replaced by the downlink telemetry subcarrier, but there is some ambiguity about this in the available documents. In the *regenerative* mode shown in Figure 18.8, the ranging subcarrier is demodulated and the symbol timing and ranging code recovered. This signal then modulates the downlink ranging subcarrier, thus avoiding the noise received in the uplink passband. In either mode, the downlink signal

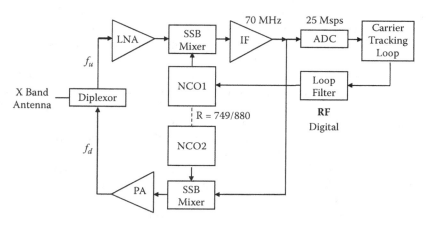

FIGURE 18.7
Turnaround ranging. ADC, analog-to-digital converter.

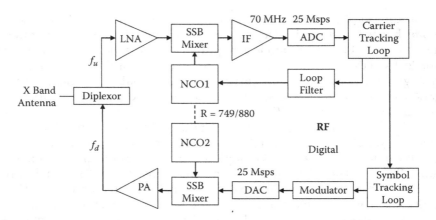

FIGURE 18.8
Regenerative ranging. ADC, analog-to-digital converter; DAC, digital-to-analog converter.

is received on Earth, and the subcarriers are individually demodulated and processed.

The DSN determines the range using the ranging subcarrier PR code and the range rate using the downlink carrier tracking loop and NCO frequency. However, the DSN range baseline can be much longer than the PR code length. While the longer baseline could be handled using a longer PR code, this would create problems in the correlation process to recover the PR code phase [17]. This point needs to be emphasized as it is the key to providing precision time transfer to vehicles served by the DSN. Note that the TWSTFT ranging signal design uses repeated PR codes of 4,095 chips and resolves the range ambiguity by modulating the code. A correlator as in the USNO modem can cope with this using a fast DSP processor; however, the DSN PR code needs a correlator with over a million chips. The way the DSN design copes with this issue is important, not only with respect to the existing time transfer method but also for understanding the method suggested in the next section.

While there are techniques that can reduce the correlator hardware requirements, including methods based on the fast Fourier transform (FFT) [18] and fast Walsh transform (FWT) [19], even these techniques are not practical for a million-chip correlator. A key design consideration described in Bryant [14] is the use of a technique that accumulates multiple cycles of the entire PR code to improve the SNR, then correlates it using a fast DSP processor. This allows a robust correlation of the ranging phase at leisurely rates compared to the chip rate. However, this makes it difficult to embed additional information by modulating the ranging signal, as in the TWSTFT method.

The DSN ranging equipment uses a clever combination of relatively short PR codes of varying lengths that can be reprogrammed for different missions. The code generator and correlator design provides much flexibility

TABLE 18.7

DSN Ranging Codes

Name	Length	Binary Code Sequence
C_1	2	1 0
C_2	7	1 1 1 0 0 1 0
C_3	11	1 1 1 0 0 0 1 0 1 1 0
C_4	15	1 1 1 1 0 0 0 1 0 0 1 1 0 1 0
C_5	19	1 1 1 1 0 1 0 1 0 0 0 0 1 1 0 1 1 0 0
C_6	23	1 1 1 1 1 0 1 0 1 1 0 0 1 1 0 0 1 0 1 0 0 0 0

in the number of codes and the design of each code. A number of "good" codes are given in Berner and Bryant [15]; Table 18.7 shows the six codes used in combination for the DSN regenerative ranging signal. Note that in these codes the number of ones is one more than the number of zeros, and that the coefficients are chosen to have a good autocorrelation function for each code and low cross-correlation functions between different codes. Since the length of each code contains no factor common to any of the others, there is no common divisor, and the composite ranging signal has length equal to the product of the PR code lengths, which in this case is 1,009,470 chips. Using a ranging clock rate near 1 MHz, this results in a range ambiguity of about 75,000 km. The ambiguity has to be resolved by other means.

The PR codes are used in a rather interesting way. First, each code is repeated as necessary for the full composite signal period. This results in six bit strings of length equal to the product of the code lengths. Then, for i from 0 to 1,009,469 bits, each bit $C(i)$ of the composite signal is

$$C(i) = C_1(i) \oplus (C_2(i) \cap C_3(i) \cap C_4(i) \cap C_5(i) \cap C_6(i)). \tag{18.1}$$

The resulting signal has a strong spectral component at half the chip frequency, as it is dominated by the C_1 component, which alternates ones and zeros. The remaining codes cause occasional phase flips at a rate about 4.6 percent of the ranging clock rate.

The downlink signal is processed by massive I and Q integrators, one for each chip of the composite code. The DSP processes six integrators in parallel, one for each PR code in Table 18.7. In effect, each integrator is a massive comb filter. Each integrator is processed at relatively low rates by a correlator implemented in a DSP chip. Eventually, after possibly long periods of integration, each correlator will produce a pulse at regular intervals depending on the code length. When all six correlators produce a pulse at the same time, the epoch of the ranging signal has been established.

While not explicit in the available documentation, the DSN calculates the time at the spacecraft and, after accounting for the space link delay and spacecraft motion, sends the time to the spacecraft in a command message in the same or a subsequent pass. Unfortunately, this method does not provide precision time transfer to the spacecraft as the time command sent over the 1553 telemetry bus is precise only to 0.5 ms. Possible remedies for this are discussed in the next section.

18.6 Parting Shots

Precision time transfer from Earth to a spacecraft could in principle be done by modulating the uplink ranging signal, as in the TWSTFT method described in Section 18.1, but this is not practical given the very low SNR and the very long integration times required. On the other hand, time transfer could be done using a technique similar to the Space Shuttle demonstration described in Section 18.2. In this technique, the spacecraft records its clock at the epoch of a ranging signal transmitted from Earth. Later, it receives the time of signal arrival as computed on Earth and adjusts the clock by the difference. The problem with this method is that it takes two uplink and one downlink passes to complete and this could take over a day for deep-space missions.

On Earth, the epoch of the ranging signal received from the spacecraft is determined using an awesome bank of integrators and correlators. In principle, the spacecraft could use the same technique, but this is hugely expensive in complexity, computing cycles, and power. However, in the regenerative ranging mode, the ranging signal is demodulated and the symbol clock recovered. The baseband signal can be used by a bank of relatively simple digital correlators and accumulators to determine the ranging signal epoch at the spacecraft. In the design suggested in Figure 18.9, there is a correlator

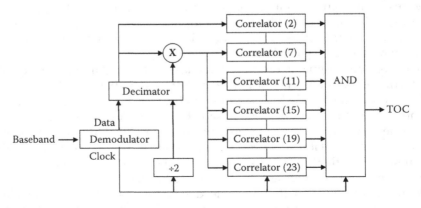

FIGURE 18.9
Ranging signal correlators.

for each of the six ranging codes shown in Table 18.7. Each correlator contains an accumulator for each chip of each code and produces a pulse at the time of the maximum accumulator value. The time of coincidence (TOC) when all six pulses fire at the same time establishes the ranging signal epoch. Note the divide-by-two counter, which is to partially despread the raw baseband signal. The reason for this is explained in this section.

The key component in this design is the decimator. In effect, it throws away 16 of the last 17 bits and keeps only the last. The reason this works is the massive coding gain possible with the DSN ranging codes. For this to work properly, the decimation factor must be relatively prime to the code lengths, and 17 is the smallest such factor. However, this also means that 17 TOC intervals are required to determine one coincidence.

Figure 18.10 shows the operations for each of the six correlators. For a correlator of N bits, the shift and coefficient registers have N bits, and there are N accumulators, one for each bit. At the in-phase sample time, the data bit overwrites the shift register at bit position j. Then, the coefficient vector at bit position k is multiplied by the shift register at bit position $j + k$ mod N and added to the accumulator at index j. Operation continues for k from 0 to $N - 1$. The multiplication operation is implemented as an exclusive OR gate followed by an inverter. The output pulse fires at the index of the accumulator with the maximum value. The TOC pulse fires when all six pulses fire at the same time.

This design provides a huge amount of integration over the 17-TOC coincidence interval; however, the integration can be continued for more coincidence intervals as necessary. Even the longest 23-chip code repeats over 43,000 times over one TOC interval, so the design should tolerate a modest error rate. The current DSN ranging infrastructure is expected to operate with SNR as low as –10 dB [14], which with binary phase-shift keying (BPSK) modulation yields an error rate of 0.327. Tests in simulation at this error rate showed the design operates reliably even without integrating more than one 17-TOC coincidence.

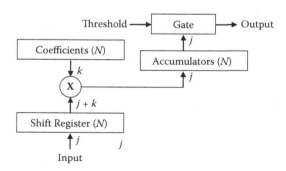

FIGURE 18.10
Correlator and accumulator.

The most obvious implementation of this method is using a commodity DSP chip, which should have no trouble keeping up with the correlator operations. With a 16-bit integer-only DSP chip such as the Texas Instruments TMS320C54X and a 16-bit FIFO, the word rate is about 3.7 kHz, which is a chip shot for any modern DSP. The chip could be implemented as a bus peripheral for the spacecraft computer and the TOC pulse used to cause a spacecraft computer interrupt. The design will need a way to flag the PPS pulse from the spacecraft clock NCO and record in the sample stream. The DSP program can use this to compensate for the delay in processing.

A crude implementation in C running on an older computer ran at about 750 kb/s, and each generated bit requires a call to the Unix random() function to simulate a bit error. The exercise turned up a couple of "gotchas." First, the ranging signal subcarrier component C_1 must be removed before correlation of the longer codes. As shown in Figure 18.9, this is done using the symbol clock, a divide-by-two counter, and an exclusive OR gate. Second, the resulting data stream has a high proportion of zeros, and this causes integrator sag, especially with the shorter codes. This is fixed simply by increasing the amplitude of positive correlations by a compromise factor of 1.3.

There are two sources of ambiguity that must be resolved in this design. The first is the phase of the divide-by-two counter. If the wrong phase, a coincidence of the five longer codes will never coincide with the C_1 code, and the device will never find a TOC. In this case, a time-out can be used to flip the counter phase. The second ambiguity is due to the inherent ambiguity of the BPSK modulation. If the subcarrier phase is inverted, a TOC will be found, but the integrator amplitudes will be much smaller than in the upright phase. In this case, a subcarrier phase flip will restore correct operation.

The spacecraft clock can be disciplined in several ways, the most natural of which is to calculate the coordinate time at which a particular TOC is to arrive at the spacecraft and embed it in the telemetry stream. The time of arrival can be determined using the iterated procedure of Section 17.4. Since the ranging subcarrier and telemetry subcarrier are modulated on the same RF carrier, this should be readily possible.

For this design to work properly, there must be some way to determine the time of each TOC in proper time on Earth and convert to coordinate time in the J2000 frame. But, since there is no need to synchronize the ranging signal TOC to UTC or any other timescale, the DSN ranging equipment probably has no hardware to do this. Note that the TOC interval is not precisely 1 s long, so the TOC interval precesses over the second relative to the DSN station clock. A time of coincidence between the TOC and the actual second occurs every 100,947 s or somewhat over 1 day.

A technique borrowed from LORAN-C can be used to establish the proper time of each TOC. This may require a minor amount of additional hardware in the DSN ranging equipment. When a coincidence is detected, it causes a computer interrupt. The computer records the UTC second from the station clock and provides it to the time transfer function. Then, the proper time of each TOC is equal to the number of proper seconds since coincidence times 9,470 in microseconds. Time transfer from Earth to a satellite can be done in the following steps:

1. Read the station clock and determine the time of the next TOC in J2000 coordinates.
2. Using the iterated procedure of Section 17.4, determine the time of arrival at the spacecraft.
3. Propagate the DSN antenna state vector to this time. This accounts for the motion due to Earth rotation and orbit revolution.
4. Insert this time in the telemetry stream.

As a final comment, this device could in fact be a key component in an autonomous navigation system, although in this application it might operate with different codes at lower rates commensurate with typical Proximity-1 space data links. From the available documentation, the Electra radio can turn the carrier around to measure the range rate but has no capability to generate or use a ranging signal to accurately measure range other than the Proximity-1 protocol described in Section 17.6. It was mentioned in briefings that the Electra FPGA was being reprogrammed to support quaternary phase-shift keying (QPSK) in addition to BPSK. This adds a quadrature channel that could in principle be used for a ranging signal similar to the DSN ranging signal. The ranging signal would be transmitted at the same rate as the data and used in the same way as described. Using the DSN ranging codes in this way would result in coincidence intervals of about 2 min. Since the SNR on Proximity-1 links is usually much higher than on DSN links and the round-trip light time is very much smaller, it is likely that shorter, more efficient PR codes could be devised.

References

1. Started, P.A., et al. Confluence of navigation, communication, and control in distributed spacecraft systems. *Proc. IEEE 2002 Aerospace Electron. Syst. Mag. 17, 5* (May 2002), 26–32.
2. Guilford, A., et al. Time dissemination alternatives for future NASA. *Proceedings 38th Precise Time and Time Interval Application and Planning Meeting* (December 2006), 319–328.
3. Hanson, D.W. Fundamentals of two-way time transfer by satellite. *Proceedings 43rd Annual Symposium on Frequency Control* (May 1989), 174–178.
4. Landis, P., and I. Galysh. NRL/USNO two-way time transfer modem design and test results. *Proceedings IEEE Frequency Control Symposium* (May 1992), 317–326.

5. Kirchner, D. Two-way time transfer via communication satellites. *Proc. IEEE 79*, 7 (July 1991), 983–990.

6. Chi, A.R. Satellite time transfer via TDRSS and applications. *Proceedings 11th Precise Time and Time Interval Application and Planning Meeting* (December 1979), 45–64.

7. Feltham, S., F. Gonzalez, and P. Puech. ACES: A time and frequency mission for the International Space Station. *Proceedings 1999 Joint Meeting EFTF-IEEE IFCS* (1999), 148–151.

8. Started, P.A., et al. A scalable small-spacecraft navigation and communication infrastructure for lunar operations. *Proceedings IEEE 2005 Aerospace Conference* (March 2005), 5–12, 595–600.

9. Edwards, C.D., et al. A Martian telecommunications network: UHF relay support of the Mars Exploration Rovers by the Mars Global Surveyor, Mars Odyssey, and Mars Express Orbiters. *Proceedings 55th International Astronautical Congress* (October 2004).

10. Edwards, C.D. Relay communications strategies for Mars exploration through 2020. *Acta Astronautica 59, 1–5* (July–September 2006), 3.

11. Miller, J., et al. NASA architecture for Solar System time distribution. *Proceedings IEEE 2007 Frequency Control Symposium* (May 2007), 1299–1303.

12. Nelson, R.A., et al. *Key Issues for Navigation and Time Dissemination in NASA's Space Exploration Program.* NASA Technical Memorandum 2006-214425, October 2006.

13. Martin-Mur, T.J., et al. *The JPL Roadmap for Deep Space Navigation.* JPL Technical Report 06-0150, AAS/AIAA SpaceFlight Mechanics Meeting, January 2006.

14. Bryant, S. Using digital signal processor technology to simplify deep space ranging. *Proceedings IEEE Aerospace Conference, Vol. 3* (March 2001), 1277–1282.

15. Berner, J.B., and S.H. Bryant. Operations comparison of deep space ranging types: Sequential tone vs. pseudo-noise. *Proceedings 2002 IEEE Aerospace Conference* (March 2002).

16. Thornton, C.L., and J.S. Border. *Radiometric Tracking Techniques for Deep-Space Navigation.* JPL Deep-Space Communications and Navigation Series, January 2005.

17. Kinman, P.W. Pseudo-noise and regenerative ranging. *Proceedings 54th International Astronautical Congress* (September 2003).

18. Kayani, J.K. A computationally efficient correlator for pseudo-random correlation systems. *Proceedings IEEE Sixth International Symposium on Spread Spectrum Techniques and Applications, 2* (September 2000), 675–680.

19. Budisin, S.Z. Fast PN sequence correlation by using FWT. *Proceedings IEEE 1989 Mediterranean Electrochemical Conference MELECON* (April 1989), 513–515.

19

Technical History of NTP

Beware the Jabberwock, my son!
The jaws that bite, the claws that catch!
Beware the Jubjub bird, and shun
The frumious Bandersnatch!

Lewis Carroll,
Through the Looking Glass

An argument can be made that the Network Time Protocol (NTP) is the longest running, continuously operating, distributed application in the Internet. As NTP is near the end of its third decade, it is of historic interest to document the origins and evolution of the architecture, protocol, and algorithms. Not incidentally, NTP was an active participant in the early development of Internet technology, and its timestamps recorded many milestones in measurement and prototyping programs.

This chapter* documents significant milestones in the evolution of computer network timekeeping technology over five generations of NTP to the present. It is intended to stand alone and does not require inhaling the technocracy of the other chapters. The NTP software distributions for Unix, Windows, and VMS have been maintained by a corps of over four dozen volunteers at various times. There are too many to list here, but the major contributors are revealed in the narrative to follow. The current NTP software distribution, documentation, and related materials and newsgroups and links are available on the Web at http://www.ntp.org. In addition, all my papers, articles, and reports cited here are in PostScript and PDF files at http://www.eecis.udel.edu/~mills. Further information, including executive summaries, project reports, and briefing slide presentations, are at the NTP project page http://www.eecis.udel.edu/~mills/ntp.html.

There are three main threads interwoven in this discussion. First is a history lesson on significant milestones for the NTP specifications, implementations, and coming-out parties. These milestones calibrate and are calibrated by developments elsewhere in the Internet community. Second is a chronology of the algorithmic refinements that led to better and better accuracy, stability, and security that continue to the present. These algorithms represent

---

* Some of the material in this chapter is drawn from Mills, D.L. *ACM Computer Communications Review, 33,* 2 (April 2003), 9–22 [1], which is not widely available. It is published here as a convenience for the reader.

the technical contributions as documented in the references. Third is a discussion of the various proof-of-performance demonstrations and surveys conducted over the years, each attempting to outdo the previous in calibrating the performance of NTP in the Internet of the epoch. Each of these three threads winds through the remainder of this narrative.

19.1 On the Antiquity of NTP

The roots of NTP can be traced to a demonstration at the National Computer Conference in 1979, believed to be the first public coming-out party of the Internet sending mail, speech, and facsimile messages over a trans-Atlantic satellite network. However, it was not until 1981 that the synchronization technology was documented in the now-historic Internet Engineering Note (IEN) series as IEN-173 [2]. The first specification of a public protocol developed from it appeared in Request for Comments (RFC) 778 [3]. The first deployment of the technology in a local network was as an integral function of the Hello routing protocol documented in RFC-891 [4], which survived for many years in a network prototyping and test-bed operating system called the Fuzzball [5].

NTP was not then and is not now the only synchronization scheme available on the Internet. Other mechanisms have been specified in the Internet Protocol (IP) suite to record and transmit the time at which an event takes place, including the Daytime [6] and Time [7] protocols and ICMP Timestamp [8] message defined as Internet standards, as well as the IP Timestamp option [9].

The Unix *timed*, which arrived in 1984 [10], was designed for use on a local Ethernet. It uses an election algorithm to designate a single host as master and the remaining hosts synchronized to it as slaves. The Digital Time Synchronization Service (DTSS) [11], which was adopted by the Enterprise community, uses a hierarchy of time providers, servers, and clerks similar to the NTP stratum model. A scheme with features similar to NTP is described in Paxson [12]. It is intended for multiserver local-area networks (LANs) in which each of a set of possibly many time servers determines its time offset relative to each of the other servers in the set using periodic timestamped messages, then determines the system clock correction using a fault-tolerant averaging algorithm. However, none of these schemes has crafted data-grooming and discipline algorithms as later developed for NTP.

What later became known as NTP Version 0 was implemented in 1985, both in Fuzzball by me and in Unix by Louis Mamakos and Michael Petry at the University of Maryland. Fragments of the Unix code survive in the software running today. RFC-958 contains the first formal specification of this version [13], but it did little more than document the NTP packet header and offset/delay calculations still used. Considering the modest speeds of networks and computers of the era, the nominal accuracy that could be achieved on an Ethernet was tens of milliseconds. Even on paths spanning the Atlantic, where the network jitter could spike over 1 s, the accuracy was generally better than 100 ms.

Version 1 of the NTP specification was documented 3 years later in RFC-1059 [14]. It contained the first comprehensive specification of the protocol and algorithms, including primitive versions of the clock filter, select, and discipline algorithms. The design of these algorithms was guided largely by a series of experiments, documented in RFC-956 [15], in which the basic theory of the clock filter algorithm was developed and refined. This was the first version that defined the use of client/server and symmetric modes and, of course, the first version to make use of the version field in the header.

A transactions article on NTP Version 1 (NTPv1) appeared in 1991 [16]. This was the first article that exposed the NTP model, including the architecture, protocol, and algorithms to the general engineering community. While this model is generally applicable today, there have been a continuing series of enhancements and new features introduced over the years, some of which are described in following sections.

The NTPv2 specification followed as RFC-1119 in 1989 [17]. A completely new implementation slavish to the specification was built by Dennis Fergusson at the University of Toronto. This was the first RFC in PostScript and as such the single most historically orthogonal document in the RFC publishing process. It was the first to include a formal model and state machine describing the protocol and pseudocode defining the operations. It introduced the NTP Control Message Protocol for use in managing NTP servers and clients and the cryptographic authentication scheme based on symmetric key cryptography, both of which survive to the present.

There was considerable discussion during 1989 about the newly announced DTSS. DTSS and NTP communities had much the same goals but somewhat different strategies for achieving them. One problem with DTSS, as viewed by the NTP community, was a possibly serious loss of accuracy since the DTSS design did not discipline the clock frequency.* The problem with the NTP design, as viewed by the DTSS community, was the lack of formal correctness principles in the design process. A key component in the DTSS design on which the correctness principles were based was an agreement algorithm invented by Keith Marzullo in his dissertation and described in Marzullo and Owicki [19].

In the finest Internet tradition of stealing good ideas, the Marzullo algorithm was integrated with the existing suite of NTP data-grooming algorithms, including the filter, cluster, and combine algorithms, which the DTSS design lacked. However, the Marzullo algorithm in its original form produced excessive jitter and seriously degraded timekeeping quality over typical Internet paths. The modified algorithm, now called the *select algorithm*, avoids this problem. The

---

* NTP is not the only scheme to discipline the frequency; this is done in the schemes described by Liao et al. [18] and Paxson [12], although the latter scheme does not operate in real time.

resulting suite of algorithms has survived substantially intact, although many modifications and improvements have been made over the years.

In 1992, the NTPv3 specification appeared as RFC-1305 [20], again in PostScript and now running some 113 pages. As the Internet Engineering Task Force (IETF) insisted on ASCII (American Standard Code for Information Interchange), the official IETF source document is the Corel Ventura document source with brutalized equations. The finished document is typeset in PDF with snazzy figures, tables, and equations but has been the only IETF document ever produced in this form. The specification includes an appendix describing a formal error analysis and an intricate error budget, including all error contributions between the reference clock over intervening servers to the eventual client. This provided the basis to support maximum error and expected error statistics, which provide a reliable characterization of timekeeping quality as well as a reliable metric for selecting the best from among a population of rowdy servers. As in the NTPv2 specification, the model was described using a formal state machine and pseudocode. This version also introduced broadcast mode and included reference clock drivers in the state machine.

Lars Mathiesen at the University of Copenhagen carefully revised the NTPv2 implementation to comply with the NTPv3 specification. There was considerable give and take between the specification and implementation, and some changes were made in each to reach consensus, so that the implementation was aligned precisely with the specification. This was a major effort that lasted over a year, during which the specification and implementation converged to a consistent formal model.

In the years since the NTPv3 specification, NTP has evolved in various ways, adding new features and algorithm revisions while still preserving interoperability with older versions. Somewhere along the line, it became clear that a new version number was needed as the state machine and pseudocode had evolved somewhat from the NTPv3 specification, so it became NTPv4. The evolution process was begun with a number of white papers, including Mills and Thyagarajan [21] and Mills [22].

Subsequently, a simplified NTPv4 model was developed for the Simple Network Time Protocol Version 4 (SNTPv4) in RFC-4330 [23]. SNTP is compatible with NTP and specified for the IPv4, IPv6, and Open System Interconnection (OSI) protocol stacks.* However, SNTPv4 does not include the crafted mitigation and discipline algorithms. These algorithms are not necessary in an implementation intended solely for a personal computer (PC) client or a server synchronized to an external time source, such as a GPS receiver. SNTPv4 has appeared (with glorious forgivable protocol booboos) in Windows XP and is used in several stand-alone NTP servers integrated with GPS receivers.

---

* An implementation of NTP using the OSI protocol stack over X.25 is described by Crowcroft and Onions [24].

19.2 On the Proliferation of NTP around the Globe

There is a certain sense of the radio amateur in the deployment of NTP around the globe. Certainly, each new country found running NTP was a new notch in the belt. A particularly satisfying conquest was when the national standards laboratory of a new country lit up an NTP primary server connected directly to the national time and frequency ensemble. Internet timekeepers Judah Levine at the NIST and Richard Schmidt at the U.S. Naval Observatory (USNO) have deployed public NTP primary servers at several locations in the United States and overseas. Several other countries, including Canada, the United Kingdom, Germany, and Japan, have public Internet NTP servers connected to national time and frequency ensembles. There was a period when NTP was well lit in the United States and Europe but dark elsewhere in South America, Africa, and the Pacific Rim. Today, the Sun never sets or even gets close to the horizon on NTP. The most rapidly growing populations are in eastern Europe and South America, but the real prize is a new one found in Antarctica. Experience in global timekeeping is documented in Mills, Thyagarajan, and Huffman [25].

One of the real problems in fielding a large, complex software distribution is porting to idiosyncratic hardware and operating systems. There are now over two dozen ports of the distribution for just about every hardware platform running Unix, Windows, and VMS marketed over the last 20 years, some of them truly historic in their own terms. Various distributions have run on everything from embedded controllers to supercomputers, even watches, spacecraft, uninterruptable power sources (UPSs), and print servers. Maintaining the configuration scripts and patch library is a truly thankless job, and getting good at it may not be a career enhancer. Volunteer Harlan Stenn currently manages this process using modern autoconfigure tools. New versions are tested first in our research net DCnet, then in bigger sandboxes like CAIRN and 6BONE, and finally put up for public release at http://www.ntp.org. The bug stream arrives at bugs@ntp.org.

At this point, the history lesson is substantially complete. However, along the way several specific advancements need to be identified. The remaining sections of this chapter discuss a number of them in detail.

19.3 Autonomous Authentication

Some time around 1985, Project Athena at the Massachusetts Institute of Technology (MIT) was developing the Kerberos security model, which provides cryptographic authentication of users and services. Fundamental to the Kerberos design is the ticket used to access computer and network services. Tickets have a designated lifetime and must be securely revoked when their lifetime expires. Thus, all Kerberos facilities must have secure time synchronization services. While the NTP protocol contains specific provisions to deflect bogus packets and replays, these provisions are inadequate to deflect more sophisticated attacks, such as masquerade. To deflect such attacks, NTP packets can be authenticated using symmetric key cryptography with keyed message digests and private keys. The original scheme used the Digital Encryption Standard operating in cipher block chaining (DES-CBC) mode.

However, provision of DES-based source authentication created problems for the public software distribution. Due to the International Trade in Arms Regulations (ITAR) at the time, DES could not be included in NTP distributions exported outside the United States and Canada. Initially, the way to deal with this was to provide two versions of DES in the source code, one operating as an empty stub and the other with the algorithm but encrypted with DES and a secret key. The idea was that if a potential user could provide proof of residence, the key was revealed. Later, this awkward and cumbersome method was replaced by maintaining two distributions, one intended for domestic use and the other for export. Recipients were placed on their honor to fetch the politically correct version.

However, there was still the need to authenticate NTP packets in the export version. Louis Mamakos at the University of Maryland adapted the MD5 message digest algorithm for NTP. This algorithm is specifically designed for the same function as the DES-CBC algorithm but is free of ITAR restrictions. In NTPv4, the export distribution has been discontinued and the DES source code deleted. The message digest algorithm interface is compatible with the OpenSSL cryptographic library widely used in the Internet of today. Presumably, OpenSSL Blowfish-CBC or IDEA-CBC could be used according to fancy.

While symmetric key source authentication has worked well, it requires secret keys, which complicates key distribution and, especially for broadcast modes, is vulnerable to compromise. The IETF has defined several cryptographic algorithms and protocols, but these require a persistent state, which is not possible in some NTP modes. Some appreciation of the problems is apparent from the observation that secure timekeeping requires secure cryptographic media, but secure media require reliable lifetime enforcement [26]. The implied circularity applies to any secure time synchronization service, including NTP [27]. However, and with particular importance to NTP, public key cryptography requires considerable processor resources and can result in poor timekeeping quality.

These problems were addressed in NTPv4 with a new security model and protocol called Autokey [28], discussed in Chapter 9. Autokey uses a combination of public key cryptography and a pseudorandom keystream. Since public key cryptography hungers for large chunks of processor resources and can degrade timekeeping quality, the algorithms are used sparingly to sign and verify time values, while the much less expensive keystream is used to authenticate packets relative to the signed values. Furthermore, Autokey is completely self-configuring, so that servers and clients can be deployed and redeployed in an arbitrary topology and automatically exchange signed values without manual intervention.

19.4 Autonomous Configuration

It became clear as the NTP development continued that a most valuable enhancement would be the capability for a number of clients and servers to automatically configure and deploy in an NTP subnet delivering the best timekeeping quality while conserving processor and network resources. Not only would this avoid the tedious chore of engineering specific configuration files for each server and client but it would also provide a robust response and reconfiguration scheme should components of the subnet fail. The DTSS model described in Digital Time Service Functional Specification Version T.1.0.5 [11] goes a long way to achieve this goal but has serious deficiencies, notably the lack of cryptographic authentication.

In NTPv3, configuration files had to be constructed manually using information found in the lists of public servers at http://www.ntp.org, although some sites partially automated the process using crafted DNS (domain name system) records. If large numbers of clients are involved, such as in large corporations with hundreds and thousands of personal computers and workstations, the method of choice is broadcast mode, which was added in NTPv3, or IPv4 multicast mode and IPv6 broadcast mode, which were added in NTPv4.

However, in NTPv3 broadcast clients did not send to servers, so there was no way to calibrate and correct for the server-client propagation delay or a way to initialize the Autokey protocol and run the identity schemes. This is provided in NTPv4 by a protocol modification in which the client, once receiving the first broadcast packet, executes a volley of client/server exchanges to calibrate the delay and run the Autokey protocol, then reverts to listen-only mode.

In spite of the protocol modification, broadcast mode provides somewhat less accuracy than client/server mode since it does not track variations due to routing changes or network loads. In addition, it is not easily adapted for autonomous deployment. In NTPv4, two new automatic server configuration schemes were added: manycast and pool. These are described in Chapter 5. In manycast mode, a client sends to a broadcast address, and any server listening on this address responds with a unicast packet, which then mobilizes an association in the client. The client processes the unicast packets from a few to a dozen servers, then winnows the population down to three using the NTP mitigation algorithms.

The pool scheme relies on a crafted, hierarchical database with members consisting of DNS zones ending in pool.ntp. For instance, the query eu.pool.ntp returns servers in Europe, and the query de.us.pool.ntp returns servers in Delaware. A server queried in one of these zones returns a number of server addresses randomized over the zone. The client proceeds as in the manycast scheme to winnow the population.

19.5 Radios, We Have Radios

For as many years as NTP has ticked on this planet, the definitive source for public NTP servers in the Internet has been a set of public lists, one for primary servers and the other for secondary servers, maintained at http://www.ntp.org. Each server in these tables is operated as a public service and maintained by a volunteer staff. Primary servers have up to several hundred clients each, and a few multiple-server deployments operated by NIST and USNO have an estimated total of 25 million clients. A primary server requires a reference clock, usually a radio or satellite receiver or telephone modem. Following is a history lesson on the development and deployment of NTP primary servers in the Internet.

The first use of radios as a reference clock was in 1981 when a Heath WWV/H receiver was connected to a Fuzzball at COMSAT (Communications Satellite Corporation) Laboratories in Clarksburg, Maryland [3]. This machine provided time synchronization for Fuzzball LANs in the United States, United Kingdom, Norway, Germany, and Italy. These LANs were used in the DARPA (Defense Advanced Research Projects Agency) Atlantic Satellite program for satellite measurements and protocol development. Later, the LANs were used to watch the national power grids of the United States, United Kingdom, and Norway swish and sway over the heating and cooling seasons [29].

DARPA purchased four Spectracom WWVB receivers, which were hooked up to Fuzzballs at MIT Lincoln Laboratories, COMSAT Laboratories, USC (University of Southern California) Information Sciences Institute, and SRI (Stanford Research Institute) International. The radios were redeployed in 1986 in the National Science Foundation (NSF) Phase I backbone network, which used Fuzzball routers [30]. It is a tribute to the manufacturer that all four radios are serviceable today; two are in regular operation at the University of Delaware, a third serves as backup spare, and the fourth is in the Boston Computer Museum.

These four radios, together with the Heath WWV/H receiver at COMSAT Laboratories and a pair of TrueTime GOES (Geosynchronous Operational

Environmental Satellites) receivers at Ford Motor Headquarters and Digital Western Research Laboratories, provided primary time synchronization services throughout the ARPANET (Advanced Research Projects Agency Network), MILnet, and dozens of college campuses, research institutions, and military installations. By 1988, two Precision Standard Time WWV/H receivers joined the flock, but these and the Heath WWV/H receiver are no longer available. From the early 1990s, these nine primary servers were joined by an increasing number of volunteer radio-equipped servers, now numbered in the hundreds in the public Internet.

As the cost of GPS receivers plummeted from the stratosphere (the first one I bought cost $17,000), GPS receivers started popping up all over the place, and the price dropped to less than $100. In the United States and Canada, the alternative to GPS is long-wave radio WWVB transmitting from Colorado. Other long-wave radio services in Europe and Japan are listed in Table 13.6. However, shortwave radio WWV/H and CHU stations have been useful sources. While GOES satellite receivers are available, the GOES satellite itself is being discontinued. GPS receivers are much less expensive and provide better accuracy. Over the years, some 44 clock driver modules supporting these and virtually every radio, satellite, and modem national standard time service in the world have been implemented for NTP.

Recent additions to the driver library include drivers for the WWV/H and CHU transmissions that work directly from an ordinary shortwave receiver and audio sound card or motherboard codec. Some of the more exotic drivers built in our laboratory include a computerized LORAN-C (Long Range Navigation System C) receiver with exceptional stability [31] and a DSP chip-based WWV/H demodulator/decoder using theoretically optimal algorithms [32].

19.6 Hunting the Nanoseconds

When the Internet first wound NTP clocksprings, computers and networks were much, much slower than today. A typical wide-area network (WAN) speed was 48 kb/s, about the speed of a telephone modem of today. A large time-sharing computer of the day was the Digital Equipment TOPS-20, which was not a whole lot faster, but it did run an awesome version of Zork. This was the heyday of the minicomputer, the most ubiquitous of which was the Digital Equipment PDP11 and its little brother, the LSI-11. NTP was born on these machines and grew up with the Fuzzball operating system. There were about two dozen Fuzzballs scattered at Internet hot spots in the United States and Europe. They functioned as hosts and gateways for network research and prototyping and so made good development platforms for NTP.

In the early days, most computer hardware clocks were driven by the power grid as the primary timing source. Power grid clocks have a resolution of 16 or 20 ms, depending on country, and the uncorrected time can wander several seconds over the day and night, especially in summertime. While power grid clocks have rather dismal performance relative to accurate civil time, they do have an interesting characteristic, at least in areas of the country that are grid synchronous. Early experiments in time synchronization and network measurement could assume that the time offsets between grid-synchronized clocks was constant, since they all ran at the same frequency and close phase, so all NTP had to do was calibrate the constant offsets.

Later, computer clocks were driven by an oscillator stabilized by a quartz crystal resonator, which is much more stable than the power grid but has the disadvantage that the intrinsic frequency offset between crystal clocks can reach several hundred parts per million or several seconds per day. In fact, over the years only Digital has paid particular attention to the manufacturing tolerance of the clock oscillator, so their machines make the best timekeepers. In fact, this is one of the reasons why all the primary servers operated by NIST are Digital Alphas.

As crystal clocks came into widespread use, the discipline algorithm was modified to adjust the frequency as well as the time. Thus, an intrinsic offset of several hundred parts per million could be reduced to a residual on the order of 0.1 PPM and residual timekeeping errors to the order of a clock tick. Later designs decreased the tick from 16 or 20 ms to 4 ms and eventually to 1 ms in the Alpha. The Fuzzballs were equipped with a hardware counter/timer with a 1-ms tick, which was considered heroic in those days.

To achieve resolutions better than one tick, some kind of auxiliary counter is required. Early Sun SPARC machines had a 1-MHz counter synchronized to the tick interrupt. In this design, the seconds are numbered by the tick interrupt, and the microseconds within the second read directly from the counter. In principle, these machines could keep time to 1 μs, assuming that NTP could discipline the clocks between machines to this order. In point of fact, performance was limited to a few milliseconds, both because of network and operating system latencies and because of small varying-frequency excursions induced by ambient temperature variations.

Analysis, simulation, and experiment led to continuing improvements in the discipline algorithm that adjusts the clock time and frequency in response to an external source, such as another NTP server or a local radio or satellite receiver, or telephone modem [33]. As a practical matter, the best timekeeping requires a directly connected radio; however, the interconnection method, usually a serial port, itself has inherent jitter. In addition, the method implemented in the operating system kernel to adjust the time generally has limitations of its own [34].

In a project originally sponsored by Digital and later by Sun, components of the discipline algorithm were implemented directly in the kernel. Also, an otherwise-unused counter was harnessed to interpolate the microseconds. In addition to these improvements, a special clock discipline loop was implemented for the pulse-per-second (PPS) signal produced by some reference clocks and precision oscillators. The complete design and application interface were reported in Mills [35], some sections of which appeared as RFC-1589 [36]. The kernel software described in Chapter 8 is now an integral component of the kernels distributed with Digital and Sun workstations and in the FreeBSD and Linux operating systems.

A systematic search for sources of jitter described in Mills [37] revealed significant contributions due to serial port drivers, input/output (I/O) system latencies, and process scheduling. Most of these latencies were avoided using crafted I/O applications in the form of BSD line disciplines and STREAMS modules. Van Jacobson and Craig Leres at the Lawrence Berkeley Laboratory built one that used the PPS signal transitions on a serial port lead to generate a precision timestamp with a latency of only 6 µs. However, these applications were in general not portable and were implemented for only a few systems.

An interesting application of the PPS signal was in Norway, where a Fuzzball NTP primary server was connected to a cesium frequency standard with PPS output. In those days, the Internet bridging the United States and Europe had notoriously high jitter, in some cases peaks reaching over 1 s. The cesium standard and kernel discipline maintained constant frequency but did not provide a way to number the seconds. NTP provided this function via the Internet and other primary servers. The experience with very high jitter resulted in special nonlinear signal-processing code, called the *popcorn spike suppressor*, in the discipline algorithm.

Still, network and computer speeds were reaching higher and higher. The time to cycle through the kernel and back, once 58 µs in a Sun SPARC IPC, was decreasing to 1 µs in a Digital Alpha and 0.4 µs in a Sun Blade 1000. To ensure a reliable ordering of events, the need was building to improve the clock resolution better than 1 µs, and the nanosecond seemed a good target. NTPv4 now implements all clock adjustments in floating double, which in principle could discipline the clock with femtosecond resolution if the underlying hardware supported it.

For ultimate accuracy, the original microsecond kernel was overhauled to support a nanosecond clock conforming to the PPS interface specified in RFC-2783 [38]. Nanosecond kernels have been built and tested for SunOS, Alpha, Linux, and FreeBSD systems, with the last two including the code in current systems [39]. The results with the new kernel demonstrate that the residual error with modern hardware and a precision PPS signal is in the order of 50 ns [40].

This represents the state of the art in current timekeeping practice. Having come this far, the machine I use now runs at 3.4 GHz and can chime with another across the country at full 100-Mb/s speeds, which raises the possibility of a picosecond clock. The inherent resolution of the NTP timestamp is about 232 ps, which suggests that we soon might approach that limit and require rethinking the NTP protocol design. At these speeds, NTP could be used to synchronize the motherboard central processing unit (CPU) and ASIC (application-specific integrated circuit) oscillators using optical interconnects.

19.7 Experimental Studies

Over the years, a good deal of effort has gone into the analysis of computer clocks and methods to stabilize them in frequency and time. As networks and computers have become faster and faster, the characterization of computer clock oscillators and the evolution of synchronization technology has continuously evolved to match. Following is a technical timeline of the significant events in this progress.

When the ICMP (Internet Control Message Protocol) divorced from the first Internet routing protocol GGP, one of the first functions added to ICMP was the ICMP Timestamp message, which is similar to the ICMP Echo message but carries timestamps with millisecond resolution [8]. Experiments with these messages used Fuzzballs and the very first implementation of ICMP. In fact, the first use of the name PING (Packet InterNet Groper) can be found in RFC-889 [41]. Related experiments were later reported by Cole and Foxcroft [42].

While the hosts and gateways did not at first have synchronized clocks, they did record timestamps with a granularity of 16 or 1 ms, which could be used to measure round-trip times and synchronize experiments after the fact. Statistics collected this way were used for the analysis and refinement of early TCP (Transmission Control Protocol) algorithms, especially the parameter estimation schemes used by the retransmission time-out algorithm.

The first comprehensive survey of NTP operating in the Internet was published in 1985 [29]. Later surveys appeared in 1990 [43] and 1997 [25]. The 1997 survey was a profound undertaking. It attempted to find and expose every NTP server and client in the public Internet using data collected by the standard NTP monitoring tools. After filtering to remove duplicates and falsetickers, the survey found over 185,000 client/server associations in over 38,000 NTP servers and clients. The results actually represented only a fraction of the total number of NTP servers and clients at that time. It is known from other sources that many thousands of NTP servers and clients lurked behind firewalls where the monitoring programs could not find them. Extrapolating from data provided about the estimated population in Norway, it is a fair statement that well over 100,000 NTP daemons were prowling the Internet in 1997, more likely several times that number. Recently, an NTP client was found hiding in a stand-alone print server and another in a battery backup power system. The next one may be found in a wireless alarm clock.

"On the Chronology and Metrology of Computer Network Timescales and Their Application to the Network Time Protocol" [44], published in *ACM*

Computer Communications Review, is a slightly tongue-in-cheek survey of the timescale, calendar, and metrology issues involved in computer network timekeeping. Of particular interest in that article is how to deal with leap seconds in the UTC timescale. While provisions are available in NTP to disseminate leap seconds throughout the NTP subnet, means to anticipate their scheduled occurrence were not implemented in radio, satellite, and modem services until relatively recently, and not all radios and only a handful of kernels support leap seconds. In fact, on the 15 leap second occasions since Internet timekeeping began in 1979, the behavior of the NTP subnet on and shortly after each leap could only be described in terms of a pinball machine. Today, there is no excuse for leap second misadventures. In NTPv4, the leap indicator is set automatically in the NIST and USNO servers and passed up the stratum tree by dependent servers and clients. Since the kernels used in many modern operating systems are leap enabled, they should behave better on the occasion of a leap.

While almost all time dissemination means in the world are based on UTC, some users have expressed the need for atomic time (TAI, International Atomic Time), including means to metricate intervals that span multiple leap seconds [45]. NTPv4 includes a simple mechanism to retrieve a table of historic leap seconds from NIST servers and distribute it throughout the NTP subnet. However, at this writing a suitable application program interface (API) has yet to be designed and implemented and then navigate the IETF standards process. Refinements to the Autokey protocol have been made to ensure the most recent copy of this table is distributed using secure means.

19.8 Theory and Algorithms

As all this was going on, there was a good deal of excitement in the theoretical community developing abstract models and algorithms for time synchronization. The fundamental abstraction from which correctness principles are based is the *happens-before* relation introduced by Lamport [46] and Lamport and Melliar-Smith [47]. It demonstrates that clocks are required to determine a reliable time value if no more than $3m + 1$ of them are falsetickers, but only $2m + 1$ clocks are required if digital signatures are used, as is the case with Autokey.

A number of fault-tolerant time synchronization algorithms have evolved in the computer science theory community, including those mentioned in Chapter 3. Drawing from this work, a cascade of four algorithms was developed for NTP: the filter, select, cluster, and combine algorithms. In a series of experiments documented in RFC-956 [29], the algorithm that emerged computes the round-trip delay for each of the last eight measurement rounds and selects the offset associated with the minimum round-trip delay. This algorithm, somewhat modified, survives.

As described in Chapter 3, the NTP select algorithm is based on the intersection algorithm of Marzullo and Owicki [19], together with a refinement algorithm similar to the self-stabilizing algorithm of Lu and Zhang [48]. This algorithm, somewhat modified to reduce jitter, was added in NTPv3 and survives today. The cluster algorithm was added in NTPv2 but has been modified in significant ways since then. The fundamentals of computer clock discipline technology were presented in the 1992 report [49], which remains valid. That report set forth mathematically precise models for error analysis, transient response, and clock discipline principles. Selected sections of that report were condensed and refined in Mills [33].

In a series of careful measurements over a period of 2 years with selected servers in the United States, Australia, and Europe, an analytical model of the idiosyncratic computer clock oscillator was developed and verified. While a considerable body of work on this subject has accreted in the literature, with few exceptions the object of study has been precision oscillators of the highest quality used as time and frequency standards. Computer oscillators have no such pedigree since there are generally no provisions to stabilize the ambient environment, in particular the crystal temperature.

The discipline algorithm in Mills [50] further extended and refined the model evolved from Mills [49]. The algorithm design was considerably influenced by a collaboration with Judah Levine at NIST. Levine's own _lockclock_ algorithm, which is used in the NTP primary servers operated by NIST, is described in his article [51]. Mills [50] introduced the concept of _Allan deviation_, a statistic useful for the characterization of clock discipline performance. This statistic is commonly displayed by a plot of stability versus averaging interval in log-log coordinates, as shown in Figure 12.2. Each Internet server is characterized by a straight line with slope −1, which is associated with white-phase noise. Each computer oscillator is characterized by a straight line with slope +0.5, which is associated with random-walk frequency noise. Knowing these two characteristics allows the optimum averaging interval to be determined for each combination of server and oscillator. Mills [50] also described a number of algorithmic improvements incorporated in the NTPv4 design, including the select algorithm and an improved discipline and hardware model for the kernel PPS signal.

Mills [52] further extended and quantified the clock discipline model developed in Mills [50]. Its primary contribution is the Allan intercept model that characterizes typical computer oscillators. The Allan intercept is the point (x, y) where the straight-line asymptotes shown in Figure 12.2 for each individual source and oscillator intersect. This work resulted in a hybrid algorithm, implemented in NTPv4, which both improves performance over typical Internet paths and allows the message poll intervals to be substantially increased without degrading accuracy. A special-purpose simulator that included substantially all the NTP algorithms was used to verify predicted behavior with both simulated and actual data over the entire envelope of frenetic Internet behaviors.

19.9 Growing Pains

In the beginning, almost all NTP servers operated in client/server mode, by which a client sends requests at intervals ranging from 1 min to tens of minutes, depending on accuracy requirements. In this mode, time values flow outward from the primary servers through possibly several layers of secondary servers to the clients. In some cases involving multiple redundant servers, peers operate in symmetric mode, and values can flow from one peer to the other or vice versa, depending on which one is closest to the reference clock according to a defined metric. Some large corporations and public institutions operate multiple primary servers in different regions of the country, each connected to one or more redundant radio or satellite receivers using different dissemination services. This forms an exceptionally robust synchronization source for both on-campus and off-campus public access.

While NTP service makes only minimal demands on the host processor, the client population of popular servers like NIST and USNO has been growing to huge proportions, with the busiest servers handling thousands of packets per second. In the Internet of today, even this flux does not daunt these servers, at least if the clients use common sense and reasonable packet rates. However, common sense is not a ubiquitous commodity even in the NTP community. Whether due to terror or ignorance, on occasion clients have sent packets as fast as possible, like 256 packets in 1 s. In Australia, where packets are counted and charged, this is an unacceptable hazard. This and other incidents like it are described in Mills et al. [53].

To defend against clogging attacks like these, a feature similar to what telephone service providers define as *call-gap* has been incorporated in the NTP design. The scheme uses a most recently used (MRU) list of IP source addresses and time values and operates to discard packets that exceed given peak and average rate limits. As an optional feature, when these limits are exceeded, a nasty kiss-o'-death (KoD) packet is returned to the client. If the client uses the public NTP software distribution and has broken the rules, the server may return a KoD and the client is forced to slow down.

19.10 As Time Goes By

In retrospect, while NTP has been a technical adventure in its own right by providing the means for accurate and dependable time synchronization, NTP has also been an enabling technology for practical uses of synchronized clocks. Using NTP for timestamping stock trades, radio and television broadcast programs, and distributed data acquisition readily springs to mind, but as Liskov pointed out [54], synchronized clocks are vital to some important distributed algorithms and could improve performance in others.

Near the end of the first decade of the new century, it is quite likely that precision timekeeping technology has evolved about as far as it can given the realities of available computer hardware and operating systems. Using specially modified kernels and creative interface devices, Poul-Henning Kamp and I have demonstrated that computer time in a modern workstation can be disciplined within some tens of nanoseconds relative to a precision source such as a cesium or rubidium frequency standard [40]. While not many computer applications would justify such heroic means, the demonstration suggests that the single most useful option for high-performance timekeeping in a modern workstation may be a temperature-compensated system clock oscillator.

It is likely that future deployment of public NTP services might well involve an optional secure timestamping service, perhaps for a fee. This agenda is being pursued as a commercial enterprise. In fact, several NIST servers are now being equipped with timestamping services. This makes public key authentication a vital component of such a service, especially if the Sun never sets on the service area.

One of the most fascinating developments in network timekeeping is the application of the technology in planetary and deep-space missions. As discussed in Chapters 17 and 18, this brings up new and exotic issues in general relativity, astrodynamics, and radiometric navigation. Perhaps the most interesting lesson to learn from the adventure is, as the timekeeping and security functions are so intertwined on Earth, the timekeeping and navigation functions are so intertwined in space.

19.11 Parting Shots

Internet timekeeping is considered by some to be a hobby, and even I have revealed a likeness to amateur radio. There seems no other explanation why the volunteer timekeeper corps has continued so long to improve the software quality, write clock drivers for every new radio that comes along, and port the stuff to new hardware and operating systems. The generals in the army have been revealed in the narrative here, but the many soldiers of the trench must be thanked as well, especially when the hardest job is convincing the boss that time tinkering is good for business. A list of important contributors is available at http://www.ntp.org and on the copyright page in the NTP software documentation.

We are done here.

References

Note: The papers and reports by D. L. Mills are available in PostScript and PDF at http://www.eecis.udel.edu/~mills.

1. Mills, D.L. A brief history of NTP time: confessions of an Internet timekeeper. *ACM Computer Commun. Rev. 33, 2* (April 2003), 9–22.

2. Mills, D.L. *Time Synchronization in DCNET Hosts.* Internet Project Report IEN-173, COMSAT Laboratories, February 1981.

3. Mills, D.L. *DCNET Internet Clock Service.* Network Working Group Report RFC-778, COMSAT Laboratories, April 1981.

4. Mills, D.L. *DCN Local-Network Protocols.* Network Working Group Report RFC-891, M/A-COM Linkabit, December 1983.

5. Mills, D.L. The Fuzzball. *Proceedings ACM SIGCOMM 88 Symposium* (Palo Alto, CA, August 1988), 115–122.

6. Postel, J. *Daytime Protocol.* Network Working Group RFC-867, Information Sciences Institute, May 1983.

7. Postel, J., and K. Herrenstien. *Time Protocol.* Network Working Group RFC-868, Information Sciences Institute, May 1983.

8. Postel, J. *Internet Control Message Protocol.* Network Working Group RFC-777. Information Sciences Institute, April 1981.

9. Su, Z. *Specification of the Internet Protocol (IP) Timestamp Option.* Network Working Group RFC-781, May 1981.

10. Gusella, R., and S. Zatti. TEMPO—a network time controller for a distributed Berkeley UNIX system. *IEEE Distributed Processing Technical Committee Newsletter 6, SI-2* (June 1984), 7–15. Also in *Proceedings Summer 1984 USENIX* (Salt Lake City, CO, June 1984).

11. *Digital Time Service Functional Specification Version T.1.0.5.* Digital Equipment Corporation, 1989.

12. Paxson, V. On calibrating measurements of packet transit times. *Proceedings Joint Internet Conference on Measurements and Modelling of Computer Systems* (Madison, June 1998), 11–21.

13. Mills, D.L. *Network Time Protocol (NTP).* Network Working Group Report RFC-958, M/A-COM Linkabit, September 1985.

14. Mills, D.L. *Network Time Protocol (Version 1) Specification and Implementation.* Network Working Group Report RFC-1059, University of Delaware, Newark, July 1988.

15. Mills, D.L. *Algorithms for Synchronizing Network Clocks.* Network Working Group Report RFC-956, M/A-COM Linkabit, September 1985.

16. Mills, D.L. Internet time synchronization: the Network Time Protocol. *IEEE Trans. Commun. COM-39, 10* (October 1991), 1482–1493.

17. Mills, D.L. *Network Time Protocol (Version 2) Specification and Implementation.* Network Working Group Report RFC-1119, University, October 1989.

18. Liao, C., M. Martonosi, and D. Clark. Experience with an adaptive globally-synchronizing clock algorithm. *Proceedings 11th Annual ACM Symposium on Parallel Algorithms and Architecture* (Saint Malo, June 1999), 106–114.

19. Marzullo, K., and S. Owicki. Maintaining the time in a distributed system. *ACM Operating Syst. Rev. 19, 3* (July 1985), 44–54.

20. Mills, D.L. *Network Time Protocol (Version 3) Specification, Implementation and Analysis*. Network Working Group Report RFC-1305, University of Delaware, Newark, March 1992.
21. Mills, D.L, and A. Thyagarajan. *Network Time Protocol Version 4 Proposed Changes*. Electrical Engineering Department Report 94-10-2, University of Delaware, Newark, October 1994.
22. Mills, D.L. *Proposed Authentication Enhancements for the Network Time Protocol Version 4*. Electrical Engineering Report 96-10-3, University of Delaware, Newark, October 1996.
23. Mills, D. *Simple Network Time Protocol (SNTP) Version 4 for IPv4, IPv6 and OSI*. Network Working Group Report RFC-4330, University of Delaware, Newark, January 2006.
24. Crocroft, J., and J.P. Onions. *Network Time Protocol (NTP) Over the OSI Remote Operations Service*. Network Working Group Report RFC-1165, University College London, June 1990.
25. Mills, D.L., A. Thyagarajan, and B.C. Huffman. Internet timekeeping around the globe. *Proceedings Precision Time and Time Interval (PTTI) Applications and Planning Meeting* (Long Beach, CA, December 1997), 365–371.
26. Mills, D.L. Cryptographic authentication for real-time network protocols. *AMS DIMACS Series in Discrete Mathematics and Theoretical Computer Science, 45* (1999), 135–144.
27. Mills, D.L. *Public Key Cryptography for the Network Time Protocol*. Electrical Engineering Report 00-5-1, University of Delaware, Newark, May 2000.
28. Mills, D.L. *The Autokey Security Architecture, Protocol and Algorithms*. Electrical Engineering Report 03-2-20, University of Delaware, Newark, February 2003.
29. Mills, D.L. *Experiments in Network Clock Synchronization*. Network Working Group Report RFC-957, M/A-COM Linkabit, September 1985.
30. Mills, D.L., and H.-W. Braun. The NSFNET Backbone Network. *Proceedings ACM SIGCOMM 87 Symposium* (Stoweflake, VT, August 1987), 191–196.
31. Mills, D.L. *A Computer-Controlled LORAN-C Receiver for Precision Timekeeping*. Electrical Engineering Department Report 92-3-1, University of Delaware, Newark, March 1992.
32. Mills, D.L. *A Precision Radio Clock for WWV Transmissions*. Electrical Engineering Report 97-8-1, University of Delaware, Newark, August 1997.
33. Mills, D.L. Precision synchronization of computer network clocks. *ACM Computer Commun. Rev. 24, 2* (April 1994), 28–43.
34. Mills, D.L. On the accuracy and stability of clocks synchronized by the Network Time Protocol in the Internet system. *ACM Computer Commun. Rev. 20, 1* (January 1990), 65–75.
35. Mills, D.L. *Unix Kernel Modifications for Precision Time Synchronization*. Electrical Engineering Department Report 94-10-1, University of Delaware, Newark, October 1994.
36. Mills, D.L. *A Kernel Model for Precision Timekeeping*. Network Working Group Report RFC-1589, University of Delaware, Newark, March 1994.

37. Mills, D.L. The network computer as precision timekeeper. *Proceedings Precision Time and Time Interval (PTTI) Applications and Planning Meeting* (Reston, VA, December 1996), 96–108.
38. Mogul, J., D. Mills, J. Brittenson, J. Stone, and U. Windl. *Pulse-per-Second API for Unix-like Operating Systems, Version 1*. Request for Comments RFC-2783, Internet Engineering Task Force, March 2000.
39. Mills, D.L. The nanokernel. Software and documentation, including test results. http://www.ntp.org.
40. Mills, D.L., and P.-H. Kamp. The nanokernel. *Proceedings Precision Time and Time Interval (PTTI) Applications and Planning Meeting* (Reston, VA, November 2000), 423–430.
41. Mills, D.L. *Internet Delay Experiments*. Network Working Group Report RFC-889, M/A-COM Linkabit, December 1983.
42. Cole, R., and C. Foxcroft. An experiment in clock synchronisation. *Computer J. 31, 6* (1988), 496–502.
43. Mills, D.L. *Measured Performance of the Network Time Protocol in the Internet System*. Network Working Group Report RFC-1128, University of Delaware, Newark, October 1989.
44. Mills, D.L. On the chronology and metrology of computer network timescales and their application to the Network Time Protocol. *ACM Computer Commun. Rev. 21, 5* (October 1991), 8–17.
45. Levine, J., and D. Mills. Using the Network Time Protocol to transmit International Atomic Time (TAI). *Proceedings Precision Time and Time Interval (PTTI) Applications and Planning Meeting* (Reston, VA, November 2000), 431–439.
46. Lamport, L. Time, clocks and the ordering of events in a distributed system. *Commun. ACM 21, 7* (July 1978), 558–565.
47. Lamport, L., and P.M. Melliar-Smith. Synchronizing clocks in the presence of faults. *JACM 32, 1* (January 1985), 52–78.
48. Lu, M., and D. Zhang. Analysis of self-stabilizing clock synchronization by means of stochastic Petri nets. *IEEE Trans. Computers 39, 5* (May 1990), 597–604.
49. Mills, D.L. *Modelling and Analysis of Computer Network Clocks*. Electrical Engineering Department Report 92-5-2, University of Delaware, Newark, May 1992.
50. Mills, D.L. Improved algorithms for synchronizing computer network clocks. *IEEE/ACM Trans. Networks 3, 3* (June 1995), 245–254.
51. Levine, J. An algorithm to synchronize the time of a computer to universal time. *IEEE/ACM Trans. Networking 3, 1* (February 1995), 42–50.
52. Mills, D.L. Adaptive hybrid discipline algorithm for the Network Time Protocol. *IEEE/ACM Trans. Networking 6, 5* (October 1998), 505–514.
53. Mills, D.L., J. Levine, R. Schmidt, and D. Plonka. Coping with overload on the Network Time Protocol public servers. *Proceedings Precision Time and Time Interval (PTTI) Applications and Planning Meeting* (Washington, DC, December 2004), 5–16.
54. Liskov, B. Practical uses of synchronized clocks in distributed systems. *Proceedings 10th Annual ACM Symposium on Principles of Distributed Computing* (Montreal, April 1991), 1–9.

Further Reading

Allan, D.W., J.E. Gray, and H.E. Machlan. The National Bureau of Standards atomic time scale: generation, stability, accuracy and accessibility. In Blair, B.E. (Ed.), *Time and Frequency Theory and Fundamentals.* National Bureau of Standards Monograph 140, U.S. Department of Commerce, 1974, 205–231.

Arvind, K. Probabilistic clock synchronization in distributed systems. *IEEE Trans. Parallel Distributed Syst. 5, 5* (May 1964), 474–487.

Cristian, F. A probabilistic approach to distributed clock synchronization. *Distributed Computing 3* (1989), 146–158.

Halpern, J.Y., B. Simons, R. Strong, and D. Dolev. Fault-tolerant clock synchronization. *Proceedings ACM Third Annual Symposium on Principles of Distributed Computing* (August 1984), 89–102.

Lindsay, W.C., and A.V. Kantak. Network synchronization of random signals. *IEEE Trans. Commun. COM-28, 8* (August 1980), 1260–1266.

Lundelius, J., and N.A. Lynch. A new fault-tolerant algorithm for clock synchronization. *Proceedings Third Annual ACM Symposium on Principles of Distributed Computing* (August 1984), 75–88.

Mills, D.L. *Clock Discipline Algorithms for the Network Time Protocol Version 4.* Electrical Engineering Report 97-3-3, University of Delaware, Newark, March 1997.

Mitra, D. Network synchronization: analysis of a hybrid of master-slave and mutual synchronization. *IEEE Trans. Commun. COM-28, 8* (August 1980), 1245–1259.

Mu, Y., and V. Varadharajan. Robust and secure broadcasting. In *Proceedings INDOCRYPT 2001, LNCS 2247,* Springer-Verlag, New York, 2001, 223–231.

Rickert, N.W. Non Byzantine clock synchronization—a programming experiment. *ACM Operating Syst. Rev. 22, 1* (January 1988), 73–78.

Schneider, F. *A Paradigm for Reliable Clock Synchronization.* Computer Science Technical Report TR 86-735, Cornell University, Ithaca, NY, February 1986.

Schnorr, C.P. Efficient signature generation for smart cards. *J. Cryptol. 4, 3* (1991), 161–174.

Srikanth, T.K., and S. Toueg. Optimal clock synchronization. *JACM 34, 3* (July 1987), 626–645.

Bibliography

Bibliomaniac (n): Someone with a lunatic's passion for acquiring books, as this word's roots imply. Chambers portrayed England's most famous bibliomaniac, Richard Heber (1773–1833) as an obsessive collector:

> The bibliomaniac collects books merely for the pleasure of collecting.... On hearing of a curious book, he was known to have put himself into a mail coach and travelled three or four hundred miles to obtain it, fearful to entrust his commission to anyone else.

Jeffrey Kacirk
Forgotten English (1997)

Abate, J., et al. AT&T's new approach to the synchronization of telecommunication networks. *IEEE Communications Magazine* (April 1989), 35–45.

Abali, B., C.B. Stunkel and C. Benveniste. Clock synchronization on a multicomputer. *J. Parallel Distributed Computing 40, 1* (1997), 118–130.

Abdel-Ghaffar, H. Analysis of synchronization algorithms with time-out control over networks with exponentially symmetric delays. *IEEE Trans. on Communications 50, 10* (October 2002), 1652–1661.

Adams, C., S. Farrell. Internet X.509 public key infrastructure certificate management protocols. Network Working Group Request for Comments RFC-2510, Entrust Technologies, March 1999, 30 pp.

Allan, D.W. Time and frequency (time-domain) estimation and prediction of precision clocks and oscillators. *IEEE Trans. on Ultrasound, Ferroelectrics, and Frequency Control UFFC-34, 6* (November 1987), 647–654. Also in: Sullivan, D.B., D.W. Allan, D.A. Howe and F.L. Walls (Eds.). *Characterization of Clocks and Oscillators.* NIST Technical Note 1337, U.S. Department of Commerce, 1990, 121–128.

Allan, D.W., J.E. Gray and H.E. Machlan. The National Bureau of Standards atomic time scale: generation, stability, accuracy and accessibility. In: Blair, B.E. (Ed.). *Time and Frequency Theory and Fundamentals.* National Bureau of Standards Monograph 140, U.S. Department of Commerce, 1974, 205–231.

Allan, D.W., J.H. Shoaf and D. Halford. Statistics of time and frequency data analysis. In: Blair, B.E. (Ed.). Time and Frequency Theory and Fundamentals. *National Bureau of Standards Monograph 140*, U.S. Department of Commerce, 1974, 151–204.

Allan, D.W., M.A. Weiss and T.K. Peppler. In search of the best clock. *IEEE Trans. Instrumentation and Measurement 38, 2* (February 1989), 624–630.

Arvind, K. Probabilistic clock synchronization in distributed systems. *IEEE Trans. Parallel and Distributed Systems 5, 5* (May 1994), 474–487.

Ashton, P. Algorithms for off-line clock synchronization. Department of Computer Science, University of Canterbury, December 1995, 30 pp.

Attiya, H., A. Herzberg and S. Rajsbaum, Optimal clock synchronization under different delay assumptions. *SIAM Journal on Computing 25*, 2 (February 1996), 369–3896.

Automated Computer Time Service (ACTS). NBS Research Material 8101, U.S. Department of Commerce, 1988.

Awerbuch, B. Complexity of network synchronization. *J ACM 32*, 4 (October 1985), 804–823.

Awerbuch, B., S. Kutten, Y. Mansour and B. Patt-Shamir. Time optimized self-stabilizing synchronization. *Proc. 25th Annual ACM Symposium on Theory of Computing* (1993), 652–661.

Aweya, J., M. Quellette, D. Montuano and K. Felske. Circuit emulation services over Ethernet-part 1: clock synchronization using timestamps. *International J. of Network Management 14*(1), 29–44, 2004.

Barak, B., S. Halevi, A. Herzberg and D. Naor. Clock synchronization with faults and recoveries. *Proc. 19th Annual ACM Symposium on Principles of Distributed Computing* (Portland, OR 2000), 133–142.

Barnes, J.A., and S.R. Stein. Application of Kalman filters and ARIMA models to digital frequency and phase-locked loops. *Proc. Nineteenth Annual Precise Time and Time Interval (PTTI) Applications and Planning Meeting*, (Redondo Beach, CA, December 1988), 311–323.

Bell Communications Research. Digital Synchronization Network Plan. Technical Advisory TA-NPL-000436, 1 November 1986.

Berthaud, J.-M. Time synchronization over networks using convex closures. *IEEE/ACM Trans. on Networking 8*, 2 (April 2000), 265–277.

Bertsekas, D., and R. Gallager. *Data Networks*. Prentice-Hall, Englewood Cliffs, NJ, 1987.

Beser, J., and B.W. Parkinson. The application of NAVSTAR differential GPS in the civilian community. *Navigation 29*, 2 (Summer 1982).

Blair, B.E. Time and frequency dissemination: an overview of principles and techniques. In: Blair, B.E. (Ed.). *Time and Frequency Theory and Fundamentals. National Bureau of Standards Monograph 140*, U.S. Department of Commerce, 1974, 233–313.

Blair, G.S., G. Coulson, M. Papathomas, P. Robin, J.-B. Stefani, F. Horn and L.A. Hazard. A programming model and system infrastructure for real-time synchronization in distributed multimedia systems. *IEEE J. Selected Areas in Communications, 14*, 1 (January 1996) 249–263.

Braun, W.B. Short term frequency effects in networks of coupled oscillators. *IEEE Trans. Communications COM-28*, 8 (August 1980), 1269–1275.

Calendar. The Encyclopaedia Britannica Macropaedia, 15th ed., vol. 15, pp. 460–477. Encyclopaedia Britannica Co., New York, NY, 1986.

Carroll, L. *The Complete Works of Lewis Carroll*. Penguin Group, London, 1988.

Chaffee, J.W. Relating the Allan variance to the diffusion coefficients of a linear stochastic differential equation model for precision oscillators. *IEEE Trans. Ultrasonics, Ferroelectrics and Frequency Control UFFC-34*, 6 (November 1987), 655–658.

Chi, A.R. Satellite time transfer via TDRSS and applications. *Proc. 11th Precise Time and Time Interval Application and Planning Meeting* (December 1979), 45–64.

Cole, R., and C. Foxcroft. An experiment in clock synchronisation. *The Computer Journal 31*, 6 (1988), 496–502.

Cristian, F. A probabilistic approach to distributed clock synchronization. *Distributed Computing 3* (1989), 146–158.

Cristian, F., H. Aghili and R. Strong. Clock synchronization in the presence of omission and performance faults, and processor joins. *Proc. Sixteenth International Symposium on Fault-Tolerant Computing* (July 1986), 218–233.

Crocroft, J., and J.P. Onions. Network Time Protocol (NTP) Over the OSI Remote Operations Service. Network Working Group Report RFC-1165, University College London, June 1990, 10 pp.

Dai, H., and R. Han TSync: a lightweight bidirectional time synchronization service for wireless sensor networks. *ACM SIGMOBILE Mobile Computing and Communications Review 8, 1* (January 2004), 125–139.

Data Encryption Standard. Federal Information Processing Standards Publication 46. National Bureau of Standards, U.S. Department of Commerce, 1977.

Deering, S.E., and D.R. Cheriton. Multicast routing in datagram internetworks and extended LANs. *ACM Trans. Computing Systems 8, 2* (May 1990), 85–100.

Dershowitz, N., and E.M. Reingold. Calendrical Calculations. *Software Practice and Experience 20, 9* (September 1990), 899–928.

DES Modes of Operation. Federal Information Processing Standards Publication 81. National Bureau of Standards, U.S. Department of Commerce, December 1980.

Digital Time Service Functional Specification Version T.1.0.5. Digital Equipment Corporation, 1989.

Dolev, D., J. Halpern and H. Strong. On the possibility and impossibility of achieving clock synchronization. *Proc. 16th Annual ACM Symposium on Theory of Computing* (Washington, DC, April 1984), 504–511.

Dolev, D., J. Halpern, B. Simons and R. Strong. Dynamic fault-tolerant clock synchronization. *JACM 42, 1* (January 1995), 143–185.

Dolev, D., N. Lynch, S. Pinter, E. Stark and W. Weihl. Reaching approximate agreement in the presence of faults. *Proc. Third Symposium on Reliability in Distributed Software and Database Systems* (October 1983, 145–154.

Dunigan, T.H. Hypercube clock synchronization. Concurrency: *Software Practice and Experience 4, 3* (May 1992), 257–268.

Dwork, C. Knowledge and common knowledge in a Byzantine environment: crash failures. *Information and Computation 88* (1990), 156–186.

Elson, J., L. Girod, D. Estrin. Fine-grained network time synchronization using reference broadcasts. *ACM SIGOPS Operating Systems Review 36, SI* (December 2002),

Frank, R.L. History of LORAN-C. *Navigation 29, 1* (Spring 1982).

Gifford, A., et al. Time dissemination alternatives for future NASA missions. *Proc. 38th Precise Time and Time Interval Application and Planning Meeting* (December 2006), 319–328.

Goud, M.G., and T. Herman. Stablizing Unison. *Information Processing Letters 35* (1990), 171–175.

Guillou, L.C., and J.-J. Quisquatar. A "paradoxical" identity-based signature scheme resulting from zero-knowledge. Proc. *CRYPTO 88 Advanced in Cryptology*, Springer-Verlag, 1990, 216–231.

Guino, B. Some properties of algorithms for atomic time scales. *Metrologia 24* (1987), 195–198.

Gurewitz, O., I. Cidon and M. Sidi. Network time synchronization using clock offset optimization. *Proc. 11th IEEE International Conference on Network Protocols* (November 2003), 212–221

Gusella, R., and S. Zatti. The Berkeley UNIX 4.3BSD time synchronization proto-col: protocol specification. Technical Report UCB/CSD 85/250, University of California, Berkeley, June 1985.

Gusella, R., and S. Zatti. TEMPO - A network time controller for a distributed Berkeley UNIX system. *IEEE Distributed Processing Technical Committee Newsletter 6, NoSI-2* (June 1984), 7–15. Also in: Proc. Summer 1984 USENIX (Salt Lake City, June 1984).

Gusella, R., and S. Zatti. An election algorithm for a distributed clock synchroniza-tion program. Technical Report UCB/CSD 86/275, University of California, Berkeley, December 1985.

Hac, A., and C. Xue. Synchronization in multimedia data retrieval. *Int. J. Network Mgmt., Vol. 7* (1997), 33–62.

Halpern, J.Y., B. Simons, R. Strong and D. Dolev. Fault-tolerant clock synchroniza-tion. *Proc. ACM Third Annual Symposium on Principles of Distributed Computing* (August 1984), 89–102.

Hanson, D.W. Fundamentals of two-way time transfer by satellite. *Proc. 43rd Annual Symposium on Frequency Control* (May 1989), 174–178.

Herring, T. The Global Positioning System. *Scientific American*, February 1996, 44–50.

Hohn, N., D. Veitch and P. Abry. Does fractal scaling at the IP level depend on TCP flow arrival processes? *Proc. Second ACM SIGCOMM workshop on Internet mea-surement* (Marseille, France 2002), 63–68.

Housley, R., et al. Internet X.509 public key infrastructure certificate and certificate revocation list (CRL) profile. Network Working Group Request for Comments RFC-3280, RSA Laboratories, April 2002, 129 pp.

Internet Control Message Protocol. Network Working Group Report RFC-792, USC Information Sciences Institute, September 1981.

Internet Protocol. Network Working Group Report RFC-791, USC Information Sciences Institute, September 1981.

Jefferson, D.R. Virtual time. *Proc. ACM Trans. Programming Languages and Systems 7, 3* (July 1985), 404–425.

Johannessen, S. Time synchronization in a local area network. *IEEE Control Systems Magazine 24, 2* (April 2004), 61–69.

Jones, R.H., and P.V. Tryon. Continuous time series models for unequally spaced data applied to modelling atomic clocks. *SIAM J. Sci. Stat. Comput. 4, 1* (January 1987), 71–81.

Jones, R.H., and P.V. Tryon. Estimating time from atomic clocks. *J. Research of the National Bureau of Standards 88, 1* (January-February 1983), 17–24.

Jordan, E.C. (Ed). *Reference Data for Engineers, Seventh Edition.* H.W. Sams & Co., New York, 1985.

Kajackas, A. On synchronization of communications networks with varying channel delays. *IEEE Trans. Communications 28, 8* (August 1980), 1267–1268.

Kaliski, B. PKCS #1: RSA Encryption Standard, Version 1.5. RSA Laboratories, November 1993, 26 pp.

Karn, P., and W. Simpson. Photuris: session-key management protocol. Request for Comments RFC-2522, Internet Engineering Task Force, March 1999, 76 pp.

Kent, S., and R. Atkinson. IP Authentication Header. Request for Comments RFC-2402, Internet Engineering Task Fors, November 1998, 22 pp.

Kent, S., and R. Atkinson. IP Encapsulating security payload (ESP). Request for Comments RFC-2406, Internet Engineering Task Force, November 1998, 22 pp.

Kent, S., and R. Atkinson, Security Architecture for the internet protocol. Request for Comments RFC-2401, Internet Engineering Task Force, November 1998, 66 pp.

Kessels, J.L.W. Two designs of a fault-tolerant clocking system. *IEEE Trans. Computers C-33, 10* (October 1984), 913–919.

Kirchner, D. Two-way time transfer via communication satellites. *Proc. IEEE 79, 7* (July 1991), 983–990.

Kopetz, H., and W. Ochsenreiter. Clock synchronization in distributed real-time systems. *IEEE Trans. Computers C-36, 8* (August 1987), 933–939.

Krishna, C.M., K.G. Shin and R.W. Butler. Ensuring fault tolerance of phase-locked clocks. *IEEE Trans. Computers COM-34, 8* (August 1985), 752–756.

Kugelmass, S.D., and K. Steiglitz. An upper bound on expected clock skew in synchronous systems. *IEEE Trans. Computers COM-39, 12* (December 1990), 1475–1477.

Lalinde-Pulido, J.G. A mixed approach to improve the NTP's filter performance. Departmento de Informatica y Sistemas, Universidad EAFIT, Medellin, Colombia, (undated), 5 pp.

Lamport, L., and P.M. Melliar-Smith. Synchronizing clocks in the presence of faults. *JACM 32, 1* (January 1985), 52–78.

Lamport, L., Time, clocks and the ordering of events in a distributed system. *Comm. ACM 21, 7* (July 1978), 558–565.

Landis, P., and I. Galysh. NRL/USNO two-way time transfer modem design and test results. *Proc. IEEE Frequency Control Symposium* (May 1992), 317–326.

Levine, J. Time synchronization over the Internet using an adaptive frequency-lock loop. *IEEE Trans. Ultrasonics, Ferroelectrics and Frequency Control 46, 4* (July 1999), 888–896.

Levine, J. Time synchronization using the Internet. *IEEE Trans. Ultrasonics, Ferroelectrics and Frequency Control 45, 2* (March 1998), 450–460.

Levine, J. An algorithm to synchronize the time of a computer to universal time. *IEEE Trans. on Networking 3, 1* (February 1995), 42–50.

Levine, J., and D. Mills. Using the Network Time Protocol to transmit International Atomic Time (TAI). *Proc. Precision Time and Time Interval (PTTI) Applications and Planning Meeting* (Reston, VA, November 2000).

Levine, J., M. Weiss, D.D. Davis, D.W. Allan, and D.B. Sullivan. The NIST automated computer time service. *J. Research National Institute of Standards and Technology 94, 5* (September-October 1989), 311–321.

Liao, C., M. Martonosi, and D. Clark. Experience with an adaptive globally-synchronizing clock algorithm. *Proc. 11th Annual ACM Symposium on Parallel Algorithms and Architecture* (Saint Malo, June 1999), 106–114.

Liao, C., M. Martonosi and D. Clark. An adaptive globally-synchronizing clock algorithm and its implementation on a Myrinet-based PC cluster. *Proc. 1999 ACM SIGMETRICS international conference on Measurement and Modelling of Computer Systems* (Atlanta, GA 1999), 200–201.

Lindsay, W.C., and A.V. Kantak. Network synchronization of random signals. *IEEE Trans. Communications COM-28, 8* (August 1980), 1260–1266.

Liskov, B. Practical uses of synchronized clocks in distributed systems. *Proc. 10th Annual ACM Symposium on Principles of Distributed Computing* (Montreal, April 1991), 1–9.

Liskov, B., L. Shrira and J. Wroclawski. Efficient at-most-once messages based on synchronized clocks. *ACM Trans. Computer Systems 9, 2* (May 1991), 125–142.

Lu, M., D. Zhang. Analysis of self-stabilizing clock synchronization by means of stochastic Petri nets. *IEEE Trans. Computers 39, 5* (May 1990), 597–604.

Lundelius, J., and N.A. Lynch. A new fault-tolerant algorithm for clock synchronization. *Proc. Third Annual ACM Symposium on Principles of Distributed Computing* (August 1984), 75–88.

Marzullo, K., and S. Owicki. Maintaining the time in a distributed system. *ACM Operating Systems Review 19, 3* (July 1985), 44–54.

Mattern, F. Virtual time and global states of distributed systems. *International Workshop on Parallel and Distributed Algorithms*, M. Cosnard, et al, (Eds), Elsevier Science Publishers B.V., 1989, 215–226.

Maughan, D., M. Schertler, M. Schneider, and J. Turner. Internet security association and key management protocol (ISAKMP). Request for Comments RFC-2408, Internet Engineering Task Force, November 1998, 86 pp.

Miller, J., et al. NASA architecture for Solar System time distribution. *Proc. IEEE 2007 Frequency Control Symposium* (May 2007), 1299–1303.

Mills, D.L. A brief history of NTP time: confessions of an Internet timekeeper. *ACM Computer Communications Review 33, 2* (April 2003), 9–22.

Mills, D.L. Public key cryptography for the Network Time Protocol. Electrical Engineering Report 00–5-1, University of Delaware, May 2000. 23 pp.

Mills, D.L. Adaptive hybrid clock discipline algorithm for the Network Time Protocol. *IEEE/ACM Trans. on Networking 6, 5* (October 1998), 505–514.

Mills, D.L. Clock discipline algorithms for the Network Time Protocol Version 4. Electrical Engineering Report 97–3-3, University of Delaware, March 1997, 35 pp.

Mills, D.L., and P.-H. Kamp. The nanokernel. *Proc. Precision Time and Time Interval (PTTI) Applications and Planning Meeting* (Reston, VA, November 2000).

Mills, D.L., J. Levine, R. Schmidt and D. Plonka. Coping with overload on the Network Time Protocol public servers. *Proc. Precision Time and Time Interval (PTTI) Applications and Planning Meeting* (Washington, DC, December 2004), 5–16.

Mills, D.L., A. Thyagarajan and B.C. Huffman. Internet timekeeping around the globe. *Proc. Precision Time and Time Interval (PTTI) Applications and Planning Meeting* (Long Beach, CA, December 1997), 365–371.

Mills, D.L. Improved algorithms for synchronizing computer network clocks. *IEEE/ACM Trans. on Networks 3, 3* (June 1995), 245–254.Mills, D.L. Precision synchronization of computer network clocks. *ACM Computer Communication Review 24, 2* (April 1994). 28–43.

Mills, D.L. Internet time synchronization: the Network Time Protocol. *IEEE Trans. Communications COM-39, 10* (October 1991), 1482–1493. Also in: Yang, Z., and T.A. Marsland (Eds.). *Global States and Time in Distributed Systems.* IEEE Computer Society Press, Los Alamitos, CA, 1994, 91–102.

Mills, D.L. Network Time Protocol (Version 3) specification, implementation and analysis. Network Working Group Report RFC-1305, University of Delaware, March 1992, 113 pp.

Mills, D.L. On the chronology and metrology of computer network timescales and their application to the Network Time Protocol. *ACM Computer Communications Review 21, 5* (October 1991), 8–17.

Mills, D.L. Measured performance of the Network Time Protocol in the Internet system. *ACM Computer Communication Review 20, 1* (January 1990), 65–75.

Mills, D.L. Network Time Protocol (version 2) - specification and implementation. DARPA Network Working Group Report RFC-1119, University of Delaware, September 1989.

Mills, D.L. Network Time Protocol (version 1) - specification and implementation. DARPA Network Working Group Report RFC-1059, University of Delaware, July 1988.

Mills, D.L. Algorithms for synchronizing network clocks. DARPA Network Working Group Report RFC-956, M/A-COM Linkabit, September 1985.

Mills, D.L. Experiments in network clock synchronization. DARPA Network Working Group Report RFC-957, M/A-COM Linkabit, September 1985.

Mills, D.L. Network Time Protocol (NTP). DARPA Network Working Group Report RFC-958, M/A-COM Linkabit, September 1985.

Mills, D.L. DCNET Internet Clock Service. DARPA Network Working Group Report RFC-778, COMSAT Laboratories, April 1981.

Mills, D.L. Time Synchronization in DCNET Hosts. DARPA Internet Project Report IEN-173, COMSAT Laboratories, February 1981.

Mills, D., D. Plonka and J. Montgomery. Simple network time protocol (SNTP) version 4 for IPv4, IPv6 and OSI. Network Working Group Report RFC-4330, University of Delaware, December 2005, 27 pp.

Minar, N. A survey of the NTP network. Technical Report, MIT Media Laboratory, December 1999, 10 pp.

Mitra, D. Network synchronization: analysis of a hybrid of master-slave and mutual synchronization. *IEEE Trans. Communications COM-28, 8* (August 1980), 1245–1259.

Mockapetris, P. Domain names - concepts and facilities. Network Working Group Report RFC-1034, USC Information Sciences Institute, November 1987.

Mogul, J., D. Mills, J. Brittenson, J. Stone and U. Windl. Pulse-per-second API for Unix-like operating systems, version 1. Request for Comments RFC-2783, Internet Engineering Task Force, March 2000, 31 pp.

Morgan, C. Global and logical time in distributed algorithms. *Information Processing Letters 20* (1985), 189–194.

Morley, S.G., G.W. Brainerd and R.J. Sharer. *The Ancient Maya, 4th ed.*, pp. 598–600. Stanford University Press, Stanford, CA, 1983.

Moyer, T.D. Transformation from proper time on Earth to coordinate time in Solar System barycentric space-time frame of reference - Part 1. *Celestial Mechanics 23* (1981), 33–56.

Moyer, T.D. Transformation from proper time on Earth to coordinate time in Solar System barycentric space-time frame of reference - Part 2. *Celestial Mechanics 23* (1981), 57–68.

Moyer, G. The Gregorian Calendar. *Scientific American 246, 5* (May 1982), 144–152.

Mu, Y., and V. Varadharajan. Robust and secure broadcasting. *Proc. INDOCRYPT 2001, LNCS 2247*, Springer Verlag, 2001, 223–231.

Munter, E.A. Synchronized clocks for the DMS-100 family. *IEEE Trans. Communications 28, 8* (August 1980), 1276–1284.

Murphy, D.L. Timekeeping enhancements in OSF/MK. The Open Group Research Institute, June 1997, 14 pp.

Neiger, G., and S. Toueg. Substituting for real time and common knowledge in asynchronous. *Proc. ACM SIGPLAN/SIGOPS Symposium on Principles of Distributed Computing* (1987), 281–293.

Nelson, R.A., et al. The leap second: its history and possible future. *Metrologia 38* (2001), 509–529.

NIST Time and Frequency Dissemination Services. NBS Special Publication 432 (Revised 1990), National Institute of Science and Technology, U.S. Department of Commerce, 1990. Reprinted with updates from: Time and Frequency Dissemination Services. NBS Special Publication 432, U.S. Department of Commerce, 1979.

O'Donoghue, K. F., and T.R. Plunkett. Development and validation of network clock measurement techniques. Naval Surface Weapons Center, Dahlgren, Virginia, (undated), 12 pp.

O'Donoghue, K. F., and D.T. Marlow. Time synchronization services aboard surface ships. Naval Surface Weapons Center, Dahlgren, Virginia, (undated), 12 pp.

Orman, H. The OAKLEY key determination protocol. Request for Comments RFC-2412, Internet Engineering Task Force, November 1998, 55 pp.

Ostrovsky, R., and B. Patt-Shamir. Optimal and efficient clock synchronization under drifting clocks. *Proc. ACM Annual Symposium on Principles of Distributed Computing* (Atlanta, May 1999), 3–12.

Pasztor, A., and D. Veitch. PC based precision timing without GPS. *Proc. 2002 ACM SIGMETRICS International Conference on Measurement and Modelling of Computer Systems* (Marina del Rey, CA), 1–10.

Patt-Shamir, B., and S. Rajsbaum. A theory of clock synchronization. *Proc. 26th Annual ACM Symposium on Theory of Computing* (Montreal, May 1994), 810–819.

Paxson, V. On calibrating measurements of packet transit times. *Proc. Joint Internet Conference on Measurements and Modelling of Computer Systems* (Madison, June 1998), 11–21.

Pease, M., R. Shostak and L. Lamport. Reaching agreement in the presence of faults. *JACM 27*, 2 (April 1980), 228–234.

Perumalla, K., and R. Fujimoto/ Virtual time synchronization over unreliable network transport. *Proc. 15th Workshop on Parallel and Distributed Simulation* (Lake Arrowhead, May 2001), 129–136.

Percival, D.B. The U.S. Naval Observatory Clock Time Scales. *IEEE Trans. Instrumentation and Measurement IM-27*, 4 (December 1978), 376–385.

Peterson, L.L. Preserving context information in an IPC abstraction. *Proc. Sixth symposium on Reliability in Distributed Software and Database Systems* (March 1987), 22–31.

Postel, J. Daytime protocol. Network Working Group Report RFC-867, USC Information Sciences Institute, May 1983.

Postel, J. Time protocol. Network Working Group Report RFC-868, USC Information Sciences Institute, May 1983. Postel, J. User Datagram Protocol. Network Working Group Report RFC-768, USC Information Sciences Institute, August 1980.

Postel, J. User Datagram Protocol. DARPA Network Working Group Report RFC-768, USC Information Sciences Institute, August 1980.

Prafullchandra, H., and J. Schaad. Diffie-Hellman proof-of-possession algorithms. Network Working Group Request for Comments RFC-2875, Critical Path, Inc., July 2000, 23 pp.

Ramanathan, P., D.D. Kandlur and K.G. Shin. Hardware-assisted software clock synchronization for homogeneous distributed systems. *IEEE Trans. Computers C-39*, 4 (April 1990), 514–524.

Ramanathan, P., K.G. Shin and R.W. Butler. Fault-tolerant clock synchronization in distributed systems. *IEEE Computer 23, 10* (October 1990), 33–42.

Rawley, L.A., J.H. Taylor, M.M. Davis and D.W. Allan. Millisecond pulsar PSR 1937 + 21: a highly stable clock. *Science 238* (6 November 1987), 761–765.

Reiter, M.K. A security architecture for fault-tolerant systems. *ACM Trans. Computer Systems 12, 4* (November 1994), 340–371.

Rickert, N.W. Non Byzantine clock synchronization - a programming experiment. *ACM Operating Systems Review 22, 1* (January 1988), 73–78.

Rivest, R. The MD5 Message-digest algorithm. Request for Comments RFC-1321, Internet Engineering Task Force, April 1992, 21 pp.

Rivest, R., A. Shamir, and L. Adleman. A method for obtaining digital signatures and public-key cryptosystems. *Communications of the ACM 21, 2* (February 1978), 120–126.

Rushby, J. A formally verified algorithm for clock synchronization under a hybrid fault model. Proc 13th Annual ACM Symposium on Principles of Distributed Computation (Los Angeles, CA 1994), 304–313.

Rybaczyk, J. *Expert Network Time Protocol: an experience in time.* Springer-Verlag, New York, 2005, 153 pp.

Schlossmaier, K. Proc 16th Annual ACM Symposium on Principles of Distributed Computing (Santa Barbara, CA 1997), 169–178.

Schneider, F.B. Understanding protocols for Byzantine clock synchronization. Department of Computer Science Report TR 87–859, Cornell University, August 1987.

Schneider, F.B. A paradigm for reliable clock synchronization. Department of Computer Science Technical Report TR 86–735, Cornell University, February 1986.

Schnorr, C.P. Efficient signature generation for smart cards. *J. Cryptology 4, 3* (1991), 161–174.

ScienceScope. Sounding out the threat of global warning. *Science 251* (8 February 1991), 615.

Sethi, A.S., H. Gao, and D.L. Mills. Management of the Network Time Protocol (NTP) with SNMP. Computer and Information Sciences Report 98–09, University of Delaware, November 1997, 32 pp.

Shin, K.G., and P. Ramanathan. Clock synchronization of a large multiprocessor system in the presence of malicious faults. *IEEE Trans. Computers C-36, 1* (January 1987), 2–12.

Shin, K.G., and P. Ramanathan. Transmission delays in hardware clock synchronization. *IEEE Trans. Computers C-37, 11* (November 1988), 1465–1467.

Smith, J. *Modern Communications Circuits.* McGraw-Hill, New York, NY, 1986.

Snow, C.R. A multi-protocol campus time server. *Software Practice and Experience 21, 9* (September 1991).

Srikanth, T.K., and S. Toueg. Optimal clock synchronization. *JACM 34, 3* (July 1987), 626–645.

Stein, S.R. Frequency and time - their measurement and characterization (Chapter 12). In: E.A. Gerber and A. Ballato (Eds.). *Precision Frequency Control, Vol. 2,* Academic Press, New York 1985, 191–232, 399–416. Also in: Sullivan, D.B., D.W. Allan, D.A. Howe and F.L. Walls (Eds.). *Characterization of Clocks and Oscillators. National Institute of Standards and Technology Technical Note 1337,* U.S. Government Printing Office (January 1990), TN61-TN119.

Steiner, J.G., C. Neuman, and J.I. Schiller. Kerberos: an authentication service for open network systems. *Proc. Winter USENIX Conference* (February 1988).

Stinson, D.R. *Cryptography - Theory and Practice.* CRC Press, Boca Raton, FA, 1995, ISBN 0-8493-8521-0.

Storz, W., and G. Beling. Transmitting time-critical data over heterogeneous subnetworks using standardized protocols. *Mobile Networks and Applications 2,* Balzer Science Publishers (1997), 243–249.

Strom, R.E., and S. Yemini. Optimistic recovery in distributed systems. *ACM Trans. on Computer Systems 3, 3* (August 1985), 204–226.

Su, Z. A specification of the Internet protocol (IP) timestamp option. Network Working Group Report-781. SRI International, May 1981.

Tel, G., E. Korach and S. Zaks. Synchronizing ABD networks. *IEEE/ACM Trans. on Networking 2, 1* (February 1994), 66–69.

Time. The Encyclopaedia Britannica Macropaedia, 15th ed., vol. 28, pp. 652–664. Encyclopaedia Britannica Co., New York, NY, 1986.

Time and Frequency Dissemination Services. *NBS Special Publication 432,* U.S. Department of Commerce, 1979.

Tripathi, S.K., and S.H. Chang. ETempo, a clock synchronization algorithm for hierarchical LANs —implementation and measurements. Systems Research Center Technical Report TR-86-48, University of Maryland, 25 pp.

Tryon, P.V., and R.H. Jones. Estimation of parameters in models for Cesium beam atomic clocks. *J. Research of the National Bureau of Standards 88, 1* (January-February 1983).

Van Dierendonck, A.J., and W.C. Melton. Applications of time transfer using NAVSTAR GPS. In: *Global Positioning System, Papers Published in Navigation, Vol. II,* Institute of Navigation, Washington, DC, 1984.

Vasanthavada, N., and P.N. Marinos. Synchronization of fault-tolerant clocks in the presence of malicious failures. *IEEE Trans. Computers C-37, 4* (April 1988), 440–448.

Vass, E.R. OMEGA navigation system: present status and plans 1977–1980. *Navigation 25, 1* (Spring 1978).

Weiss, M.A., D.W. Allan and T.K. Peppler. A study of the NBS time scale algorithm. *IEEE Trans. Instrumentation and Measurement 38, 2* (April 1989), 631–635.

Welch, J.L. Simulating synchronous processors. *Information and Computation 74, 2* (August 1987), 159–171.

Wilcox, D.R. Backplane bus distributed realtime clock synchronization. Technical Report 1400, Naval Ocean Systems Center, December 1990, 42 pp.

Wilcox, D.R. Local area network distributed realtime clock synchronization. Technical Report 1466, Naval Ocean Systems Center, November 1991, 70 pp.

Zarros, P.N., M.J. Lee and T.N. Saadawi. Interparticipant synchronization in realtime multimedia conferencing using feedback. *IEEE/ACM Trans. Networking 4, 2* (April 1996), 172–180.

Zhao, Y., W. Zhou, E. Lanham, S. Yu and M. Lan. Self-adaptive clock synchronization based on clock precision differences. *Proc. 25th Australian Computer Science Conference ACSC2003* (Adelaide, Australia 2003), 181–187.

Acronyms

AH: Authentication Header
AOS: acquisition of signal
ARIMA: autoregressive integrated moving average
ATSC: Advanced Television Systems Committee
BC: boundary clock (PTP)
BCE: before Common Era (BC)
BCD: binary coded decimal
BIPM: Bureau International des Poids (Paris)
BPSK: binary phase shift keying
CA: certificate authority
CCSDS: Consultative Committee on Space Data Systems
CDF: cumulative distribution function
CDMA: code division multiple access
CE: Common Era (AD)
CHU: CRC time/frequency radio station (Canada)
CIC: concatenated integrate-comb filter
CPU: central processing unit
CRC: Canadian Research Council
DCF77: PTB time/frequency radio station (Germany)
DH: Diffiie-Helman
DNS: Domain Name System
DSA: Digital Signature Algorithm
DSL: digital subscriber loop
DSN: Deep Space Network
DSP: digital signal processor
DST: daylight saving time
DTE: direct to earth
DTSS: Digital Time Synchronization Service
DTTL: digital transition tracking loop

DUT1: UT1 – UTC
DVMRP: Distance Vector Multicast Routing Protocol
ECI: Earth-centered inertial frame
ESA: European Space Agency
ESP: Encapsulated Security Payload
ET: ephemeris time
FFT: Fast Fourier Transform
FH: frequency hopping
FIFO: first in first-out
FLL: frequency-lock loop
FPGA: field-programmable gate array
FTA: fault-tolerant average
FWT: Fast Walsh Transform
GM: gravity-mass constant/PTP grandmaster
GOES: Geostationary Operational Environmental Satellite
GPS: Global Positioning System (Navstar)
GQ: Guillou-Quisquater identity scheme
HBG: METAS time/frequency radio station (Switzerland)
HQ: Have Quick (US military radio)
IANA: Internet Assigned Numbers Authority
ICMP: InterContinental Mounted Police
ICMP: Internet Group Management Protocol
IERS: International Earth Rotation Service
IETF: Internet Engineering Task Force
IF: intermediate frequency
IFF: Schnorr identity scheme
IPSEC: Internet Protocol Security Engineering

IPv4: Internet Protocol Version 4
IPv6: Internet Protocol Version 6
ISDN: International Standard for Data Networks
ITU: International Telecommunications Union
J2000: Solar System inertial epoch
JDN: Julian day number
JJY: Japan time/frequency radio station
JPL: Jet Propulsion Laboratory
LCI: Moon-centered inertial frame
LFSR: linear feedback shift register
LI: leap indicator
LNA: low-noise amplifier
LORAN-C: Long Range Navigation System
LOS: loss of signal
LRU: least recently used
LT: Lunar Dynamic Time
MAC: message authentication code/ media access layer
MCI: Mars-centered inertial frame
MD5: Message Digest Algorithm
MER: Mars Exploration Rovers
METAS: National Metrology Institute (Switzerland)
MEX: Mars Express
MII: media-independent interface
MIT: Massachusetts Institute of Technology
MLT: multi-level transport
MRO: Mars Reconnaissance Orbiter
MRU: most recently used
MSF: NPL time/frequency radio station (UK)
MSL: Mars Science Laboratory
MT: Mars Dynamic Time
MV: Mu-Varadharajan identity scheme
NAIF: Navigation and Astronomy Information Facility
NASA: National Aeronautics and Space Administration

NATO: North Atlantic Treaty Organization
NCO: numeric-controlled oscillator
NIC: network interface card
NIST: National Institute of Science and Technology (US)
NPL: National Physical Laboratory (UK)
NTP: Network Time Protocol
NTPv3: NTP Version 3
NTPv4: NTP Version 4
NTSC: National Television Systems Committee
OC: ordinary clock (PTP)
ODY: Mars Odyssey
OSI: open system interconnection
PA: power amplifier
PC: private certificate/personal computer
PCC: Processor Cycle Counter (Alpha)
PDU: protocol data unit
PHY: physical layer/Phoenix (Mars lander)
PIMP: Protocol Independent Multicast Protocol
PITS: Proximity Interleaved Time Service
PKI: Public Key Infrastructure
PLL: phase-lock loop
POSIX: Portable Operating System Interface
PPM: parts per million
PPS: pulse per second
PR: pseudo random
PTB: National Metrology Institute (Germany)
PTP: Precision Time Protocol (IEEE 1588)
PTTI: precise time and time interval
QPSK: quadrature phase shift keying
RF: radio frequency
RFC: request for comments (IETF)

RFI: radio frequency interference
RMS: root mean square
RPC: remote procedure call
RS: Reed-Solomon
RSA: Rivest-Schamir-Addelman
RTC: real-time clock
SC: spacecraft computer
SCLK: spacecraft clock
SDR: software defined radio
SHA: Secure Hash Algorithm
SI: Standard Second
SINCGARS: Single Channel Ground and Airborne Radio System
SNR: signal to noise ratio
SNTP: Simple Network Time Protocol
SOF: start of field
SSB: Solar System barycenter
SSO: sufficiently stable oscillator
STANAG: NATO Standard
STS: Space Transportation System (Shuttle)
TA: trusted authority
TAI: International Atomic Time
TC: trusted certificate/transparent clock (PTP)
TCA: Mars Aerocentric Coordinate Time (Mars)
TCB: Barycentric Coordinate Time (Solar System)
TCG: Geocentric Coordinate Time (Earth)

TCP: Transmission Control Protocol
TCS: Selenocentric Coordinate Time (Moon)
TDB: Barycentric Dynamic Time (Solar System)
TDRS: Tracking and Data Relay Satellite
TH: trusted host
TOC: time of coincidence/ time of century
TSC: Time Stamp Counter (Intel)
TT: Terrestrial Dynamic Time
TWSTFT: Two-Way Satellite Time and Frequency Transfer
UDP: User Datagram Protocol
USNO: United States Naval Observatory
USO: ultra stable oscillator
UT: Universal Time
UT1: mean solar time
UTC: Universal Coordinated Time
UUID: universal unique clock identifier (PTP)
VFO: variable frequency oscillator
VLBI: Very Long Baseline Interferometry
VSAT: very small antenna terminal
WWV/B: NIST time/frequency radio station (Colorado)
WWVH: NIST time/frequency radio station (Hawaii)

Index

"f" indicates material in figures.
"n" indicates material in footnotes.
"t" indicates material in tables.